# SIX-GUN GORILLA™

CW00820555

BOOM!™ STUDIOS

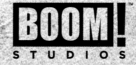

**BOOM! STUDIOS**

**ROSS RICHIE** CEO & Founder • **JACK CUMMINS** President • **MARK SMYLIE** Founder of Archaia • **MATT GAGNON** Editor-in-Chief • **FILIP SABLIK** VP of Publishing & Marketing • **STEPHEN CHRISTY** VP of Development
**LANCE KREITER** VP of Licensing & Merchandising • **PHIL BARBARO** VP of Finance • **BRYCE CARLSON** Managing Editor • **MEL CAYLO** Marketing Manager • **SCOTT NEWMAN** Production Design Manager • **IRENE BRADISH** Operations Manager
**DAFNA PLEBAN** Editor • **SHANNON WATTERS** Editor • **ERIC HARBURN** Editor • **REBECCA TAYLOR** Editor • **IAN BRILL** Editor • **CHRIS ROSA** Assistant Editor • **ALEX GALER** Assistant Editor • **WHITNEY LEOPARD** Assistant Editor
**JASMINE AMIRI** Assistant Editor • **CAMERON CHITTOCK** Assistant Editor • **HANNAH NANCE PARTLOW** Production Designer • **KELSEY DIETERICH** Production Designer • **EMI YONEMURA BROWN** Production Designer
**DEVIN FUNCHES** E-Commerce & Inventory Coordinator • **ANDY LIEGL** Event Coordinator • **BRIANNA HART** Executive Assistant • **AARON FERRARA** Operations Assistant • **JOSÉ MEZA** Sales Assistant • **ELIZABETH LOUGHRIDGE** Accounting Assistant

**SIX-GUN GORILLA, June 2014.** Published by BOOM! Studios, a division of Boom Entertainment, Inc. Six-Gun Gorilla is ™ & © 2014 Boom Entertainment, Inc. Originally published in single magazine form as SIX-GUN GORILLA No. 1–6. ™ & © 2013 Boom Entertainment, Inc. All rights reserved. BOOM! Studios™ and the BOOM! Studios logo are trademarks of Boom Entertainment, Inc., registered in various countries and categories. All characters, events, and institutions depicted herein are fictional. Any similarity between any of the names, characters, persons, events, and/or institutions in this publication to actual names, characters, and persons, whether living or dead, events, and/or institutions is unintended and purely coincidental. BOOM! Studios does not read or accept unsolicited submissions of ideas, stories, or artwork.

A catalog record of this book is available from OCLC and from the BOOM! Studios website, www.boom-studios.com, on the Librarians Page.

BOOM! Studios, 5670 Wilshire Boulevard, Suite 450, Los Angeles, CA 90036-5679. Printed in China. First Printing.
Hardcover ISBN: 978-1-60886-448-5, Softcover ISBN: 978-1-60886-390-7, eISBN: 978-1-61398-244-0

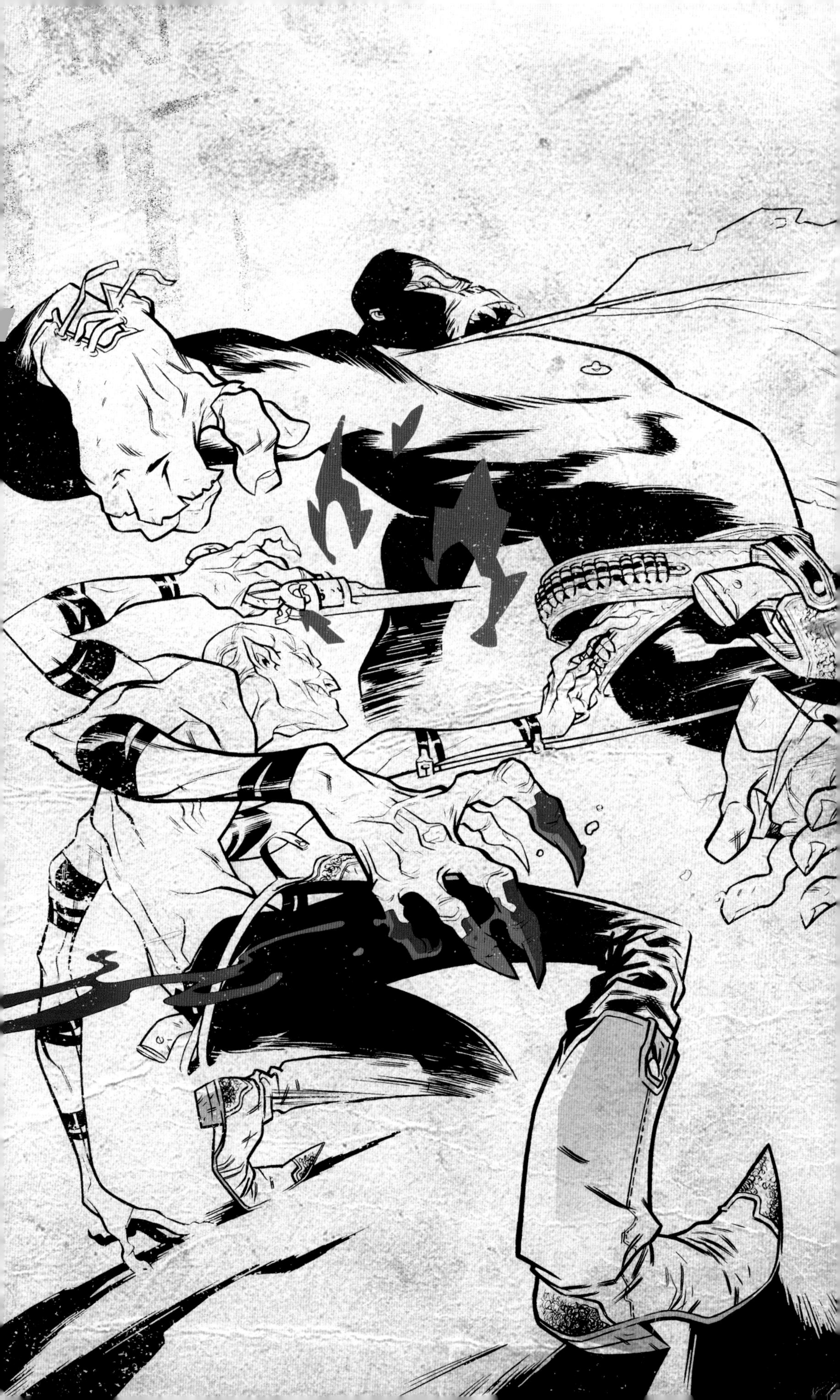

CREATED & WRITTEN BY
# SIMON SPURRIER

COLORS BY
**ANDRÉ MAY**

LETTERS BY
**STEVE WANDS**

COVER BY
**RAMÓN PÉREZ**

LIMITED EDITION
COVER BY
**CHRIS WESTON**

ART BY
# JEFF STOKELY

TRADE DESIGNER
## KELSEY DIETERICH
WITH SPECIAL THANKS TO
**MIKE LOPEZ**

EDITOR
## ERIC HARBURN

# SIX-GUN GORILLA

DEDICATED TO
## CREATORS UNKNOWN
WHOSE WORKS
OUTLIVED THEIR CREDIT


WITH THANKS
TO JESS NEVINS

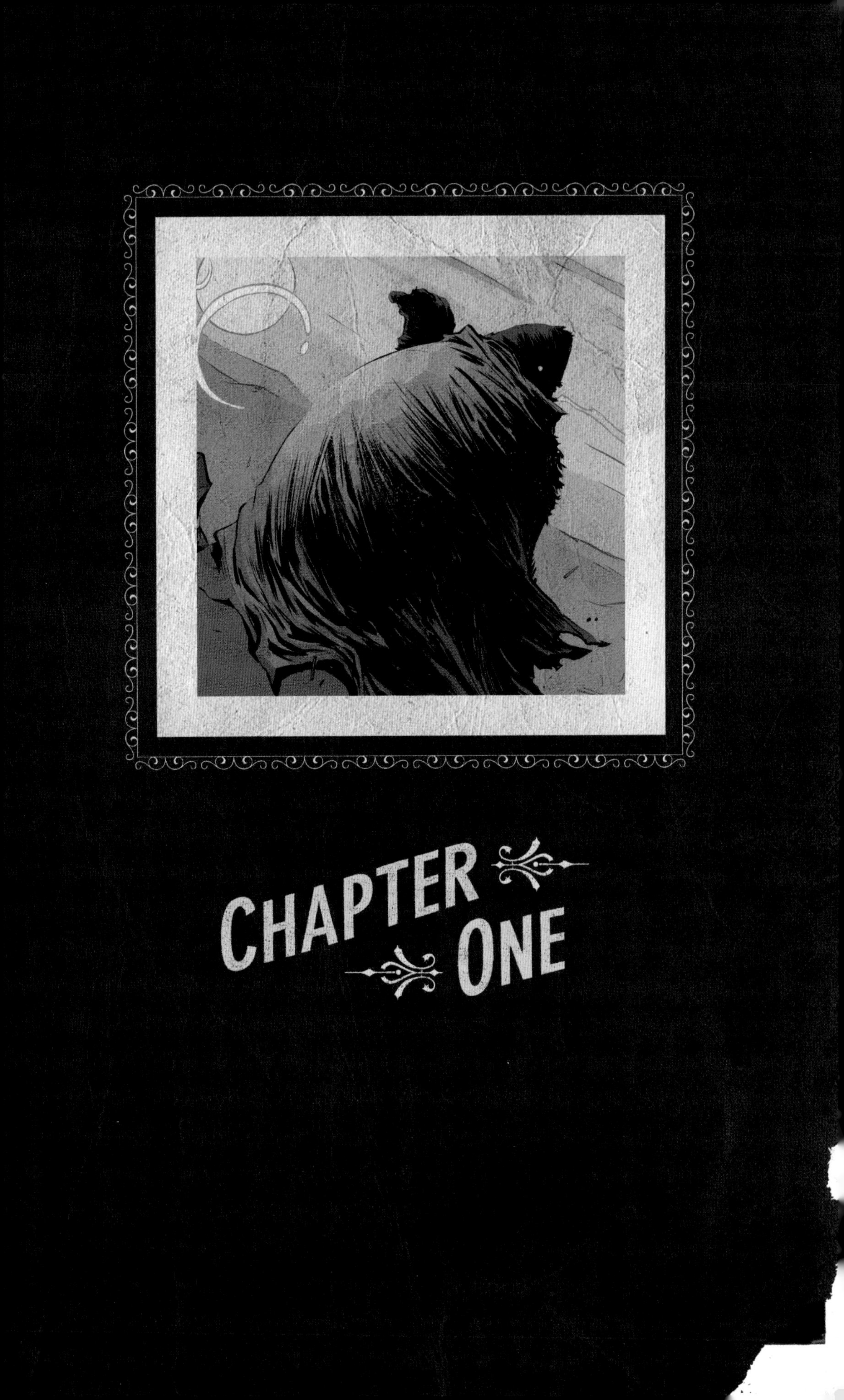

# CHAPTER ONE

# SIX-GUN GORILLA (Continued from page 8.)

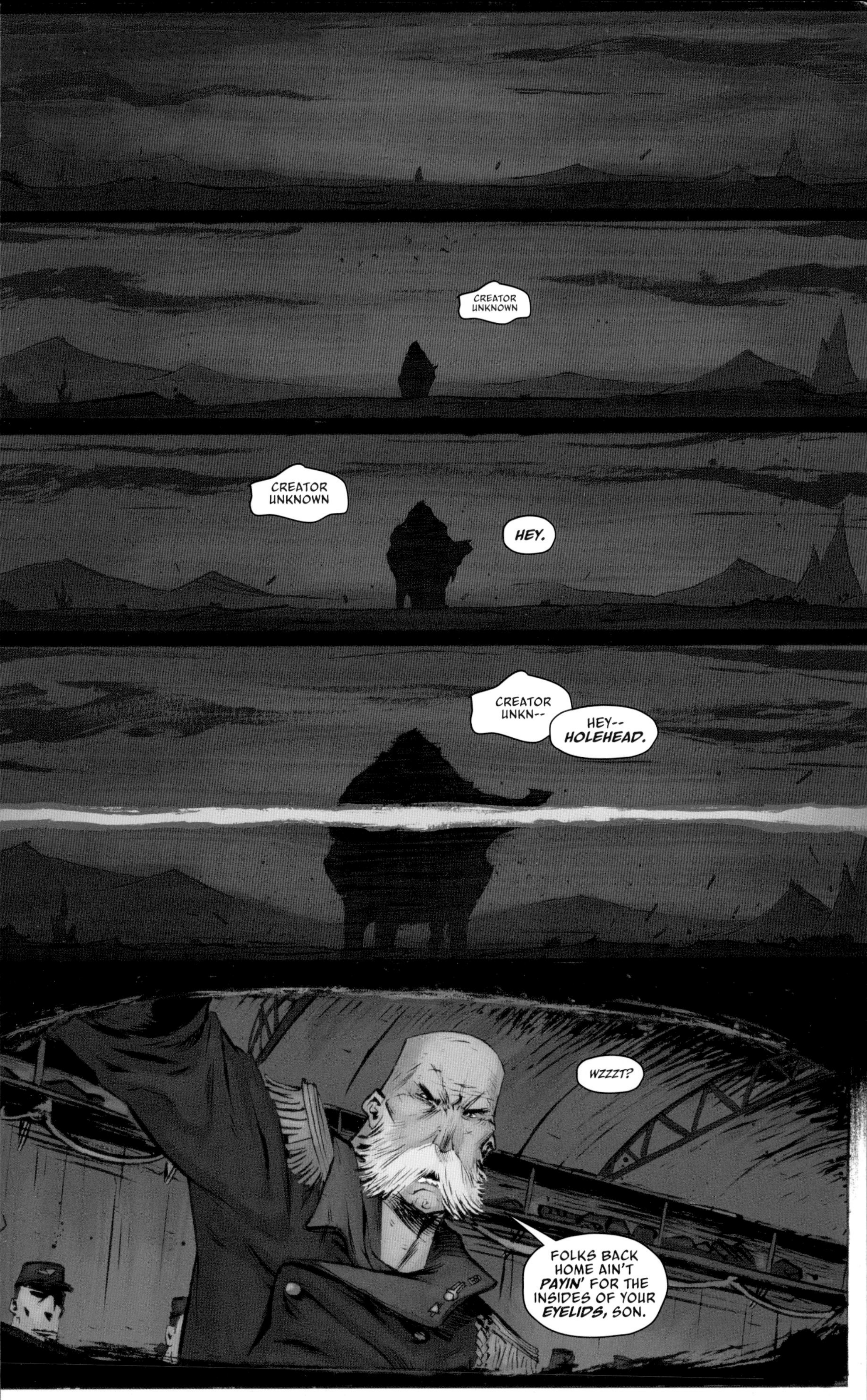
CREATOR
UNKNOWN
CREATOR
UNKNOWN
HEY.
CREATOR
UNKN--
HEY--
HOLEHEAD.
WZZZT?
FOLKS BACK HOME AIN'T PAYIN' FOR THE INSIDES OF YOUR EYELIDS, SON.

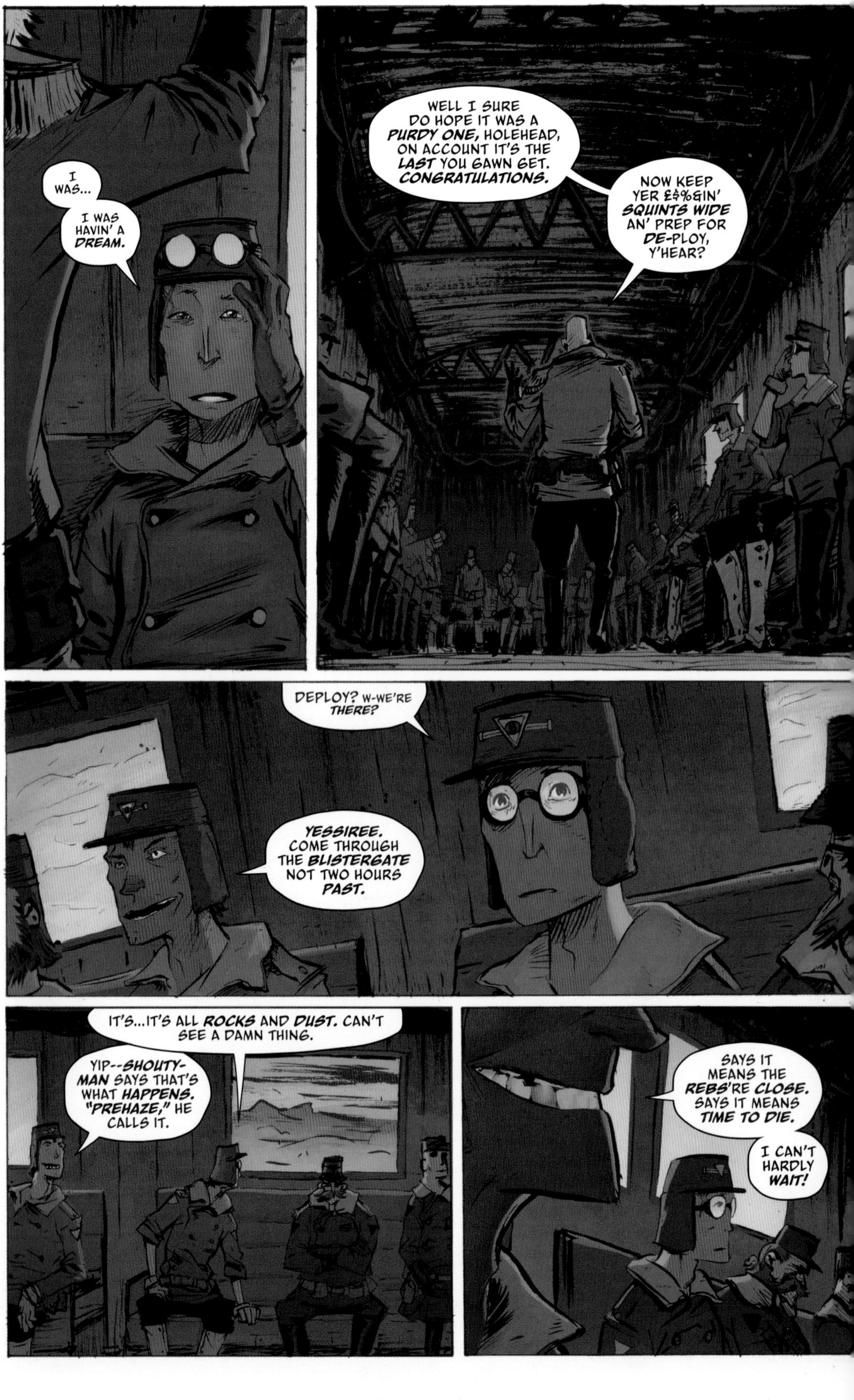
I WAS...
I WAS HAVIN' A DREAM.
WELL I SURE DO HOPE IT WAS A PURDY ONE, HOLEHEAD, ON ACCOUNT IT'S THE LAST YOU GAWN GET. CONGRATULATIONS.
NOW KEEP YER £$%&IN' SQUINTS WIDE AN' PREP FOR DE-PLOY, Y'HEAR?
DEPLOY? W-WE'RE THERE?
YESSIREE. COME THROUGH THE BLISTERGATE NOT TWO HOURS PAST.
IT'S...IT'S ALL ROCKS AND DUST. CAN'T SEE A DAMN THING.
YIP--SHOUTY-MAN SAYS THAT'S WHAT HAPPENS. "PREHAZE," HE CALLS IT.
SAYS IT MEANS THE REBS'RE CLOSE. SAYS IT MEANS TIME TO DIE.
I CAN'T HARDLY WAIT!

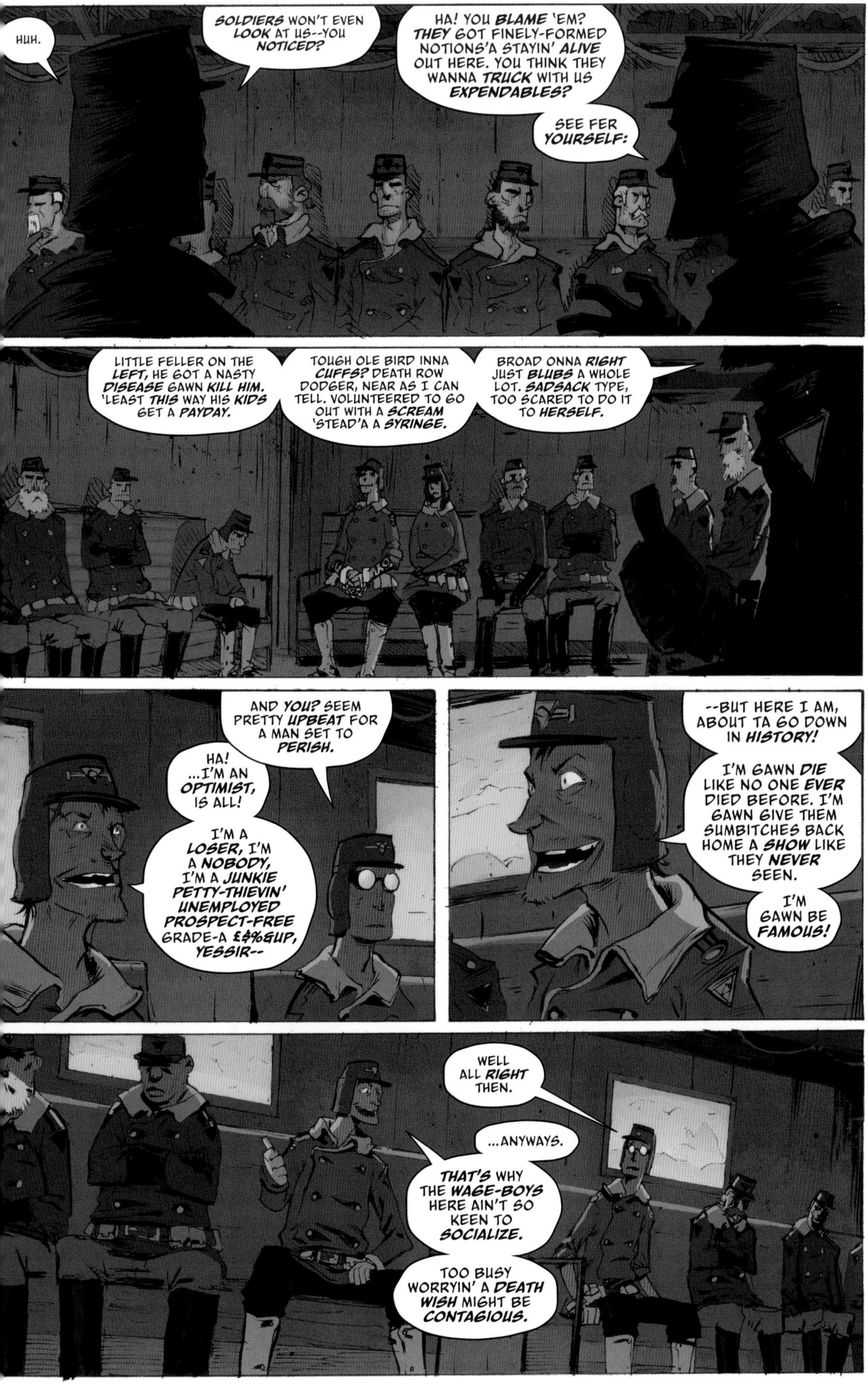
HUH.
SOLDIERS WON'T EVEN LOOK AT US--YOU NOTICED?
HA! YOU BLAME 'EM? THEY GOT FINELY-FORMED NOTIONS'A STAYIN' ALIVE OUT HERE. YOU THINK THEY WANNA TRUCK WITH US EXPENDABLES?
SEE FER YOURSELF:
LITTLE FELLER ON THE LEFT, HE GOT A NASTY DISEASE GAWN KILL HIM. 'LEAST THIS WAY HIS KIDS GET A PAYDAY.
TOUGH OLE BIRD INNA CUFFS? DEATH ROW DODGER, NEAR AS I CAN TELL. VOLUNTEERED TO GO OUT WITH A SCREAM 'STEAD'A A SYRINGE.
BROAD ONNA RIGHT JUST BLUBS A WHOLE LOT. SADSACK TYPE, TOO SCARED TO DO IT TO HERSELF.
AND YOU? SEEM PRETTY UPBEAT FOR A MAN SET TO PERISH.
HA! ...I'M AN OPTIMIST, IS ALL!
I'M A LOSER, I'M A NOBODY, I'M A JUNKIE PETTY-THIEVIN' UNEMPLOYED PROSPECT-FREE GRADE-A £$%&UP, YESSIR--
--BUT HERE I AM, ABOUT TA GO DOWN IN HISTORY!
I'M GAWN DIE LIKE NO ONE EVER DIED BEFORE. I'M GAWN GIVE THEM SUMBITCHES BACK HOME A SHOW LIKE THEY NEVER SEEN.
I'M GAWN BE FAMOUS!
WELL ALL RIGHT THEN.
...ANYWAYS.
THAT'S WHY THE WAGE-BOYS HERE AIN'T SO KEEN TO SOCIALIZE.
TOO BUSY WORRYIN' A DEATH WISH MIGHT BE CONTAGIOUS.

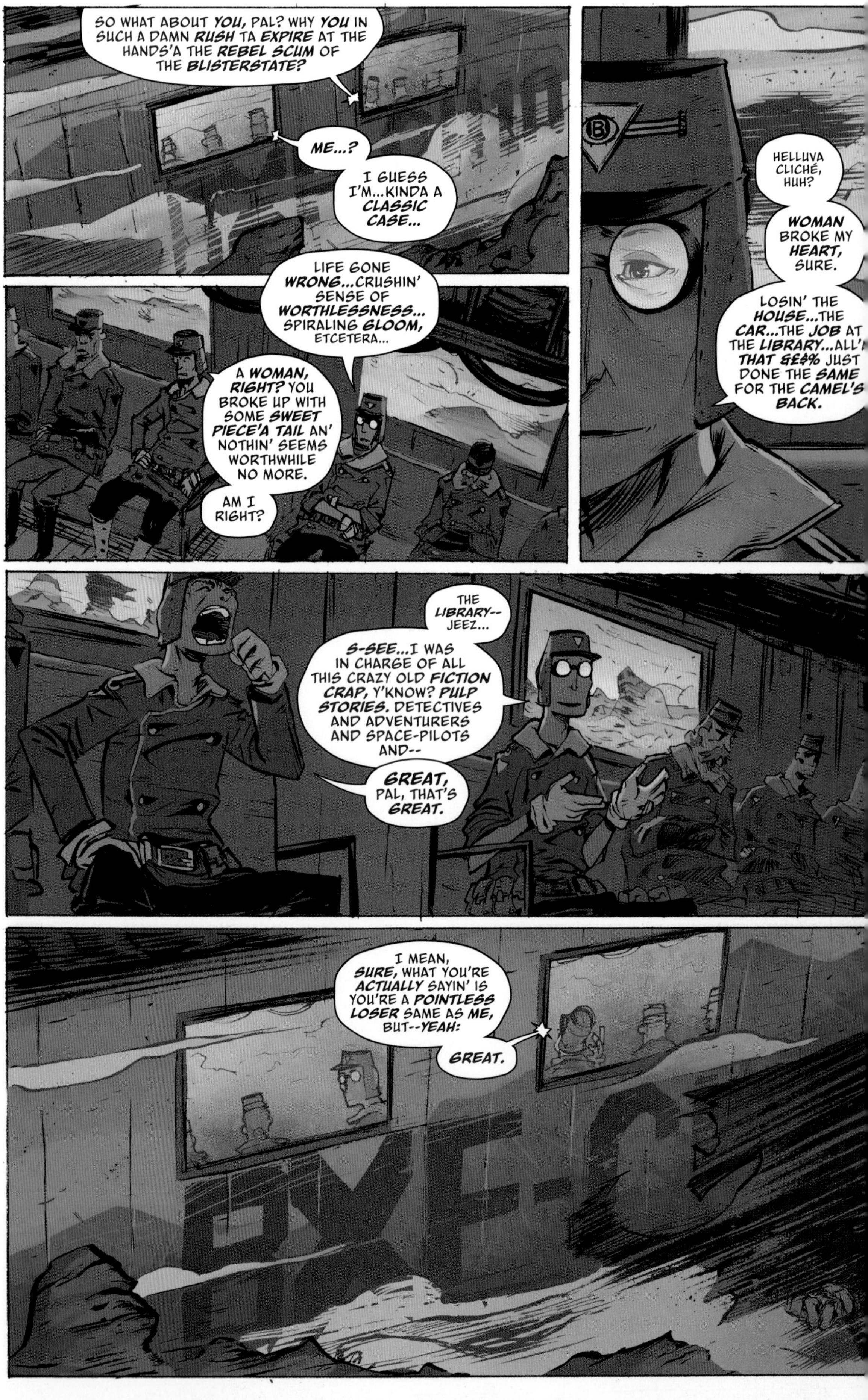
SO WHAT ABOUT YOU, PAL? WHY YOU IN SUCH A DAMN RUSH TA EXPIRE AT THE HANDS'A THE REBEL SCUM OF THE BLISTERSTATE?
ME...?
I GUESS I'M...KINDA A CLASSIC CASE...
LIFE GONE WRONG...CRUSHIN' SENSE OF WORTHLESSNESS... SPIRALING GLOOM, ETCETERA...
A WOMAN, RIGHT? YOU BROKE UP WITH SOME SWEET PIECE'A TAIL AN' NOTHIN' SEEMS WORTHWHILE NO MORE.
AM I RIGHT?
HELLUVA CLICHÉ, HUH?
WOMAN BROKE MY HEART, SURE.
LOSIN' THE HOUSE...THE CAR...THE JOB AT THE LIBRARY...ALL'A THAT &$% JUST DONE THE SAME FOR THE CAMEL'S BACK.
THE LIBRARY-- JEEZ...
S-SEE...I WAS IN CHARGE OF ALL THIS CRAZY OLD FICTION CRAP, Y'KNOW? PULP STORIES. DETECTIVES AND ADVENTURERS AND SPACE-PILOTS AND--
GREAT, PAL, THAT'S GREAT.
I MEAN, SURE, WHAT YOU'RE ACTUALLY SAYIN' IS YOU'RE A POINTLESS LOSER SAME AS ME, BUT--YEAH:
GREAT.

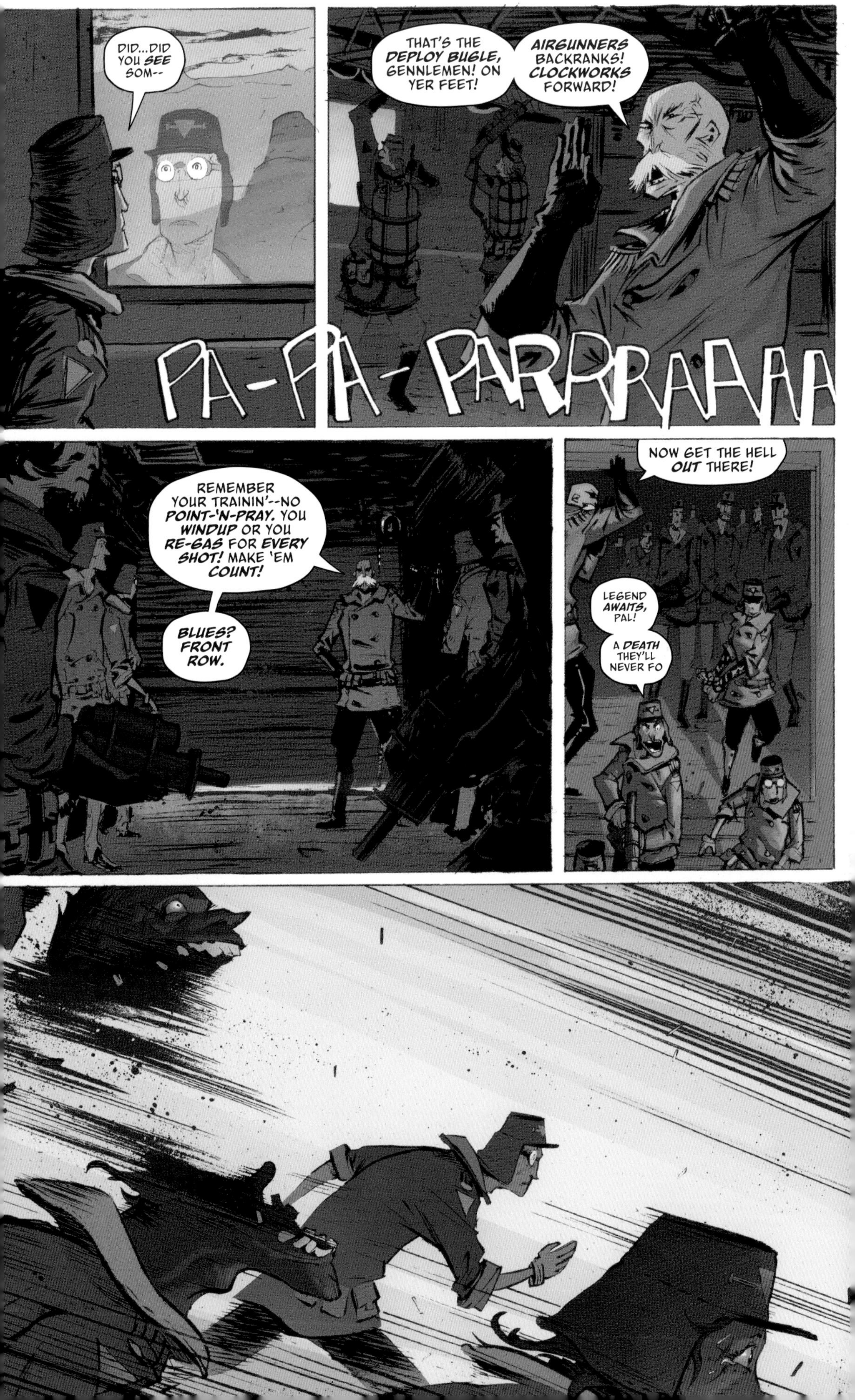
DID...DID YOU SEE SOM--
THAT'S THE DEPLOY BUGLE, GENNLEMEN! ON YER FEET!
AIRGUNNERS BACKRANKS! CLOCKWORKS FORWARD!
PA-PA-PARRRAAAA
REMEMBER YOUR TRAININ'--NO POINT-'N-PRAY. YOU WINDUP OR YOU RE-GAS FOR EVERY SHOT! MAKE 'EM COUNT!
BLUES? FRONT ROW.
NOW GET THE HELL OUT THERE!
LEGEND AWAITS, PAL!
A DEATH THEY'LL NEVER FO

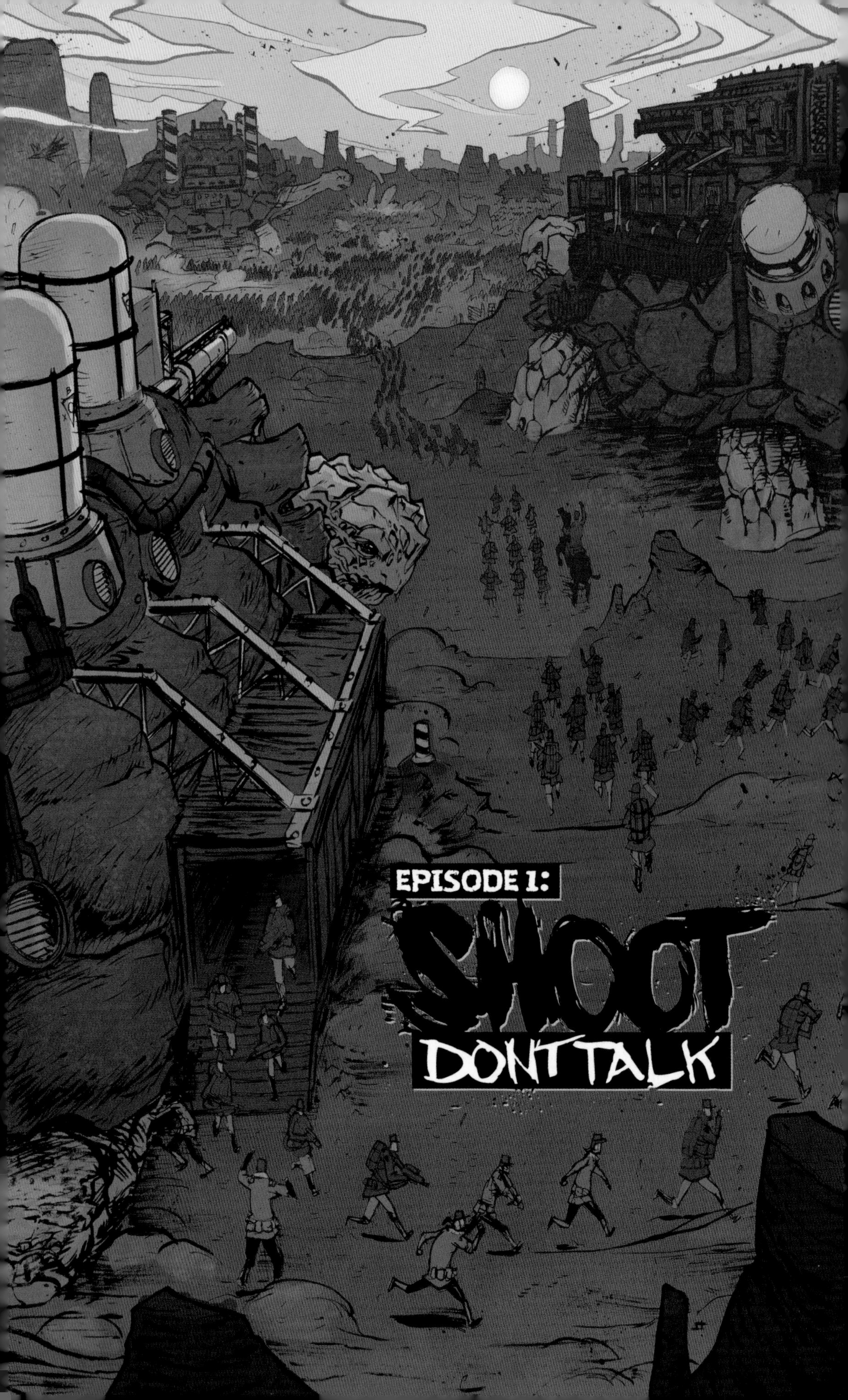
EPISODE 1:
SHOOT
DON'T TALK

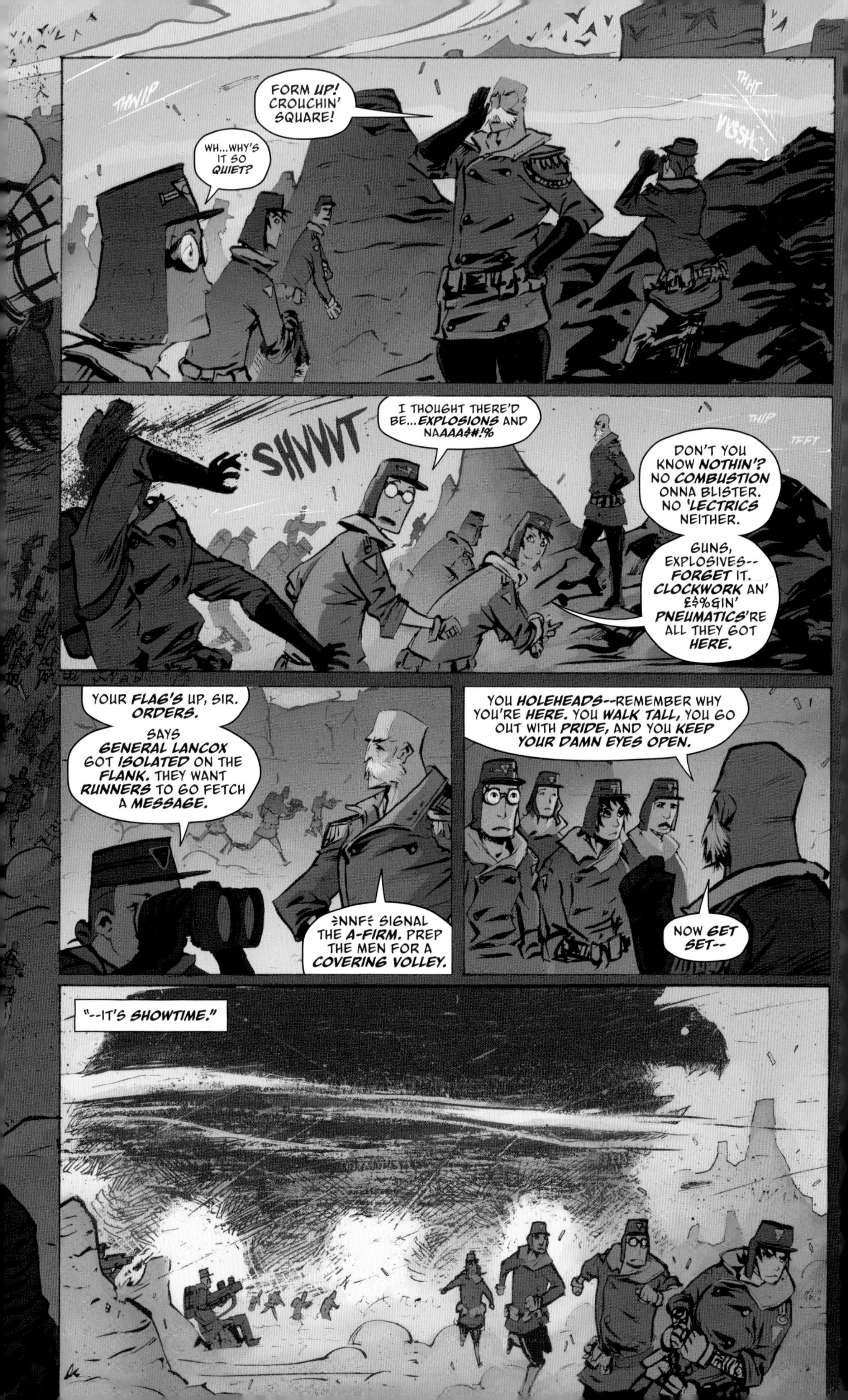
THWIP
FORM UP! CROUCHIN' SQUARE!
WH...WHY'S IT SO QUIET?
THHT
VISSH
I THOUGHT THERE'D BE...EXPLOSIONS AND NAAAA$#!%
SHVVVT
THIP
TFFT
DON'T YOU KNOW NOTHIN'? NO COMBUSTION ONNA BLISTER. NO 'LECTRICS NEITHER.
GUNS, EXPLOSIVES--FORGET IT. CLOCKWORK AN' £$%&IN' PNEUMATICS'RE ALL THEY GOT HERE.
YOUR FLAG'S UP, SIR. ORDERS.
SAYS GENERAL LANCOX GOT ISOLATED ON THE FLANK. THEY WANT RUNNERS TO GO FETCH A MESSAGE.
ƎNNF€ SIGNAL THE A-FIRM. PREP THE MEN FOR A COVERING VOLLEY.
YOU HOLEHEADS--REMEMBER WHY YOU'RE HERE. YOU WALK TALL, YOU GO OUT WITH PRIDE, AND YOU KEEP YOUR DAMN EYES OPEN.
NOW GET SET--
"--IT'S SHOWTIME."

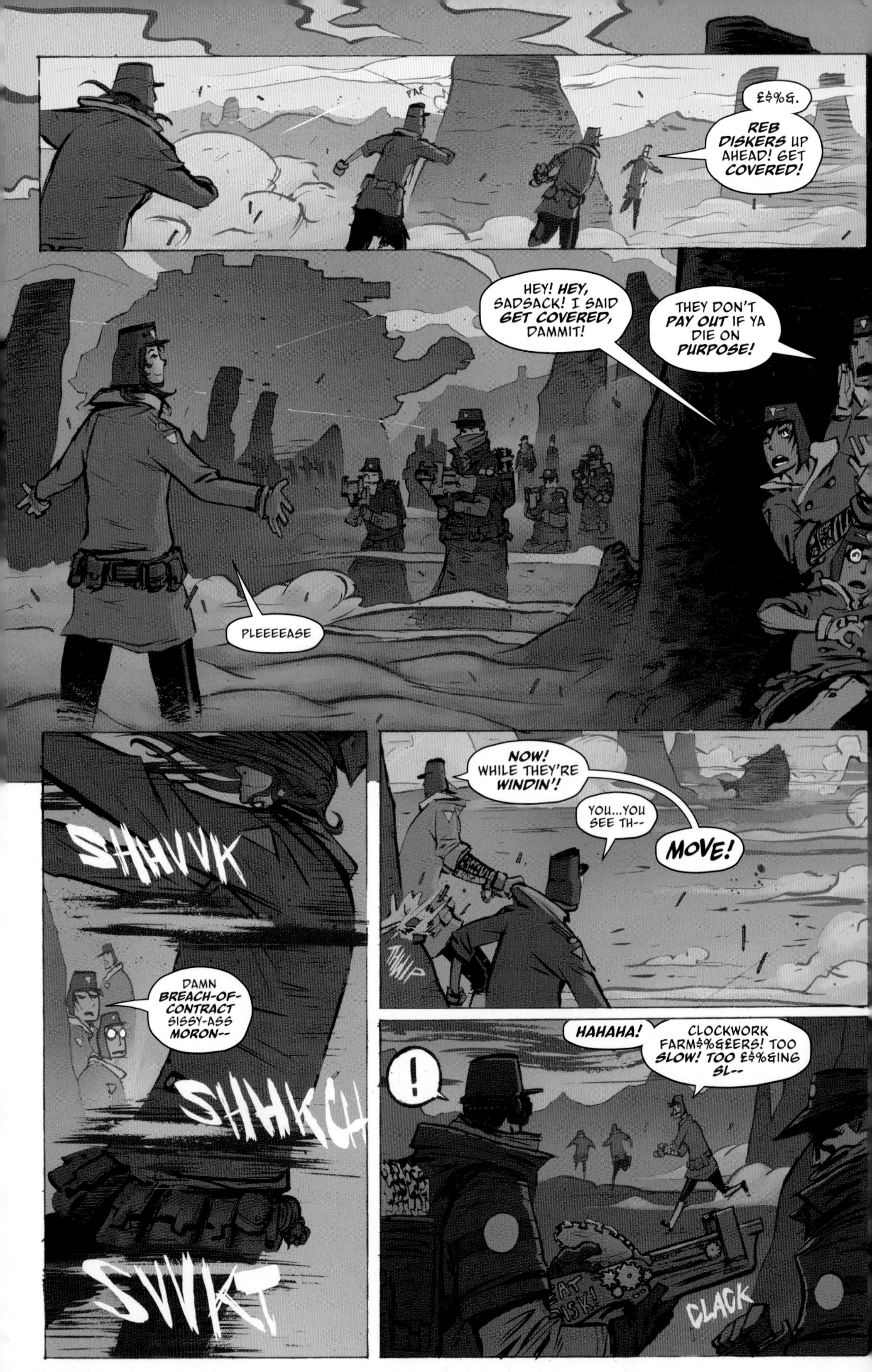
PAF
£$%G.
REB DISKERS UP AHEAD! GET COVERED!
HEY! HEY, SADSACK! I SAID GET COVERED, DAMMIT!
THEY DON'T PAY OUT IF YA DIE ON PURPOSE!
PLEEEEASE
SHHVVK
DAMN BREACH-OF-CONTRACT SISSY-ASS MORON--
SHHKCH
SVVKT
NOW! WHILE THEY'RE WINDIN'!
YOU...YOU SEE TH--
MOVE!
THWIP
HAHAHA!
CLOCKWORK FARM$%&EERS! TOO SLOW! TOO £$%&ING SL--
!
EAT DISK!
CLACK

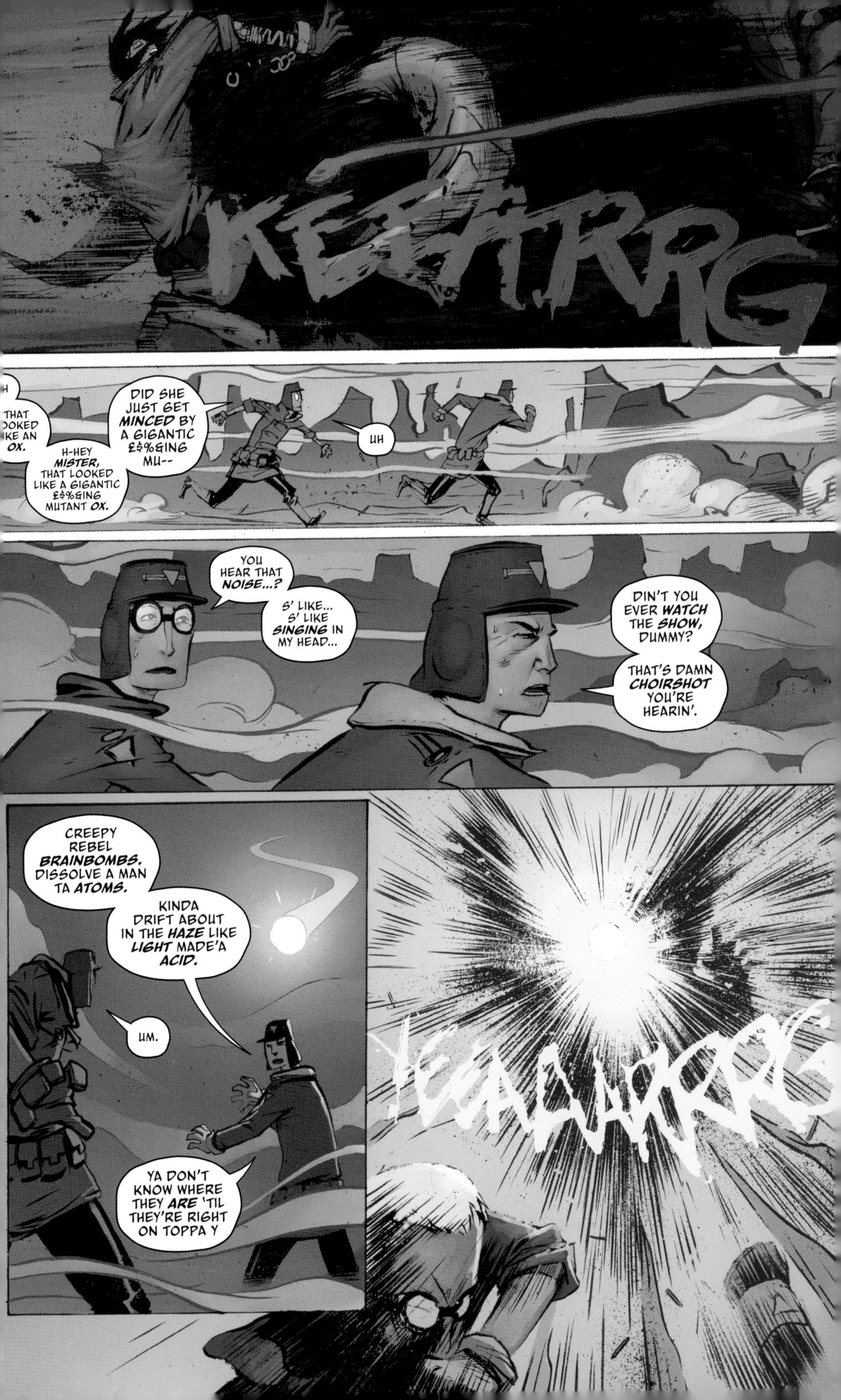
THAT OOKED IKE AN OX.
H-HEY MISTER, THAT LOOKED LIKE A GIGANTIC £$%&ING MUTANT OX.
DID SHE JUST GET MINCED BY A GIGANTIC £$%&ING MU--
UH
YOU HEAR THAT NOISE...?
S' LIKE... S' LIKE SINGING IN MY HEAD...
DIN'T YOU EVER WATCH THE SHOW, DUMMY?
THAT'S DAMN CHOIRSHOT YOU'RE HEARIN'.
CREEPY REBEL BRAINBOMBS. DISSOLVE A MAN TA ATOMS.
KINDA DRIFT ABOUT IN THE HAZE LIKE LIGHT MADE'A ACID.
UM.
YA DON'T KNOW WHERE THEY ARE 'TIL THEY'RE RIGHT ON TOPPA Y

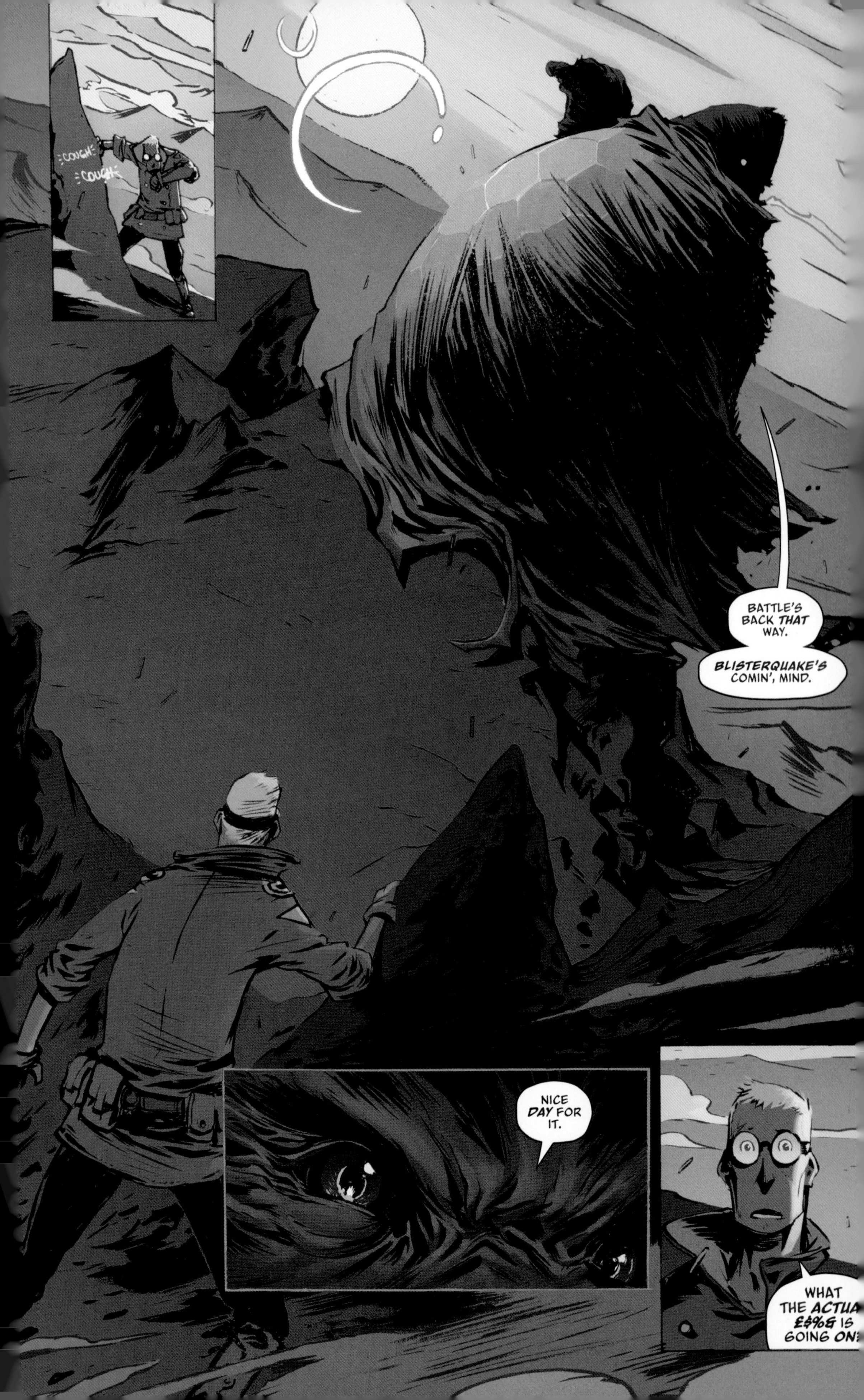
COUGH
COUGH
BATTLE'S BACK *THAT* WAY.
*BLISTERQUAKE'S* COMIN', MIND.
NICE *DAY* FOR IT.
WHAT THE *ACTUA* £$%& IS GOING *ON*

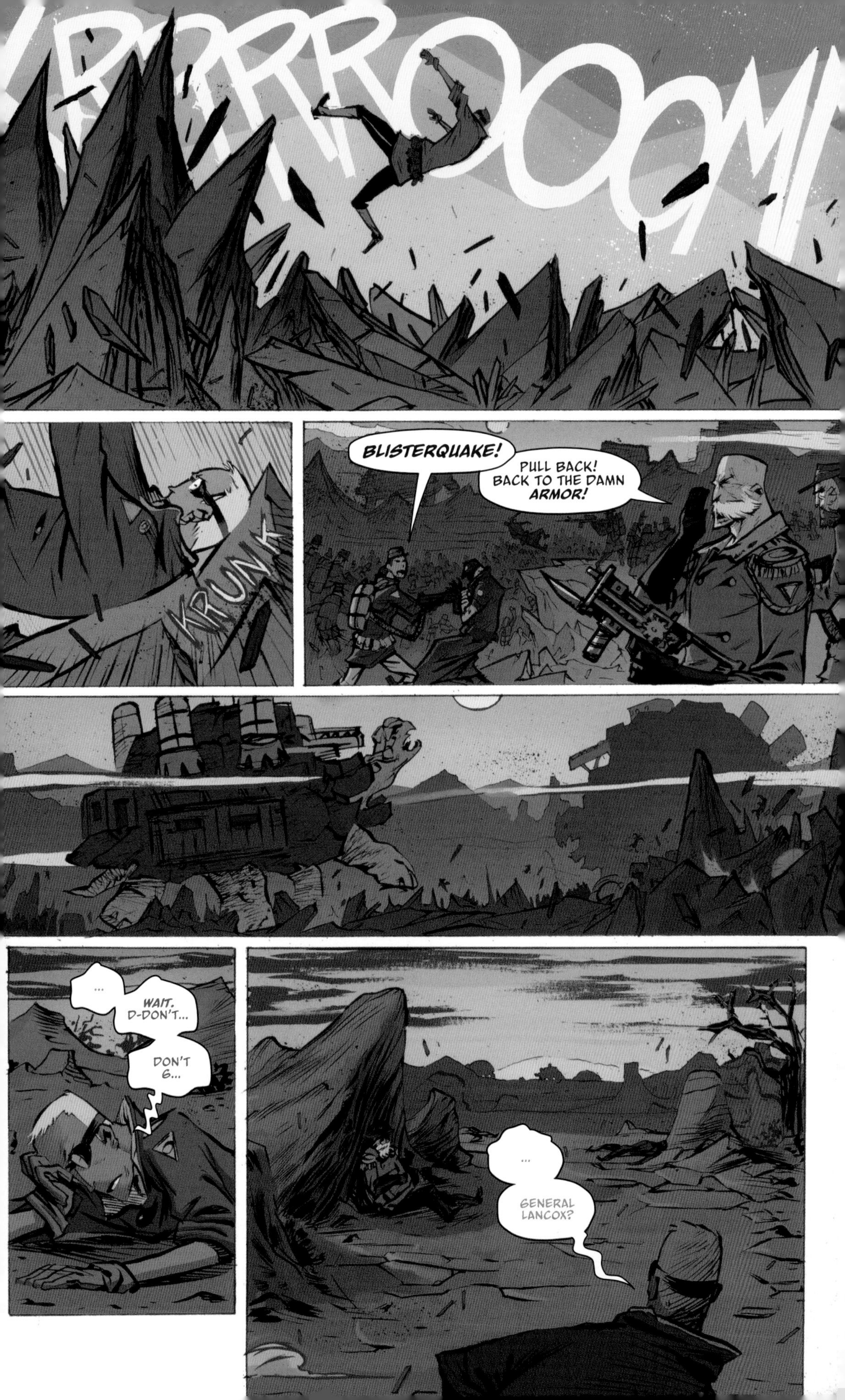
KRRRROOOM!
KRUNK
BLISTERQUAKE!
PULL BACK! BACK TO THE DAMN ARMOR!
...
WAIT. D-DON'T...
DON'T G...
...
GENERAL LANCOX?

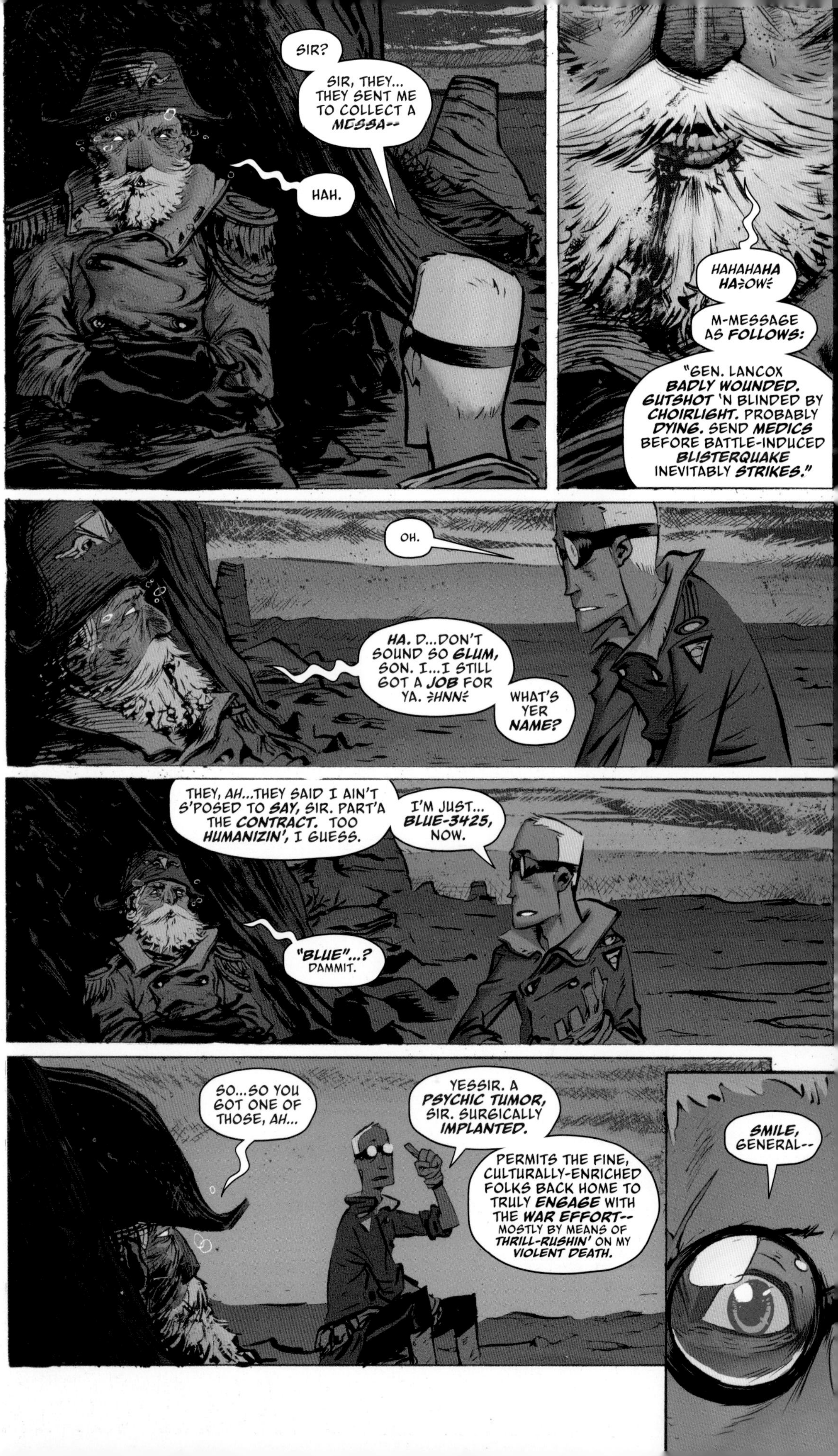
SIR?
SIR, THEY... THEY SENT ME TO COLLECT A MESSA--
HAH.
HAHAHAHA HA-OW-
M-MESSAGE AS FOLLOWS:
"GEN. LANCOX BADLY WOUNDED. GUTSHOT 'N BLINDED BY CHOIRLIGHT. PROBABLY DYING. SEND MEDICS BEFORE BATTLE-INDUCED BLISTERQUAKE INEVITABLY STRIKES."
OH.
HA. D...DON'T SOUND SO GLUM, SON. I...I STILL GOT A JOB FOR YA. -HNN-
WHAT'S YER NAME?
THEY, AH...THEY SAID I AIN'T S'POSED TO SAY, SIR. PART'A THE CONTRACT. TOO HUMANIZIN', I GUESS.
I'M JUST... BLUE-3425, NOW.
"BLUE"...? DAMMIT.
SO...SO YOU GOT ONE OF THOSE, AH...
YESSIR. A PSYCHIC TUMOR, SIR. SURGICALLY IMPLANTED.
PERMITS THE FINE, CULTURALLY-ENRICHED FOLKS BACK HOME TO TRULY ENGAGE WITH THE WAR EFFORT-- MOSTLY BY MEANS OF THRILL-RUSHIN' ON MY VIOLENT DEATH.
SMILE, GENERAL--

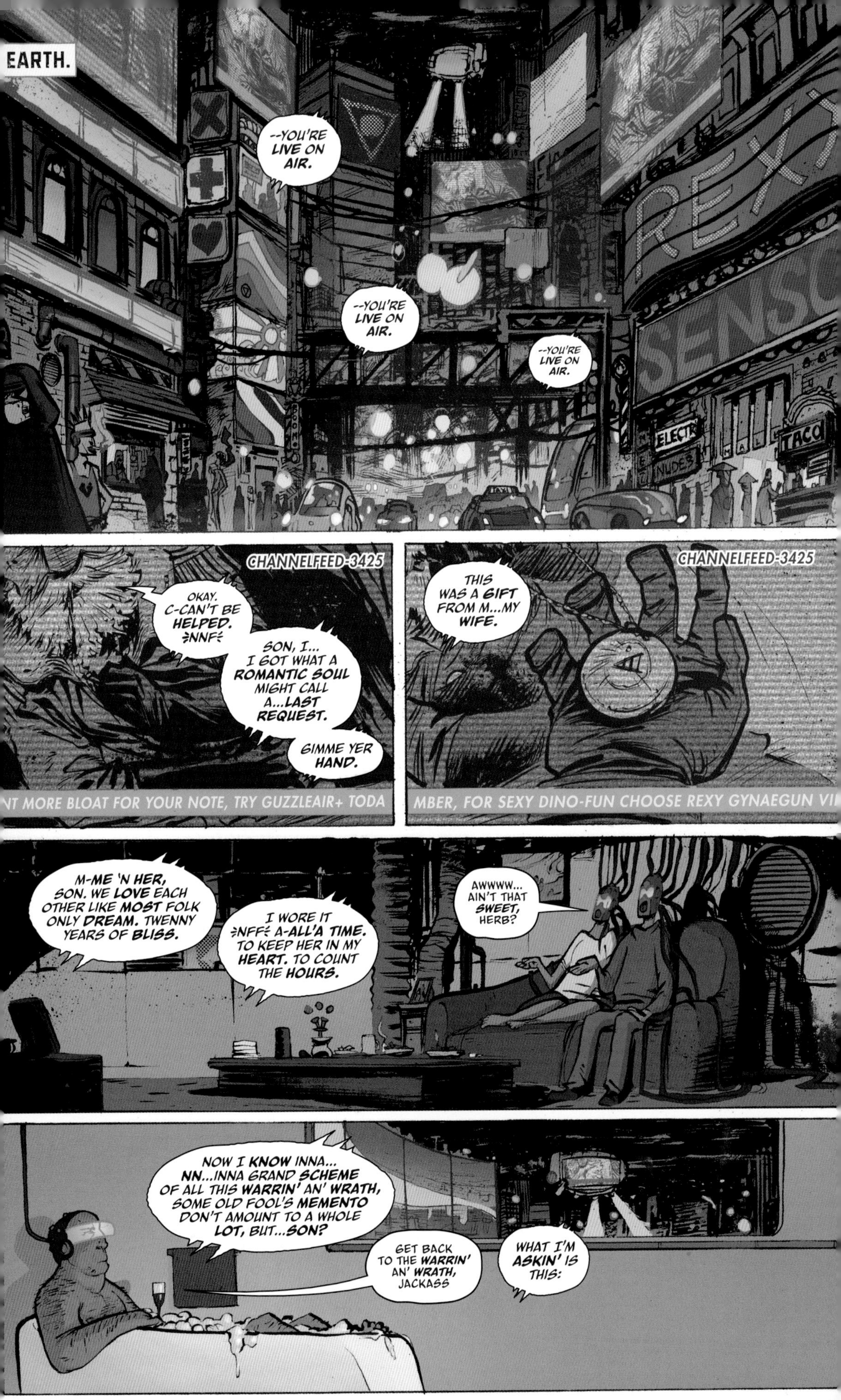
EARTH.
--YOU'RE LIVE ON AIR.
--YOU'RE LIVE ON AIR.
--YOU'RE LIVE ON AIR.
REXY
SENSO
ELECTR
NUDES
TACO
CHANNELFEED-3425
OKAY. C-CAN'T BE HELPED. NNF
SON, I... I GOT WHAT A ROMANTIC SOUL MIGHT CALL A...LAST REQUEST.
GIMME YER HAND.
NT MORE BLOAT FOR YOUR NOTE, TRY GUZZLEAIR+ TODA
CHANNELFEED-3425
THIS WAS A GIFT FROM M...MY WIFE.
MBER, FOR SEXY DINO-FUN CHOOSE REXY GYNAEGUN VI
M-ME 'N HER, SON. WE LOVE EACH OTHER LIKE MOST FOLK ONLY DREAM. TWENNY YEARS OF BLISS.
I WORE IT NFF A-ALL'A TIME. TO KEEP HER IN MY HEART. TO COUNT THE HOURS.
AWWWW... AIN'T THAT SWEET, HERB?
NOW I KNOW INNA... NN...INNA GRAND SCHEME OF ALL THIS WARRIN' AN' WRATH, SOME OLD FOOL'S MEMENTO DON'T AMOUNT TO A WHOLE LOT, BUT...SON?
GET BACK TO THE WARRIN' AN' WRATH, JACKASS
WHAT I'M ASKIN' IS THIS:

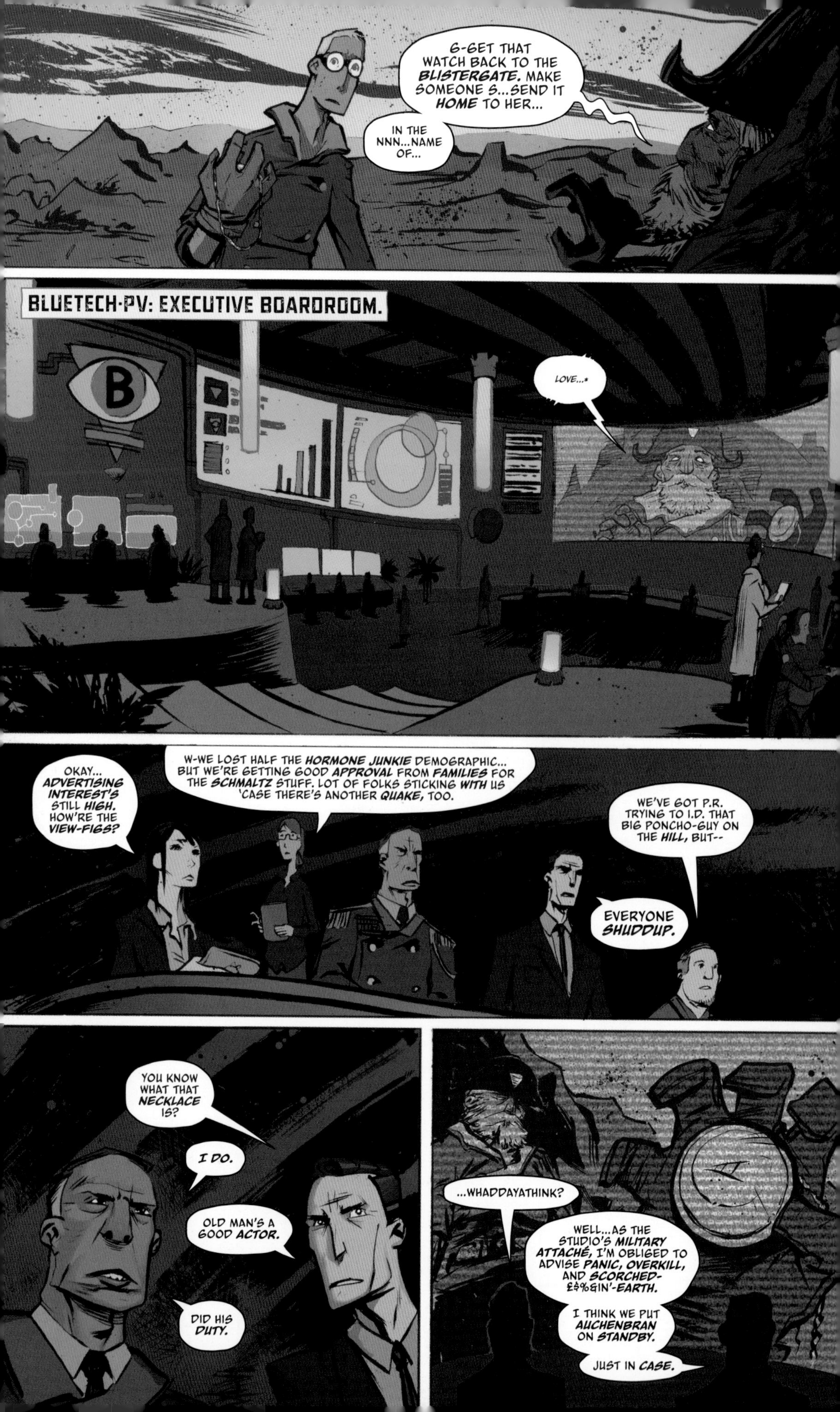
G-GET THAT WATCH BACK TO THE BLISTERGATE. MAKE SOMEONE S...SEND IT HOME TO HER...
IN THE NNN...NAME OF...
BLUETECH·PV: EXECUTIVE BOARDROOM.
LOVE...*
OKAY... ADVERTISING INTEREST'S STILL HIGH. HOW'RE THE VIEW-FIGS?
W-WE LOST HALF THE HORMONE JUNKIE DEMOGRAPHIC... BUT WE'RE GETTING GOOD APPROVAL FROM FAMILIES FOR THE SCHMALTZ STUFF. LOT OF FOLKS STICKING WITH US 'CASE THERE'S ANOTHER QUAKE, TOO.
WE'VE GOT P.R. TRYING TO I.D. THAT BIG PONCHO-GUY ON THE HILL, BUT--
EVERYONE SHUDDUP.
YOU KNOW WHAT THAT NECKLACE IS?
I DO.
OLD MAN'S A GOOD ACTOR.
DID HIS DUTY.
...WHADDAYATHINK?
WELL...AS THE STUDIO'S MILITARY ATTACHÉ, I'M OBLIGED TO ADVISE PANIC, OVERKILL, AND SCORCHED-£$%&IN'-EARTH.
I THINK WE PUT AUCHENBRAN ON STANDBY.
JUST IN CASE.

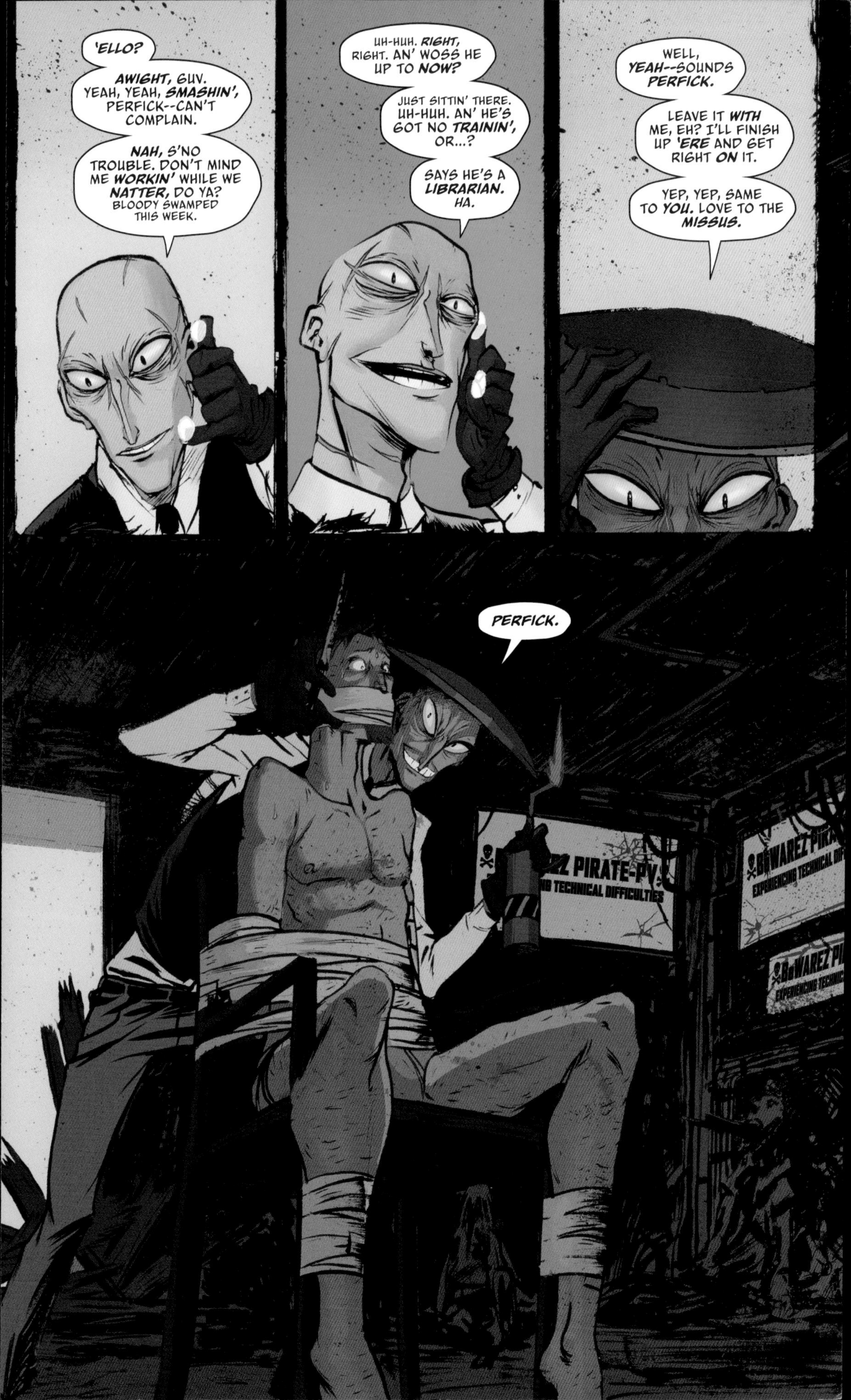
'ELLO?
AWIGHT, GUV. YEAH, YEAH, SMASHIN', PERFICK--CAN'T COMPLAIN.
NAH, S'NO TROUBLE. DON'T MIND ME WORKIN' WHILE WE NATTER, DO YA? BLOODY SWAMPED THIS WEEK.
UH-HUH. RIGHT, RIGHT. AN' WOSS HE UP TO NOW?
JUST SITTIN' THERE. UH-HUH. AN' HE'S GOT NO TRAININ', OR...?
SAYS HE'S A LIBRARIAN. HA.
WELL, YEAH--SOUNDS PERFICK.
LEAVE IT WITH ME, EH? I'LL FINISH UP 'ERE AND GET RIGHT ON IT.
YEP, YEP, SAME TO YOU. LOVE TO THE MISSUS.
PERFICK.

LOVE.

"IN THE NAME OF LOVE," HE SAYS.

FACT *IS*, SIR, WHEN YOU'RE TALKIN' TO A BITTER HEARTBROKE LOSER EX-LIBRARIAN *DIVORCÉ*--

--PARTICULARLY ONE SEEKIN' *SUICIDE* BY MEANS OF THE HARD-FOUGHT *COLONIAL WAR* BEEN RAGING FOR *YEARS*--

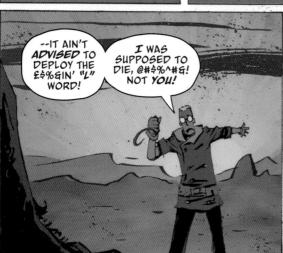

--IT AIN'T *ADVISED* TO DEPLOY THE £$%&IN' *"L"* WORD!

I WAS SUPPOSED TO DIE, @#$%^#&! NOT *YOU*!

@#$% YOUR *"NAME OF LOVE."*

AND £$%& *YOU*!

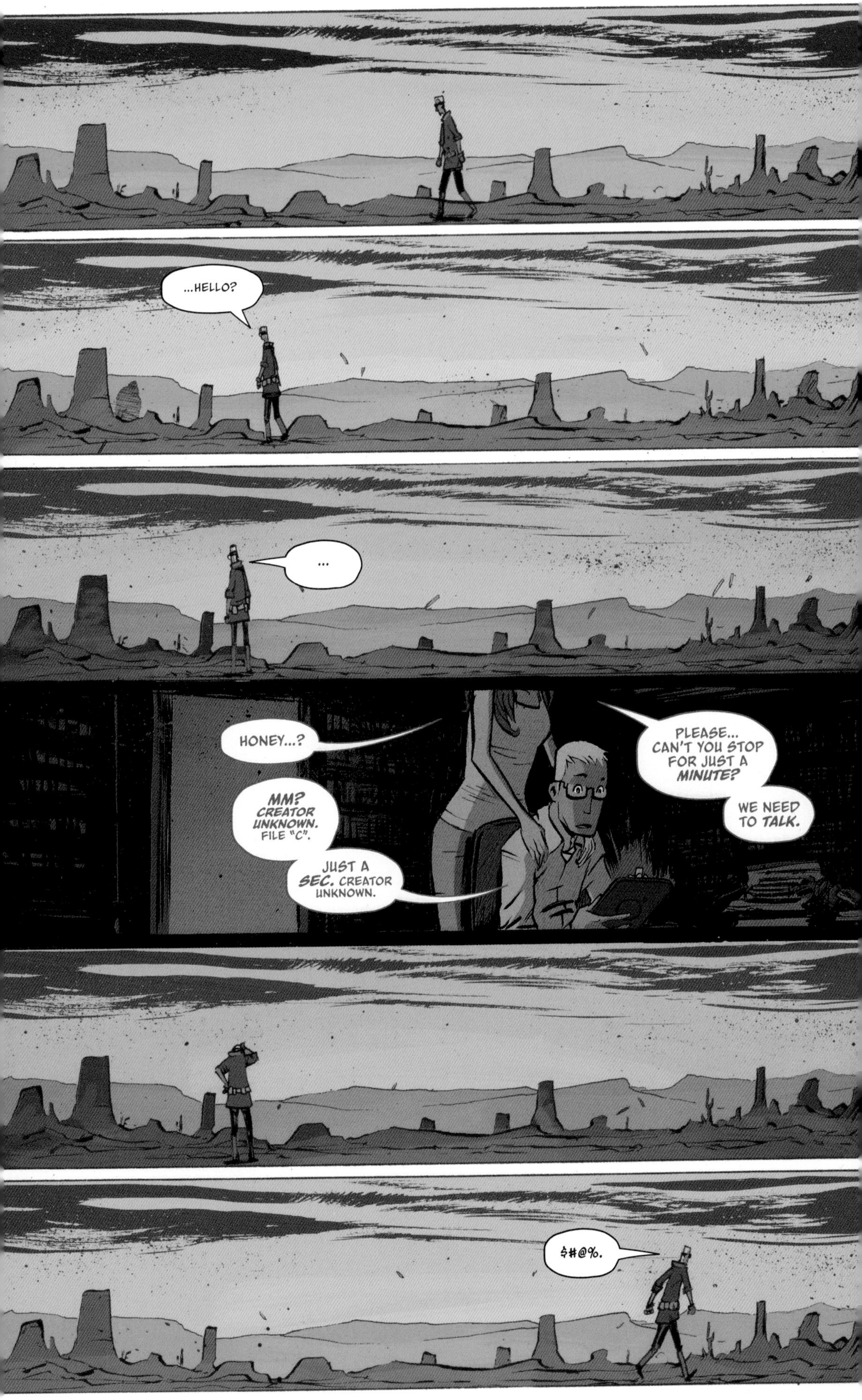
...HELLO?
...
HONEY...?
PLEASE... CAN'T YOU STOP FOR JUST A MINUTE?
WE NEED TO TALK.
MM? CREATOR UNKNOWN. FILE "C".
JUST A SEC. CREATOR UNKNOWN.
$#@%.

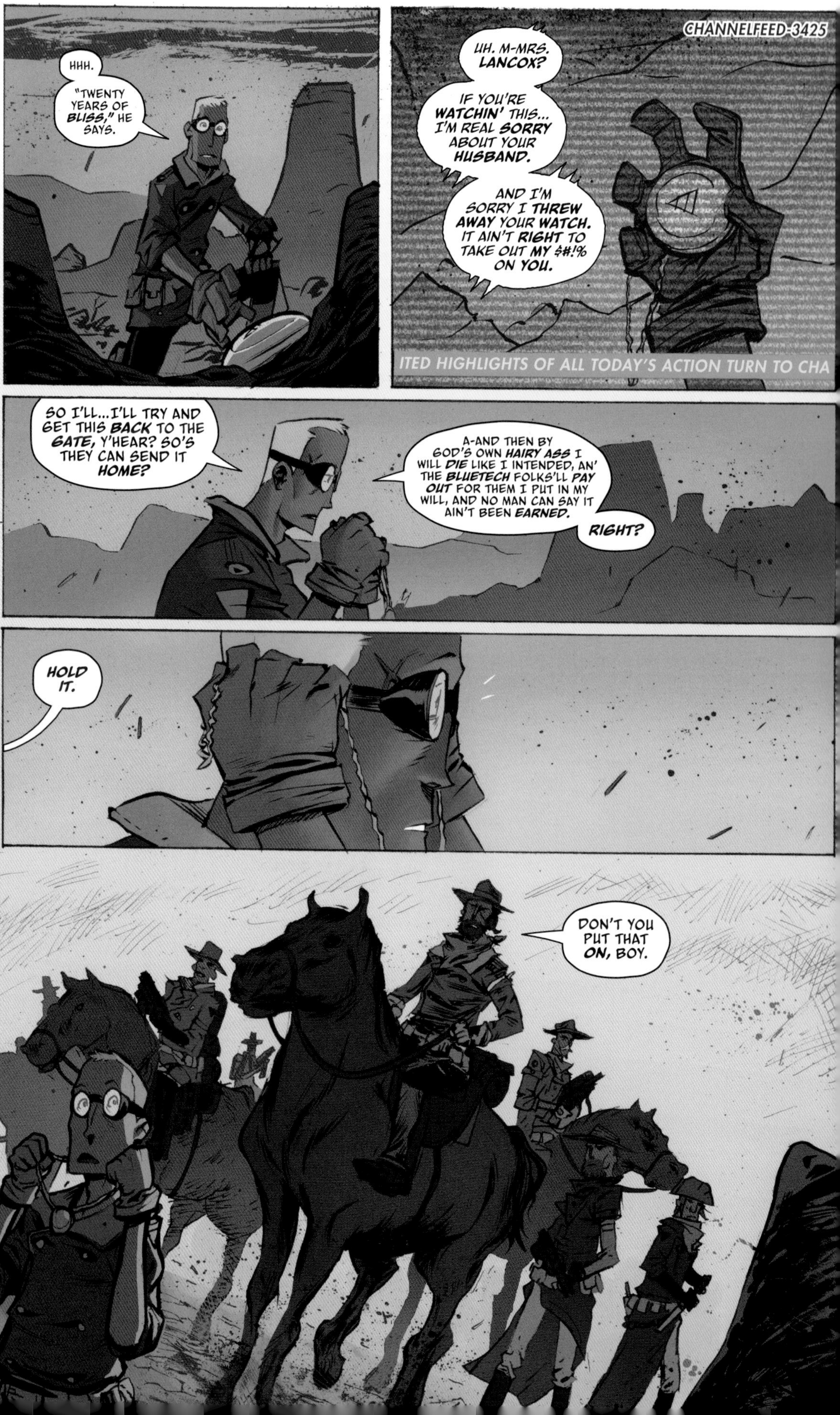

HHH.
"TWENTY YEARS OF BLISS," HE SAYS.
CHANNELFEED-3425
UH. M-MRS. LANCOX?
IF YOU'RE WATCHIN' THIS... I'M REAL SORRY ABOUT YOUR HUSBAND.
AND I'M SORRY I THREW AWAY YOUR WATCH. IT AIN'T RIGHT TO TAKE OUT MY $#!% ON YOU.
ITED HIGHLIGHTS OF ALL TODAY'S ACTION TURN TO CHA
SO I'LL...I'LL TRY AND GET THIS BACK TO THE GATE, Y'HEAR? SO'S THEY CAN SEND IT HOME?
A-AND THEN BY GOD'S OWN HAIRY ASS I WILL DIE LIKE I INTENDED, AN' THE BLUETECH FOLKS'LL PAY OUT FOR THEM I PUT IN MY WILL, AND NO MAN CAN SAY IT AIN'T BEEN EARNED.
RIGHT?
HOLD IT.
DON'T YOU PUT THAT ON, BOY.

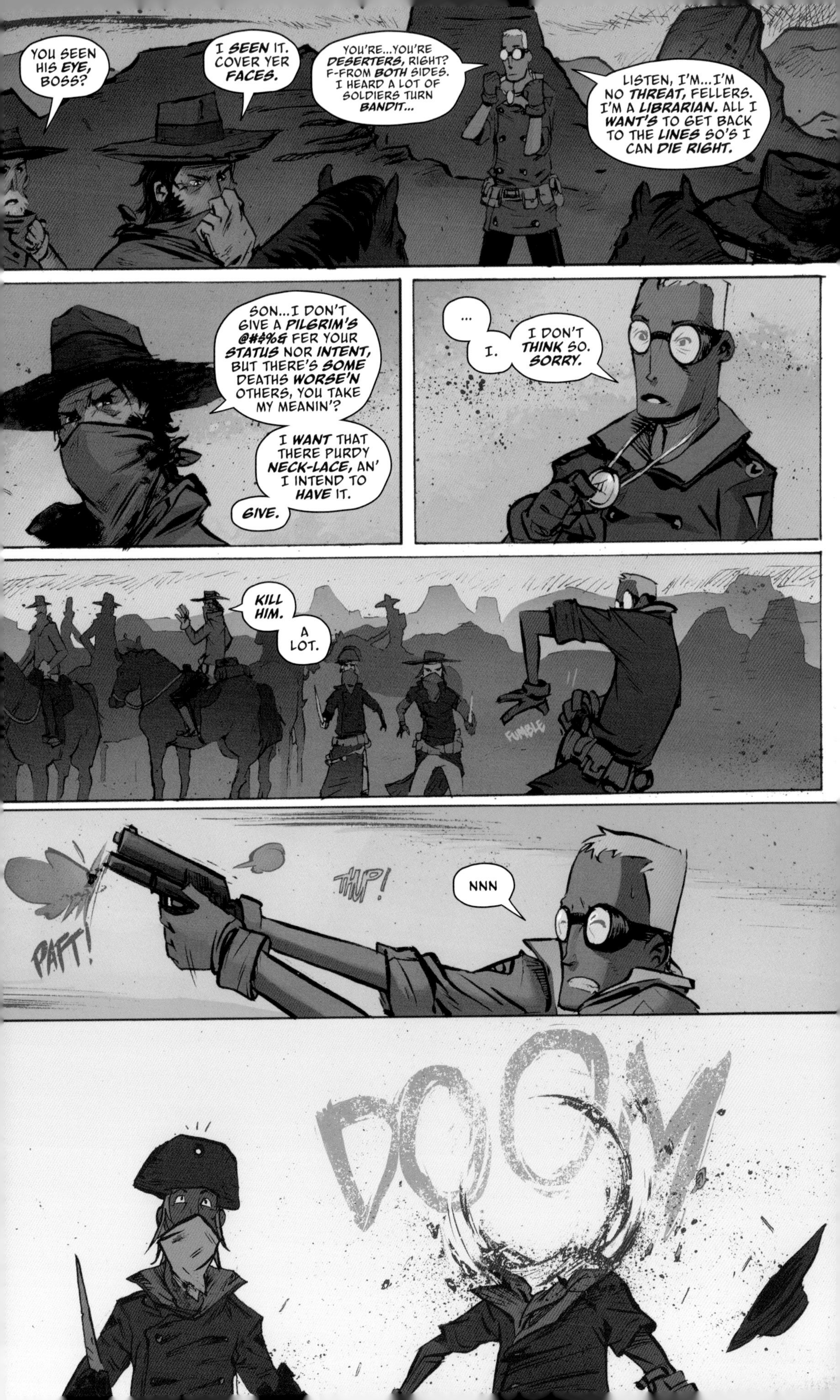
YOU SEEN HIS EYE, BOSS?
I SEEN IT. COVER YER FACES.
YOU'RE...YOU'RE DESERTERS, RIGHT? F-FROM BOTH SIDES. I HEARD A LOT OF SOLDIERS TURN BANDIT...
LISTEN, I'M...I'M NO THREAT, FELLERS. I'M A LIBRARIAN. ALL I WANT'S TO GET BACK TO THE LINES SO'S I CAN DIE RIGHT.
SON...I DON'T GIVE A PILGRIM'S @#$%& FER YOUR STATUS NOR INTENT, BUT THERE'S SOME DEATHS WORSE'N OTHERS, YOU TAKE MY MEANIN'?
I WANT THAT THERE PURDY NECK-LACE, AN' I INTEND TO HAVE IT.
GIVE.
...
I.
I DON'T THINK SO. SORRY.
KILL HIM.
A LOT.
FUMBLE
THUP!
PAFT!
NNN
DOOM

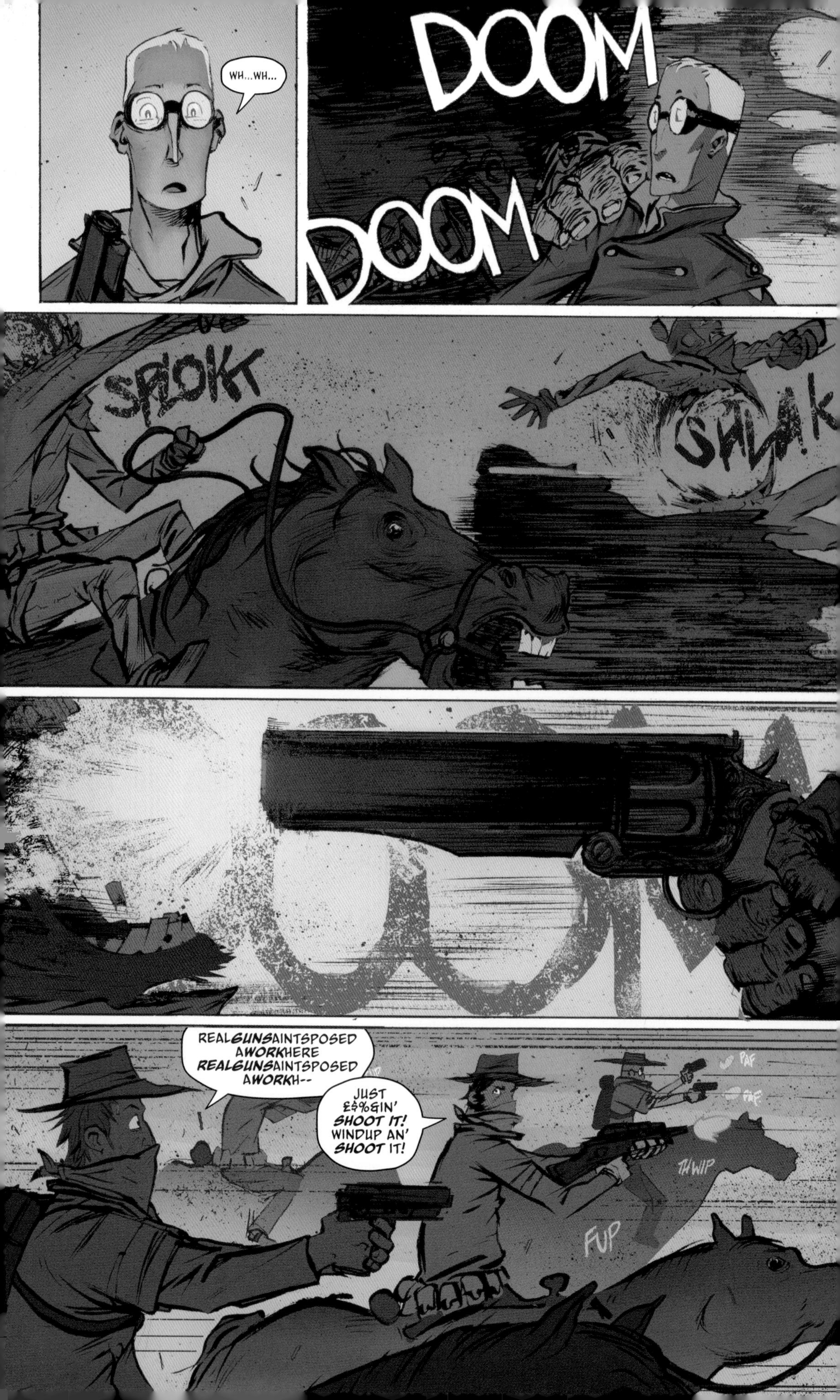
WH...WH...
DOOM
DOOM
SPLOKT
SHLAK
REALGUNSAINTSPOSED AWORKHERE REALGUNSAINTSPOSED AWORKH--
JUST £$%&IN' SHOOT IT! WINDUP AN' SHOOT IT!
PAF
PAF
THWIP
FUP

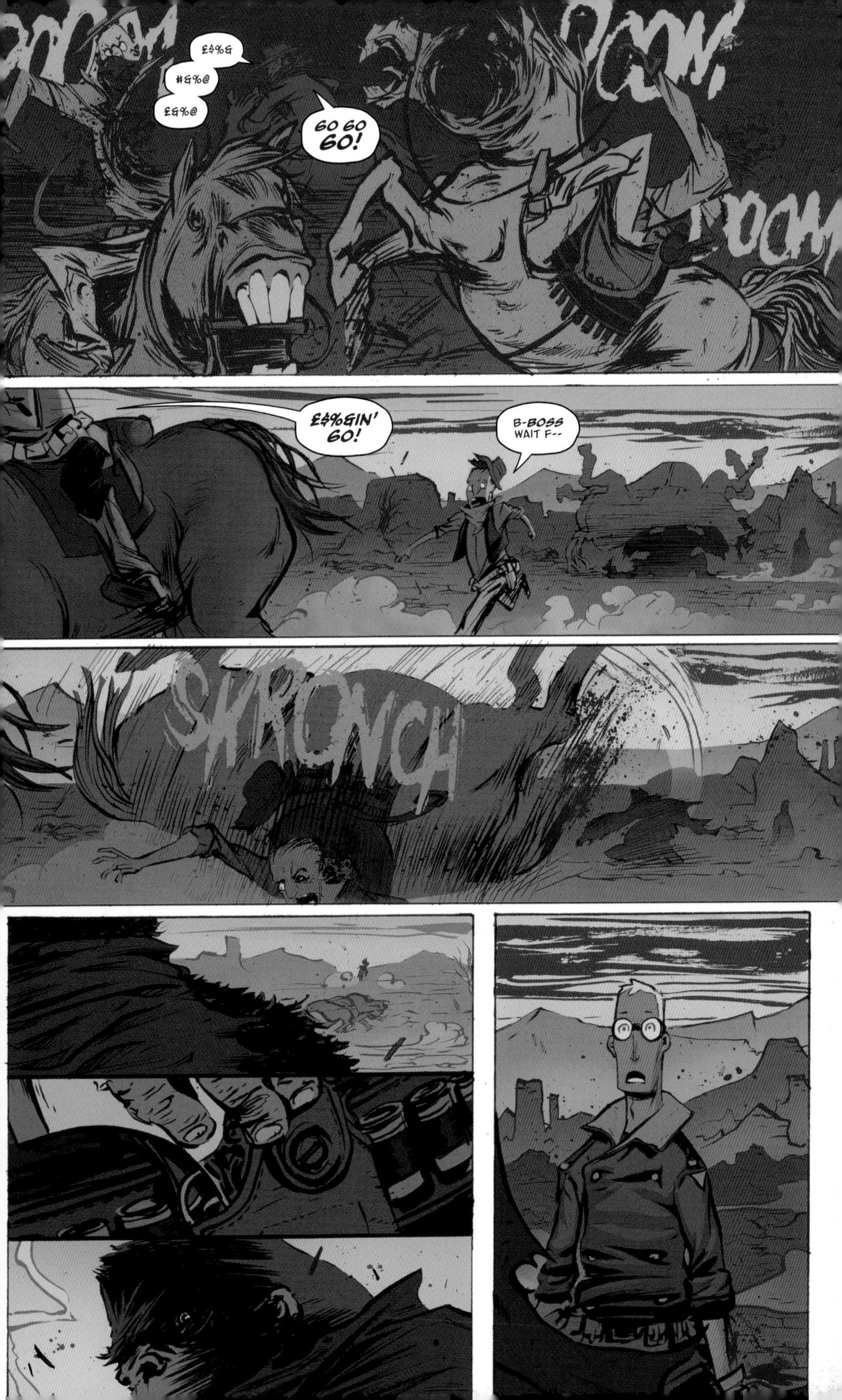
BOOM!
£$%G
#&%@
£&%@
GO GO GO!
BOOM!
BOOM
£$%GIN' GO!
B-BOSS WAIT F--
SKRONCH!

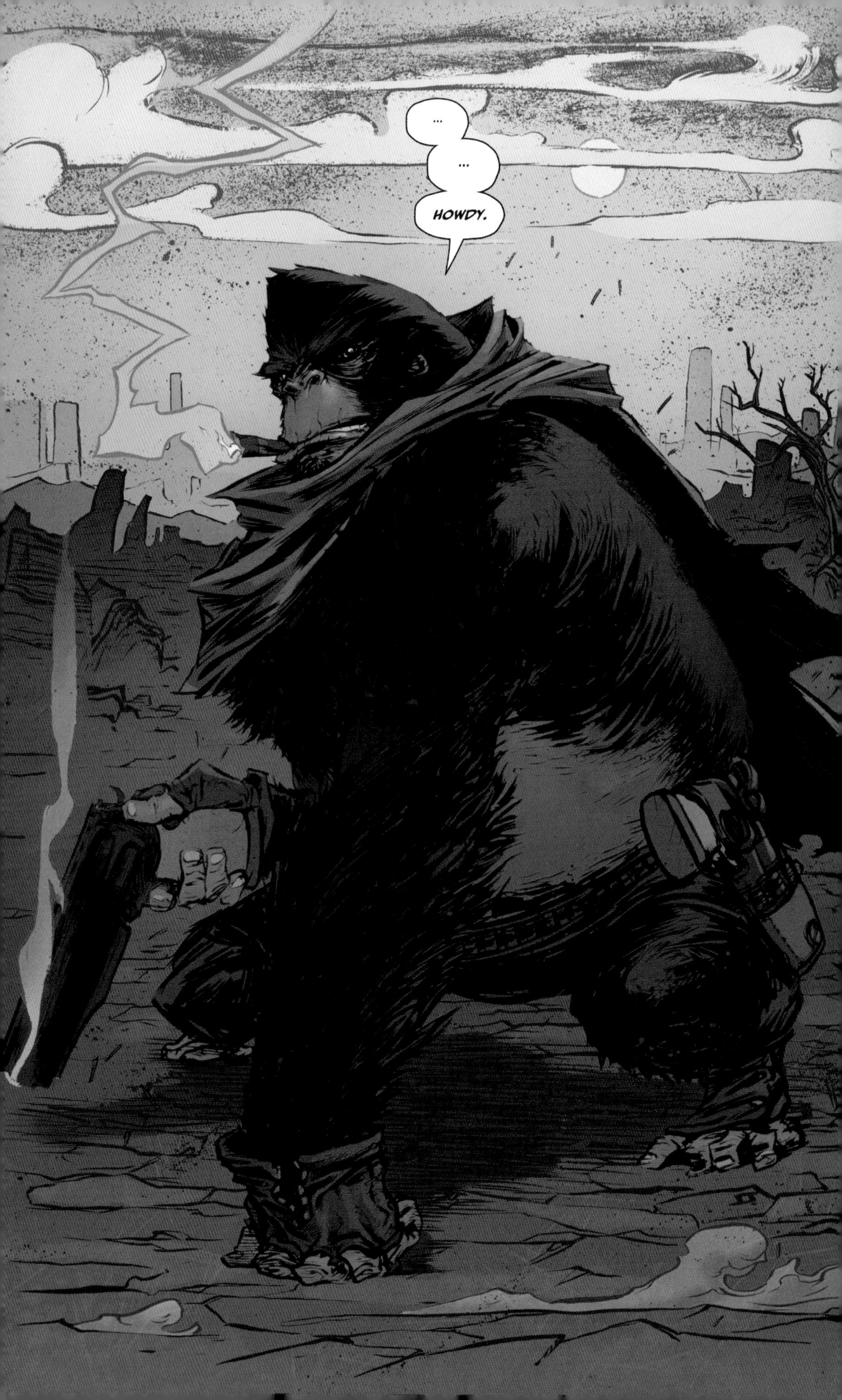
...
...
HOWDY.

# CHAPTER TWO

# SIX-GUN GORILLA

(Continued from page 8.)

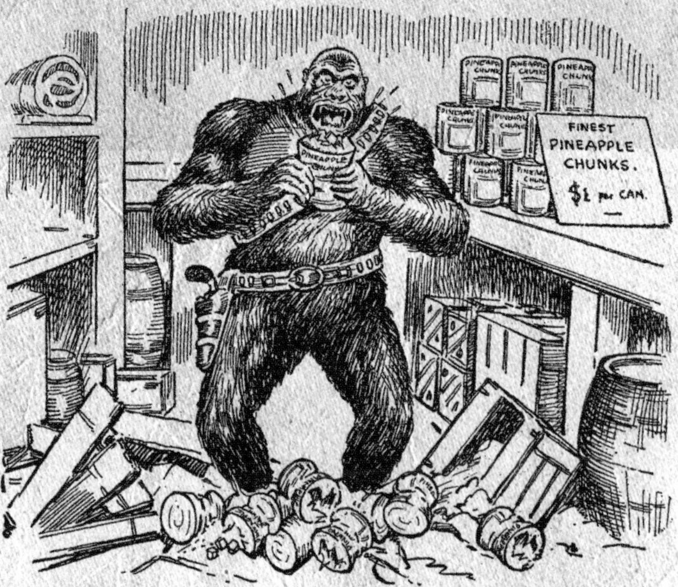
FINEST
PINEAPPLE
CHUNKS.
$1 per CAN.

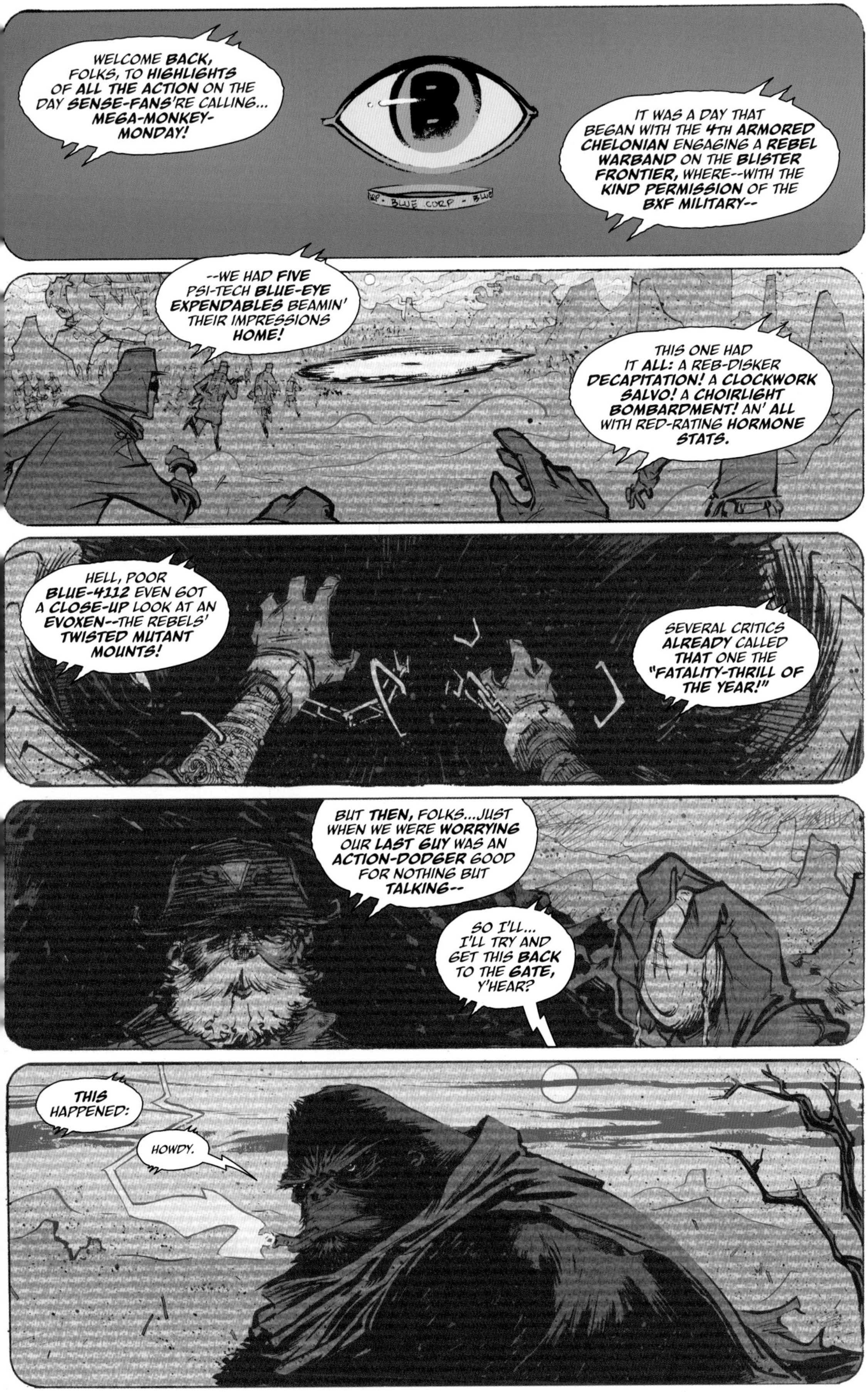
WELCOME BACK, FOLKS, TO HIGHLIGHTS OF ALL THE ACTION ON THE DAY SENSE-FANS'RE CALLING... MEGA-MONKEY-MONDAY!
BLUE.CORP - BLUE
IT WAS A DAY THAT BEGAN WITH THE 4th ARMORED CHELONIAN ENGAGING A REBEL WARBAND ON THE BLISTER FRONTIER, WHERE--WITH THE KIND PERMISSION OF THE BXF MILITARY--
--WE HAD FIVE PSI-TECH BLUE-EYE EXPENDABLES BEAMIN' THEIR IMPRESSIONS HOME!
THIS ONE HAD IT ALL: A REB-DISKER DECAPITATION! A CLOCKWORK SALVO! A CHOIRLIGHT BOMBARDMENT! AN' ALL WITH RED-RATING HORMONE STATS.
HELL, POOR BLUE-4112 EVEN GOT A CLOSE-UP LOOK AT AN EVOXEN--THE REBELS' TWISTED MUTANT MOUNTS!
SEVERAL CRITICS ALREADY CALLED THAT ONE THE "FATALITY-THRILL OF THE YEAR!"
BUT THEN, FOLKS...JUST WHEN WE WERE WORRYING OUR LAST GUY WAS AN ACTION-DODGER GOOD FOR NOTHING BUT TALKING--
SO I'LL... I'LL TRY AND GET THIS BACK TO THE GATE, Y'HEAR?
THIS HAPPENED:
HOWDY.

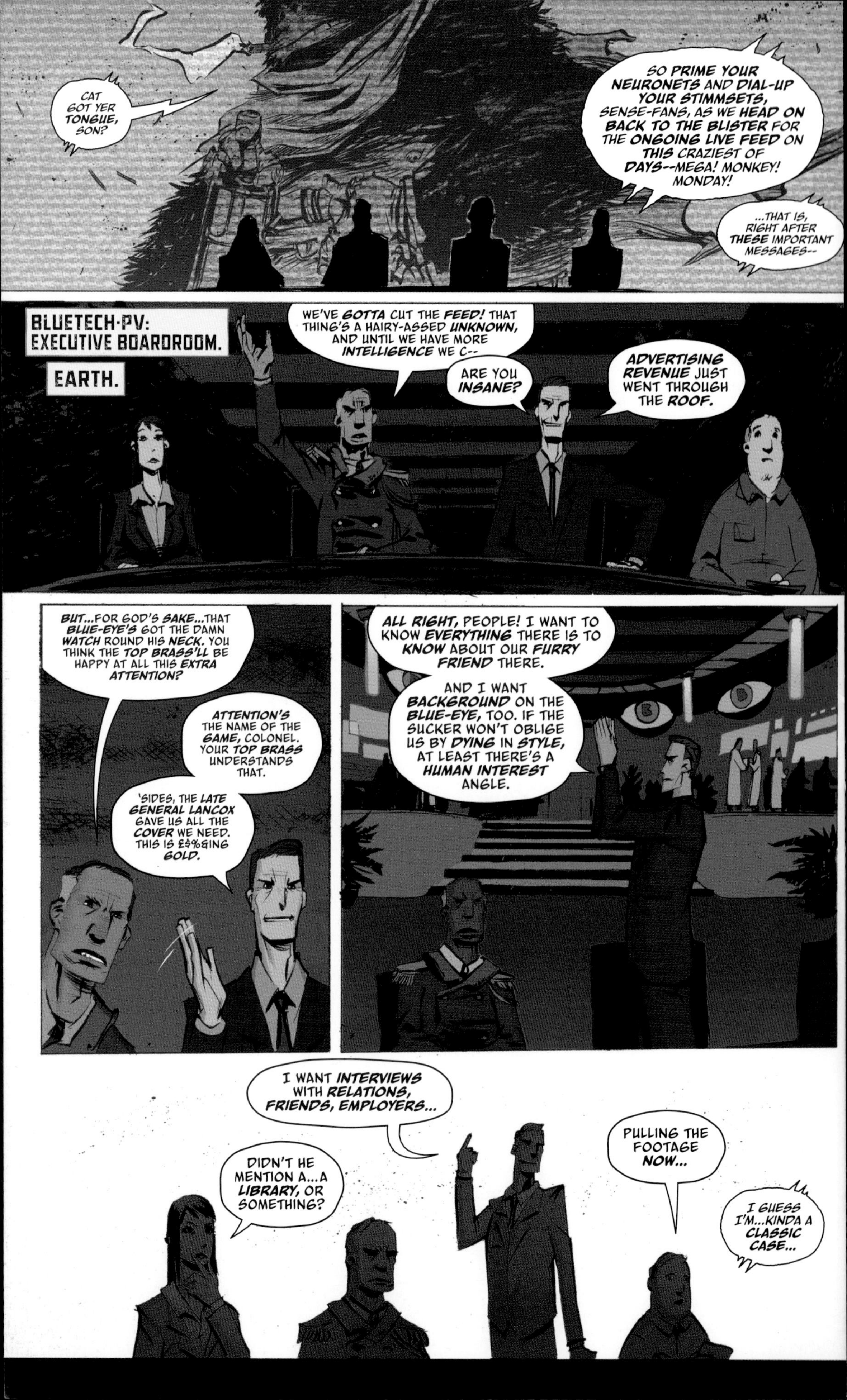
CAT GOT YER TONGUE, SON?
SO PRIME YOUR NEURONETS AND DIAL-UP YOUR STIMMSETS, SENSE-FANS, AS WE HEAD ON BACK TO THE BLISTER FOR THE ONGOING LIVE FEED ON THIS CRAZIEST OF DAYS--MEGA! MONKEY! MONDAY!
...THAT IS, RIGHT AFTER THESE IMPORTANT MESSAGES--
BLUETECH-PV: EXECUTIVE BOARDROOM.
EARTH.
WE'VE GOTTA CUT THE FEED! THAT THING'S A HAIRY-ASSED UNKNOWN, AND UNTIL WE HAVE MORE INTELLIGENCE WE C--
ARE YOU INSANE?
ADVERTISING REVENUE JUST WENT THROUGH THE ROOF.
BUT...FOR GOD'S SAKE...THAT BLUE-EYE'S GOT THE DAMN WATCH ROUND HIS NECK. YOU THINK THE TOP BRASS'LL BE HAPPY AT ALL THIS EXTRA ATTENTION?
ATTENTION'S THE NAME OF THE GAME, COLONEL. YOUR TOP BRASS UNDERSTANDS THAT.
'SIDES, THE LATE GENERAL LANCOX GAVE US ALL THE COVER WE NEED. THIS IS £$%&ING GOLD.
ALL RIGHT, PEOPLE! I WANT TO KNOW EVERYTHING THERE IS TO KNOW ABOUT OUR FURRY FRIEND THERE.
AND I WANT BACKGROUND ON THE BLUE-EYE, TOO. IF THE SUCKER WON'T OBLIGE US BY DYING IN STYLE, AT LEAST THERE'S A HUMAN INTEREST ANGLE.
I WANT INTERVIEWS WITH RELATIONS, FRIENDS, EMPLOYERS...
DIDN'T HE MENTION A...A LIBRARY, OR SOMETHING?
PULLING THE FOOTAGE NOW...
I GUESS I'M...KINDA A CLASSIC CASE...

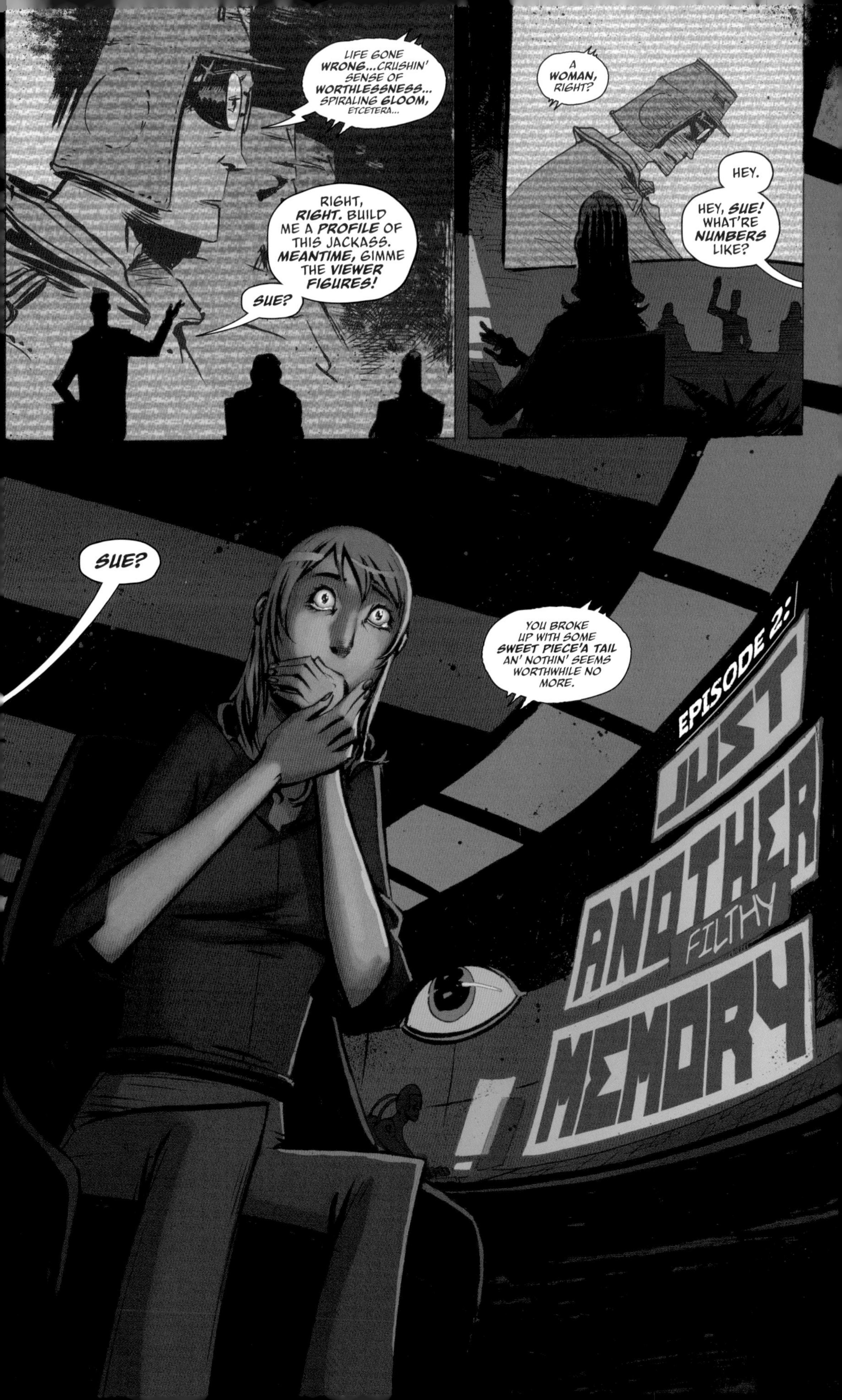

LIFE GONE WRONG...CRUSHIN' SENSE OF WORTHLESSNESS... SPIRALING GLOOM, ETCETERA...
RIGHT, RIGHT. BUILD ME A PROFILE OF THIS JACKASS. MEANTIME, GIMME THE VIEWER FIGURES!
SUE?
A WOMAN, RIGHT?
HEY.
HEY, SUE! WHAT'RE NUMBERS LIKE?
SUE?
YOU BROKE UP WITH SOME SWEET PIECE'A TAIL AN' NOTHIN' SEEMS WORTHWHILE NO MORE.
EPISODE 2:
JUST ANOTHER FILTHY MEMORY

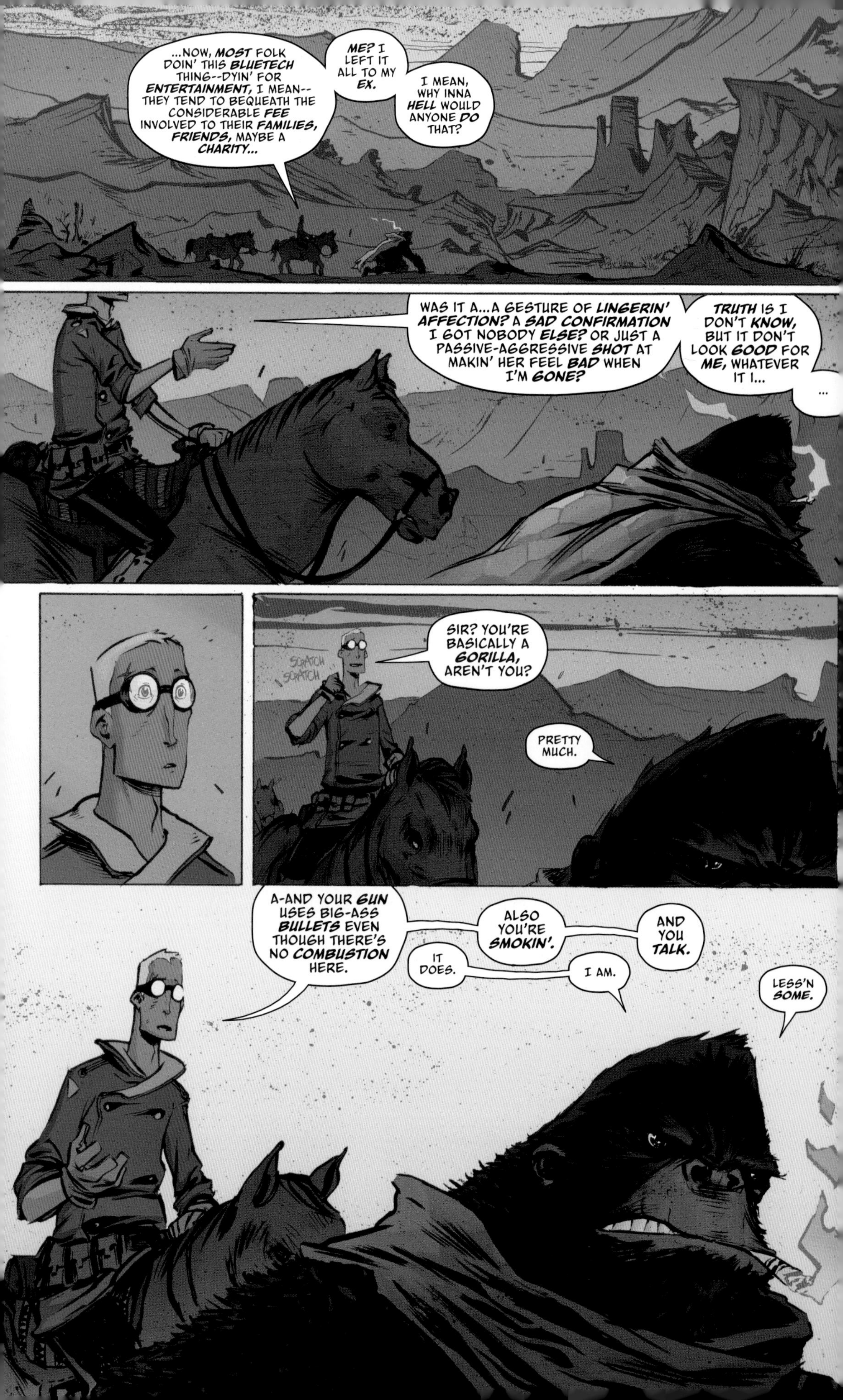
...NOW, MOST FOLK DOIN' THIS BLUETECH THING--DYIN' FOR ENTERTAINMENT, I MEAN--THEY TEND TO BEQUEATH THE CONSIDERABLE FEE INVOLVED TO THEIR FAMILIES, FRIENDS, MAYBE A CHARITY...
ME? I LEFT IT ALL TO MY EX.
I MEAN, WHY INNA HELL WOULD ANYONE DO THAT?
WAS IT A...A GESTURE OF LINGERIN' AFFECTION? A SAD CONFIRMATION I GOT NOBODY ELSE? OR JUST A PASSIVE-AGGRESSIVE SHOT AT MAKIN' HER FEEL BAD WHEN I'M GONE?
TRUTH IS I DON'T KNOW, BUT IT DON'T LOOK GOOD FOR ME, WHATEVER IT I...
...
SCRATCH SCRATCH
SIR? YOU'RE BASICALLY A GORILLA, AREN'T YOU?
PRETTY MUCH.
A-AND YOUR GUN USES BIG-ASS BULLETS EVEN THOUGH THERE'S NO COMBUSTION HERE.
IT DOES.
ALSO YOU'RE SMOKIN'.
I AM.
AND YOU TALK.
LESS'N SOME.

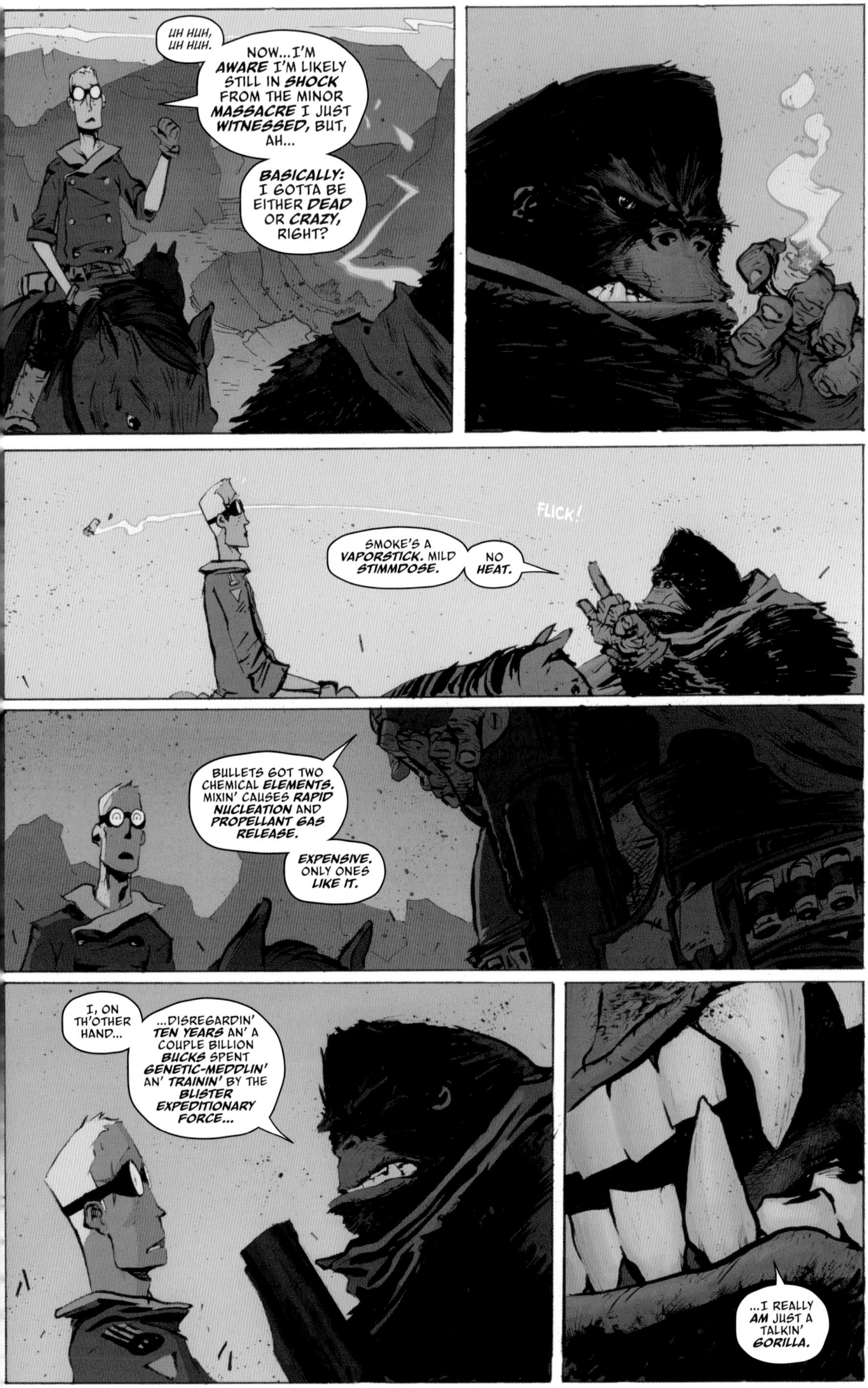
UH HUH, UH HUH.
NOW...I'M AWARE I'M LIKELY STILL IN SHOCK FROM THE MINOR MASSACRE I JUST WITNESSED, BUT, AH...
BASICALLY: I GOTTA BE EITHER DEAD OR CRAZY, RIGHT?
FLICK!
SMOKE'S A VAPORSTICK. MILD STIMMDOSE.
NO HEAT.
BULLETS GOT TWO CHEMICAL ELEMENTS. MIXIN' CAUSES RAPID NUCLEATION AND PROPELLANT GAS RELEASE.
EXPENSIVE. ONLY ONES LIKE IT.
I, ON TH'OTHER HAND...
...DISREGARDIN' TEN YEARS AN' A COUPLE BILLION BUCKS SPENT GENETIC-MEDDLIN' AN' TRAININ' BY THE BLISTER EXPEDITIONARY FORCE...
...I REALLY AM JUST A TALKIN' GORILLA.

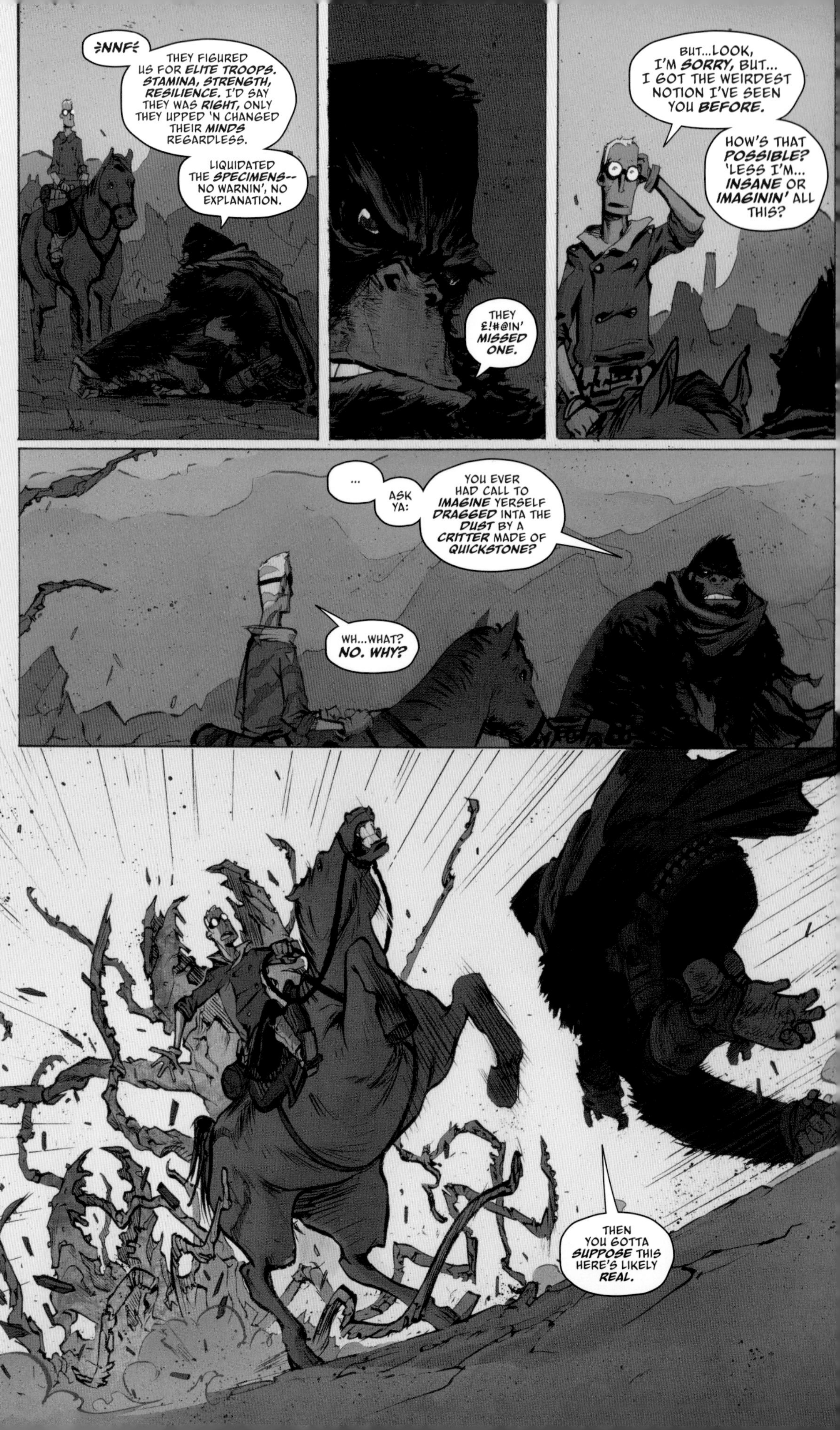

NNF
THEY FIGURED US FOR ELITE TROOPS. STAMINA, STRENGTH, RESILIENCE. I'D SAY THEY WAS RIGHT, ONLY THEY UPPED 'N CHANGED THEIR MINDS REGARDLESS.
LIQUIDATED THE SPECIMENS-- NO WARNIN', NO EXPLANATION.
THEY £!#@IN' MISSED ONE.
BUT...LOOK, I'M SORRY, BUT... I GOT THE WEIRDEST NOTION I'VE SEEN YOU BEFORE.
HOW'S THAT POSSIBLE? 'LESS I'M... INSANE OR IMAGININ' ALL THIS?
...
ASK YA:
YOU EVER HAD CALL TO IMAGINE YERSELF DRAGGED INTA THE DUST BY A CRITTER MADE OF QUICKSTONE?
WH...WHAT? NO. WHY?
THEN YOU GOTTA SUPPOSE THIS HERE'S LIKELY REAL.

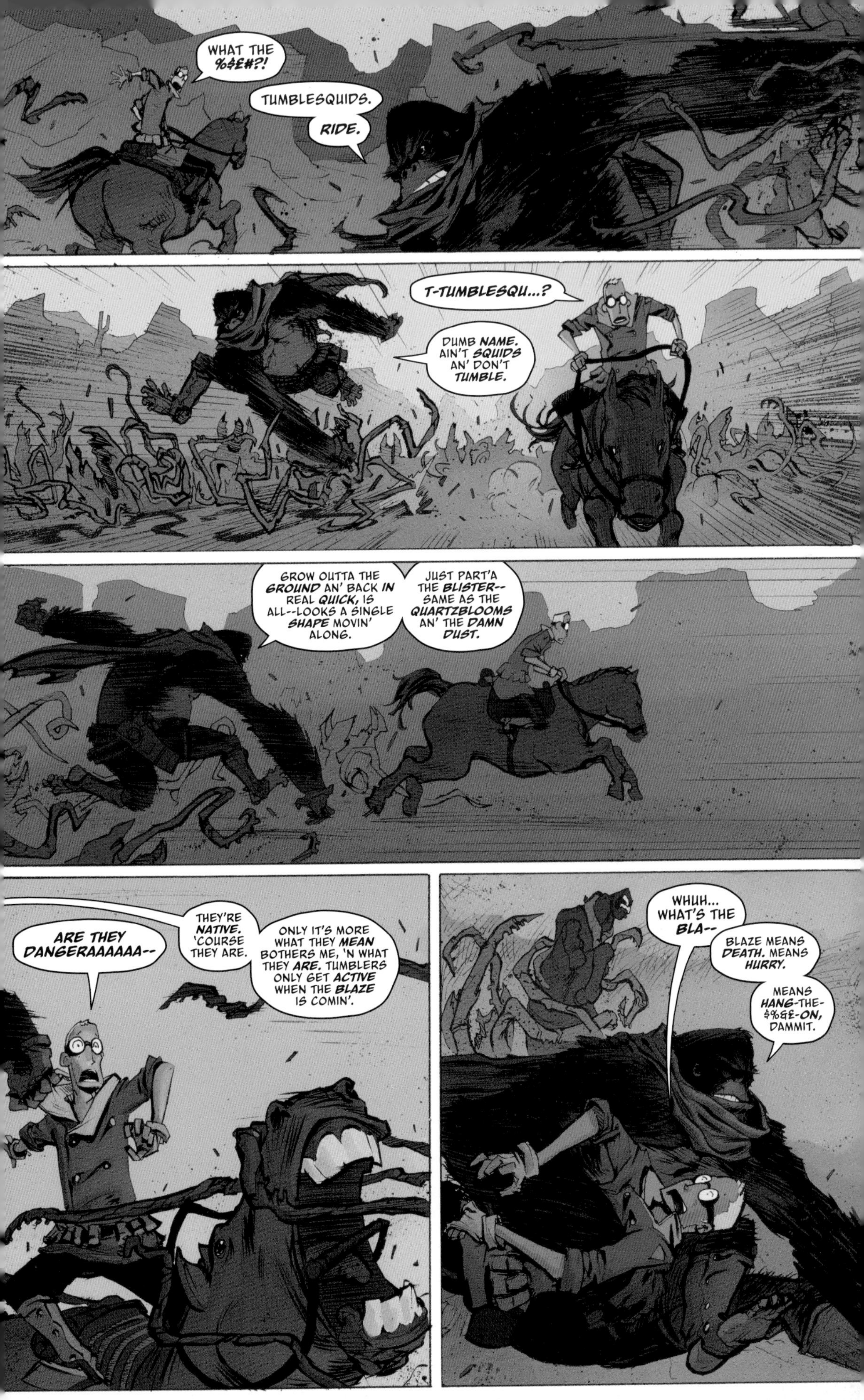

WHAT THE %$£#?!
TUMBLESQUIDS.
RIDE.
T-TUMBLESQU...?
DUMB NAME. AIN'T SQUIDS AN' DON'T TUMBLE.
GROW OUTTA THE GROUND AN' BACK IN REAL QUICK, IS ALL--LOOKS A SINGLE SHAPE MOVIN' ALONG.
JUST PART'A THE BLISTER--SAME AS THE QUARTZBLOOMS AN' THE DAMN DUST.
ARE THEY DANGERAAAAAA--
THEY'RE NATIVE. 'COURSE THEY ARE.
ONLY IT'S MORE WHAT THEY MEAN BOTHERS ME, 'N WHAT THEY ARE. TUMBLERS ONLY GET ACTIVE WHEN THE BLAZE IS COMIN'.
WHUH... WHAT'S THE BLA--
BLAZE MEANS DEATH. MEANS HURRY.
MEANS HANG-THE-$%&£-ON, DAMMIT.

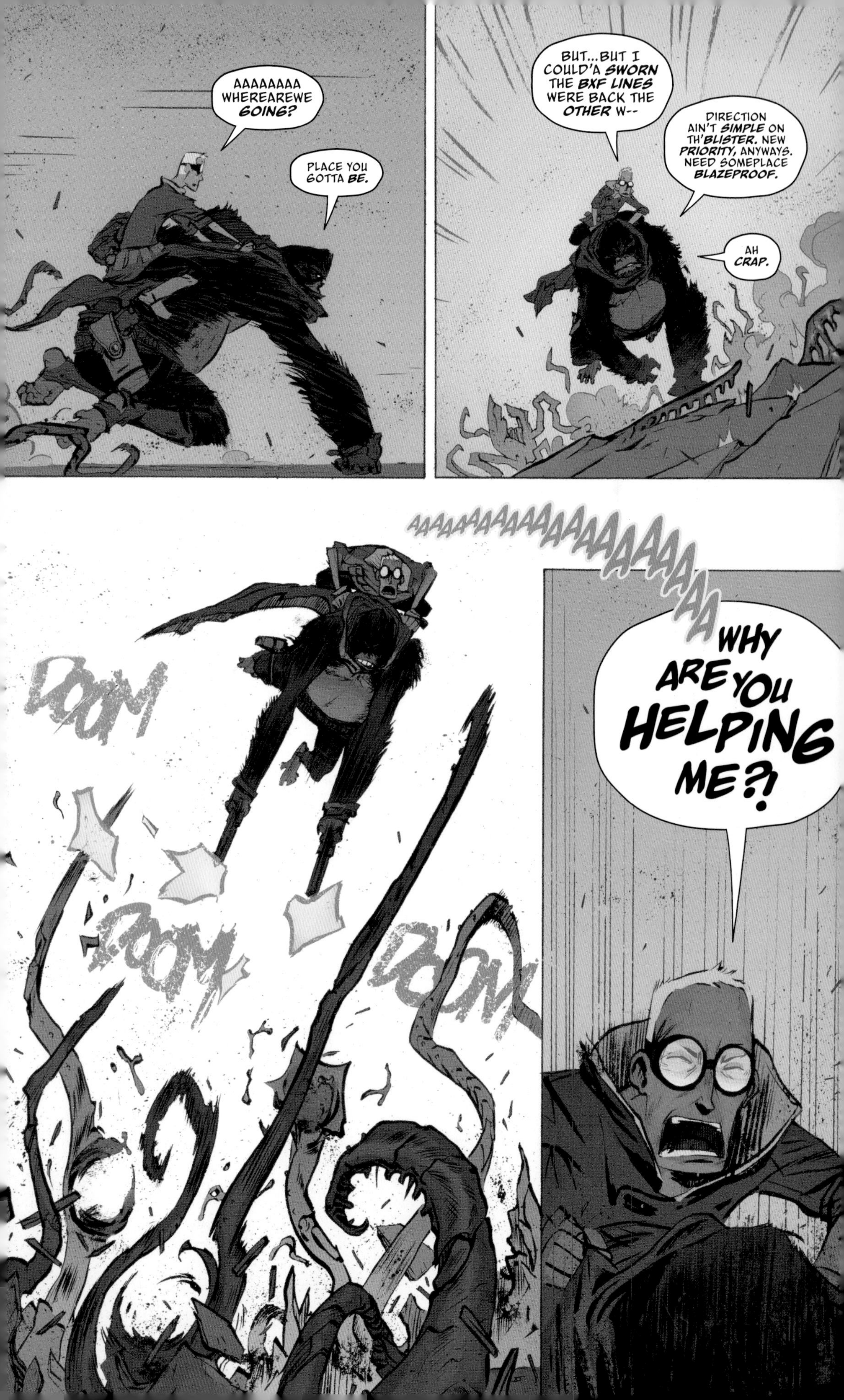
AAAAAAAA WHEREAREWE GOING?
PLACE YOU GOTTA BE.
BUT...BUT I COULD'A SWORN THE BXF LINES WERE BACK THE OTHER W--
DIRECTION AIN'T SIMPLE ON TH'BLISTER. NEW PRIORITY, ANYWAYS. NEED SOMEPLACE BLAZEPROOF.
AH CRAP.
AAAAAAAAAAAAAAAAAAAAA
DOOM
DOOM
DOOM
WHY ARE YOU HELPING ME?!

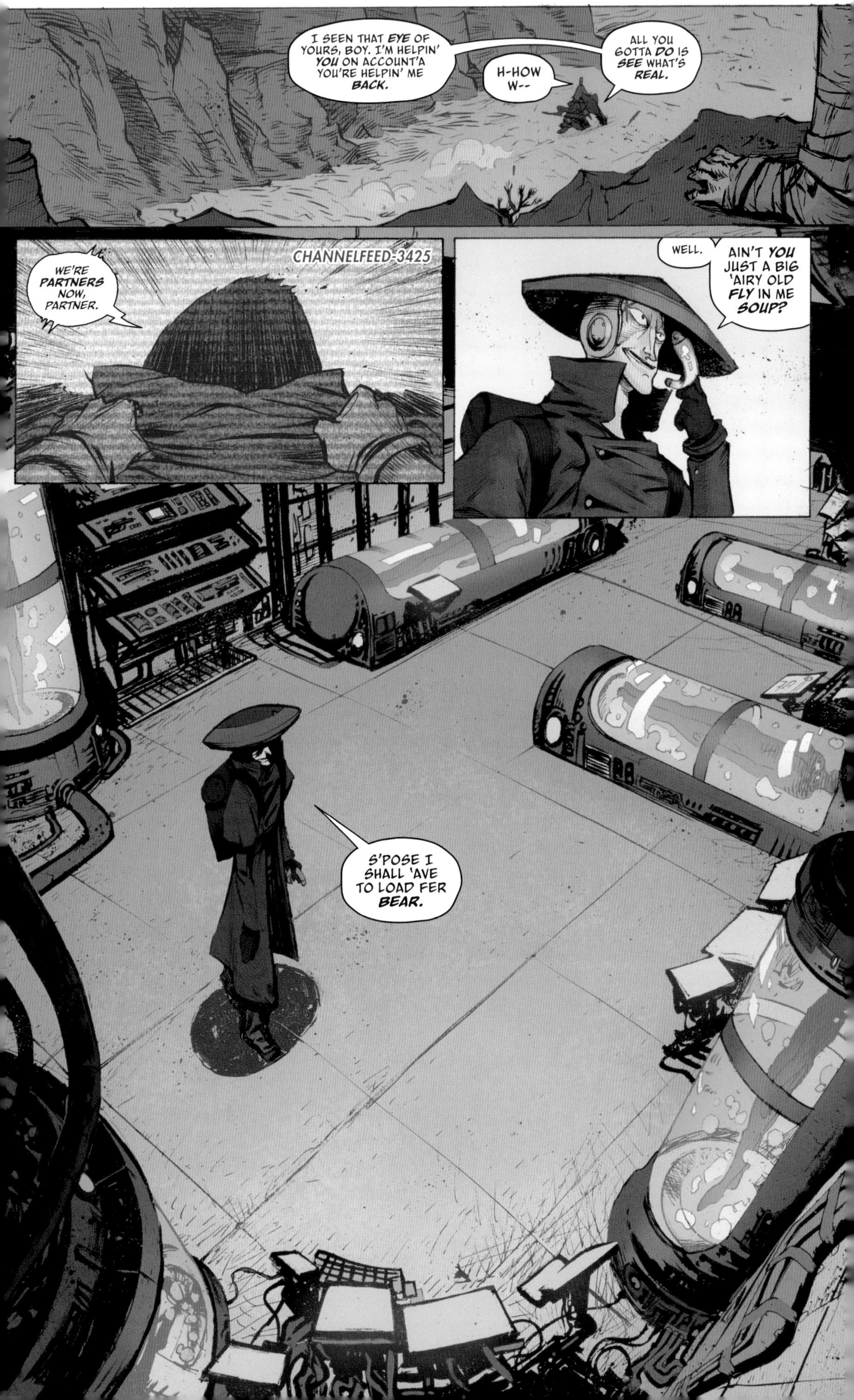
I SEEN THAT EYE OF YOURS, BOY. I'M HELPIN' YOU ON ACCOUNT'A YOU'RE HELPIN' ME BACK.
H-HOW W--
ALL YOU GOTTA DO IS SEE WHAT'S REAL.
CHANNELFEED-3425
WE'RE PARTNERS NOW, PARTNER.
WELL.
AIN'T YOU JUST A BIG 'AIRY OLD FLY IN ME SOUP?
S'POSE I SHALL 'AVE TO LOAD FER BEAR.

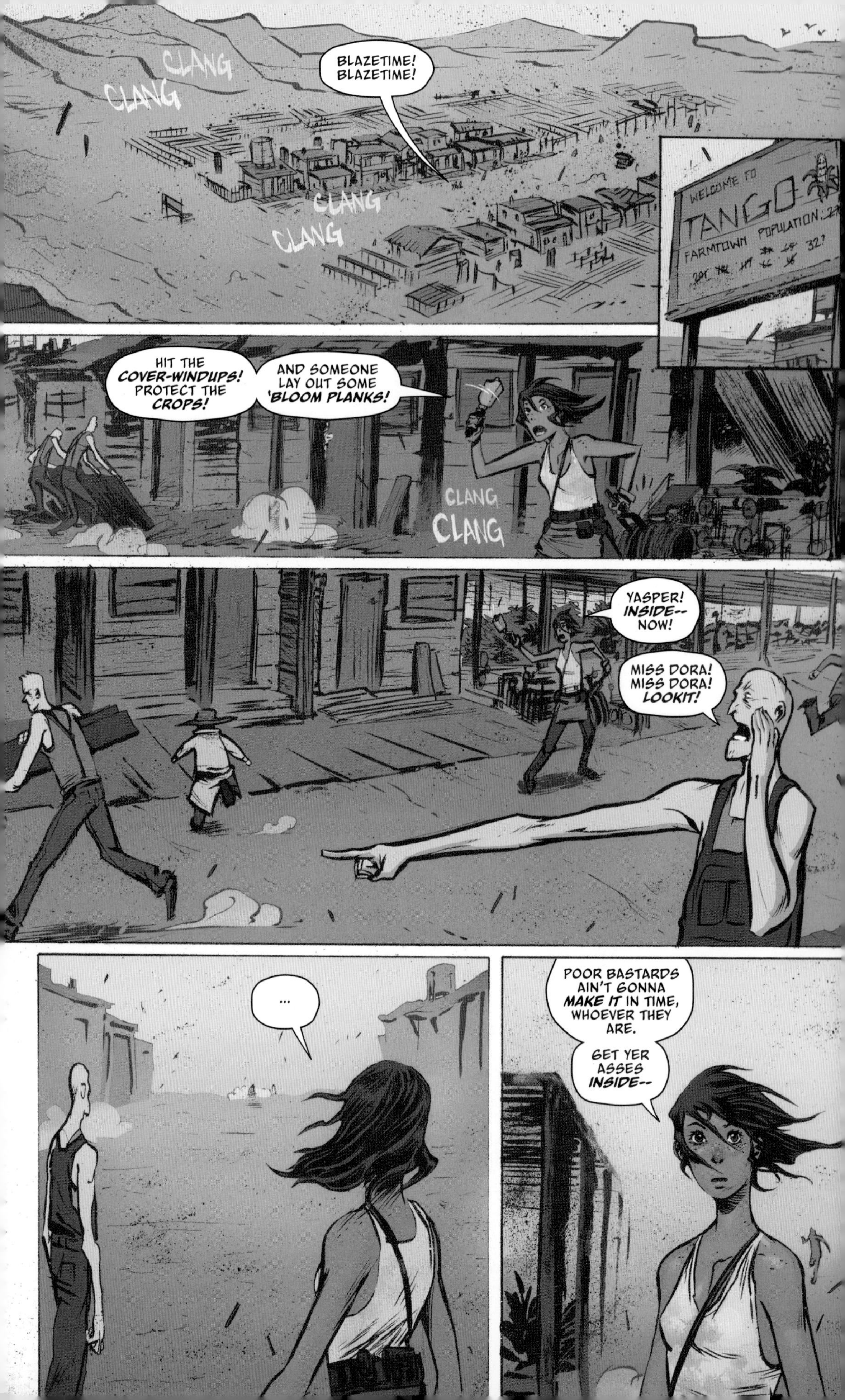
CLANG
CLANG
BLAZETIME! BLAZETIME!
CLANG
CLANG
WELCOME TO
TANGO
FARMTOWN POPULATION:
32?
HIT THE *COVER-WINDUPS!* PROTECT THE *CROPS!*
AND SOMEONE LAY OUT SOME *'BLOOM PLANKS!*
CLANG
CLANG
YASPER! *INSIDE--* NOW!
MISS DORA! MISS DORA! *LOOKIT!*
...
POOR BASTARDS AIN'T GONNA *MAKE IT* IN TIME, WHOEVER THEY ARE.
GET YER ASSES *INSIDE--*

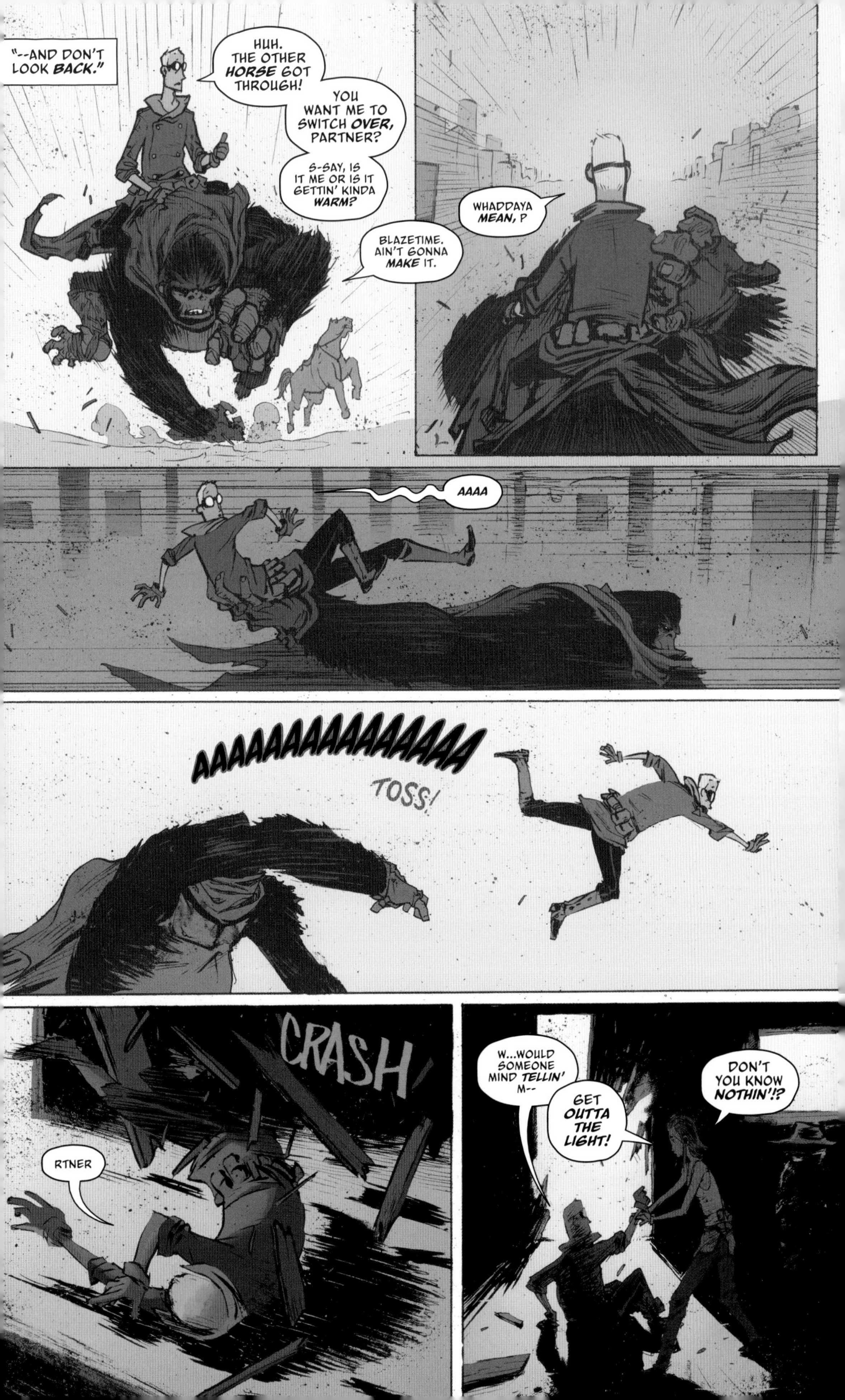
"--AND DON'T LOOK BACK."
HUH. THE OTHER HORSE GOT THROUGH!
YOU WANT ME TO SWITCH OVER, PARTNER?
S-SAY, IS IT ME OR IS IT GETTIN' KINDA WARM?
BLAZETIME. AIN'T GONNA MAKE IT.
WHADDAYA MEAN, P
AAAA
AAAAAAAAAAAAAA
TOSS!
CRASH
RTNER
W...WOULD SOMEONE MIND TELLIN' M--
GET OUTTA THE LIGHT!
DON'T YOU KNOW NOTHIN'!?

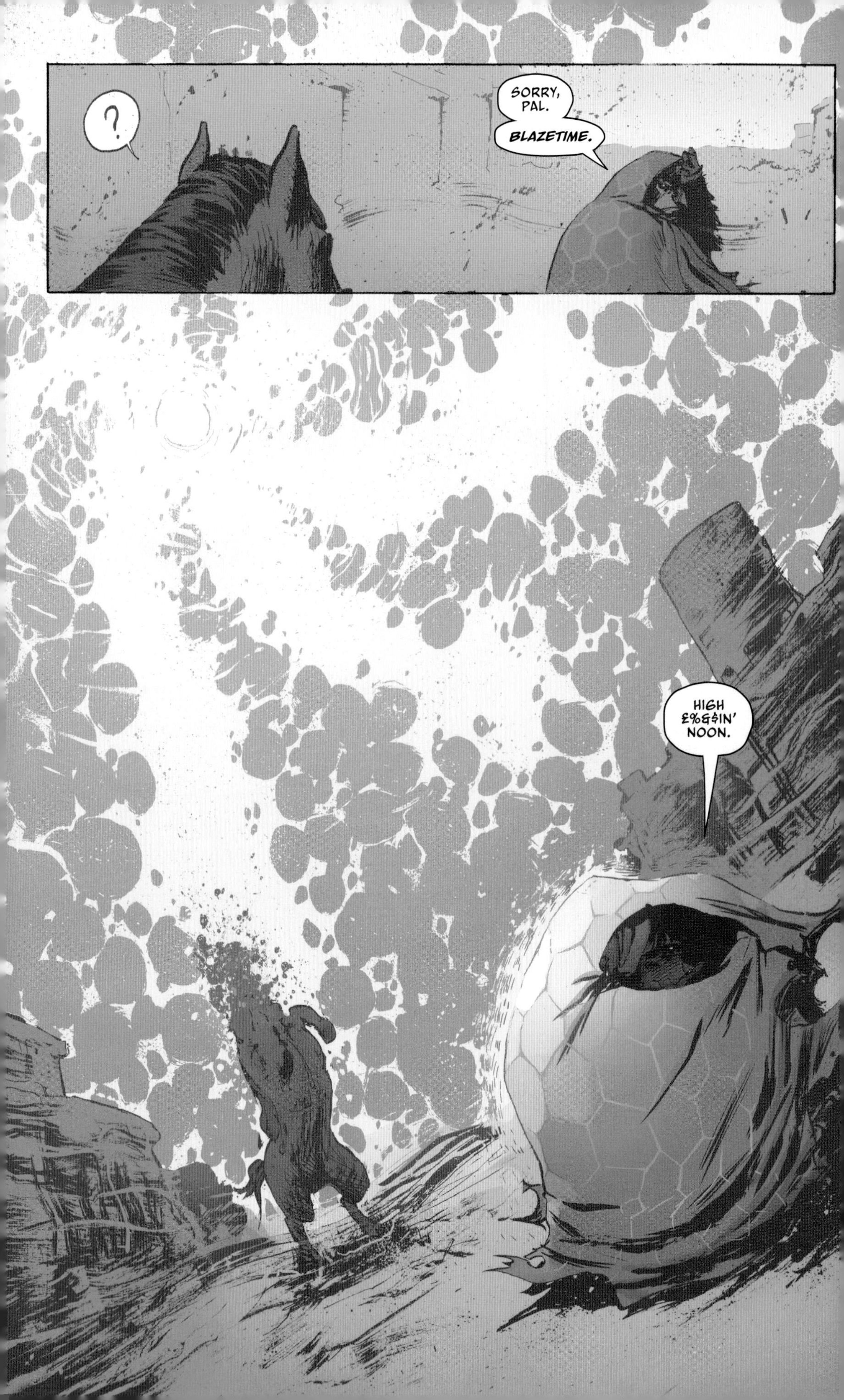
?
SORRY, PAL.
BLAZETIME.
HIGH £%&$IN' NOON.

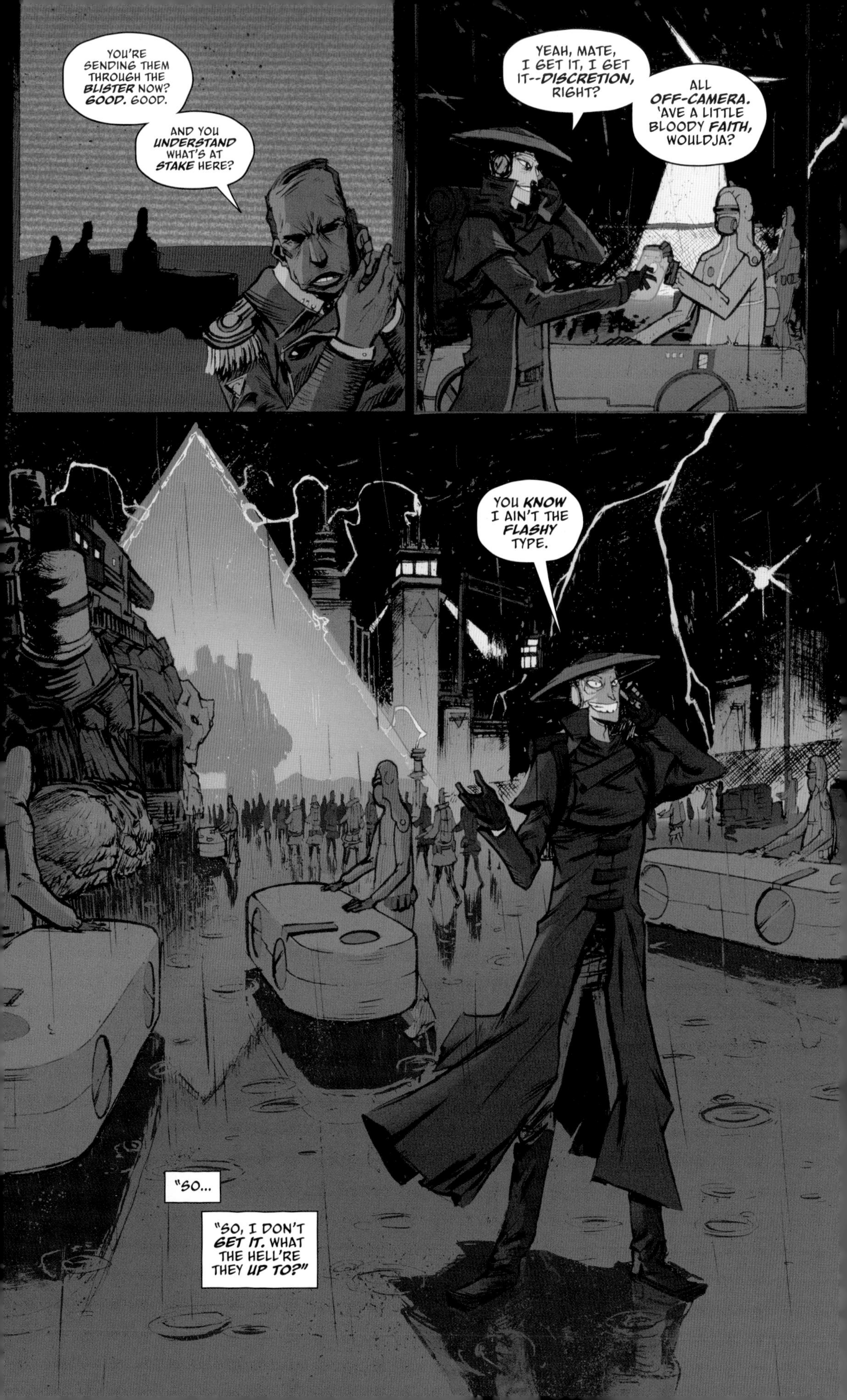
YOU'RE SENDING THEM THROUGH THE BLISTER NOW? GOOD. GOOD.
AND YOU UNDERSTAND WHAT'S AT STAKE HERE?
YEAH, MATE, I GET IT, I GET IT--DISCRETION, RIGHT?
ALL OFF-CAMERA. 'AVE A LITTLE BLOODY FAITH, WOULDJA?
YOU KNOW I AIN'T THE FLASHY TYPE.
"SO...
"SO, I DON'T GET IT. WHAT THE HELL'RE THEY UP TO?"

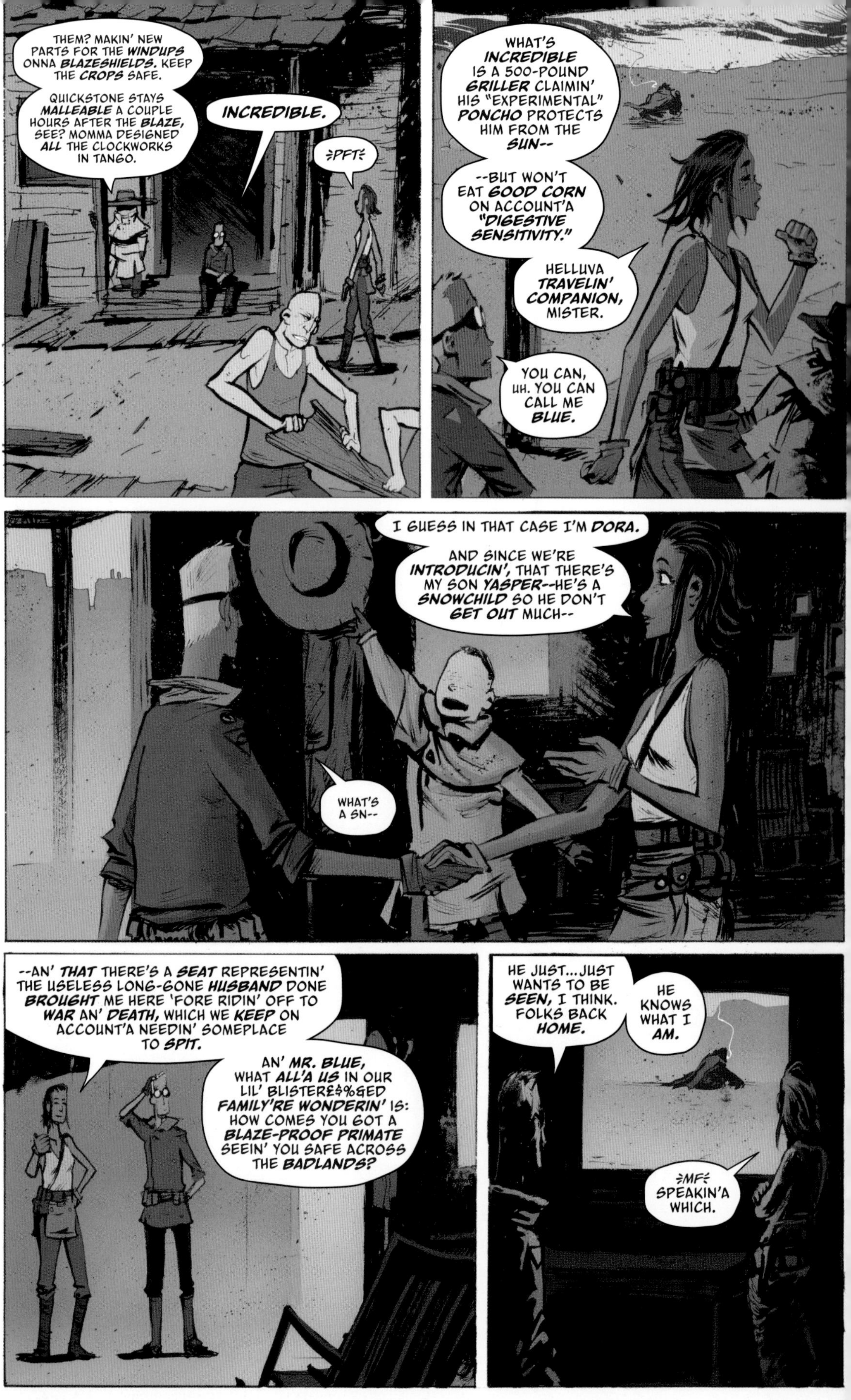
THEM? MAKIN' NEW PARTS FOR THE WINDUPS ONNA BLAZESHIELDS. KEEP THE CROPS SAFE.
QUICKSTONE STAYS MALLEABLE A COUPLE HOURS AFTER THE BLAZE, SEE? MOMMA DESIGNED ALL THE CLOCKWORKS IN TANGO.
INCREDIBLE.
PFT
WHAT'S INCREDIBLE IS A 500-POUND GRILLER CLAIMIN' HIS "EXPERIMENTAL" PONCHO PROTECTS HIM FROM THE SUN--
--BUT WON'T EAT GOOD CORN ON ACCOUNT'A "DIGESTIVE SENSITIVITY."
HELLUVA TRAVELIN' COMPANION, MISTER.
YOU CAN, UH. YOU CAN CALL ME BLUE.
I GUESS IN THAT CASE I'M DORA.
AND SINCE WE'RE INTRODUCIN', THAT THERE'S MY SON YASPER--HE'S A SNOWCHILD SO HE DON'T GET OUT MUCH--
WHAT'S A SN--
--AN' THAT THERE'S A SEAT REPRESENTIN' THE USELESS LONG-GONE HUSBAND DONE BROUGHT ME HERE 'FORE RIDIN' OFF TO WAR AN' DEATH, WHICH WE KEEP ON ACCOUNT'A NEEDIN' SOMEPLACE TO SPIT.
AN' MR. BLUE, WHAT ALL'A US IN OUR LIL' BLISTER£$%&ED FAMILY'RE WONDERIN' IS: HOW COMES YOU GOT A BLAZE-PROOF PRIMATE SEEIN' YOU SAFE ACROSS THE BADLANDS?
HE JUST...JUST WANTS TO BE SEEN, I THINK. FOLKS BACK HOME.
HE KNOWS WHAT I AM.
MF
SPEAKIN'A WHICH.

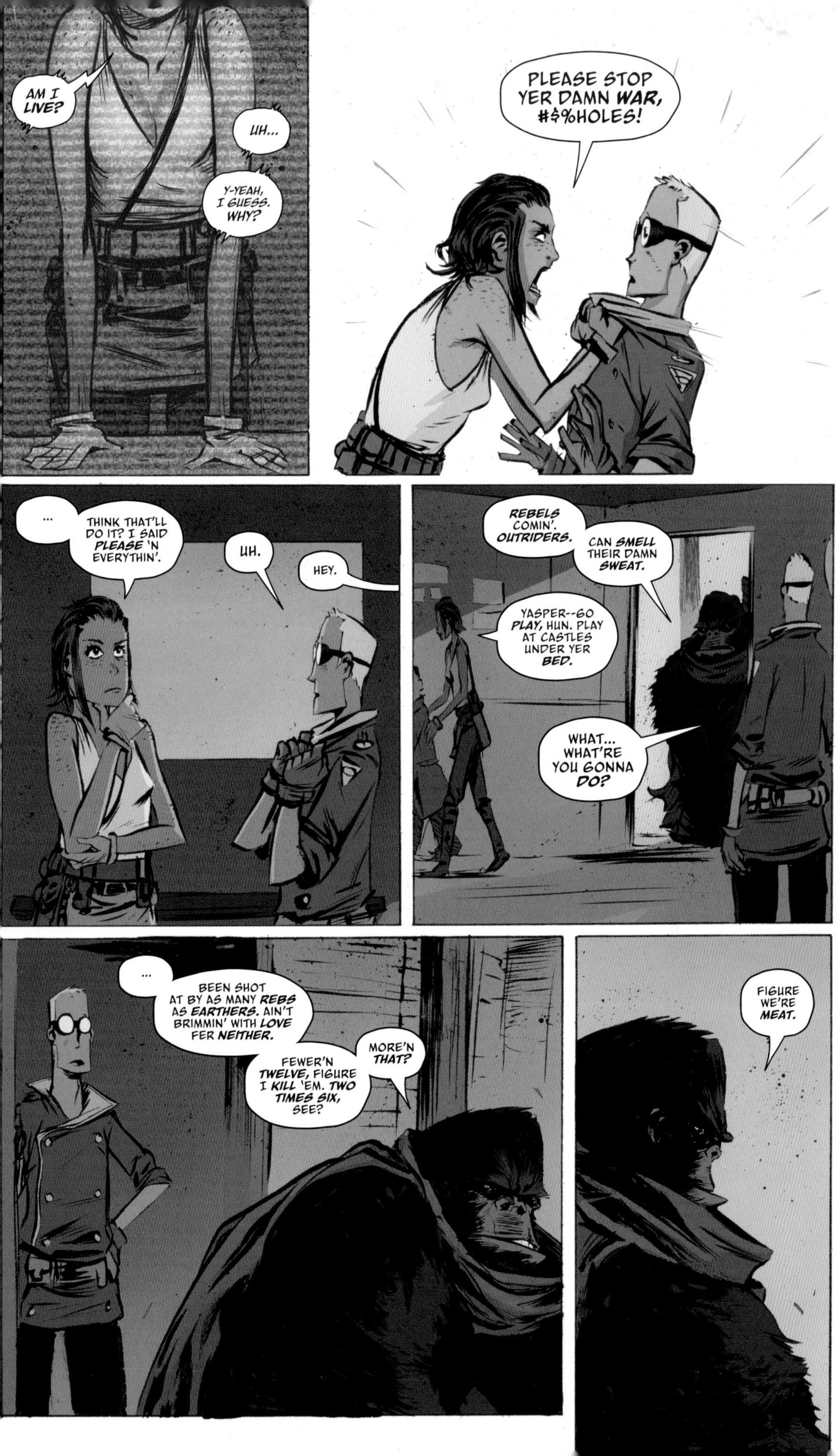
AM I LIVE?
UH...
Y-YEAH, I GUESS. WHY?
PLEASE STOP YER DAMN WAR, #$%HOLES!
...
THINK THAT'LL DO IT? I SAID PLEASE 'N EVERYTHIN'.
UH.
HEY.
REBELS COMIN'. OUTRIDERS.
CAN SMELL THEIR DAMN SWEAT.
YASPER--GO PLAY, HUN. PLAY AT CASTLES UNDER YER BED.
WHAT... WHAT'RE YOU GONNA DO?
...
BEEN SHOT AT BY AS MANY REBS AS EARTHERS. AIN'T BRIMMIN' WITH LOVE FER NEITHER.
FEWER'N TWELVE, FIGURE I KILL 'EM. TWO TIMES SIX, SEE?
MORE'N THAT?
FIGURE WE'RE MEAT.

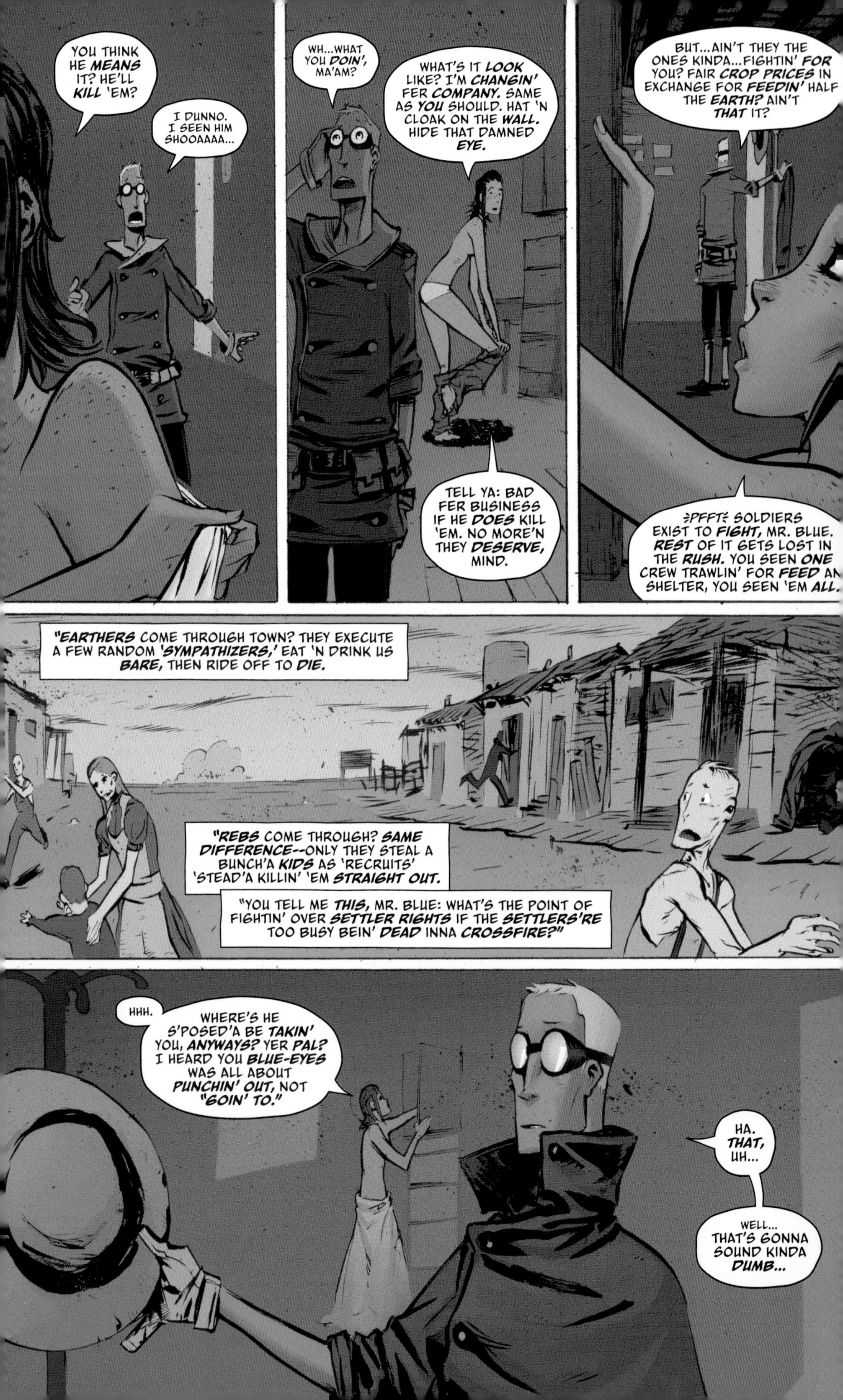
YOU THINK HE MEANS IT? HE'LL KILL 'EM?
I DUNNO. I SEEN HIM SHOOAAAA...
WH...WHAT YOU DOIN', MA'AM?
WHAT'S IT LOOK LIKE? I'M CHANGIN' FER COMPANY. SAME AS YOU SHOULD. HAT 'N CLOAK ON THE WALL. HIDE THAT DAMNED EYE.
TELL YA: BAD FER BUSINESS IF HE DOES KILL 'EM. NO MORE'N THEY DESERVE, MIND.
BUT...AIN'T THEY THE ONES KINDA...FIGHTIN' FOR YOU? FAIR CROP PRICES IN EXCHANGE FOR FEEDIN' HALF THE EARTH? AIN'T THAT IT?
PFFT SOLDIERS EXIST TO FIGHT, MR. BLUE. REST OF IT GETS LOST IN THE RUSH. YOU SEEN ONE CREW TRAWLIN' FOR FEED AN SHELTER, YOU SEEN 'EM ALL.
"EARTHERS COME THROUGH TOWN? THEY EXECUTE A FEW RANDOM 'SYMPATHIZERS,' EAT 'N DRINK US BARE, THEN RIDE OFF TO DIE.
"REBS COME THROUGH? SAME DIFFERENCE--ONLY THEY STEAL A BUNCH'A KIDS AS 'RECRUITS' 'STEAD'A KILLIN' 'EM STRAIGHT OUT.
"YOU TELL ME THIS, MR. BLUE: WHAT'S THE POINT OF FIGHTIN' OVER SETTLER RIGHTS IF THE SETTLERS'RE TOO BUSY BEIN' DEAD INNA CROSSFIRE?"
HHH.
WHERE'S HE S'POSED'A BE TAKIN' YOU, ANYWAYS? YER PAL? I HEARD YOU BLUE-EYES WAS ALL ABOUT PUNCHIN' OUT, NOT "GOIN' TO."
HA. THAT, UH...
WELL... THAT'S GONNA SOUND KINDA DUMB...

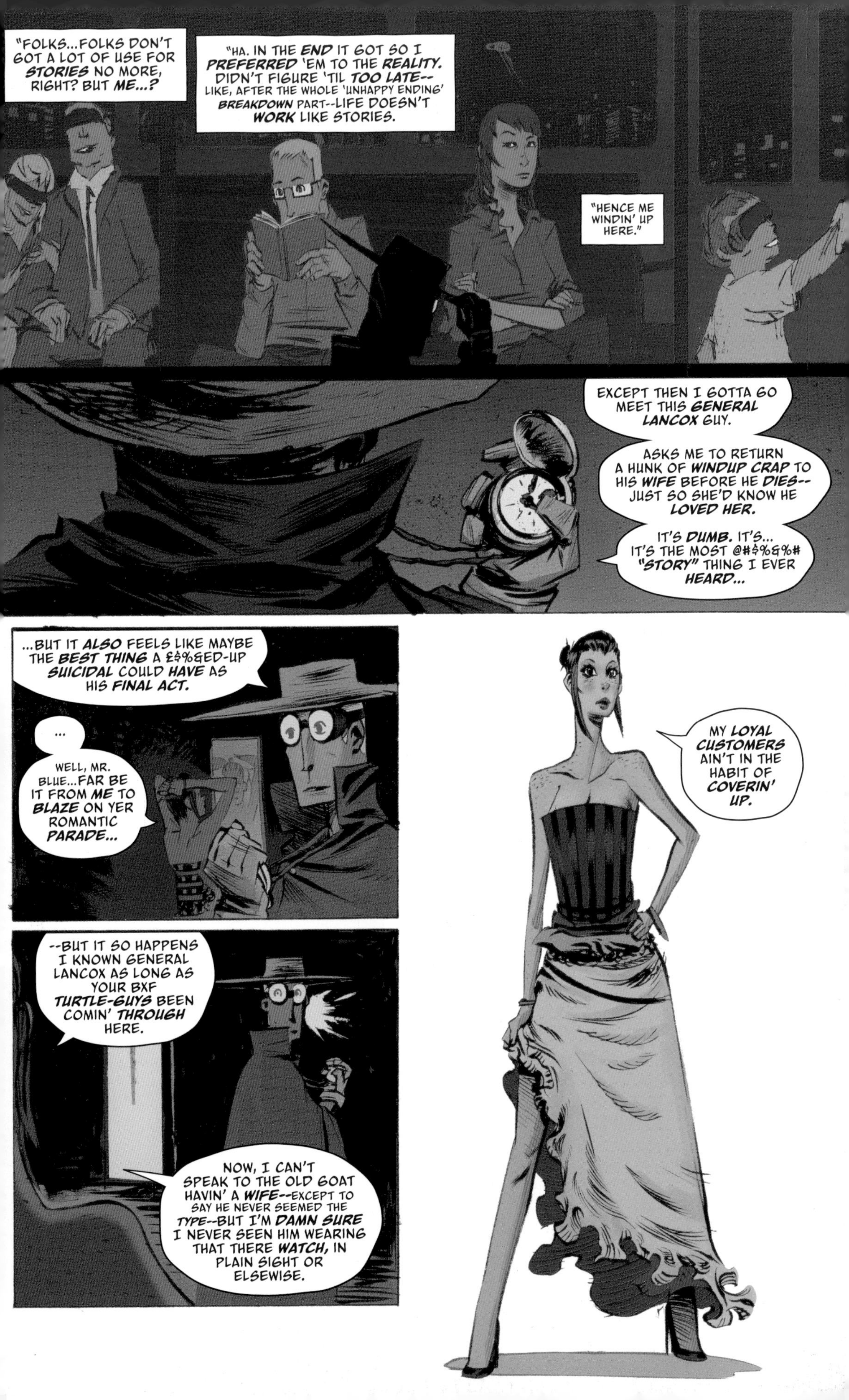
"FOLKS...FOLKS DON'T GOT A LOT OF USE FOR STORIES NO MORE, RIGHT? BUT ME...?
"HA. IN THE END IT GOT SO I PREFERRED 'EM TO THE REALITY. DIDN'T FIGURE 'TIL TOO LATE--LIKE, AFTER THE WHOLE 'UNHAPPY ENDING' BREAKDOWN PART--LIFE DOESN'T WORK LIKE STORIES.
"HENCE ME WINDIN' UP HERE."
EXCEPT THEN I GOTTA GO MEET THIS GENERAL LANCOX GUY.
ASKS ME TO RETURN A HUNK OF WINDUP CRAP TO HIS WIFE BEFORE HE DIES--JUST SO SHE'D KNOW HE LOVED HER.
IT'S DUMB. IT'S... IT'S THE MOST @#$%&%# "STORY" THING I EVER HEARD...
...BUT IT ALSO FEELS LIKE MAYBE THE BEST THING A £$%&ED-UP SUICIDAL COULD HAVE AS HIS FINAL ACT.
...
WELL, MR. BLUE...FAR BE IT FROM ME TO BLAZE ON YER ROMANTIC PARADE...
--BUT IT SO HAPPENS I KNOWN GENERAL LANCOX AS LONG AS YOUR BXF TURTLE-GUYS BEEN COMIN' THROUGH HERE.
NOW, I CAN'T SPEAK TO THE OLD GOAT HAVIN' A WIFE--EXCEPT TO SAY HE NEVER SEEMED THE TYPE--BUT I'M DAMN SURE I NEVER SEEN HIM WEARING THAT THERE WATCH, IN PLAIN SIGHT OR ELSEWISE.
MY LOYAL CUSTOMERS AIN'T IN THE HABIT OF COVERIN' UP.

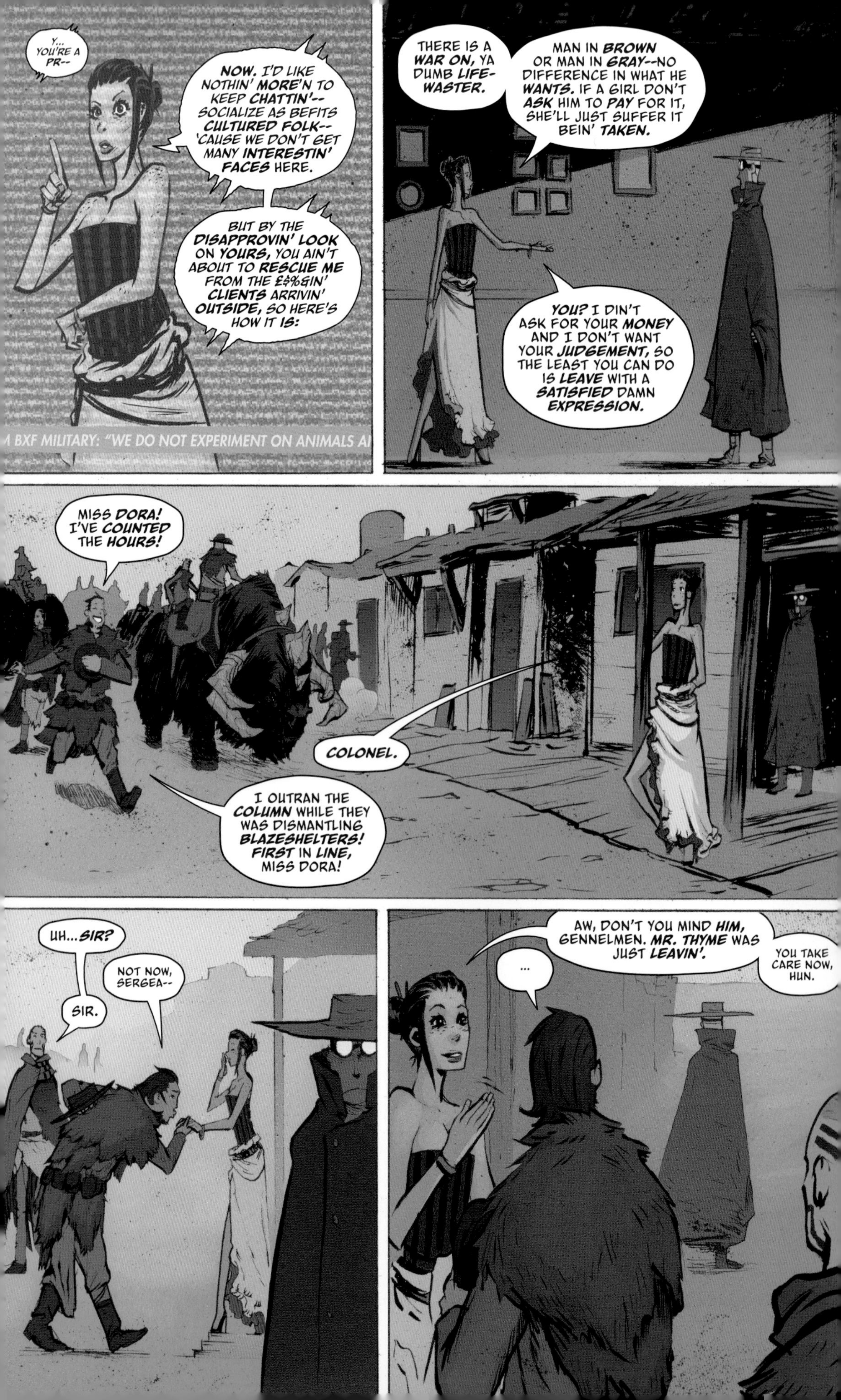
Y... YOU'RE A PR--
NOW. I'D LIKE NOTHIN' MORE'N TO KEEP CHATTIN'-- SOCIALIZE AS BEFITS CULTURED FOLK-- 'CAUSE WE DON'T GET MANY INTERESTIN' FACES HERE.
BUT BY THE DISAPPROVIN' LOOK ON YOURS, YOU AIN'T ABOUT TO RESCUE ME FROM THE £$%&IN' CLIENTS ARRIVIN' OUTSIDE, SO HERE'S HOW IT IS:
A BXF MILITARY: "WE DO NOT EXPERIMENT ON ANIMALS A
THERE IS A WAR ON, YA DUMB LIFE-WASTER.
MAN IN BROWN OR MAN IN GRAY--NO DIFFERENCE IN WHAT HE WANTS. IF A GIRL DON'T ASK HIM TO PAY FOR IT, SHE'LL JUST SUFFER IT BEIN' TAKEN.
YOU? I DIN'T ASK FOR YOUR MONEY AND I DON'T WANT YOUR JUDGEMENT, SO THE LEAST YOU CAN DO IS LEAVE WITH A SATISFIED DAMN EXPRESSION.
MISS DORA! I'VE COUNTED THE HOURS!
COLONEL.
I OUTRAN THE COLUMN WHILE THEY WAS DISMANTLING BLAZESHELTERS! FIRST IN LINE, MISS DORA!
UH...SIR?
NOT NOW, SERGEA--
SIR.
AW, DON'T YOU MIND HIM, GENNELMEN. MR. THYME WAS JUST LEAVIN'.
...
YOU TAKE CARE NOW, HUN.

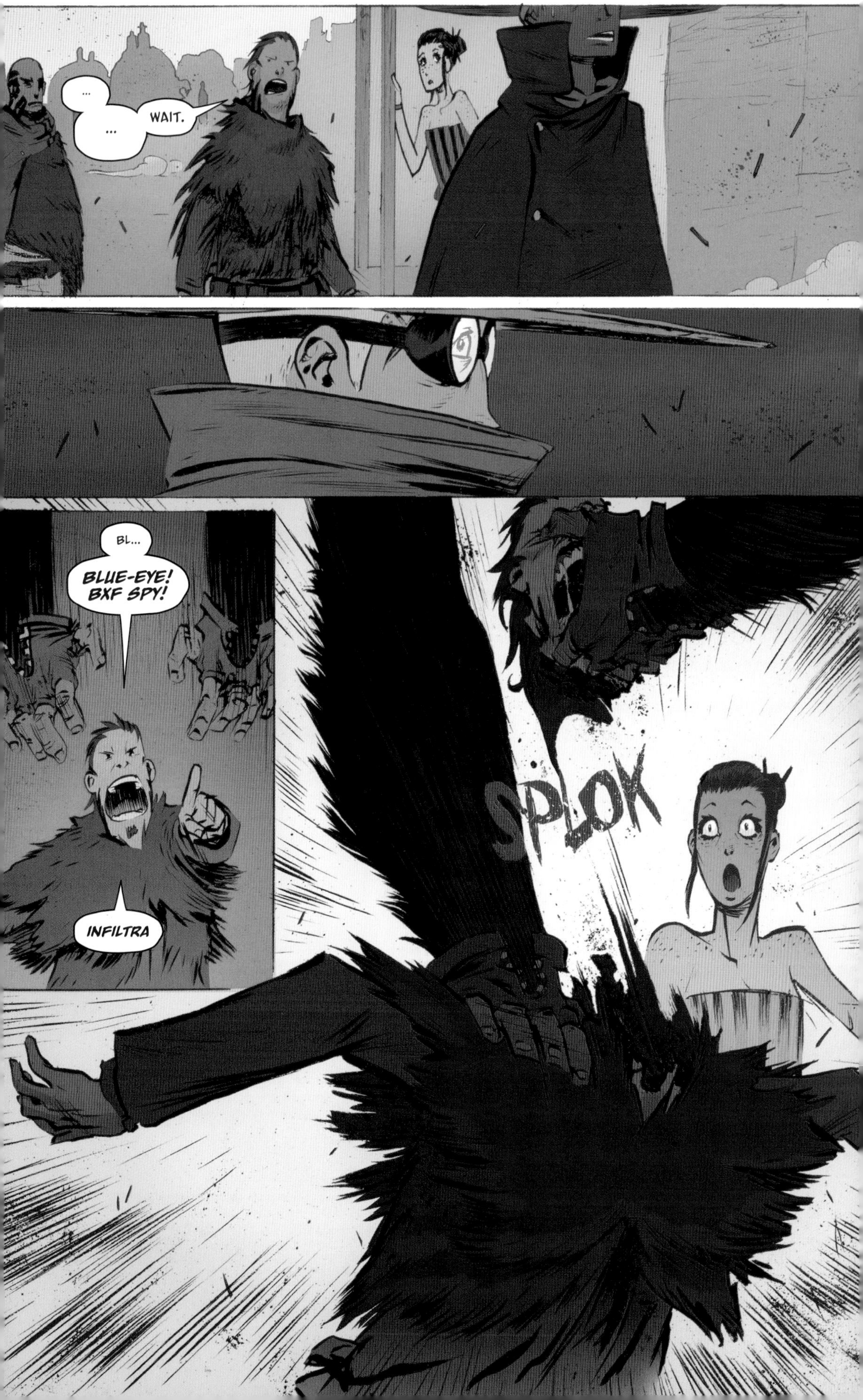
...
...
WAIT.
BL...
BLUE-EYE! BXF SPY!
INFILTRA
SPLOK

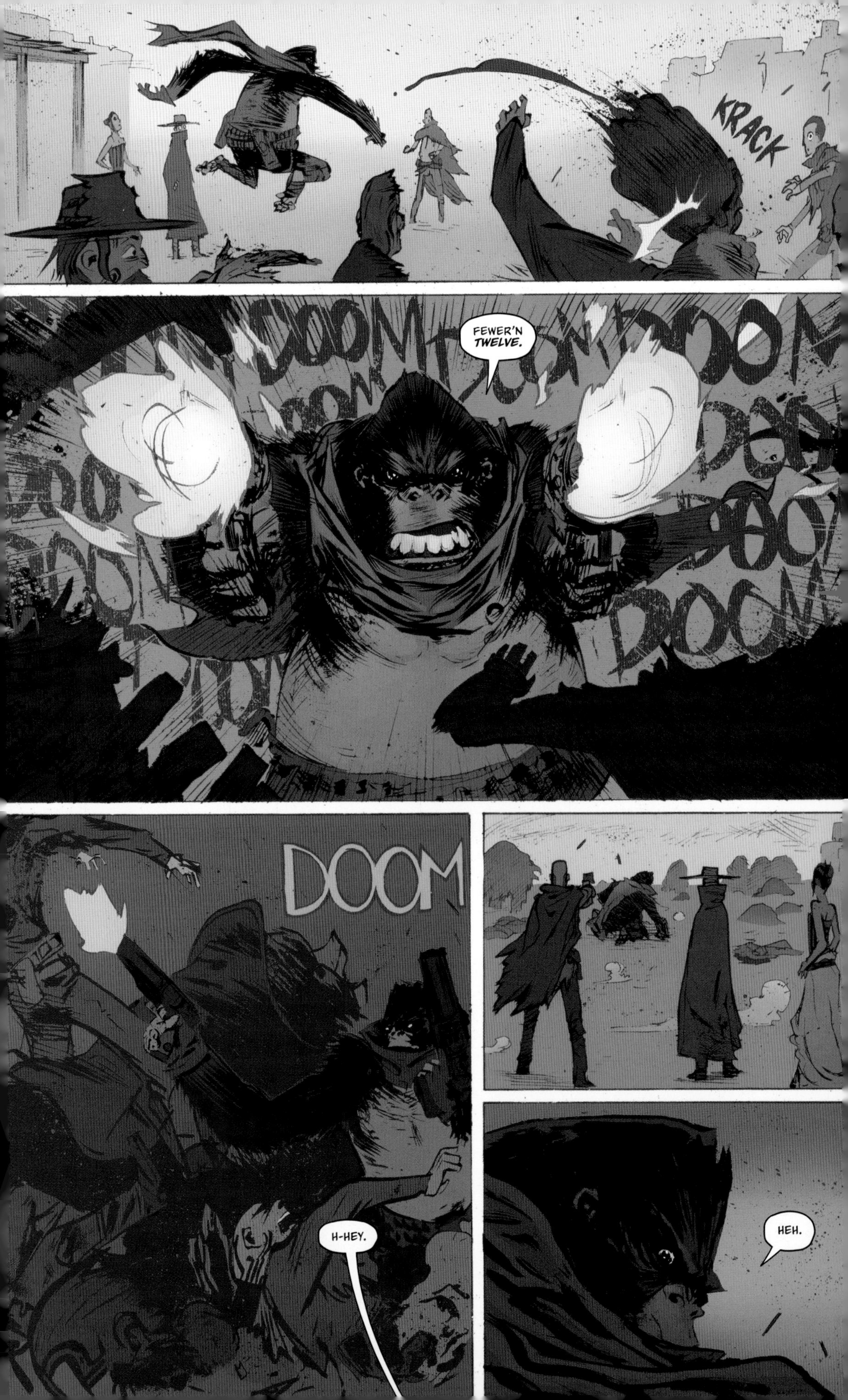
KRACK
DOOM DOOM DOOM DOOM
FEWER'N TWELVE.
DOOM
DOOM
H-HEY.
HEH.

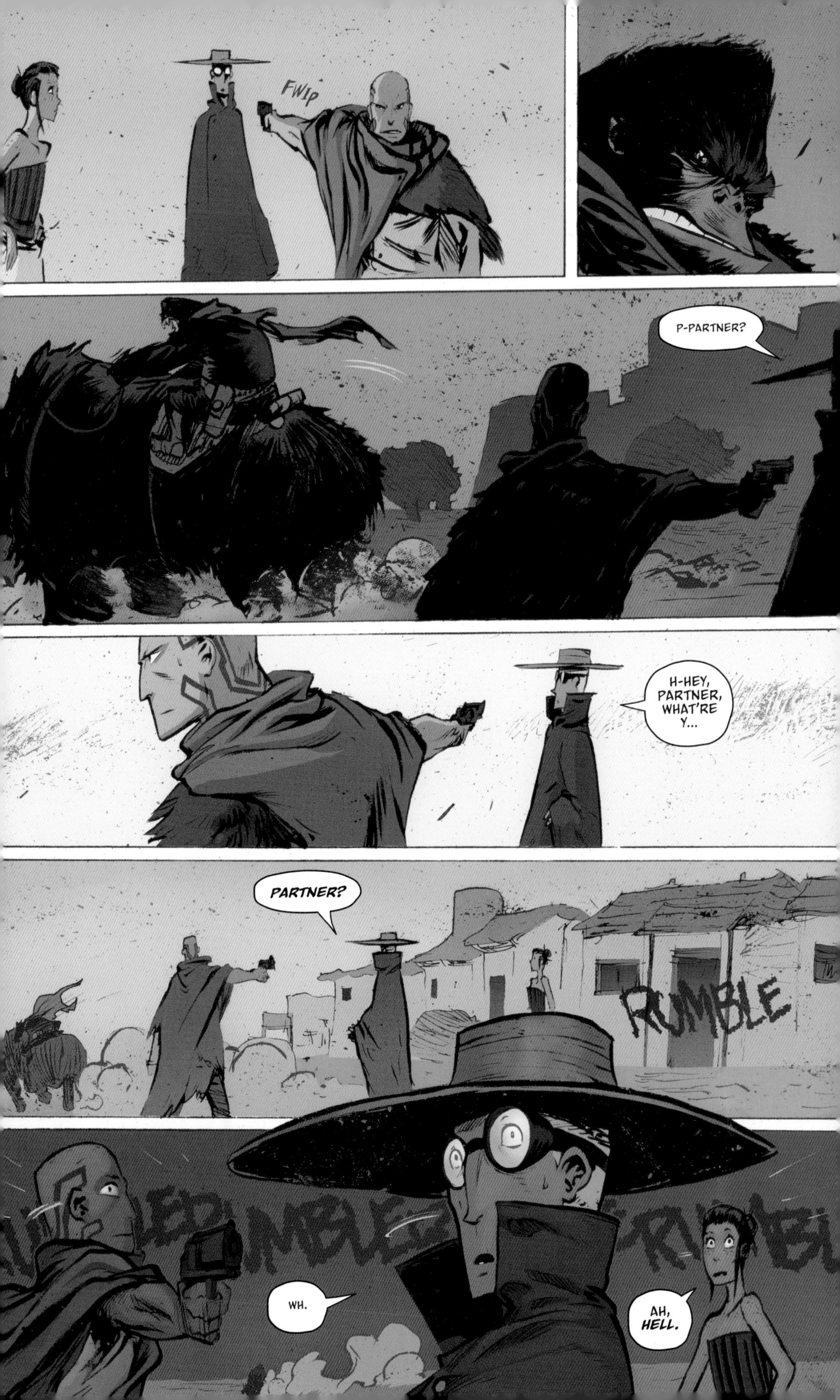
FWIP
P-PARTNER?
H-HEY, PARTNER, WHAT'RE Y...
PARTNER?
RUMBLE
WH.
AH, HELL.

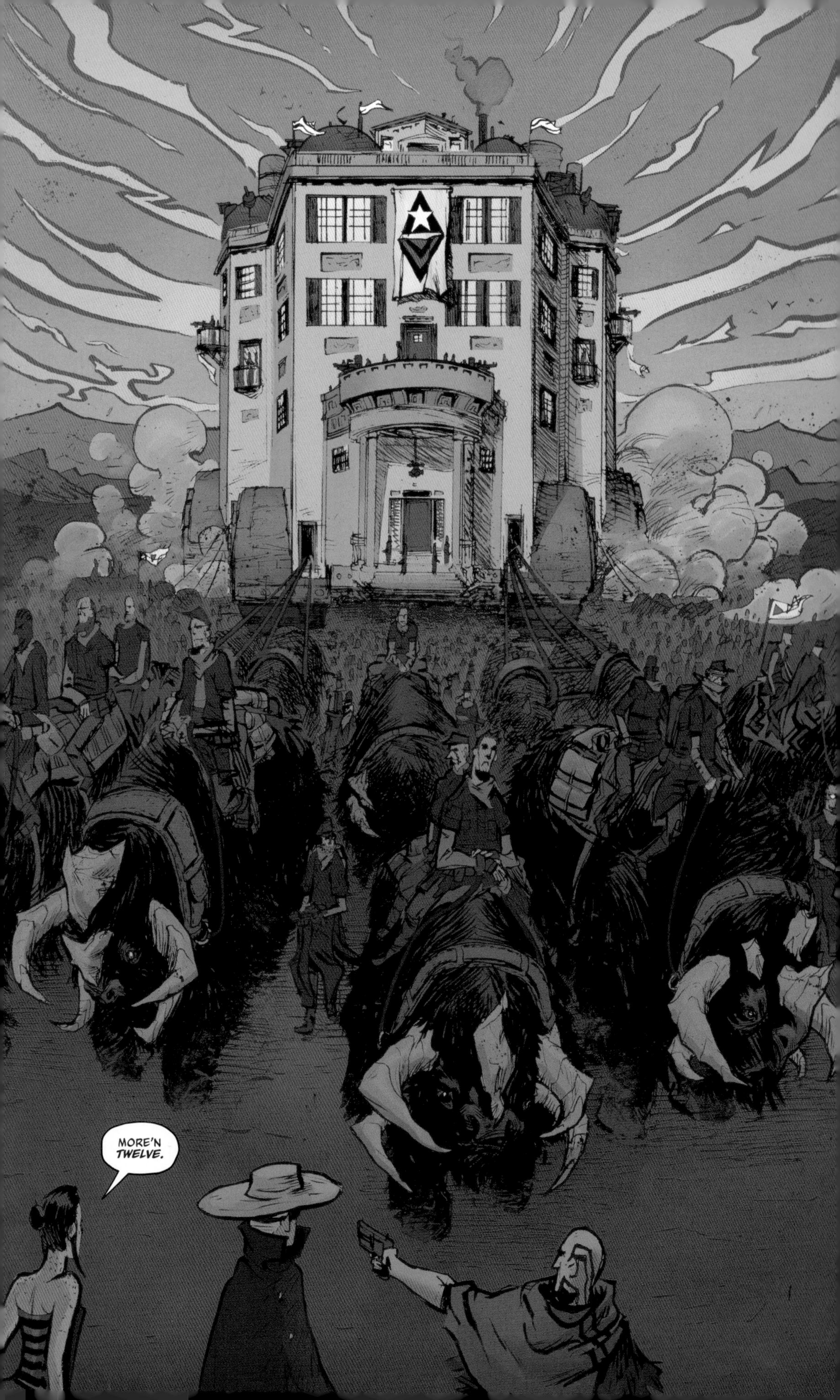
MORE'N *TWELVE.*

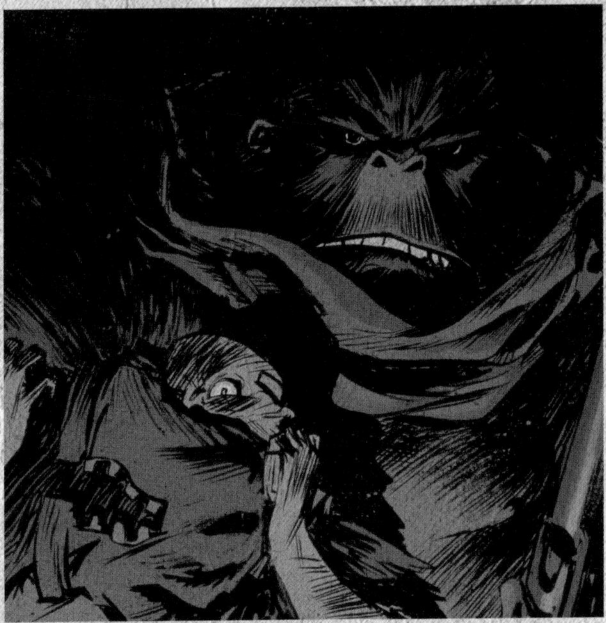

# CHAPTER THREE

# SIX-GUN GORILLA

(Continued from page 8.)

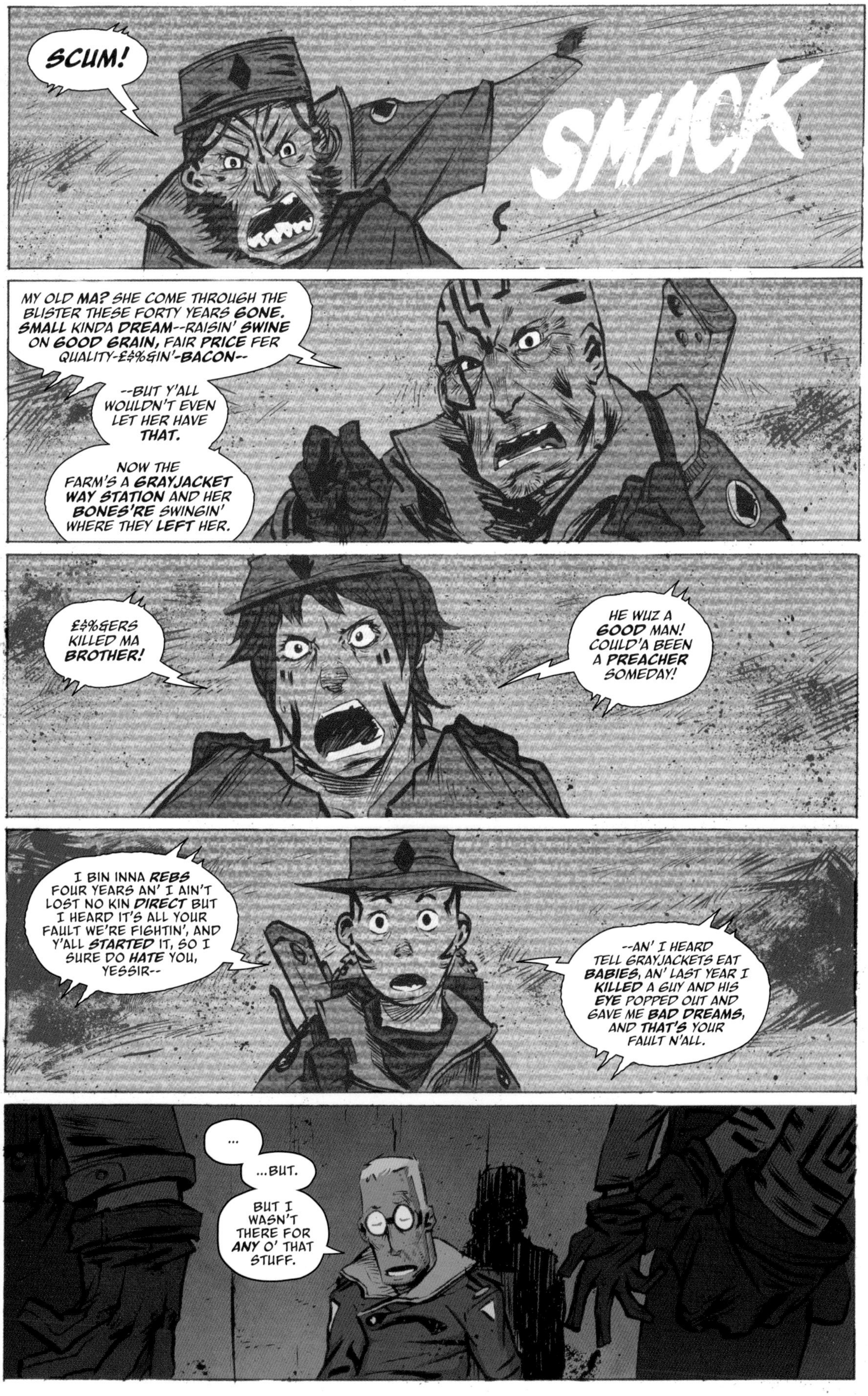
SCUM!
SMACK
MY OLD MA? SHE COME THROUGH THE BLISTER THESE FORTY YEARS GONE. SMALL KINDA DREAM--RAISIN' SWINE ON GOOD GRAIN, FAIR PRICE FER QUALITY-£$%&IN'-BACON--
--BUT Y'ALL WOULDN'T EVEN LET HER HAVE THAT.
NOW THE FARM'S A GRAYJACKET WAY STATION AND HER BONES'RE SWINGIN' WHERE THEY LEFT HER.
£$%&ERS KILLED MA BROTHER!
HE WUZ A GOOD MAN! COULD'A BEEN A PREACHER SOMEDAY!
I BIN INNA REBS FOUR YEARS AN' I AIN'T LOST NO KIN DIRECT BUT I HEARD IT'S ALL YOUR FAULT WE'RE FIGHTIN', AND Y'ALL STARTED IT, SO I SURE DO HATE YOU, YESSIR--
--AN' I HEARD TELL GRAYJACKETS EAT BABIES, AN' LAST YEAR I KILLED A GUY AND HIS EYE POPPED OUT AND GAVE ME BAD DREAMS, AND THAT'S YOUR FAULT N'ALL.
...
...BUT.
BUT I WASN'T THERE FOR ANY O' THAT STUFF.

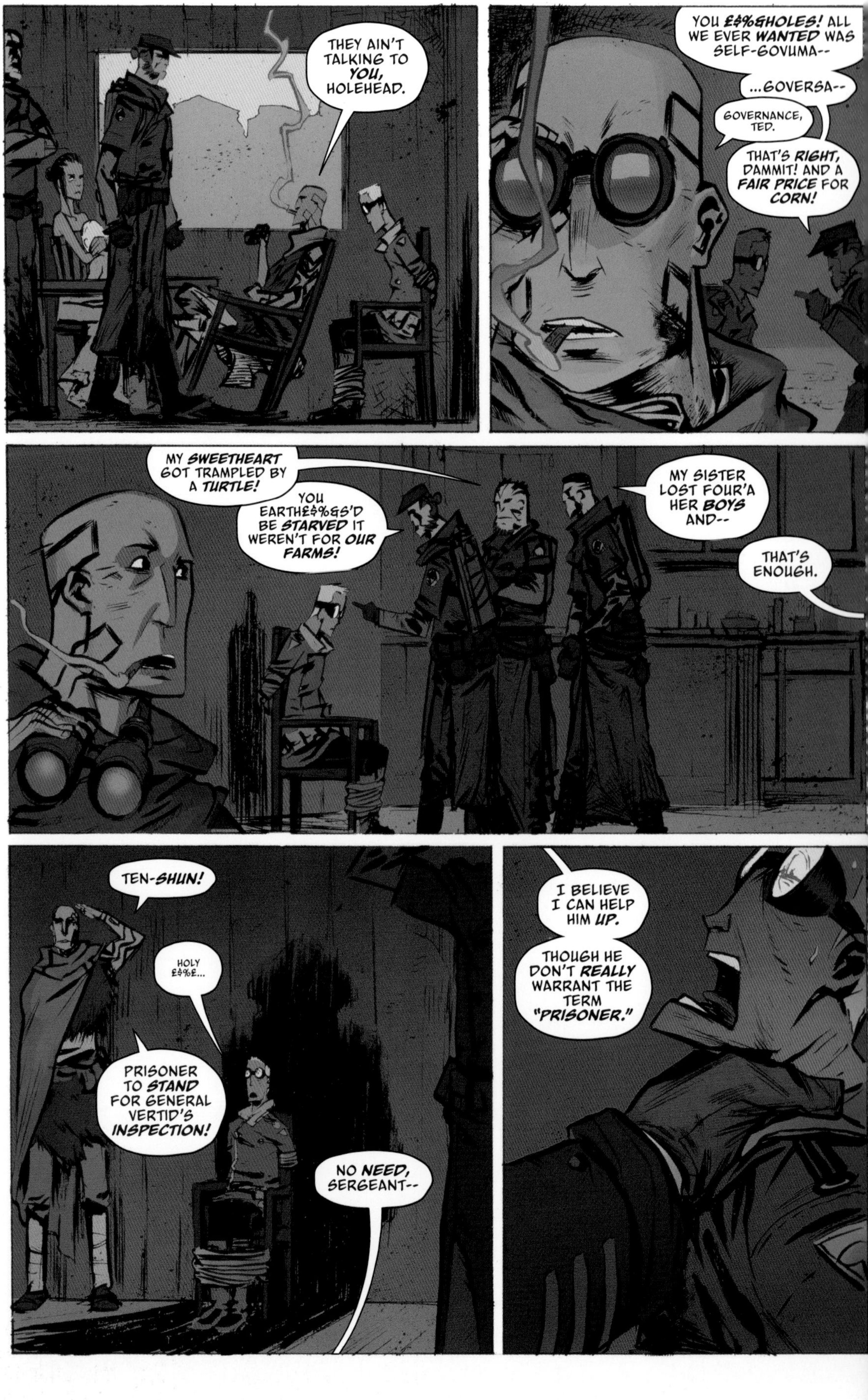
THEY AIN'T TALKING TO YOU, HOLEHEAD.
YOU £$%GHOLES! ALL WE EVER WANTED WAS SELF-GOVUMA--
...GOVERSA--
GOVERNANCE, TED.
THAT'S RIGHT, DAMMIT! AND A FAIR PRICE FOR CORN!
MY SWEETHEART GOT TRAMPLED BY A TURTLE!
YOU EARTH£$%&S'D BE STARVED IT WEREN'T FOR OUR FARMS!
MY SISTER LOST FOUR'A HER BOYS AND--
THAT'S ENOUGH.
TEN-SHUN!
HOLY £$%£...
PRISONER TO STAND FOR GENERAL VERTID'S INSPECTION!
NO NEED, SERGEANT--
I BELIEVE I CAN HELP HIM UP.
THOUGH HE DON'T REALLY WARRANT THE TERM "PRISONER."

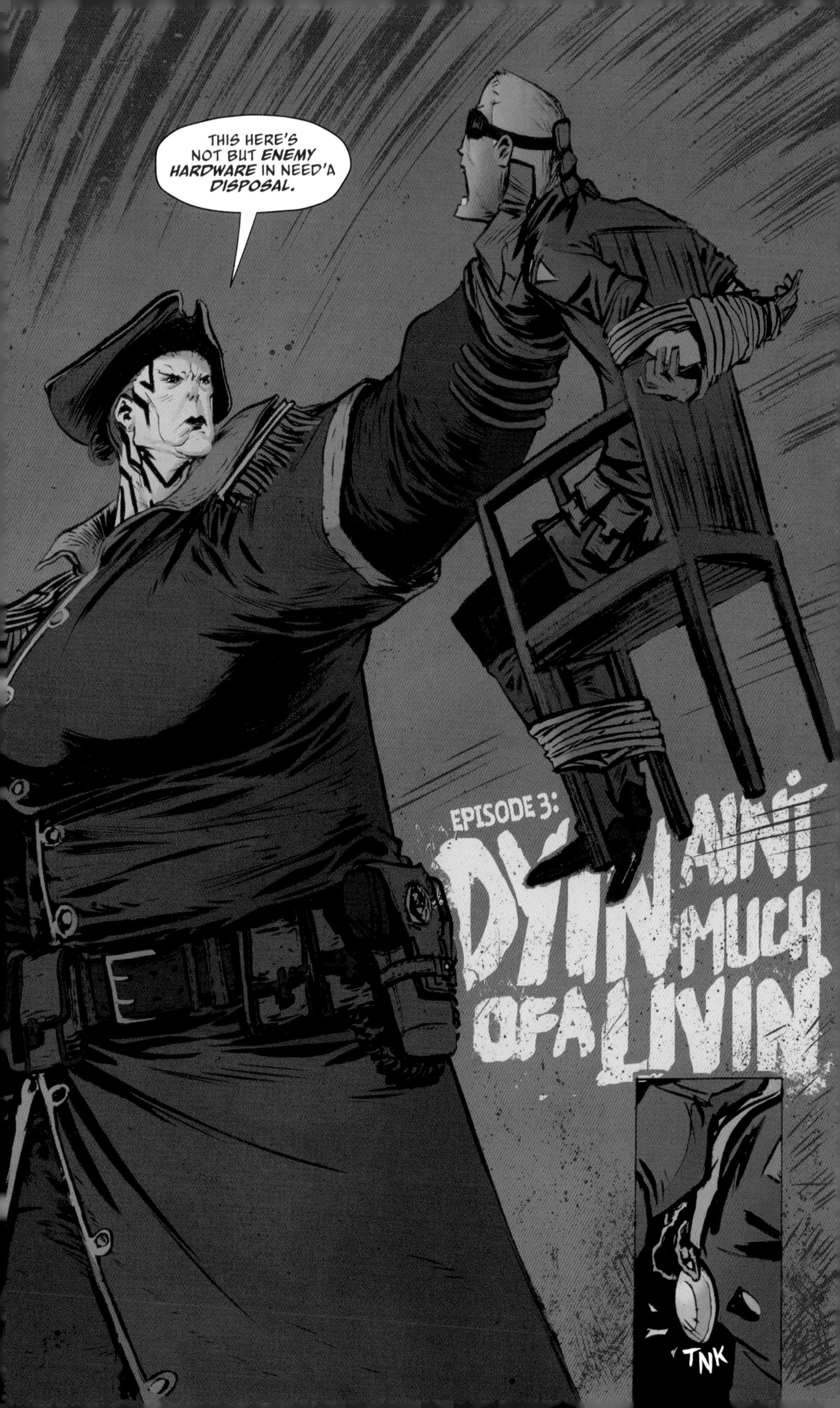
THIS HERE'S NOT BUT ENEMY HARDWARE IN NEED'A DISPOSAL.
EPISODE 3:
DYIN AINT MUCH OF A LIVIN
TNK

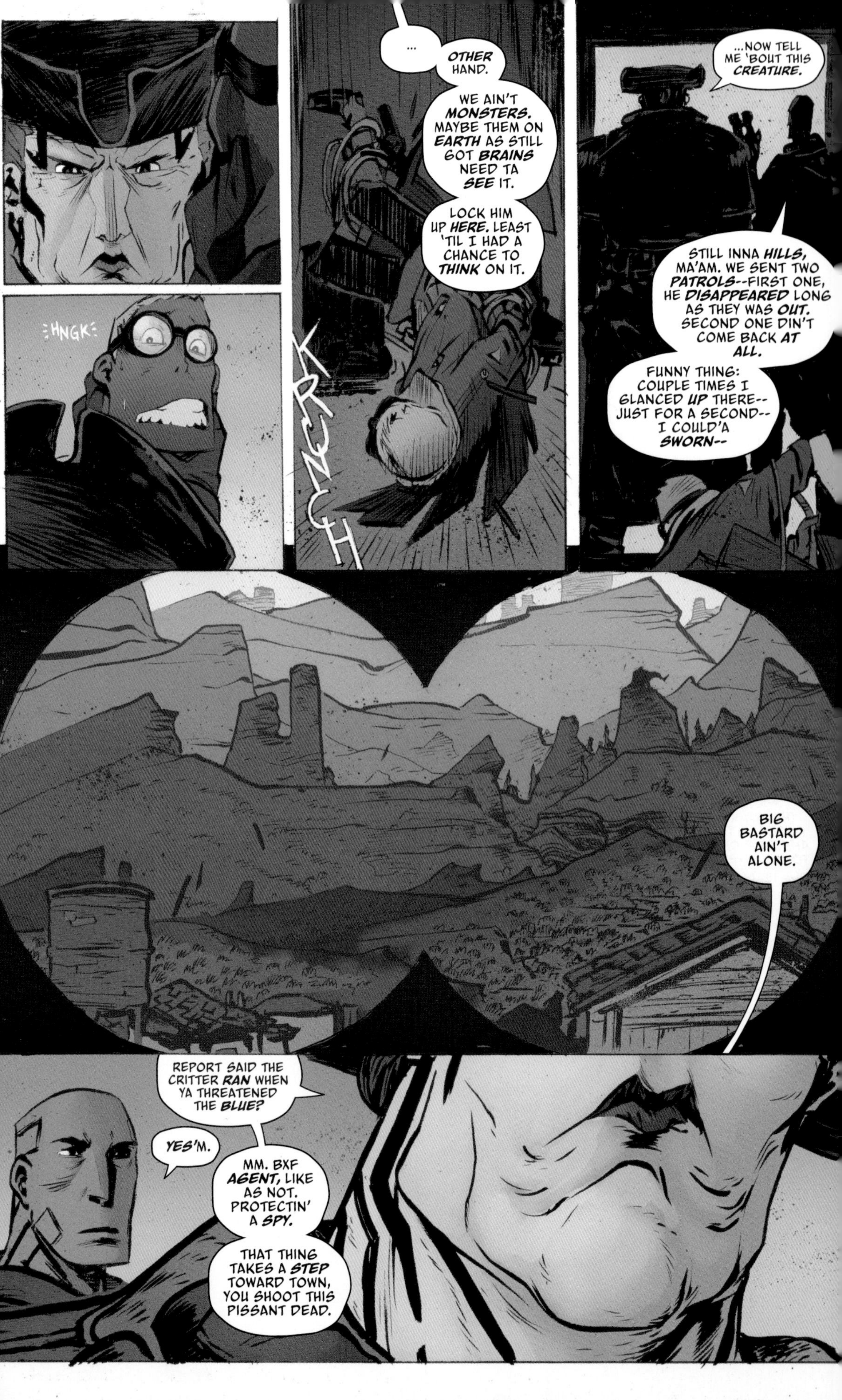
HNGK
...
OTHER HAND.
WE AIN'T MONSTERS. MAYBE THEM ON EARTH AS STILL GOT BRAINS NEED TA SEE IT.
LOCK HIM UP HERE. LEAST 'TIL I HAD A CHANCE TO THINK ON IT.
KRUNCH
...NOW TELL ME 'BOUT THIS CREATURE.
STILL INNA HILLS, MA'AM. WE SENT TWO PATROLS--FIRST ONE, HE DISAPPEARED LONG AS THEY WAS OUT. SECOND ONE DIN'T COME BACK AT ALL.
FUNNY THING: COUPLE TIMES I GLANCED UP THERE--JUST FOR A SECOND--I COULD'A SWORN--
BIG BASTARD AIN'T ALONE.
REPORT SAID THE CRITTER RAN WHEN YA THREATENED THE BLUE?
YES'M.
MM. BXF AGENT, LIKE AS NOT. PROTECTIN' A SPY.
THAT THING TAKES A STEP TOWARD TOWN, YOU SHOOT THIS PISSANT DEAD.

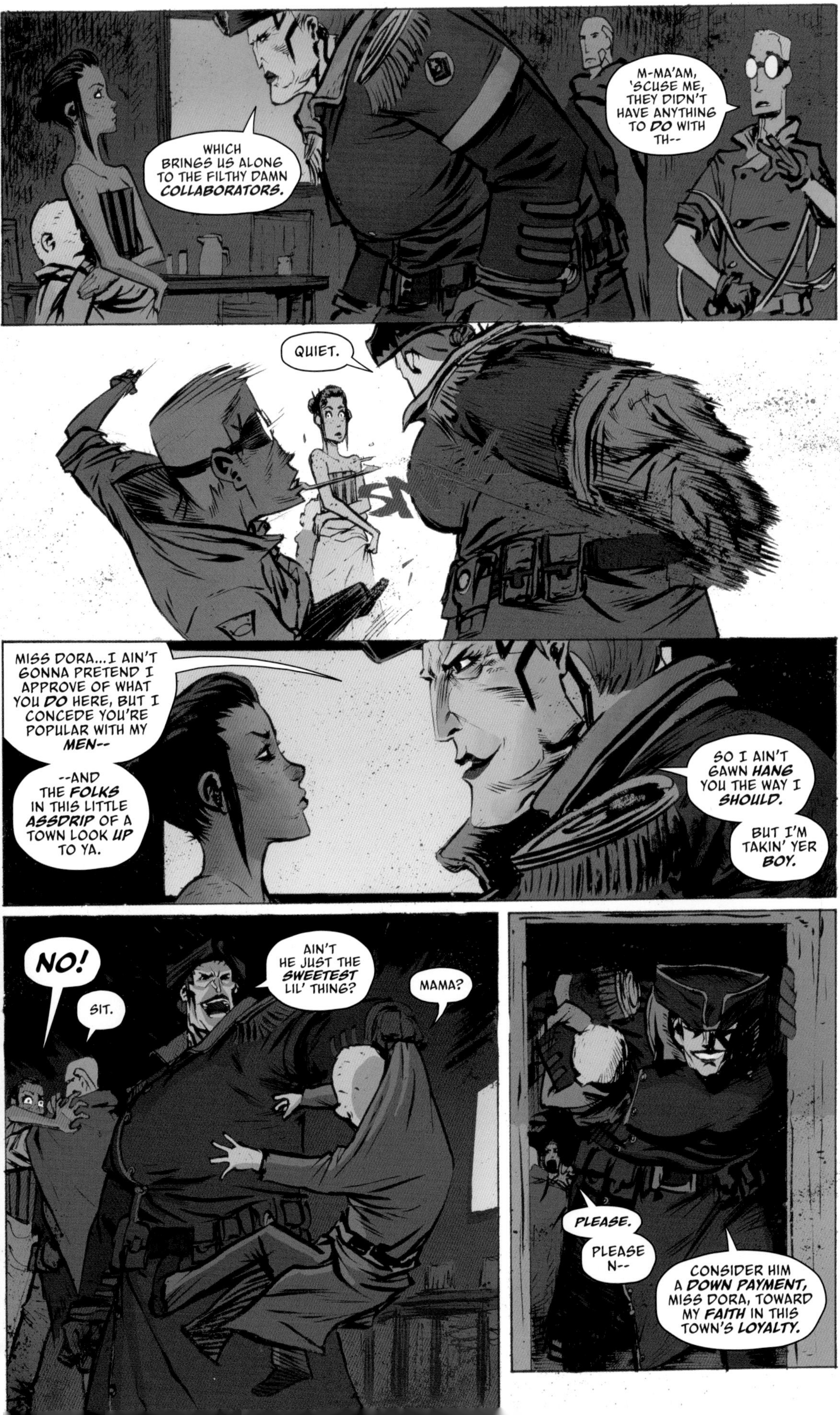
WHICH BRINGS US ALONG TO THE FILTHY DAMN COLLABORATORS.
M-MA'AM, 'SCUSE ME, THEY DIDN'T HAVE ANYTHING TO DO WITH TH--
QUIET.
MISS DORA...I AIN'T GONNA PRETEND I APPROVE OF WHAT YOU DO HERE, BUT I CONCEDE YOU'RE POPULAR WITH MY MEN--
--AND THE FOLKS IN THIS LITTLE ASSDRIP OF A TOWN LOOK UP TO YA.
SO I AIN'T GAWN HANG YOU THE WAY I SHOULD.
BUT I'M TAKIN' YER BOY.
NO!
SIT.
AIN'T HE JUST THE SWEETEST LIL' THING?
MAMA?
PLEASE.
PLEASE N--
CONSIDER HIM A DOWN PAYMENT, MISS DORA, TOWARD MY FAITH IN THIS TOWN'S LOYALTY.

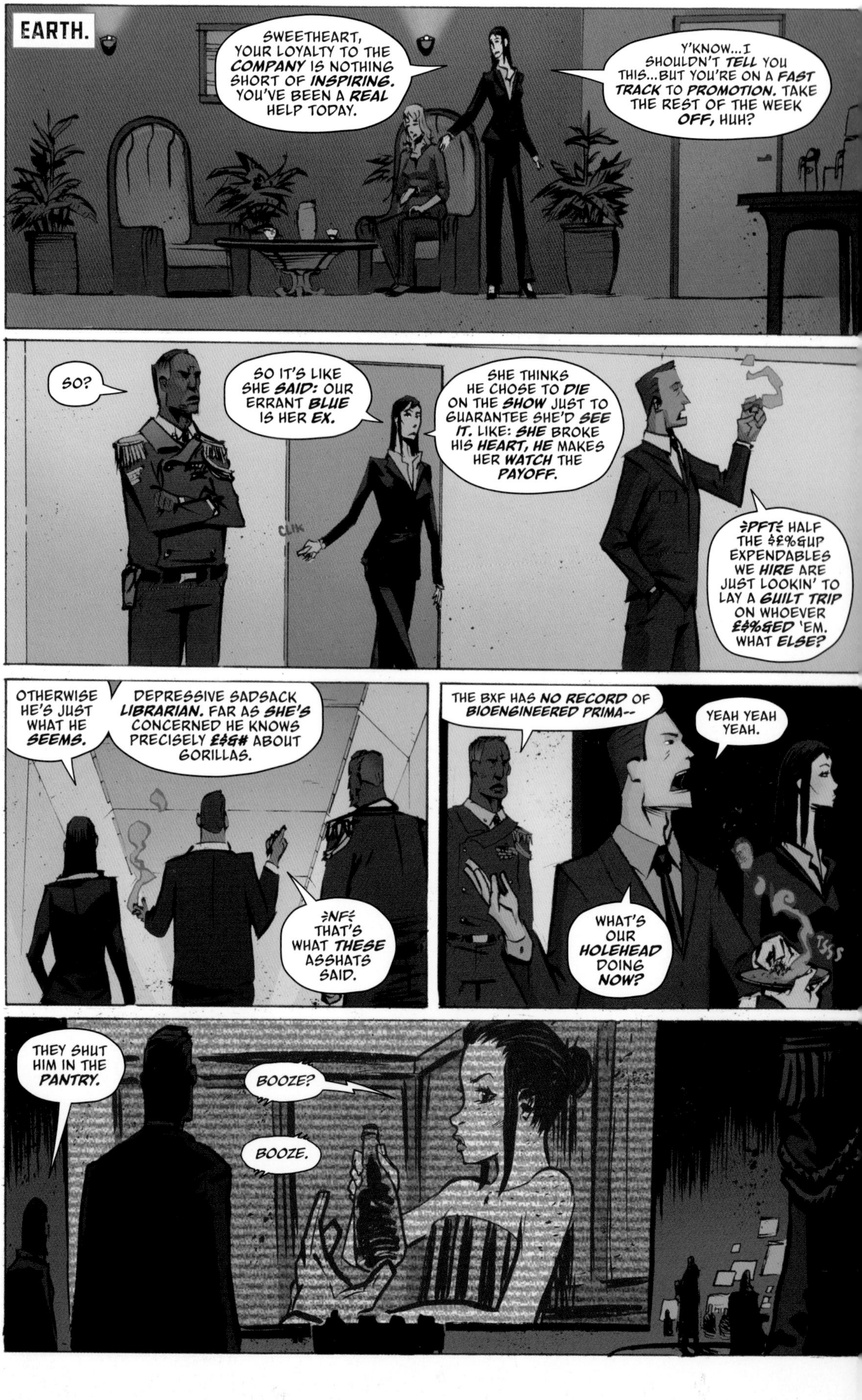
EARTH.
SWEETHEART, YOUR LOYALTY TO THE COMPANY IS NOTHING SHORT OF INSPIRING. YOU'VE BEEN A REAL HELP TODAY.
Y'KNOW...I SHOULDN'T TELL YOU THIS...BUT YOU'RE ON A FAST TRACK TO PROMOTION. TAKE THE REST OF THE WEEK OFF, HUH?
SO?
SO IT'S LIKE SHE SAID: OUR ERRANT BLUE IS HER EX.
CLIK
SHE THINKS HE CHOSE TO DIE ON THE SHOW JUST TO GUARANTEE SHE'D SEE IT. LIKE: SHE BROKE HIS HEART, HE MAKES HER WATCH THE PAYOFF.
≠PFT≠ HALF THE $£%&UP EXPENDABLES WE HIRE ARE JUST LOOKIN' TO LAY A GUILT TRIP ON WHOEVER £$%&ED 'EM. WHAT ELSE?
OTHERWISE HE'S JUST WHAT HE SEEMS.
DEPRESSIVE SADSACK LIBRARIAN. FAR AS SHE'S CONCERNED HE KNOWS PRECISELY £$&# ABOUT GORILLAS.
≠NF≠ THAT'S WHAT THESE ASSHATS SAID.
THE BXF HAS NO RECORD OF BIOENGINEERED PRIMA--
YEAH YEAH YEAH.
WHAT'S OUR HOLEHEAD DOING NOW?
TSSS
THEY SHUT HIM IN THE PANTRY.
BOOZE?
BOOZE.

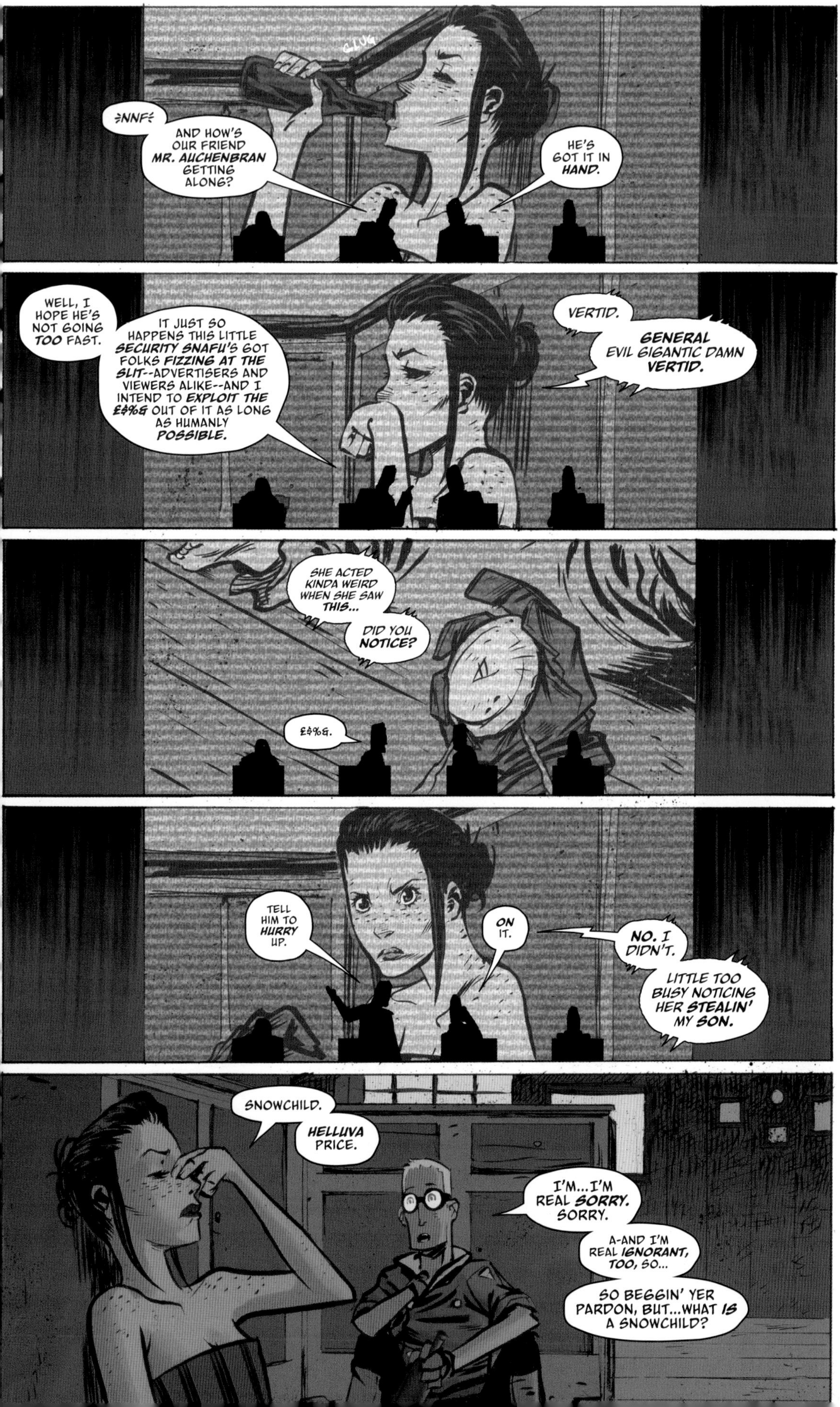
GLUG
SNNF
AND HOW'S OUR FRIEND MR. AUCHENBRAN GETTING ALONG?
HE'S GOT IT IN HAND.
WELL, I HOPE HE'S NOT GOING TOO FAST.
IT JUST SO HAPPENS THIS LITTLE SECURITY SNAFU'S GOT FOLKS FIZZING AT THE SLIT--ADVERTISERS AND VIEWERS ALIKE--AND I INTEND TO EXPLOIT THE £$%& OUT OF IT AS LONG AS HUMANLY POSSIBLE.
VERTID.
GENERAL EVIL GIGANTIC DAMN VERTID.
SHE ACTED KINDA WEIRD WHEN SHE SAW THIS...
DID YOU NOTICE?
£$%&.
TELL HIM TO HURRY UP.
ON IT.
NO. I DIDN'T.
LITTLE TOO BUSY NOTICING HER STEALIN' MY SON.
SNOWCHILD.
HELLUVA PRICE.
I'M...I'M REAL SORRY. SORRY.
A-AND I'M REAL IGNORANT, TOO, SO...
SO BEGGIN' YER PARDON, BUT...WHAT IS A SNOWCHILD?

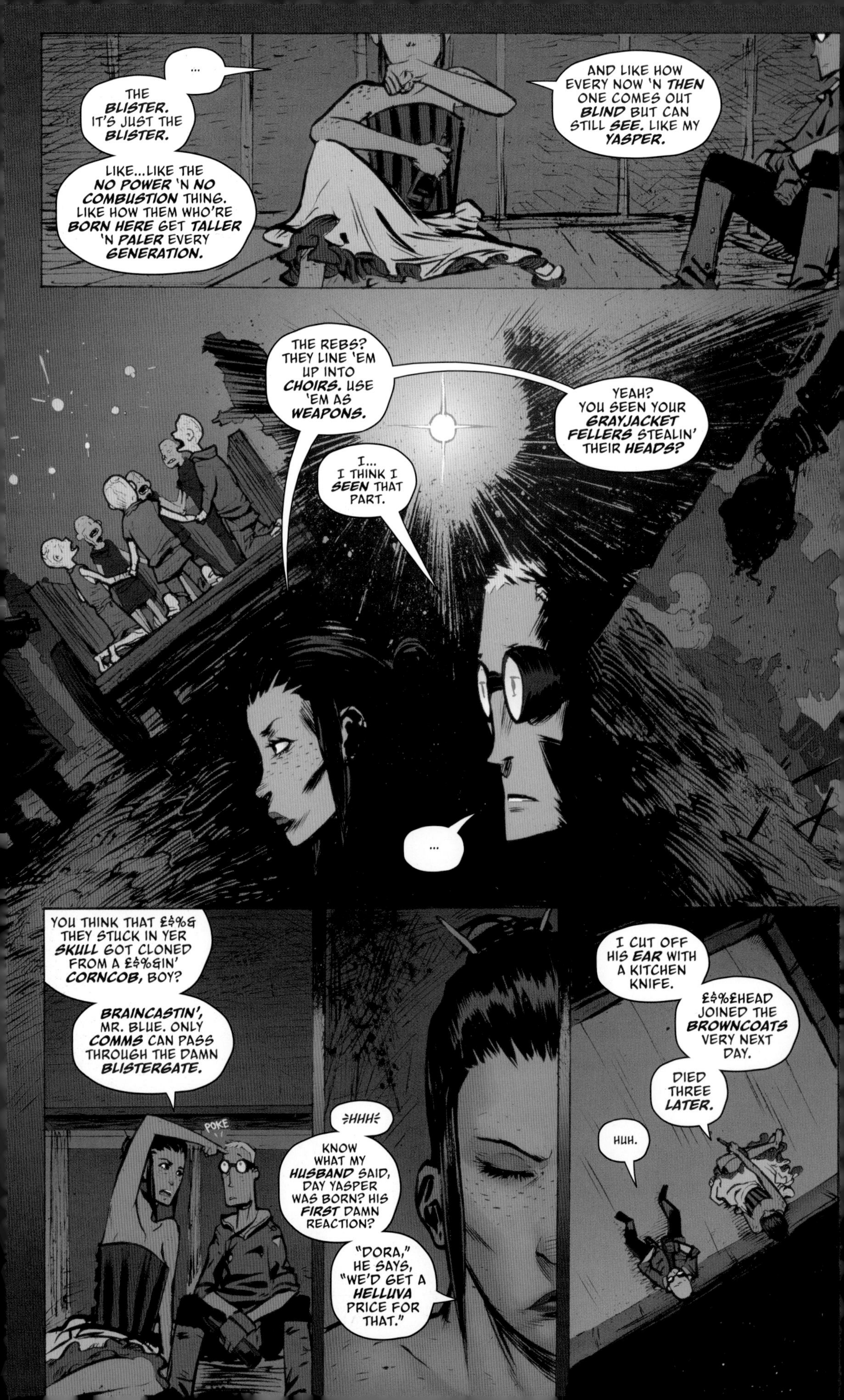

...
THE BLISTER. IT'S JUST THE BLISTER.
LIKE...LIKE THE NO POWER 'N NO COMBUSTION THING. LIKE HOW THEM WHO'RE BORN HERE GET TALLER 'N PALER EVERY GENERATION.
AND LIKE HOW EVERY NOW 'N THEN ONE COMES OUT BLIND BUT CAN STILL SEE. LIKE MY YASPER.
THE REBS? THEY LINE 'EM UP INTO CHOIRS. USE 'EM AS WEAPONS.
YEAH? YOU SEEN YOUR GRAYJACKET FELLERS STEALIN' THEIR HEADS?
I... I THINK I SEEN THAT PART.
...
YOU THINK THAT £$%& THEY STUCK IN YER SKULL GOT CLONED FROM A £$%&IN' CORNCOB, BOY?
BRAINCASTIN', MR. BLUE. ONLY COMMS CAN PASS THROUGH THE DAMN BLISTERGATE.
POKE
≈HHH≈
KNOW WHAT MY HUSBAND SAID, DAY YASPER WAS BORN? HIS FIRST DAMN REACTION?
"DORA," HE SAYS, "WE'D GET A HELLUVA PRICE FOR THAT."
I CUT OFF HIS EAR WITH A KITCHEN KNIFE.
£$%£HEAD JOINED THE BROWNCOATS VERY NEXT DAY.
DIED THREE LATER.
HUH.

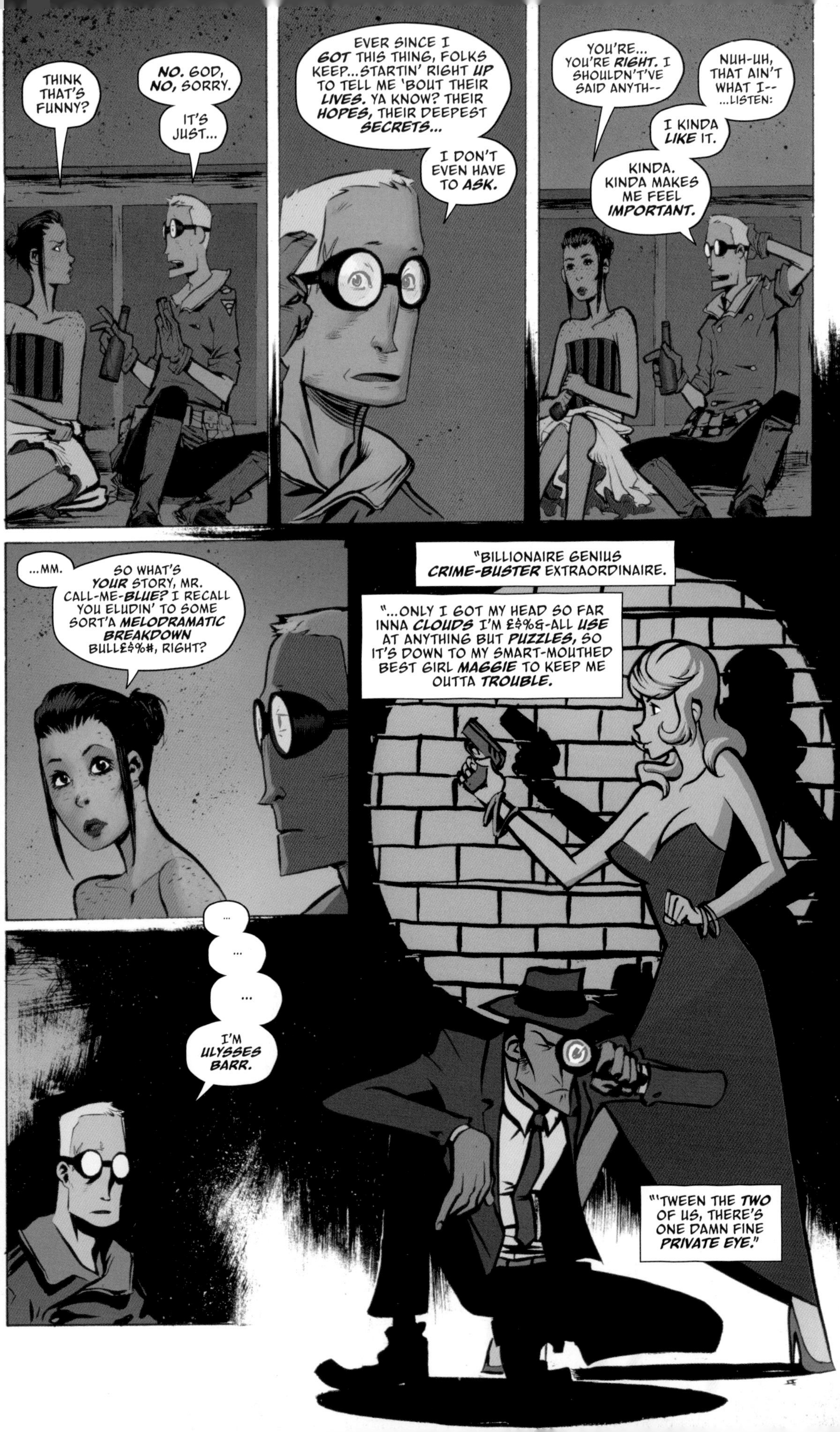
THINK THAT'S FUNNY?
NO. GOD, NO, SORRY.
IT'S JUST...
EVER SINCE I GOT THIS THING, FOLKS KEEP...STARTIN' RIGHT UP TO TELL ME 'BOUT THEIR LIVES. YA KNOW? THEIR HOPES, THEIR DEEPEST SECRETS...
I DON'T EVEN HAVE TO ASK.
YOU'RE... YOU'RE RIGHT. I SHOULDN'T'VE SAID ANYTH--
NUH-UH, THAT AIN'T WHAT I-- ...LISTEN:
I KINDA LIKE IT.
KINDA. KINDA MAKES ME FEEL IMPORTANT.
...MM.
SO WHAT'S YOUR STORY, MR. CALL-ME-BLUE? I RECALL YOU ELUDIN' TO SOME SORT'A MELODRAMATIC BREAKDOWN BULL£$%#, RIGHT?
"BILLIONAIRE GENIUS CRIME-BUSTER EXTRAORDINAIRE.
"...ONLY I GOT MY HEAD SO FAR INNA CLOUDS I'M £$%&-ALL USE AT ANYTHING BUT PUZZLES, SO IT'S DOWN TO MY SMART-MOUTHED BEST GIRL MAGGIE TO KEEP ME OUTTA TROUBLE.
...
...
...
I'M ULYSSES BARR.
"'TWEEN THE TWO OF US, THERE'S ONE DAMN FINE PRIVATE EYE."

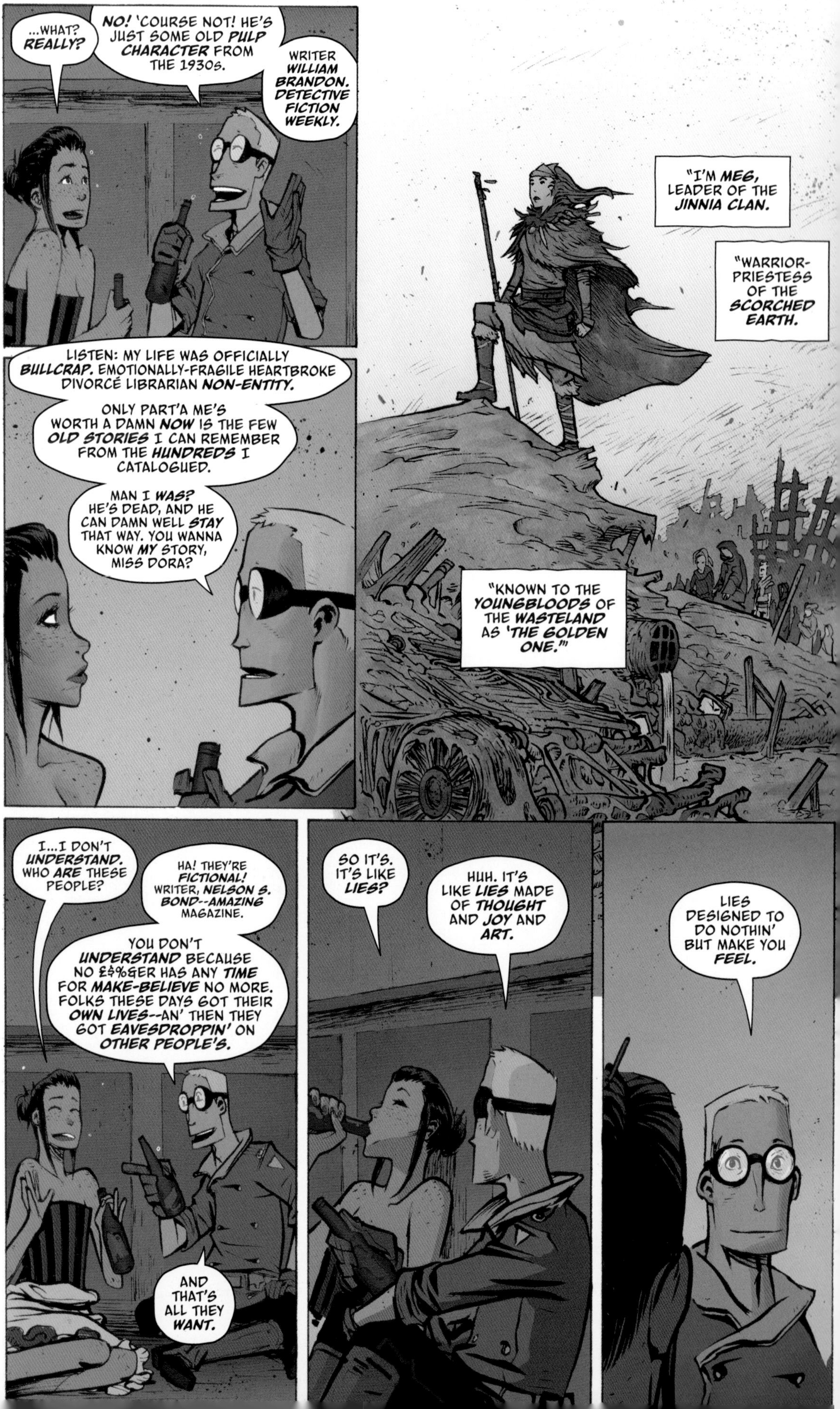
...WHAT? REALLY?
NO! 'COURSE NOT! HE'S JUST SOME OLD PULP CHARACTER FROM THE 1930s.
WRITER WILLIAM BRANDON. DETECTIVE FICTION WEEKLY.
"I'M MEG, LEADER OF THE JINNIA CLAN.
"WARRIOR-PRIESTESS OF THE SCORCHED EARTH.
"KNOWN TO THE YOUNGBLOODS OF THE WASTELAND AS 'THE GOLDEN ONE.'"
LISTEN: MY LIFE WAS OFFICIALLY BULLCRAP. EMOTIONALLY-FRAGILE HEARTBROKE DIVORCÉ LIBRARIAN NON-ENTITY.
ONLY PART'A ME'S WORTH A DAMN NOW IS THE FEW OLD STORIES I CAN REMEMBER FROM THE HUNDREDS I CATALOGUED.
MAN I WAS? HE'S DEAD, AND HE CAN DAMN WELL STAY THAT WAY. YOU WANNA KNOW MY STORY, MISS DORA?
I...I DON'T UNDERSTAND. WHO ARE THESE PEOPLE?
HA! THEY'RE FICTIONAL! WRITER, NELSON S. BOND--AMAZING MAGAZINE.
YOU DON'T UNDERSTAND BECAUSE NO £$%&ER HAS ANY TIME FOR MAKE-BELIEVE NO MORE. FOLKS THESE DAYS GOT THEIR OWN LIVES--AN' THEN THEY GOT EAVESDROPPIN' ON OTHER PEOPLE'S.
AND THAT'S ALL THEY WANT.
SO IT'S. IT'S LIKE LIES?
HUH. IT'S LIKE LIES MADE OF THOUGHT AND JOY AND ART.
LIES DESIGNED TO DO NOTHIN' BUT MAKE YOU FEEL.

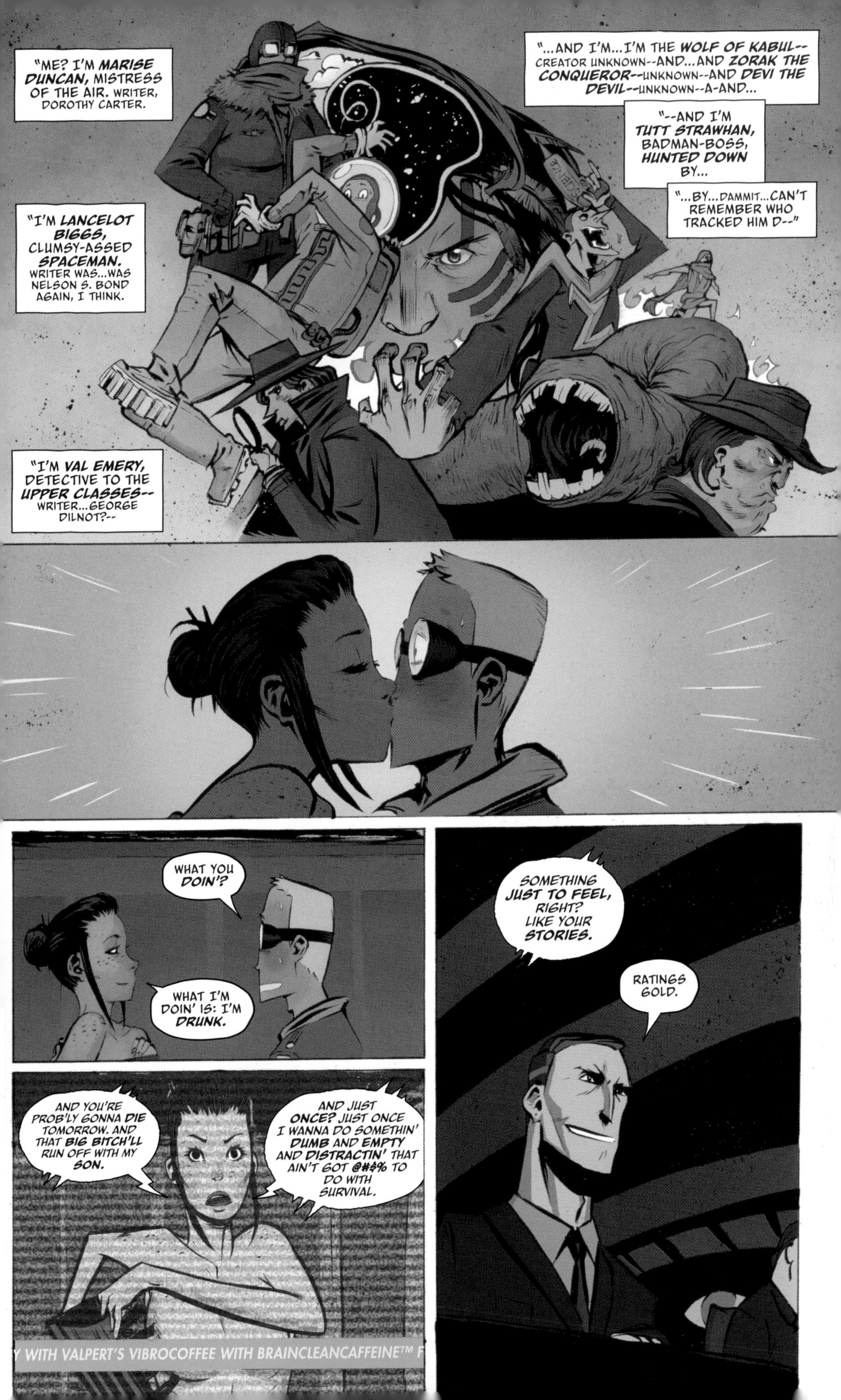
"ME? I'M MARISE DUNCAN, MISTRESS OF THE AIR. WRITER, DOROTHY CARTER.
"...AND I'M...I'M THE WOLF OF KABUL--CREATOR UNKNOWN--AND...AND ZORAK THE CONQUEROR--UNKNOWN--AND DEVI THE DEVIL--UNKNOWN--A-AND...
"--AND I'M TUTT STRAWHAN, BADMAN-BOSS, HUNTED DOWN BY...
"...BY...DAMMIT...CAN'T REMEMBER WHO TRACKED HIM D--"
"I'M LANCELOT BIGGS, CLUMSY-ASSED SPACEMAN. WRITER WAS...WAS NELSON S. BOND AGAIN, I THINK.
"I'M VAL EMERY, DETECTIVE TO THE UPPER CLASSES--WRITER...GEORGE DILNOT?--
WHAT YOU DOIN'?
WHAT I'M DOIN' IS: I'M DRUNK.
AND YOU'RE PROB'LY GONNA DIE TOMORROW. AND THAT BIG BITCH'LL RUN OFF WITH MY SON.
AND JUST ONCE? JUST ONCE I WANNA DO SOMETHIN' DUMB AND EMPTY AND DISTRACTIN' THAT AIN'T GOT @#$% TO DO WITH SURVIVAL.
Y WITH VALPERT'S VIBROCOFFEE WITH BRAINCLEANCAFFEINE™ F
SOMETHING JUST TO FEEL, RIGHT? LIKE YOUR STORIES.
RATINGS GOLD.

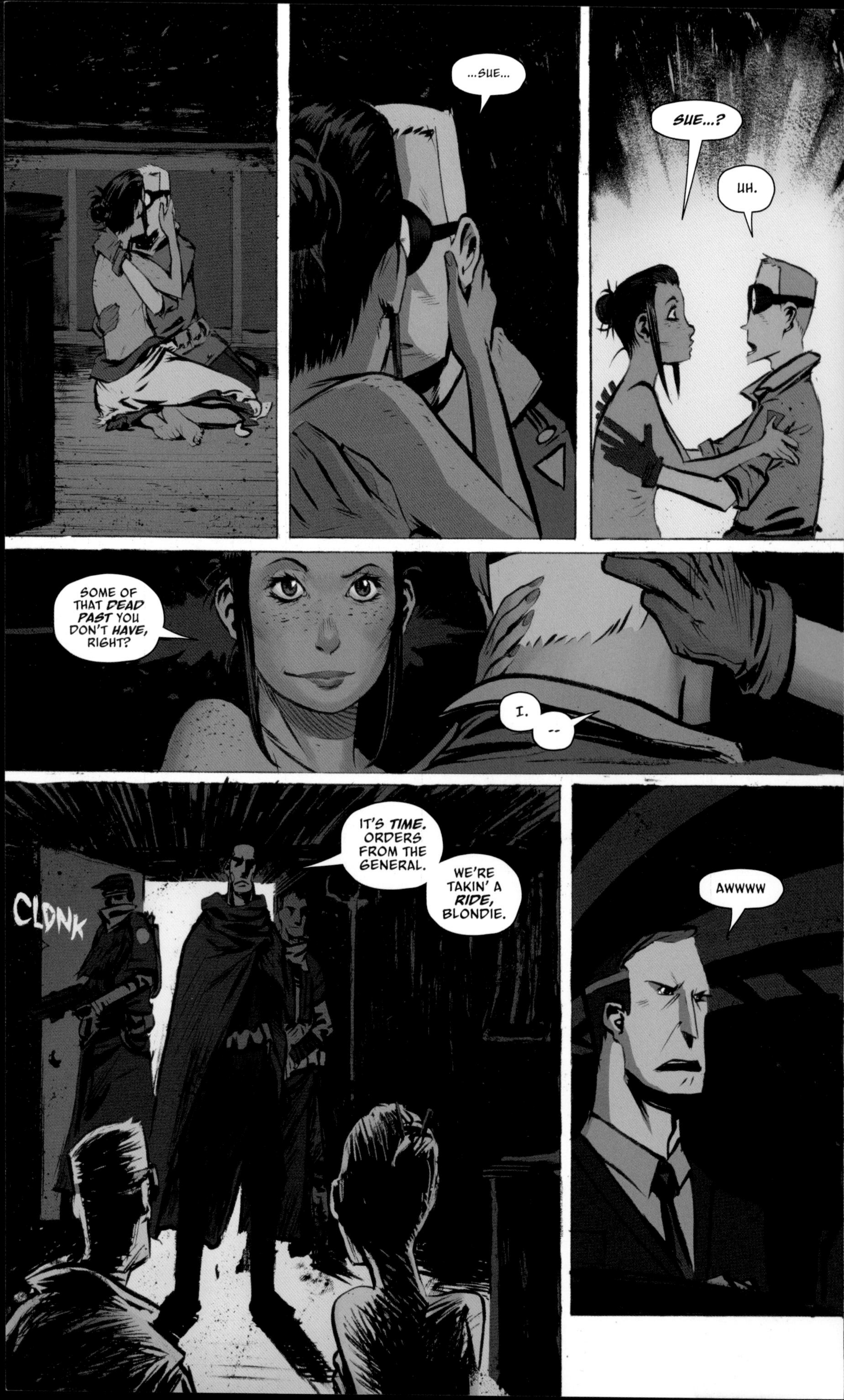
...SUE...
SUE...?
UH.
SOME OF THAT DEAD PAST YOU DON'T HAVE, RIGHT?
I.
--
CLONK
IT'S TIME. ORDERS FROM THE GENERAL.
WE'RE TAKIN' A RIDE, BLONDIE.
AWWWW

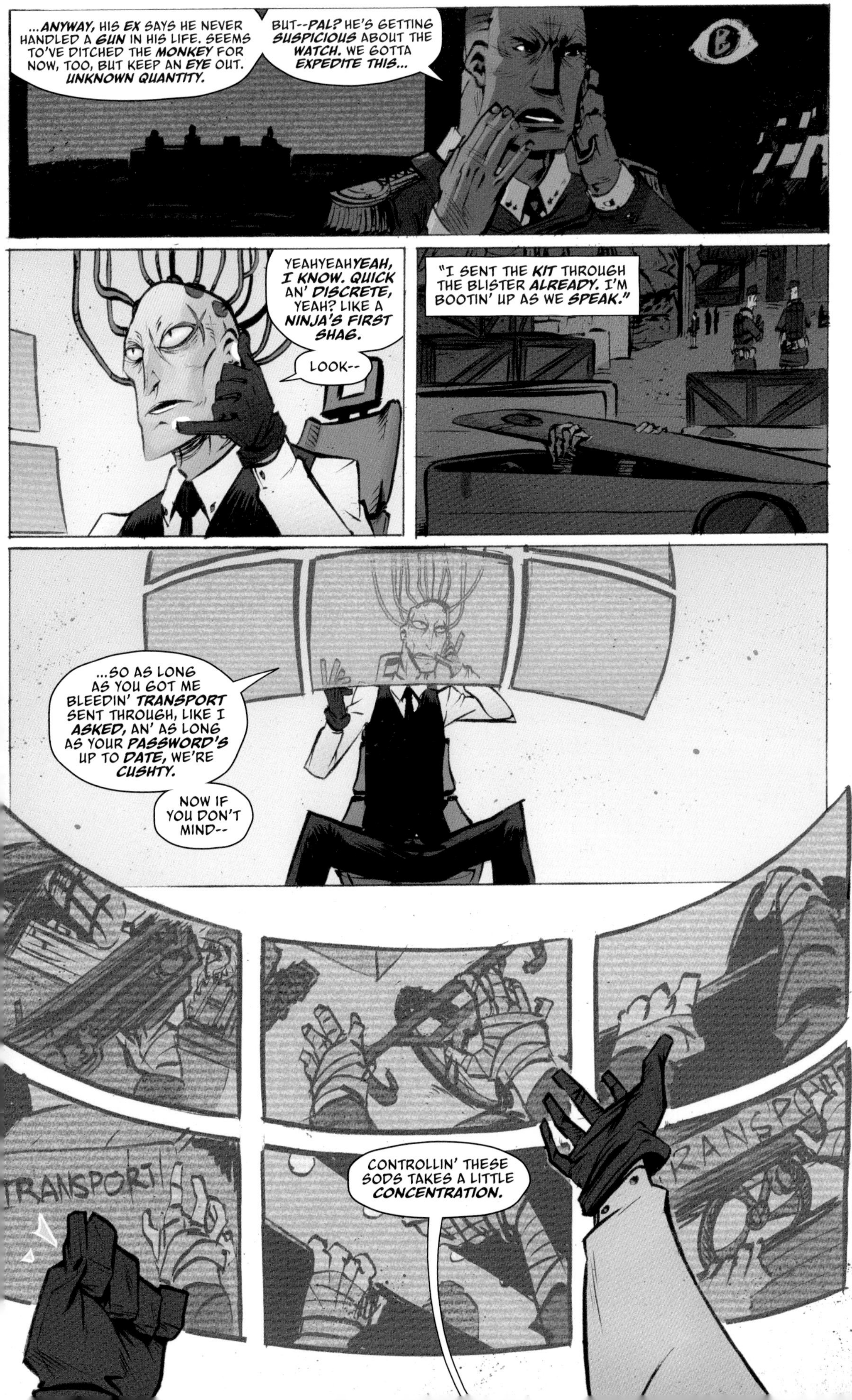
...ANYWAY, HIS EX SAYS HE NEVER HANDLED A GUN IN HIS LIFE. SEEMS TO'VE DITCHED THE MONKEY FOR NOW, TOO, BUT KEEP AN EYE OUT. UNKNOWN QUANTITY.
BUT--PAL? HE'S GETTING SUSPICIOUS ABOUT THE WATCH. WE GOTTA EXPEDITE THIS...
YEAHYEAHYEAH, I KNOW. QUICK AN' DISCRETE, YEAH? LIKE A NINJA'S FIRST SHAG.
LOOK--
"I SENT THE KIT THROUGH THE BLISTER ALREADY. I'M BOOTIN' UP AS WE SPEAK."
...SO AS LONG AS YOU GOT ME BLEEDIN' TRANSPORT SENT THROUGH, LIKE I ASKED, AN' AS LONG AS YOUR PASSWORD'S UP TO DATE, WE'RE CUSHTY.
NOW IF YOU DON'T MIND--
TRANSPORT
CONTROLLIN' THESE SODS TAKES A LITTLE CONCENTRATION.

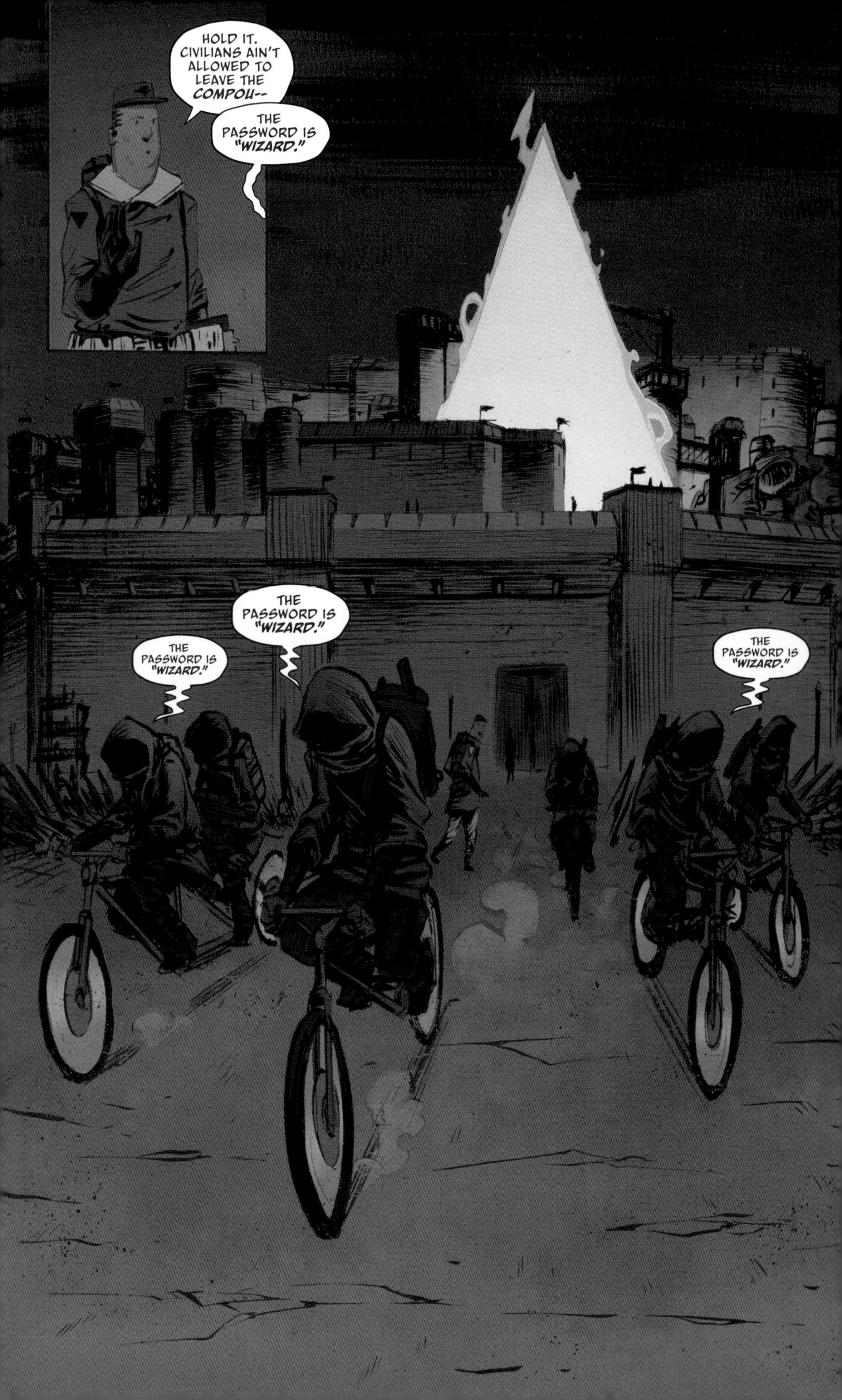
HOLD IT. CIVILIANS AIN'T ALLOWED TO LEAVE THE COMPOU--
THE PASSWORD IS "WIZARD."
THE PASSWORD IS "WIZARD."
THE PASSWORD IS "WIZARD."
THE PASSWORD IS "WIZARD."

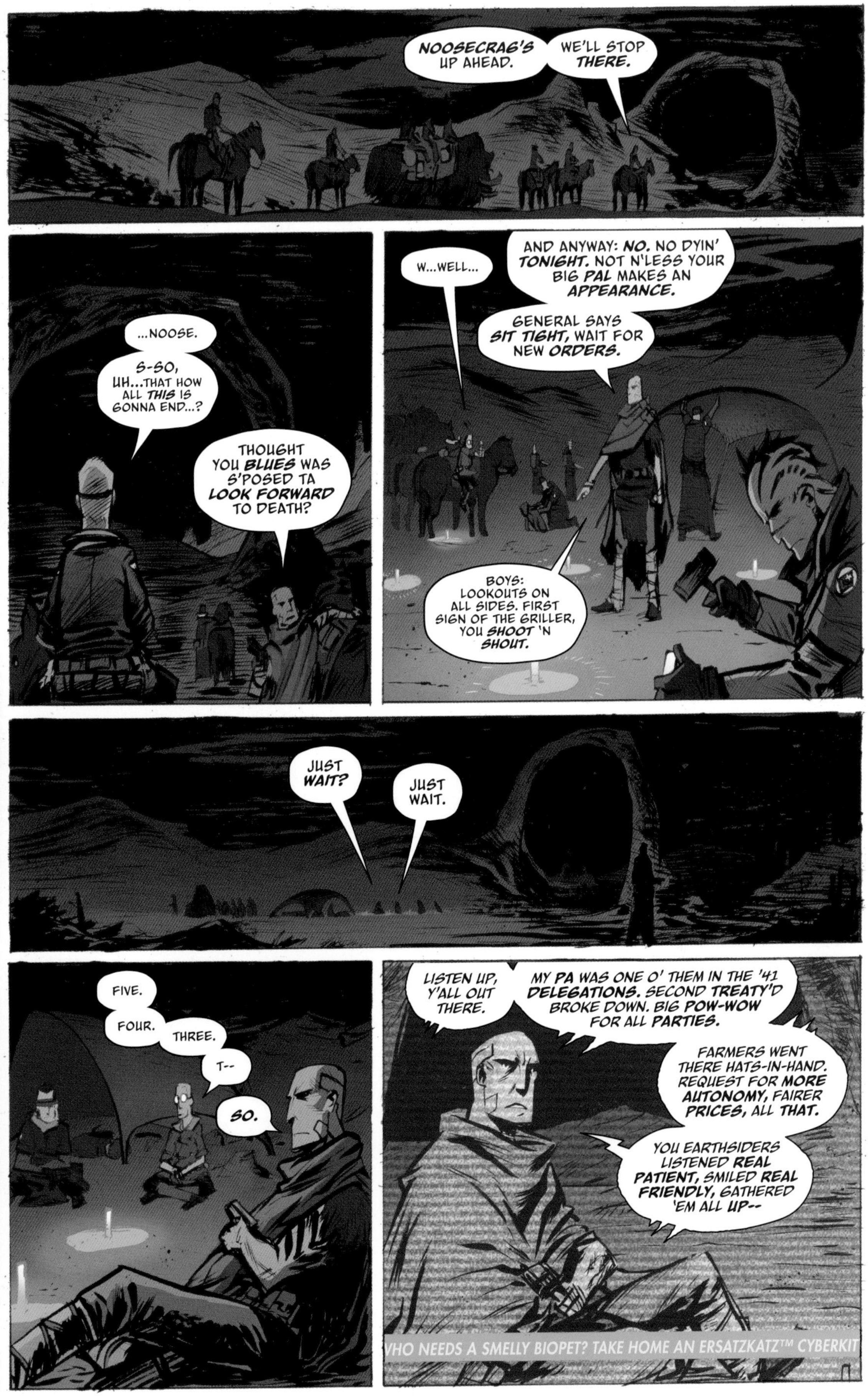
NOOSECRAG'S UP AHEAD.
WE'LL STOP THERE.
...NOOSE.
S-SO, UH...THAT HOW ALL THIS IS GONNA END...?
THOUGHT YOU BLUES WAS S'POSED TA LOOK FORWARD TO DEATH?
W...WELL...
AND ANYWAY: NO. NO DYIN' TONIGHT. NOT N'LESS YOUR BIG PAL MAKES AN APPEARANCE.
GENERAL SAYS SIT TIGHT, WAIT FOR NEW ORDERS.
BOYS: LOOKOUTS ON ALL SIDES. FIRST SIGN OF THE GRILLER, YOU SHOOT 'N SHOUT.
JUST WAIT?
JUST WAIT.
FIVE.
FOUR.
THREE.
T--
SO.
LISTEN UP, Y'ALL OUT THERE.
MY PA WAS ONE O' THEM IN THE '41 DELEGATIONS. SECOND TREATY'D BROKE DOWN. BIG POW-WOW FOR ALL PARTIES.
FARMERS WENT THERE HATS-IN-HAND. REQUEST FOR MORE AUTONOMY, FAIRER PRICES, ALL THAT.
YOU EARTHSIDERS LISTENED REAL PATIENT, SMILED REAL FRIENDLY, GATHERED 'EM ALL UP--
VHO NEEDS A SMELLY BIOPET? TAKE HOME AN ERSATZKATZ™ CYBERKIT

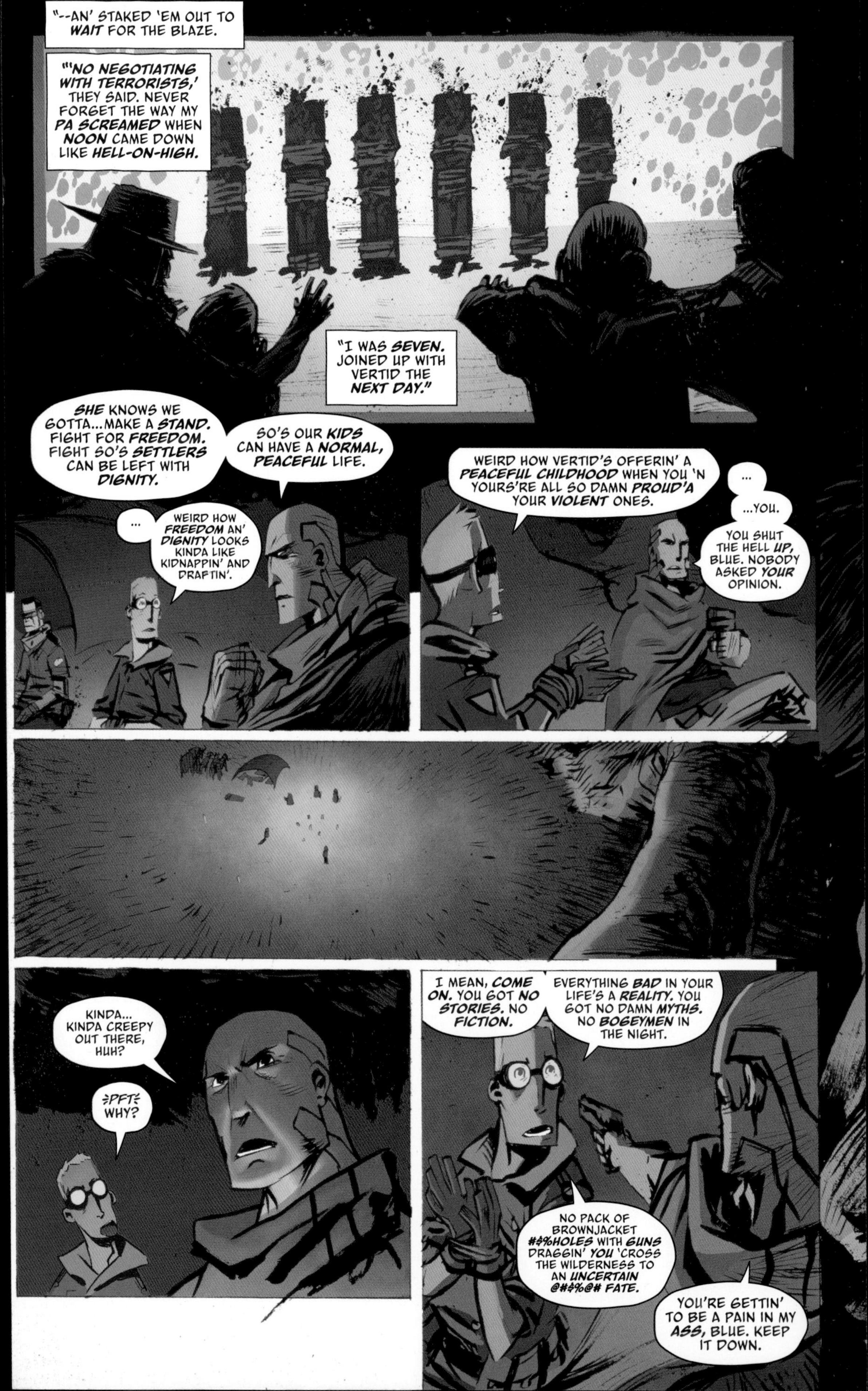
"--AN' STAKED 'EM OUT TO WAIT FOR THE BLAZE.
"'NO NEGOTIATING WITH TERRORISTS,' THEY SAID. NEVER FORGET THE WAY MY PA SCREAMED WHEN NOON CAME DOWN LIKE HELL-ON-HIGH.
"I WAS SEVEN. JOINED UP WITH VERTID THE NEXT DAY."
SHE KNOWS WE GOTTA...MAKE A STAND. FIGHT FOR FREEDOM. FIGHT SO'S SETTLERS CAN BE LEFT WITH DIGNITY.
SO'S OUR KIDS CAN HAVE A NORMAL, PEACEFUL LIFE.
...
WEIRD HOW FREEDOM AN' DIGNITY LOOKS KINDA LIKE KIDNAPPIN' AND DRAFTIN'.
WEIRD HOW VERTID'S OFFERIN' A PEACEFUL CHILDHOOD WHEN YOU 'N YOURS'RE ALL SO DAMN PROUD'A YOUR VIOLENT ONES.
...
...YOU.
YOU SHUT THE HELL UP, BLUE. NOBODY ASKED YOUR OPINION.
KINDA... KINDA CREEPY OUT THERE, HUH?
≠PFT≠ WHY?
I MEAN, COME ON. YOU GOT NO STORIES. NO FICTION.
EVERYTHING BAD IN YOUR LIFE'S A REALITY. YOU GOT NO DAMN MYTHS. NO BOGEYMEN IN THE NIGHT.
NO PACK OF BROWNJACKET #$%HOLES WITH GUNS DRAGGIN' YOU 'CROSS THE WILDERNESS TO AN UNCERTAIN @#$%@# FATE.
YOU'RE GETTIN' TO BE A PAIN IN MY ASS, BLUE. KEEP IT DOWN.

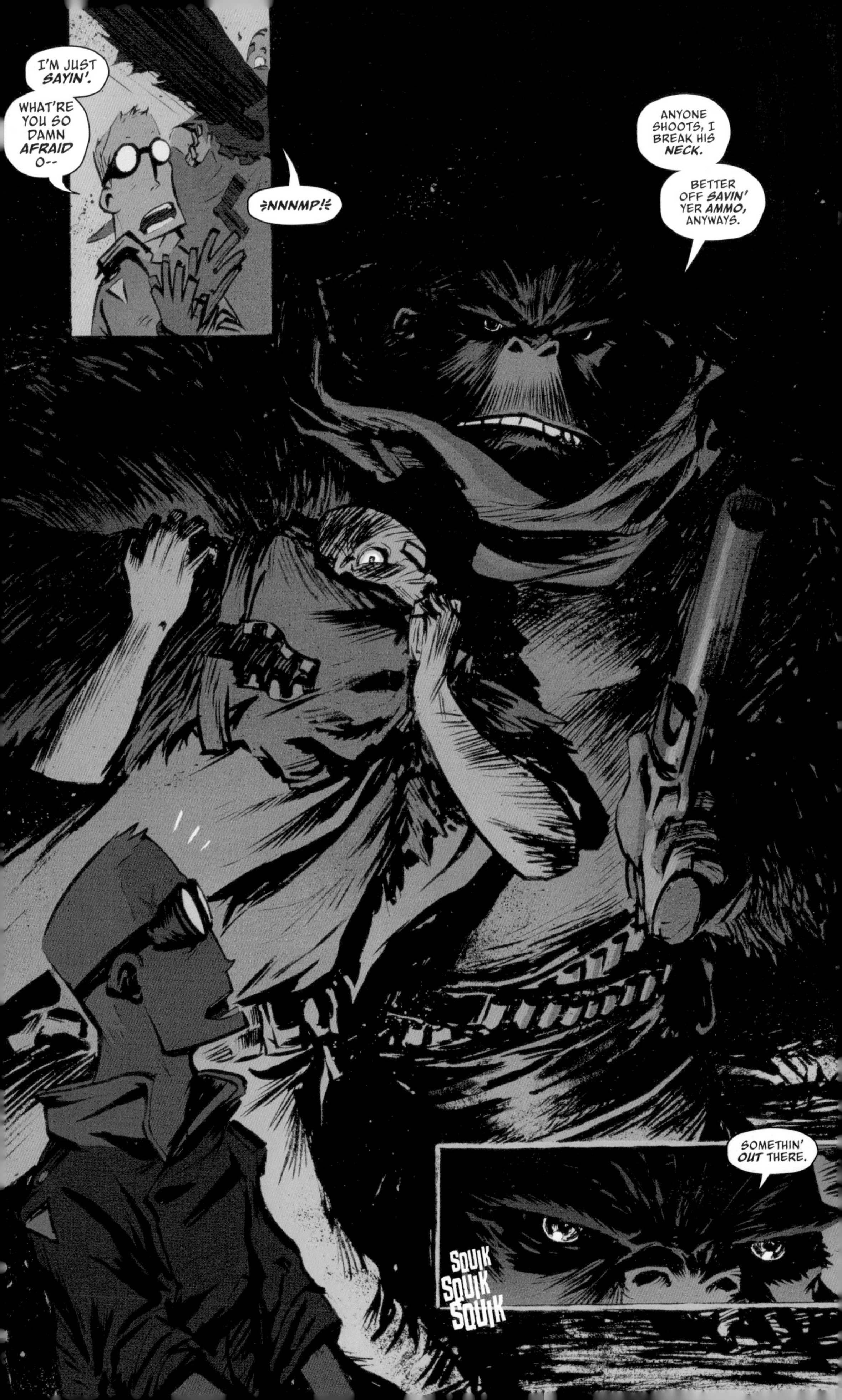
I'M JUST SAYIN'.
WHAT'RE YOU SO DAMN AFRAID O--
≠NNNMP!≠
ANYONE SHOOTS, I BREAK HIS NECK.
BETTER OFF SAVIN' YER AMMO, ANYWAYS.
SOMETHIN' OUT THERE.
SQUIK SQUIK SQUIK

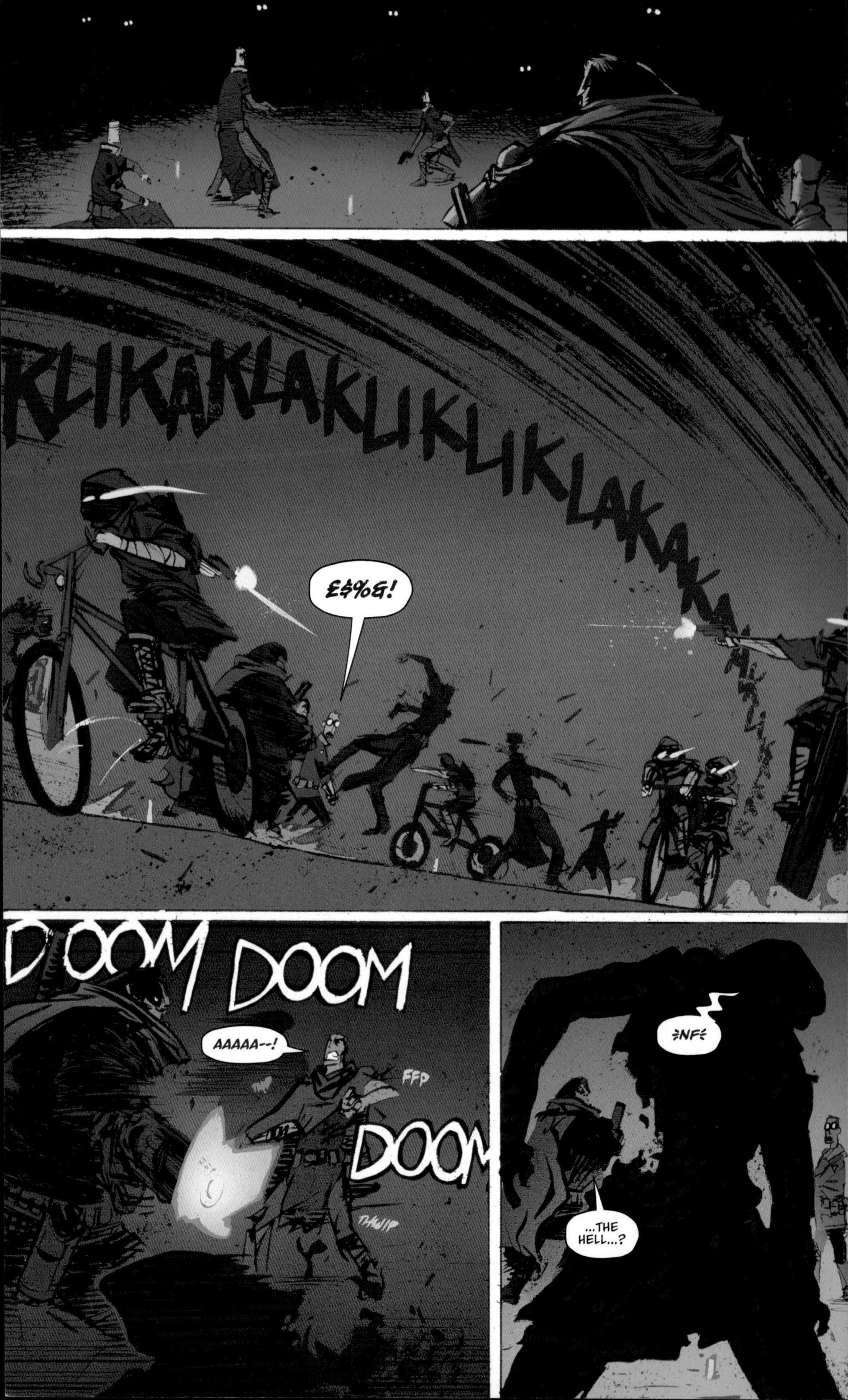
KLIKAKLAKLIKLIKLAKAKA
£$%&!
DOOM DOOM
AAAAA--!
FFP
DOOM
THWIP
NF
...THE HELL...?

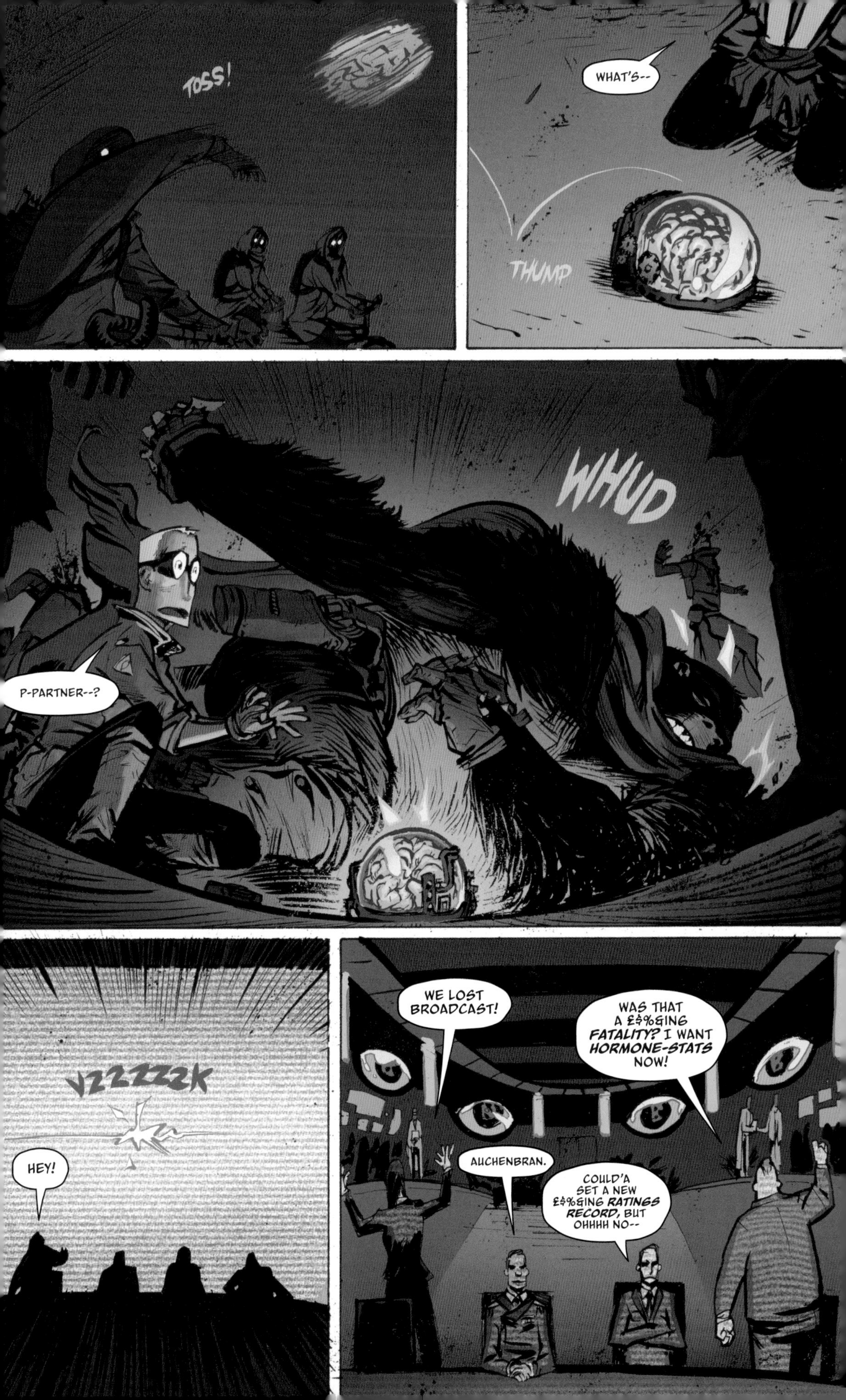
TOSS!
WHAT'S--
THUMP
WHUD
P-PARTNER--?
VZZZZZK
HEY!
WE LOST BROADCAST!
WAS THAT A £$%&ING FATALITY? I WANT HORMONE-STATS NOW!
AUCHENBRAN.
COULD'A SET A NEW £$%&ING RATINGS RECORD, BUT OHHHH NO--

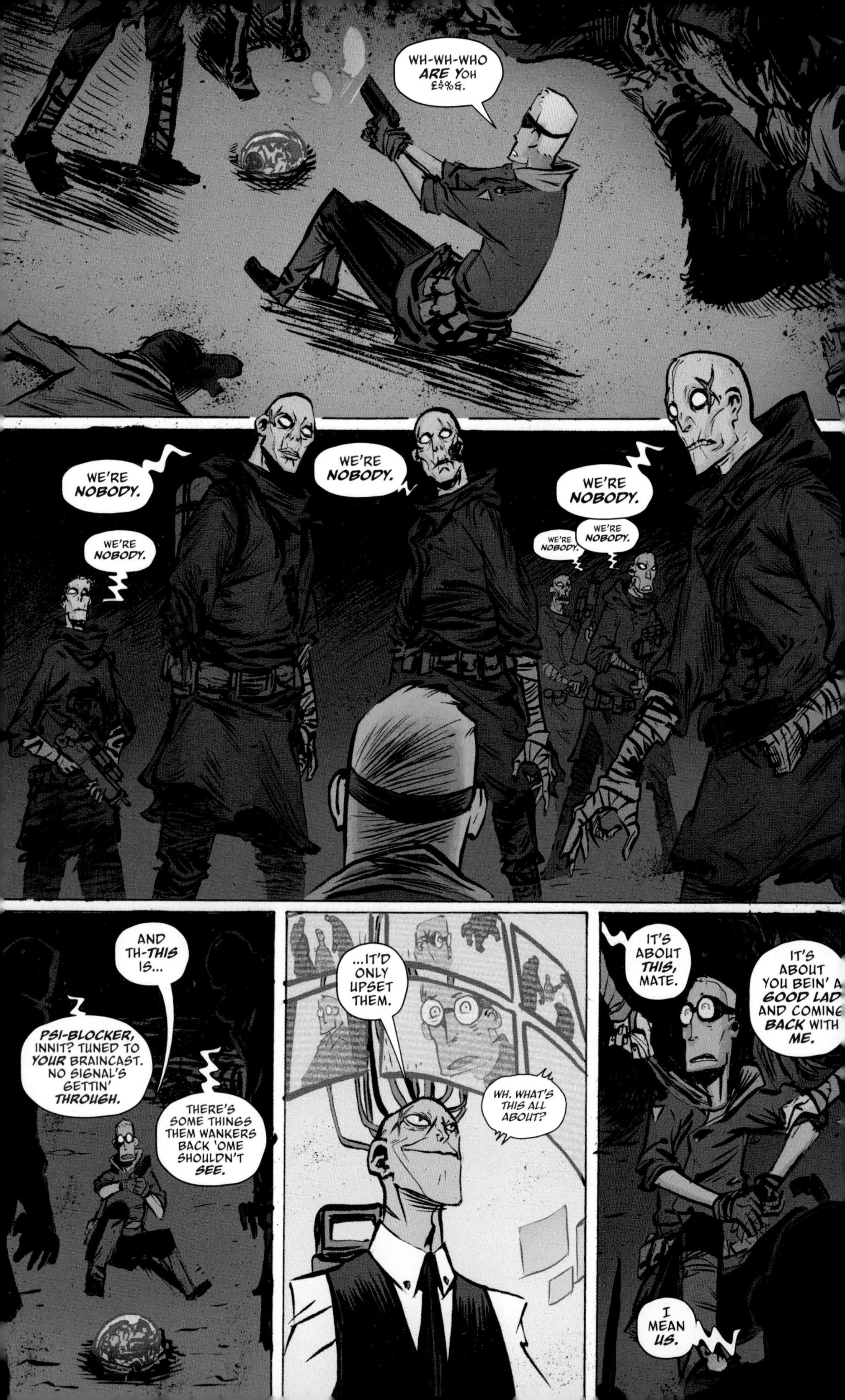
WH-WH-WHO ARE YOH £$%G.
WE'RE NOBODY.
WE'RE NOBODY.
WE'RE NOBODY.
WE'RE NOBODY.
WE'RE NOBODY.
WE'RE NOBODY.
AND TH-THIS IS...
PSI-BLOCKER, INNIT? TUNED TO YOUR BRAINCAST. NO SIGNAL'S GETTIN' THROUGH.
THERE'S SOME THINGS THEM WANKERS BACK 'OME SHOULDN'T SEE.
...IT'D ONLY UPSET THEM.
WH. WHAT'S THIS ALL ABOUT?
IT'S ABOUT THIS, MATE.
IT'S ABOUT YOU BEIN' A GOOD LAD AND COMING BACK WITH ME.
I MEAN US.

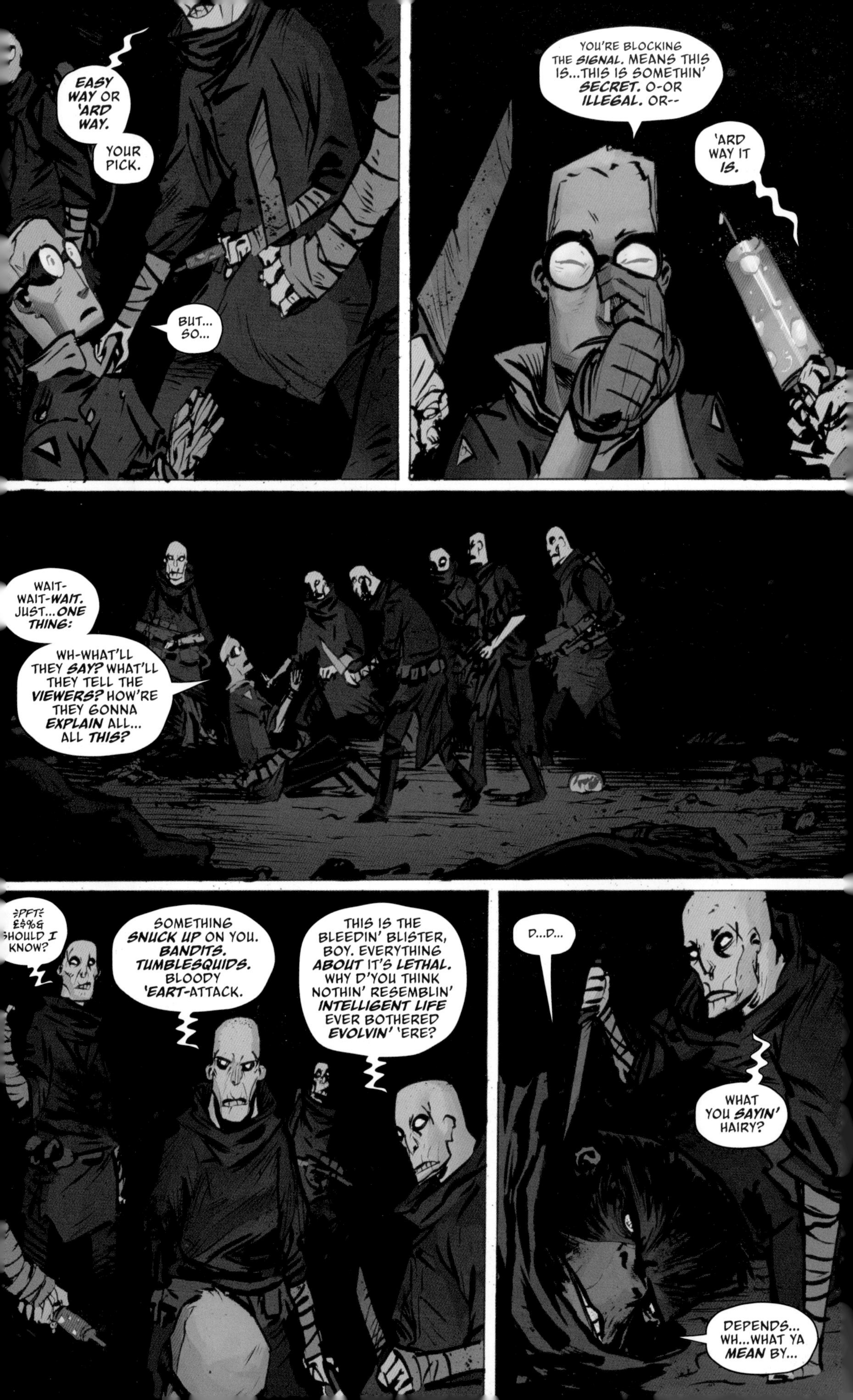
EASY WAY OR 'ARD WAY.
YOUR PICK.
BUT... SO...
YOU'RE BLOCKING THE SIGNAL. MEANS THIS IS...THIS IS SOMETHIN' SECRET. O-OR ILLEGAL. OR--
'ARD WAY IT IS.
WAIT-WAIT-WAIT. JUST...ONE THING:
WH-WHAT'LL THEY SAY? WHAT'LL THEY TELL THE VIEWERS? HOW'RE THEY GONNA EXPLAIN ALL... ALL THIS?
PFT £$%& HOULD I KNOW?
SOMETHING SNUCK UP ON YOU. BANDITS. TUMBLESQUIDS. BLOODY 'EART-ATTACK.
THIS IS THE BLEEDIN' BLISTER, BOY. EVERYTHING ABOUT IT'S LETHAL. WHY D'YOU THINK NOTHIN' RESEMBLIN' INTELLIGENT LIFE EVER BOTHERED EVOLVIN' 'ERE?
D...D...
WHAT YOU SAYIN' HAIRY?
DEPENDS... WH...WHAT YA MEAN BY...

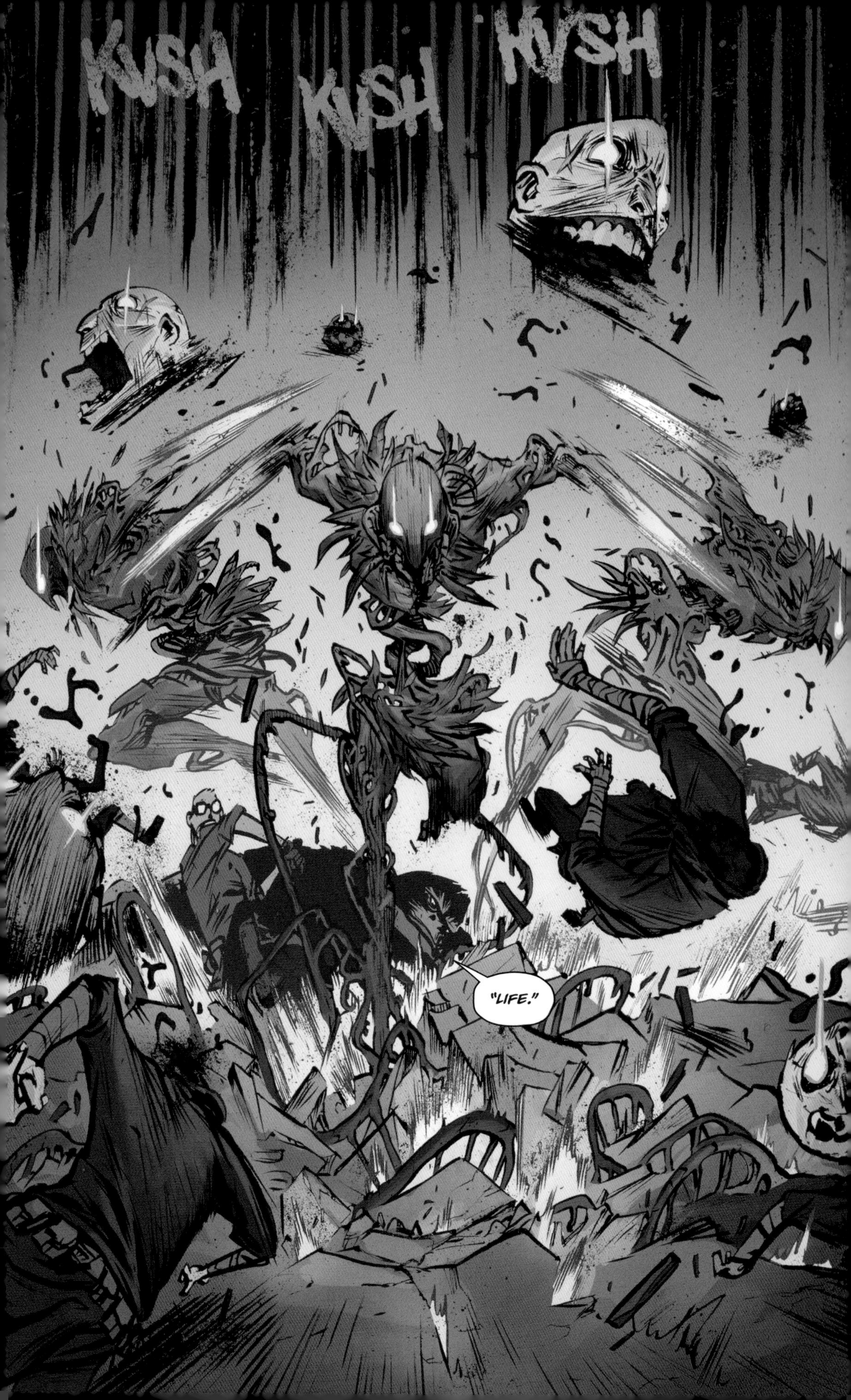
KUSH
KUSH
KUSH
"LIFE."

# CHAPTER FOUR

# SIX-GUN GORILLA

(Continued from page 8.)

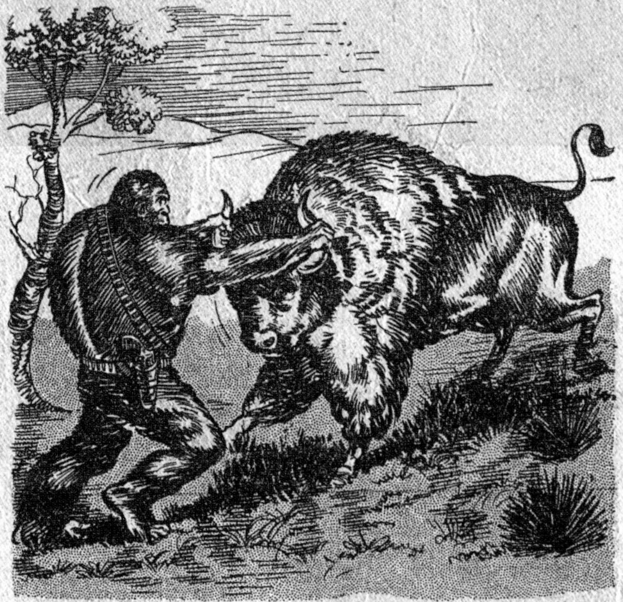



STAMPS.—300 different, including Airmail, beautiful uncommon sets, pictorials, Colonials. You'll be delighted. Price 6d. White, Stamps, Lye, Stourbridge.

ASTRID Packet Free.—Astrid (mourning) stamp, obsolete Morocco, Agencies (Windsor), fine set scarce Airmail, Belgium Tin Hat, Roumania (King Charles), 50 different, new large anniversary stamp. Remember we give 50% discount. Enclose 2d and request approvals. Robinson Bros. (D), Moreton, Wirral.

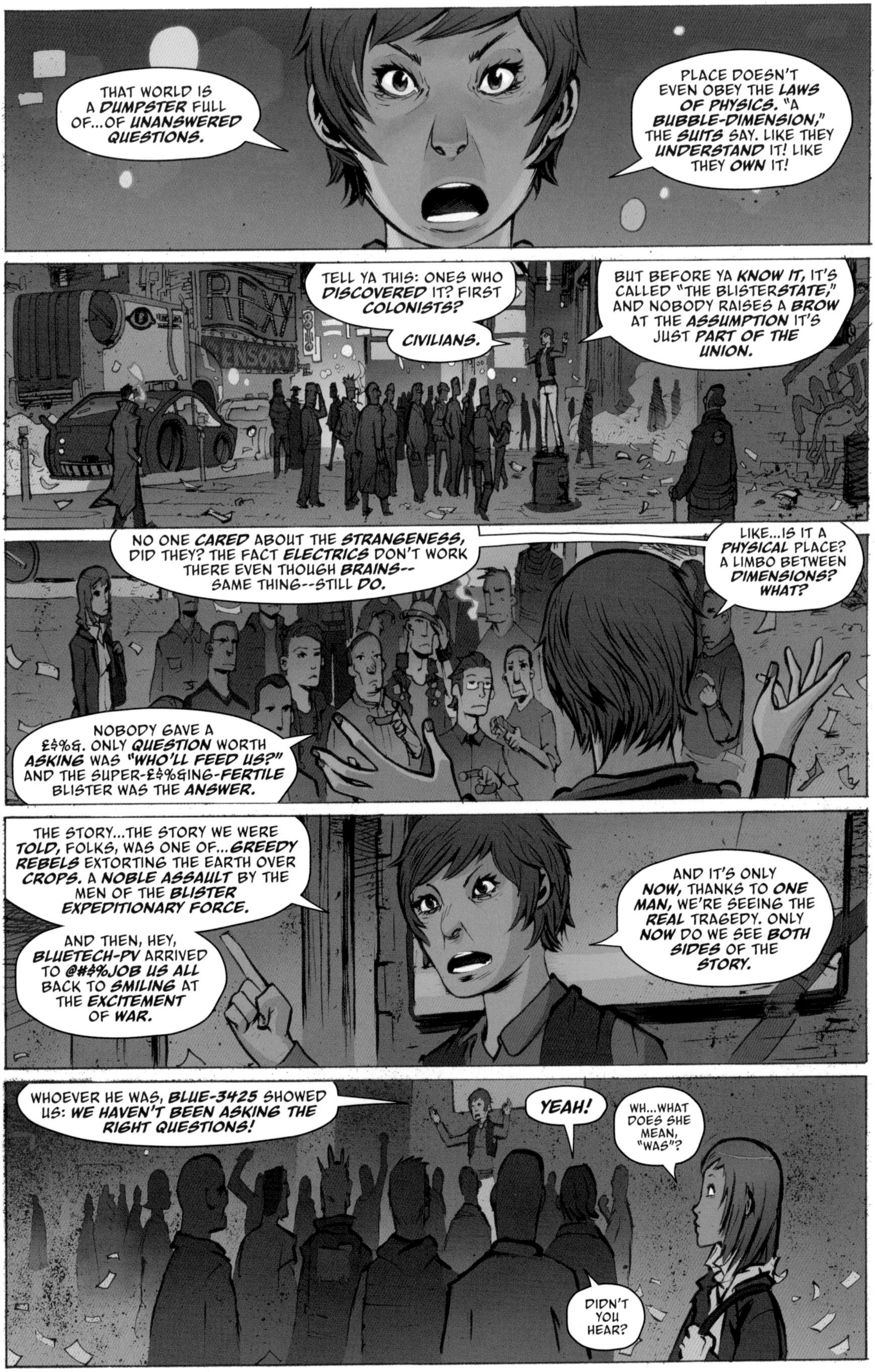
THAT WORLD IS A DUMPSTER FULL OF...OF UNANSWERED QUESTIONS.
PLACE DOESN'T EVEN OBEY THE LAWS OF PHYSICS. "A BUBBLE-DIMENSION," THE SUITS SAY. LIKE THEY UNDERSTAND IT! LIKE THEY OWN IT!
TELL YA THIS: ONES WHO DISCOVERED IT? FIRST COLONISTS?
CIVILIANS.
BUT BEFORE YA KNOW IT, IT'S CALLED "THE BLISTERSTATE," AND NOBODY RAISES A BROW AT THE ASSUMPTION IT'S JUST PART OF THE UNION.
REXY
NO ONE CARED ABOUT THE STRANGENESS, DID THEY? THE FACT ELECTRICS DON'T WORK THERE EVEN THOUGH BRAINS--SAME THING--STILL DO.
LIKE...IS IT A PHYSICAL PLACE? A LIMBO BETWEEN DIMENSIONS? WHAT?
NOBODY GAVE A £$%&. ONLY QUESTION WORTH ASKING WAS "WHO'LL FEED US?" AND THE SUPER-£$%&ING-FERTILE BLISTER WAS THE ANSWER.
THE STORY...THE STORY WE WERE TOLD, FOLKS, WAS ONE OF...GREEDY REBELS EXTORTING THE EARTH OVER CROPS. A NOBLE ASSAULT BY THE MEN OF THE BLISTER EXPEDITIONARY FORCE.
AND THEN, HEY, BLUETECH-PV ARRIVED TO @#$%JOB US ALL BACK TO SMILING AT THE EXCITEMENT OF WAR.
AND IT'S ONLY NOW, THANKS TO ONE MAN, WE'RE SEEING THE REAL TRAGEDY. ONLY NOW DO WE SEE BOTH SIDES OF THE STORY.
WHOEVER HE WAS, BLUE-3425 SHOWED US: WE HAVEN'T BEEN ASKING THE RIGHT QUESTIONS!
YEAH!
WH...WHAT DOES SHE MEAN, "WAS"?
DIDN'T YOU HEAR?

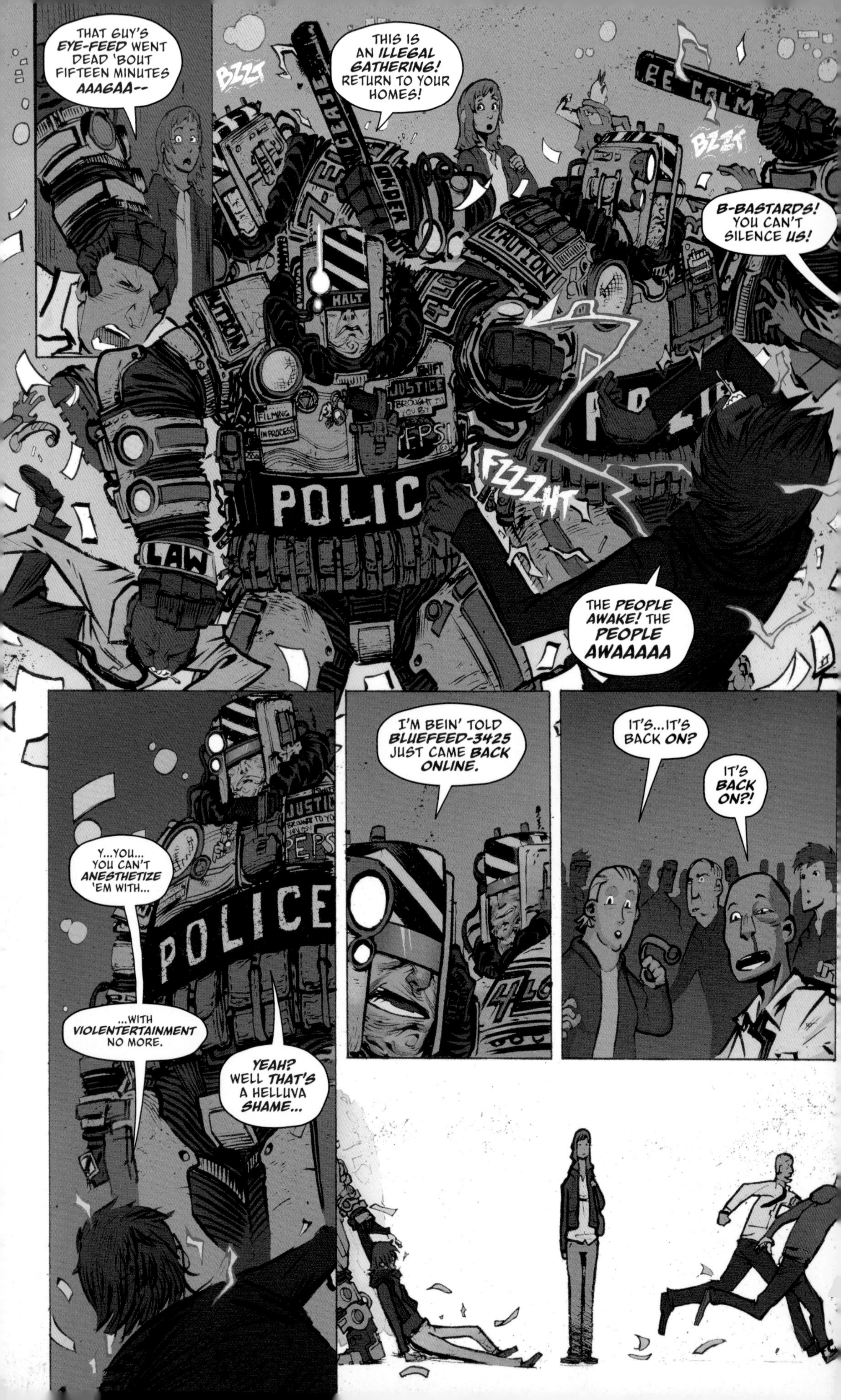

THAT GUY'S EYE-FEED WENT DEAD 'BOUT FIFTEEN MINUTES AAAGAA--
BZZT
THIS IS AN ILLEGAL GATHERING! RETURN TO YOUR HOMES!
CEASE
ORDER
BE CALM
BZZT
B-BASTARDS! YOU CAN'T SILENCE US!
CAUTION
CAUTION
HALT
JUSTICE BROUGHT TO YOU BY PEPSI
FILMING IN PROCESS
POLIC
FZZZHT
LAW
THE PEOPLE AWAKE! THE PEOPLE AWAAAAAA
Y...YOU... YOU CAN'T ANESTHETIZE 'EM WITH...
...WITH VIOLENTERTAINMENT NO MORE.
POLICE
YEAH? WELL THAT'S A HELLUVA SHAME...
I'M BEIN' TOLD BLUEFEED-3425 JUST CAME BACK ONLINE.
IT'S...IT'S BACK ON?
IT'S BACK ON?!

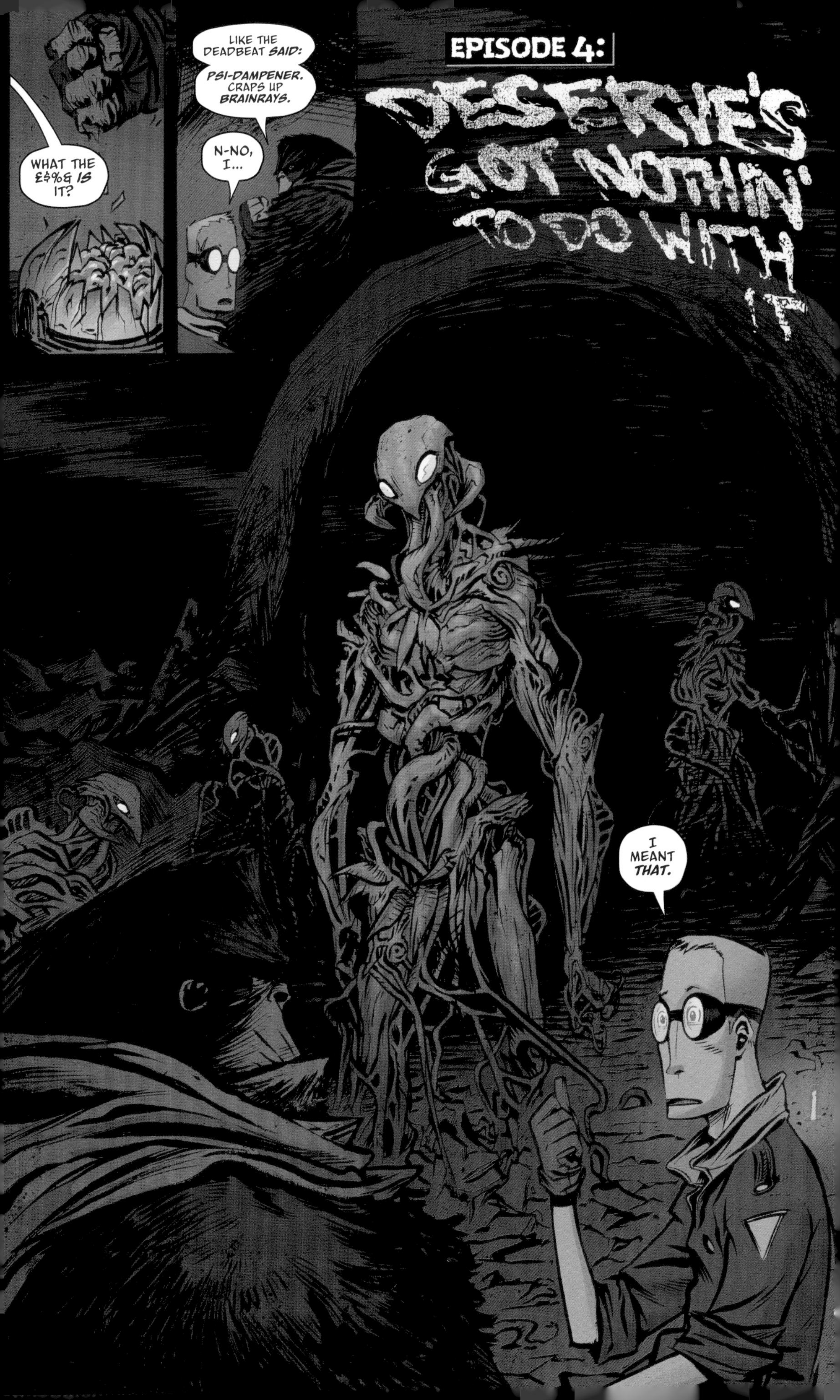

WHAT THE £$%& IS IT?
LIKE THE DEADBEAT SAID:
PSI-DAMPENER. CRAPS UP BRAINRAYS.
N-NO, I...
EPISODE 4:
DESERVE'S GOT NOTHIN' TO DO WITH IT
I MEANT THAT.

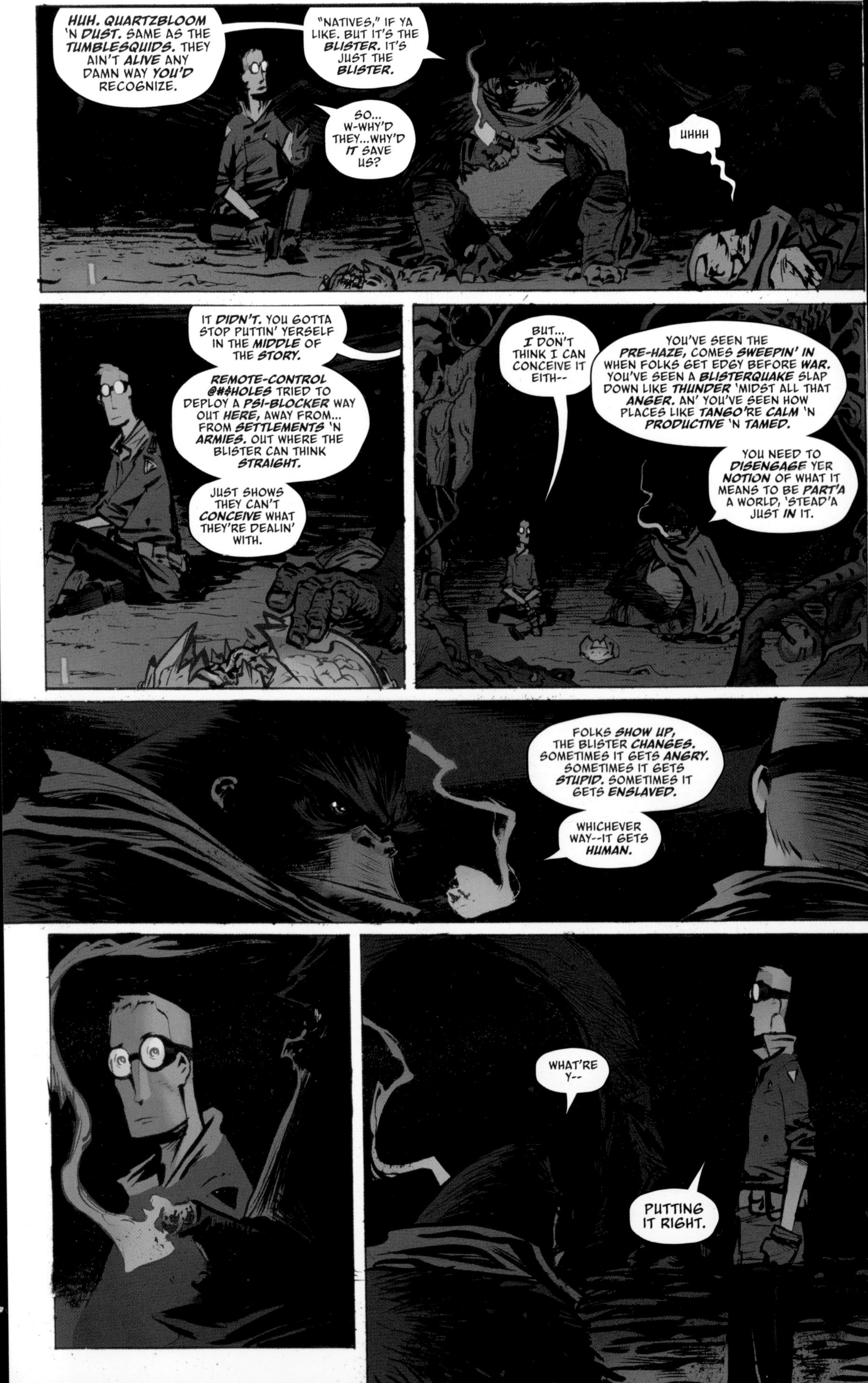
HUH. QUARTZBLOOM 'N DUST. SAME AS THE TUMBLESQUIDS. THEY AIN'T ALIVE ANY DAMN WAY YOU'D RECOGNIZE.
"NATIVES," IF YA LIKE. BUT IT'S THE BLISTER. IT'S JUST THE BLISTER.
SO... W-WHY'D THEY...WHY'D IT SAVE US?
UHHH
IT DIDN'T. YOU GOTTA STOP PUTTIN' YERSELF IN THE MIDDLE OF THE STORY.
REMOTE-CONTROL @#$HOLES TRIED TO DEPLOY A PSI-BLOCKER WAY OUT HERE, AWAY FROM... FROM SETTLEMENTS 'N ARMIES. OUT WHERE THE BLISTER CAN THINK STRAIGHT.
JUST SHOWS THEY CAN'T CONCEIVE WHAT THEY'RE DEALIN' WITH.
BUT... I DON'T THINK I CAN CONCEIVE IT EITH--
YOU'VE SEEN THE PRE-HAZE, COMES SWEEPIN' IN WHEN FOLKS GET EDGY BEFORE WAR. YOU'VE SEEN A BLISTERQUAKE SLAP DOWN LIKE THUNDER 'MIDST ALL THAT ANGER. AN' YOU'VE SEEN HOW PLACES LIKE TANGO'RE CALM 'N PRODUCTIVE 'N TAMED.
YOU NEED TO DISENGAGE YER NOTION OF WHAT IT MEANS TO BE PART'A A WORLD, 'STEAD'A JUST IN IT.
FOLKS SHOW UP, THE BLISTER CHANGES. SOMETIMES IT GETS ANGRY. SOMETIMES IT GETS STUPID. SOMETIMES IT GETS ENSLAVED.
WHICHEVER WAY--IT GETS HUMAN.
WHAT'RE Y--
PUTTING IT RIGHT.

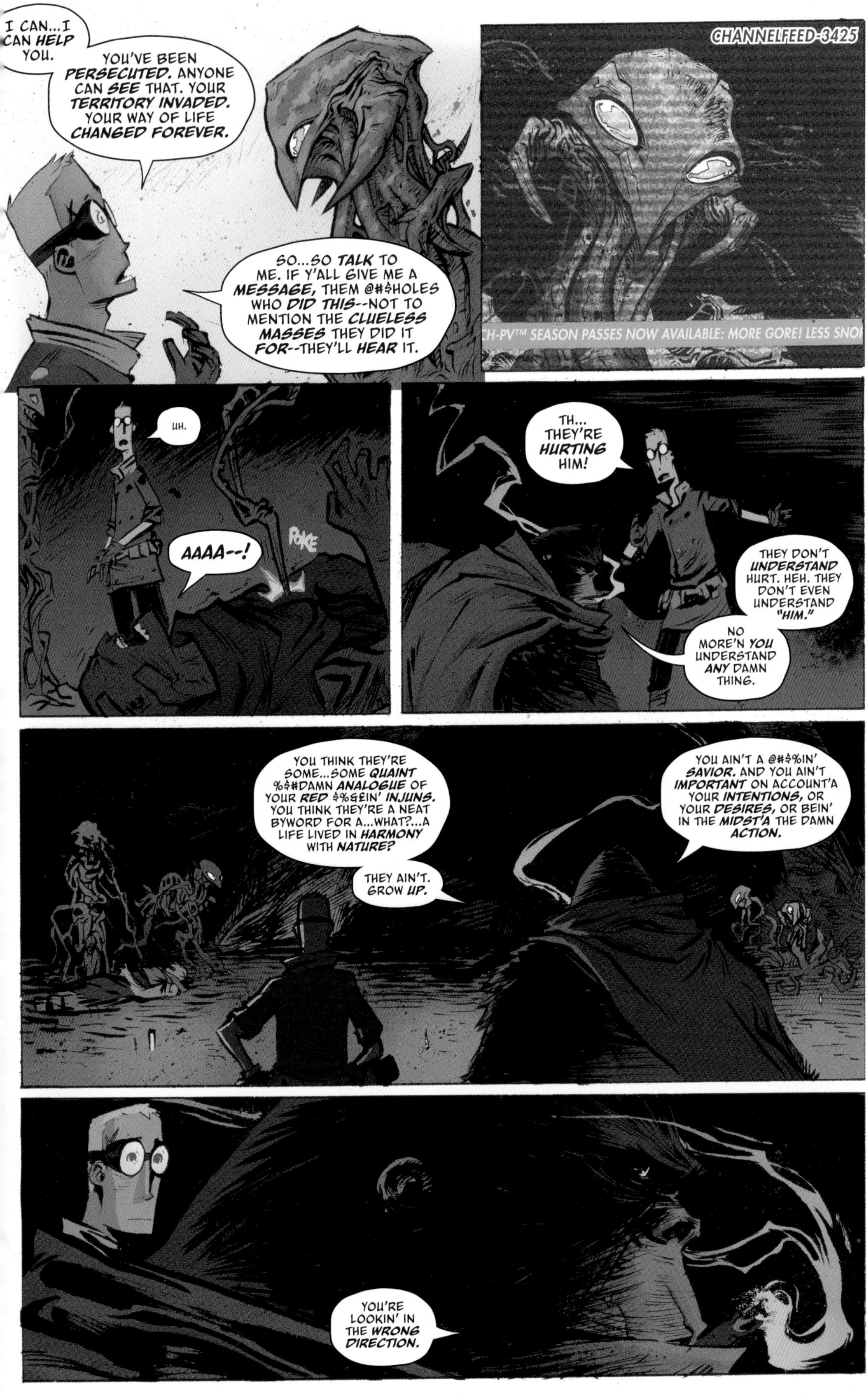
I CAN...I CAN HELP YOU.
YOU'VE BEEN PERSECUTED. ANYONE CAN SEE THAT. YOUR TERRITORY INVADED. YOUR WAY OF LIFE CHANGED FOREVER.
CHANNELFEED-3425
SO...SO TALK TO ME. IF Y'ALL GIVE ME A MESSAGE, THEM @#$HOLES WHO DID THIS--NOT TO MENTION THE CLUELESS MASSES THEY DID IT FOR--THEY'LL HEAR IT.
CH-PV™ SEASON PASSES NOW AVAILABLE: MORE GORE! LESS SNO
UH.
AAAA--!
POKE
TH... THEY'RE HURTING HIM!
THEY DON'T UNDERSTAND HURT. HEH. THEY DON'T EVEN UNDERSTAND "HIM."
NO MORE'N YOU UNDERSTAND ANY DAMN THING.
YOU THINK THEY'RE SOME...SOME QUAINT %$#DAMN ANALOGUE OF YOUR RED $%&IN' INJUNS. YOU THINK THEY'RE A NEAT BYWORD FOR A...WHAT?...A LIFE LIVED IN HARMONY WITH NATURE?
THEY AIN'T. GROW UP.
YOU AIN'T A @#$%IN' SAVIOR. AND YOU AIN'T IMPORTANT ON ACCOUNT'A YOUR INTENTIONS, OR YOUR DESIRES, OR BEIN' IN THE MIDST'A THE DAMN ACTION.
YOU'RE LOOKIN' IN THE WRONG DIRECTION.

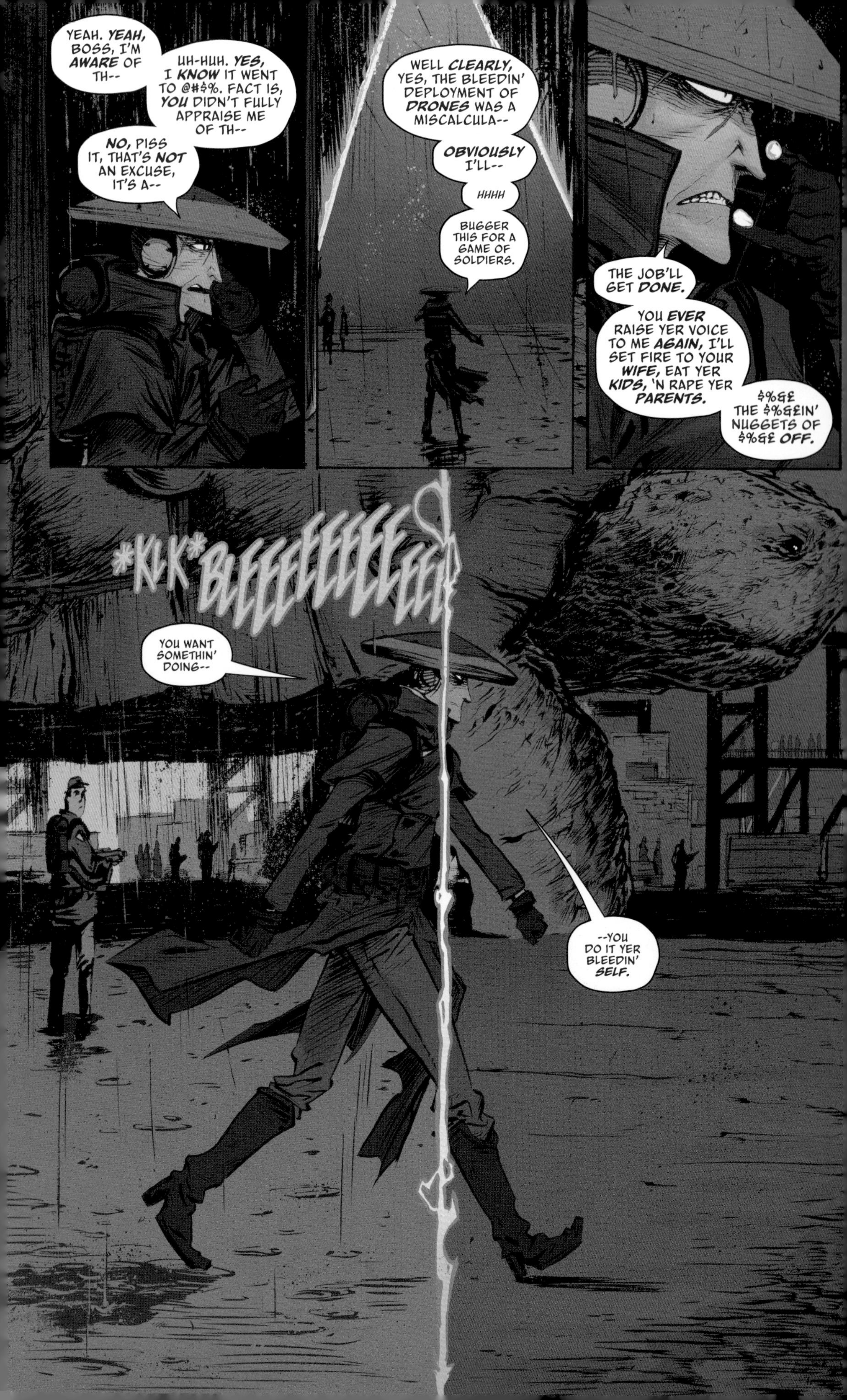
YEAH. YEAH, BOSS, I'M AWARE OF TH--
UH-HUH. YES, I KNOW IT WENT TO @#$%. FACT IS, YOU DIDN'T FULLY APPRAISE ME OF TH--
NO, PISS IT, THAT'S NOT AN EXCUSE, IT'S A--
WELL CLEARLY, YES, THE BLEEDIN' DEPLOYMENT OF DRONES WAS A MISCALCULA--
OBVIOUSLY I'LL--
HHHH
BUGGER THIS FOR A GAME OF SOLDIERS.
THE JOB'LL GET DONE.
YOU EVER RAISE YER VOICE TO ME AGAIN, I'LL SET FIRE TO YOUR WIFE, EAT YER KIDS, 'N RAPE YER PARENTS.
$%&£ THE $%&£IN' NUGGETS OF $%&£ OFF.
*KLK*BLEEEEEEEEEEEEP
YOU WANT SOMETHIN' DOING--
--YOU DO IT YER BLEEDIN' SELF.

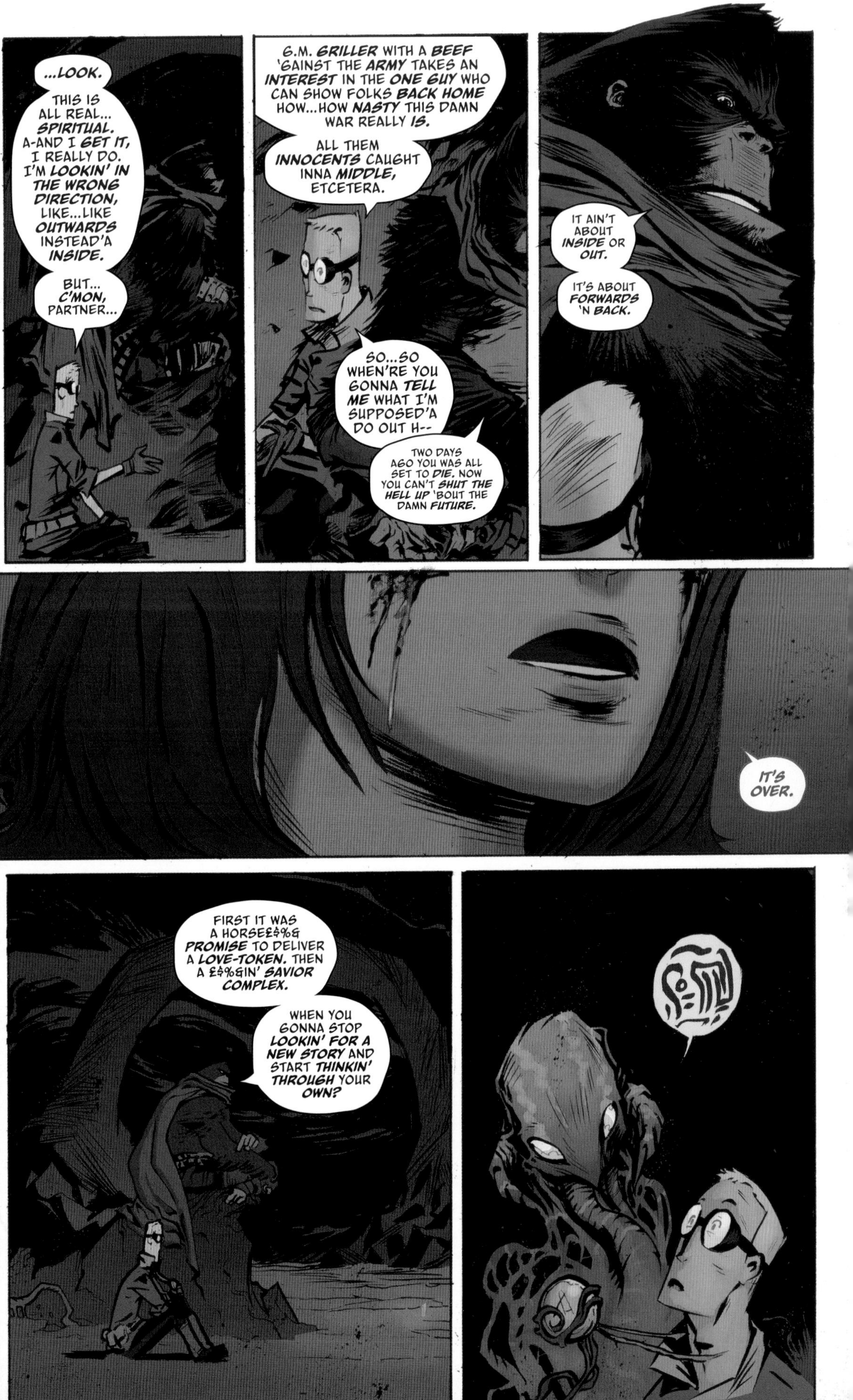

...LOOK.
THIS IS ALL REAL... SPIRITUAL. A-AND I GET IT, I REALLY DO. I'M LOOKIN' IN THE WRONG DIRECTION, LIKE...LIKE OUTWARDS INSTEAD'A INSIDE.
BUT... C'MON, PARTNER...
G.M. GRILLER WITH A BEEF 'GAINST THE ARMY TAKES AN INTEREST IN THE ONE GUY WHO CAN SHOW FOLKS BACK HOME HOW...HOW NASTY THIS DAMN WAR REALLY IS.
ALL THEM INNOCENTS CAUGHT INNA MIDDLE, ETCETERA.
SO...SO WHEN'RE YOU GONNA TELL ME WHAT I'M SUPPOSED'A DO OUT H--
TWO DAYS AGO YOU WAS ALL SET TO DIE. NOW YOU CAN'T SHUT THE HELL UP 'BOUT THE DAMN FUTURE.
IT AIN'T ABOUT INSIDE OR OUT.
IT'S ABOUT FORWARDS 'N BACK.
IT'S OVER.
FIRST IT WAS A HORSE£$%& PROMISE TO DELIVER A LOVE-TOKEN. THEN A £$%&IN' SAVIOR COMPLEX.
WHEN YOU GONNA STOP LOOKIN' FOR A NEW STORY AND START THINKIN' THROUGH YOUR OWN?

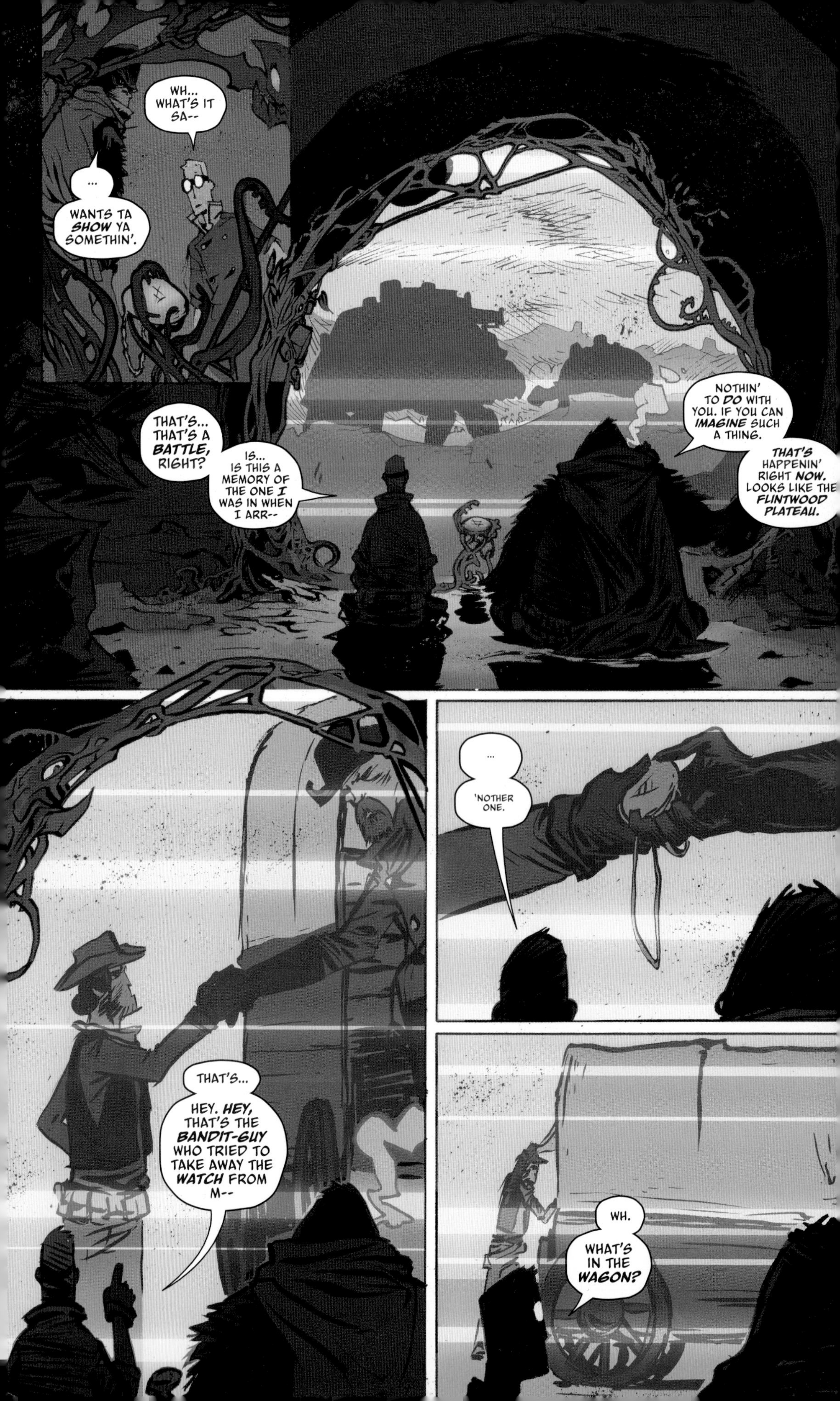

WH... WHAT'S IT SA--
...
WANTS TA SHOW YA SOMETHIN'.
THAT'S... THAT'S A BATTLE, RIGHT?
IS... IS THIS A MEMORY OF THE ONE I WAS IN WHEN I ARR--
NOTHIN' TO DO WITH YOU. IF YOU CAN IMAGINE SUCH A THING.
THAT'S HAPPENIN' RIGHT NOW. LOOKS LIKE THE FLINTWOOD PLATEAU.
THAT'S...
HEY. HEY, THAT'S THE BANDIT-GUY WHO TRIED TO TAKE AWAY THE WATCH FROM M--
...
'NOTHER ONE.
WH.
WHAT'S IN THE WAGON?

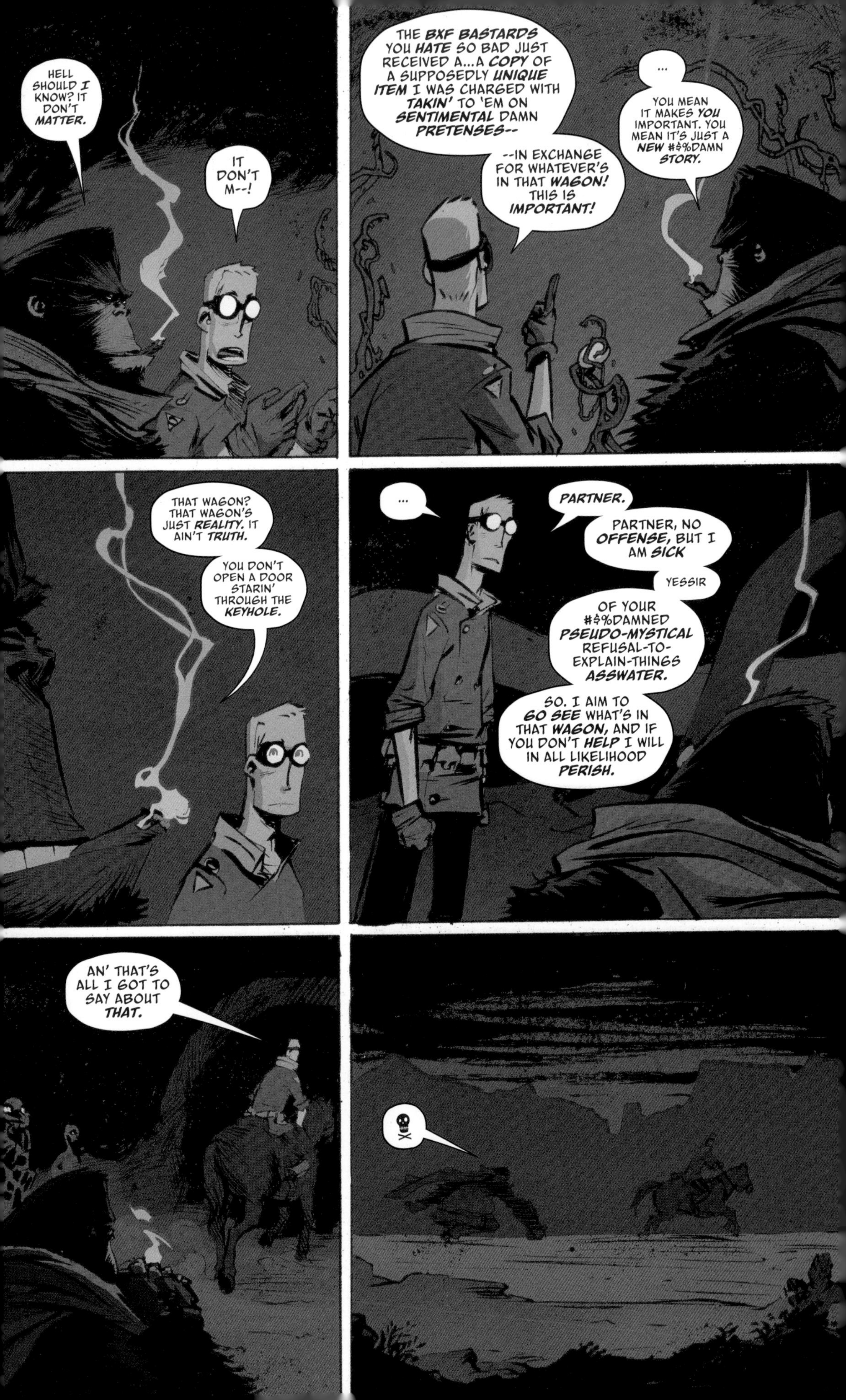
HELL SHOULD I KNOW? IT DON'T MATTER.
IT DON'T M--!
THE BXF BASTARDS YOU HATE SO BAD JUST RECEIVED A...A COPY OF A SUPPOSEDLY UNIQUE ITEM I WAS CHARGED WITH TAKIN' TO 'EM ON SENTIMENTAL DAMN PRETENSES--
--IN EXCHANGE FOR WHATEVER'S IN THAT WAGON! THIS IS IMPORTANT!
...
YOU MEAN IT MAKES YOU IMPORTANT. YOU MEAN IT'S JUST A NEW #$%DAMN STORY.
THAT WAGON? THAT WAGON'S JUST REALITY. IT AIN'T TRUTH.
YOU DON'T OPEN A DOOR STARIN' THROUGH THE KEYHOLE.
...
PARTNER.
PARTNER, NO OFFENSE, BUT I AM SICK
YESSIR
OF YOUR #$%DAMNED PSEUDO-MYSTICAL REFUSAL-TO-EXPLAIN-THINGS ASSWATER.
SO. I AIM TO GO SEE WHAT'S IN THAT WAGON, AND IF YOU DON'T HELP I WILL IN ALL LIKELIHOOD PERISH.
AN' THAT'S ALL I GOT TO SAY ABOUT THAT.

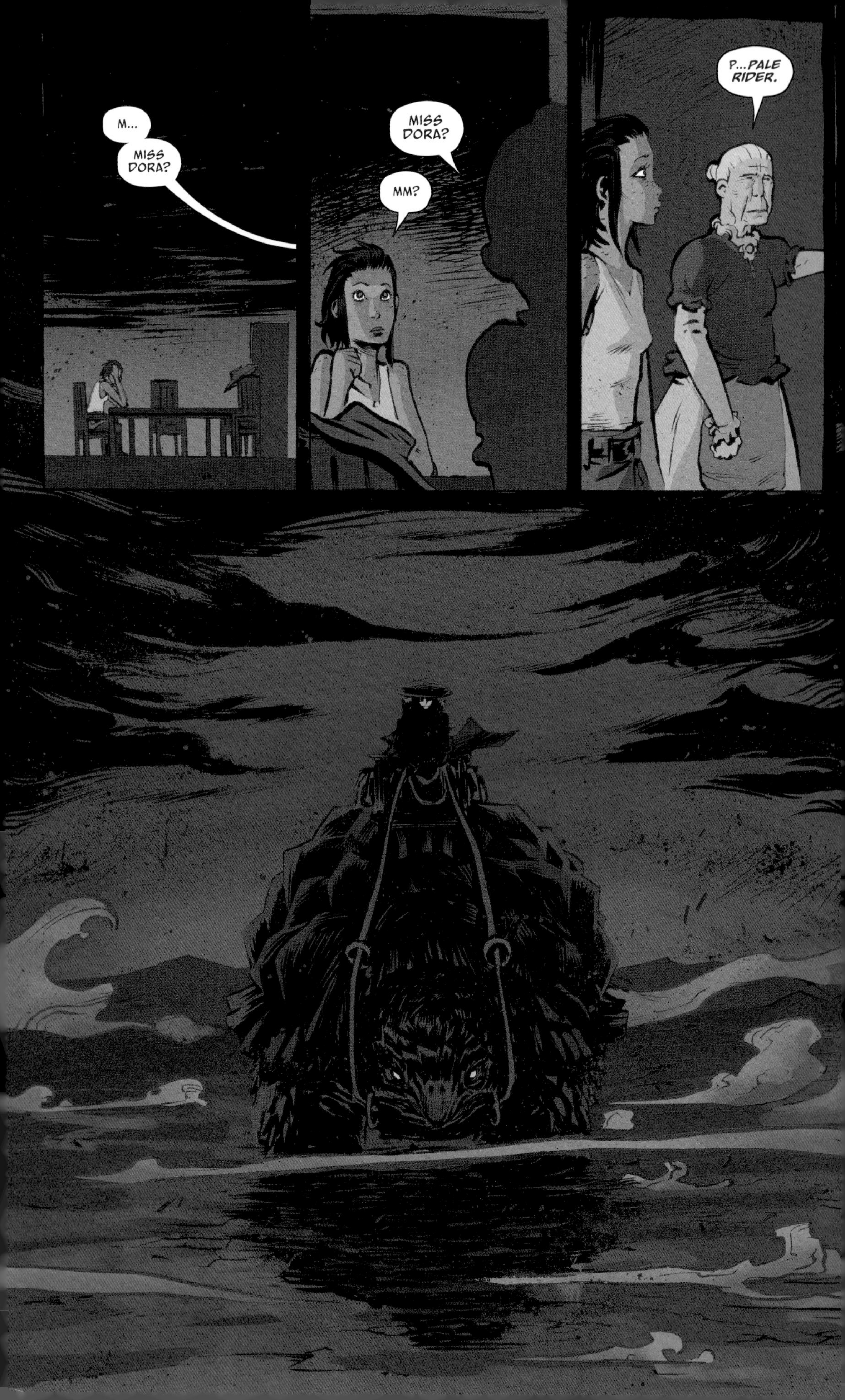
M...
MISS DORA?
MISS DORA?
MM?
P...PALE RIDER.

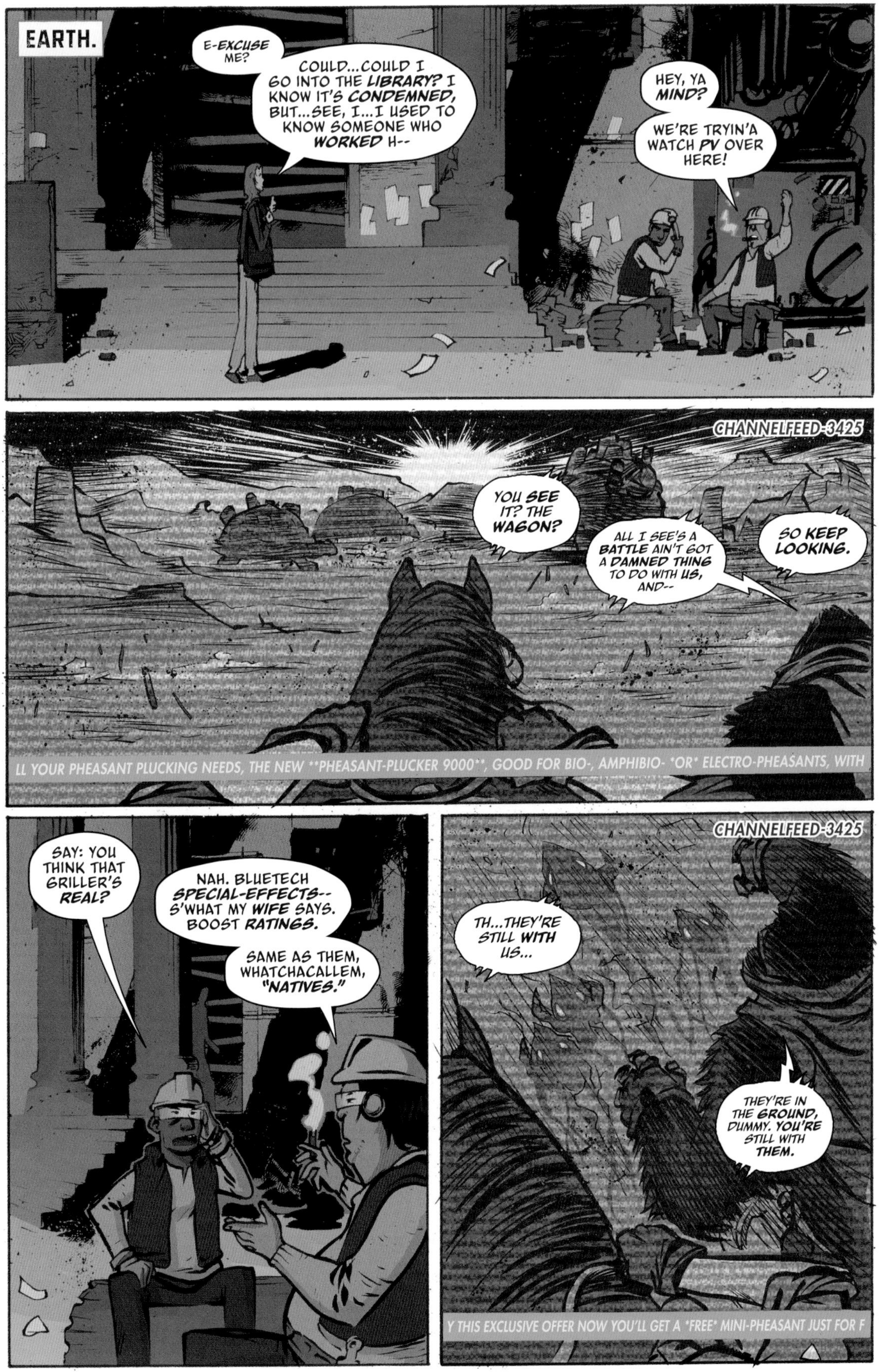

EARTH.
E-EXCUSE ME?
COULD...COULD I GO INTO THE LIBRARY? I KNOW IT'S CONDEMNED, BUT...SEE, I...I USED TO KNOW SOMEONE WHO WORKED H--
HEY, YA MIND?
WE'RE TRYIN'A WATCH PV OVER HERE!
CHANNELFEED-3425
YOU SEE IT? THE WAGON?
ALL I SEE'S A BATTLE AIN'T GOT A DAMNED THING TO DO WITH US, AND--
SO KEEP LOOKING.
LL YOUR PHEASANT PLUCKING NEEDS, THE NEW **PHEASANT-PLUCKER 9000**, GOOD FOR BIO-, AMPHIBIO- *OR* ELECTRO-PHEASANTS, WITH
SAY: YOU THINK THAT GRILLER'S REAL?
NAH. BLUETECH SPECIAL-EFFECTS--S'WHAT MY WIFE SAYS. BOOST RATINGS.
SAME AS THEM, WHATCHACALLEM, "NATIVES."
CHANNELFEED-3425
TH...THEY'RE STILL WITH US...
THEY'RE IN THE GROUND, DUMMY. YOU'RE STILL WITH THEM.
Y THIS EXCLUSIVE OFFER NOW YOU'LL GET A *FREE* MINI-PHEASANT JUST FOR F

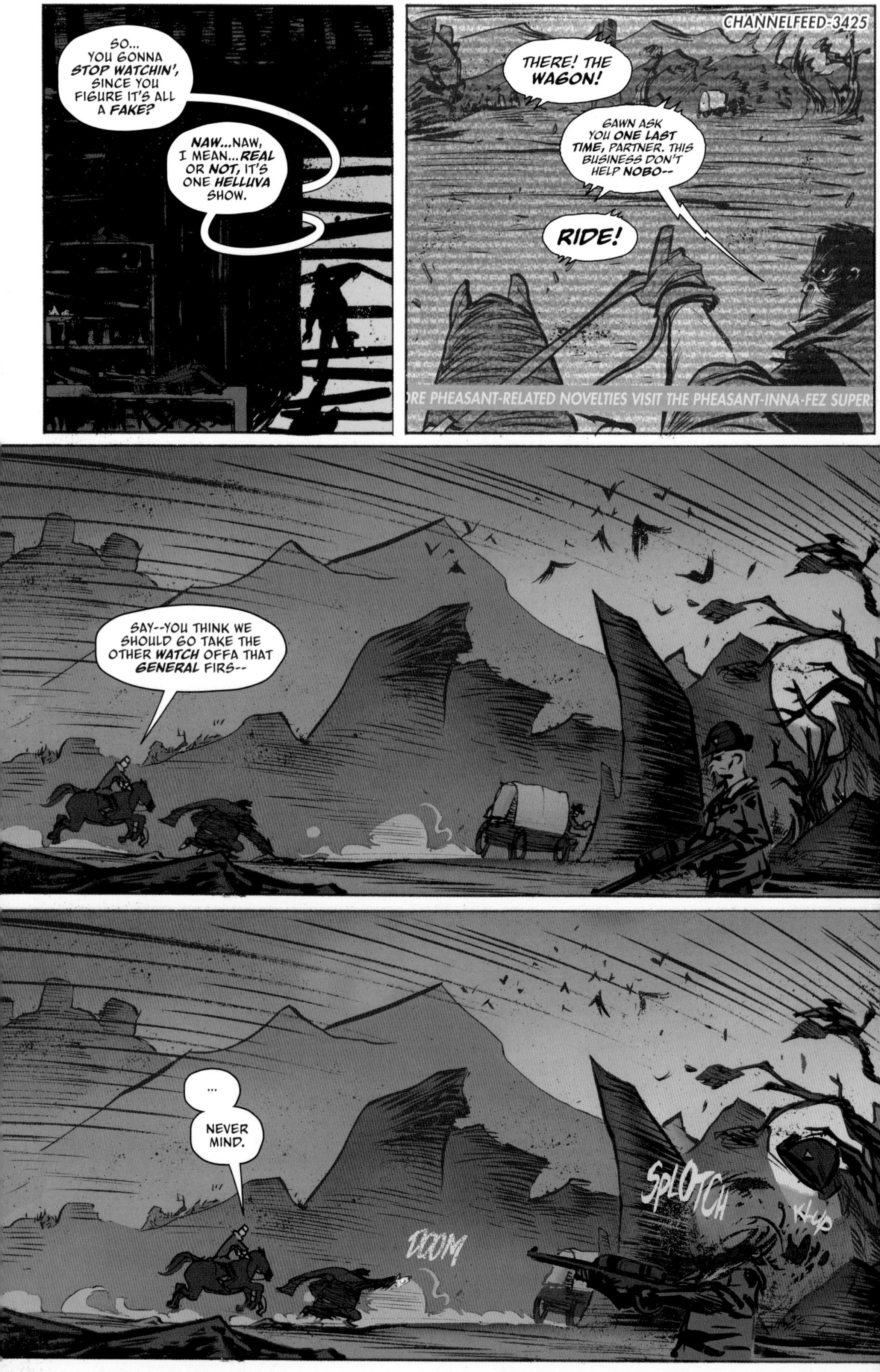
SO... YOU GONNA STOP WATCHIN', SINCE YOU FIGURE IT'S ALL A FAKE?
NAW...NAW, I MEAN...REAL OR NOT, IT'S ONE HELLUVA SHOW.
CHANNELFEED-3425
THERE! THE WAGON!
GAWN ASK YOU ONE LAST TIME, PARTNER. THIS BUSINESS DON'T HELP NOBO--
RIDE!
ORE PHEASANT-RELATED NOVELTIES VISIT THE PHEASANT-INNA-FEZ SUPERS
SAY--YOU THINK WE SHOULD GO TAKE THE OTHER WATCH OFFA THAT GENERAL FIRS--
...
NEVER MIND.
DOOM
SPLOTCH
KLUP

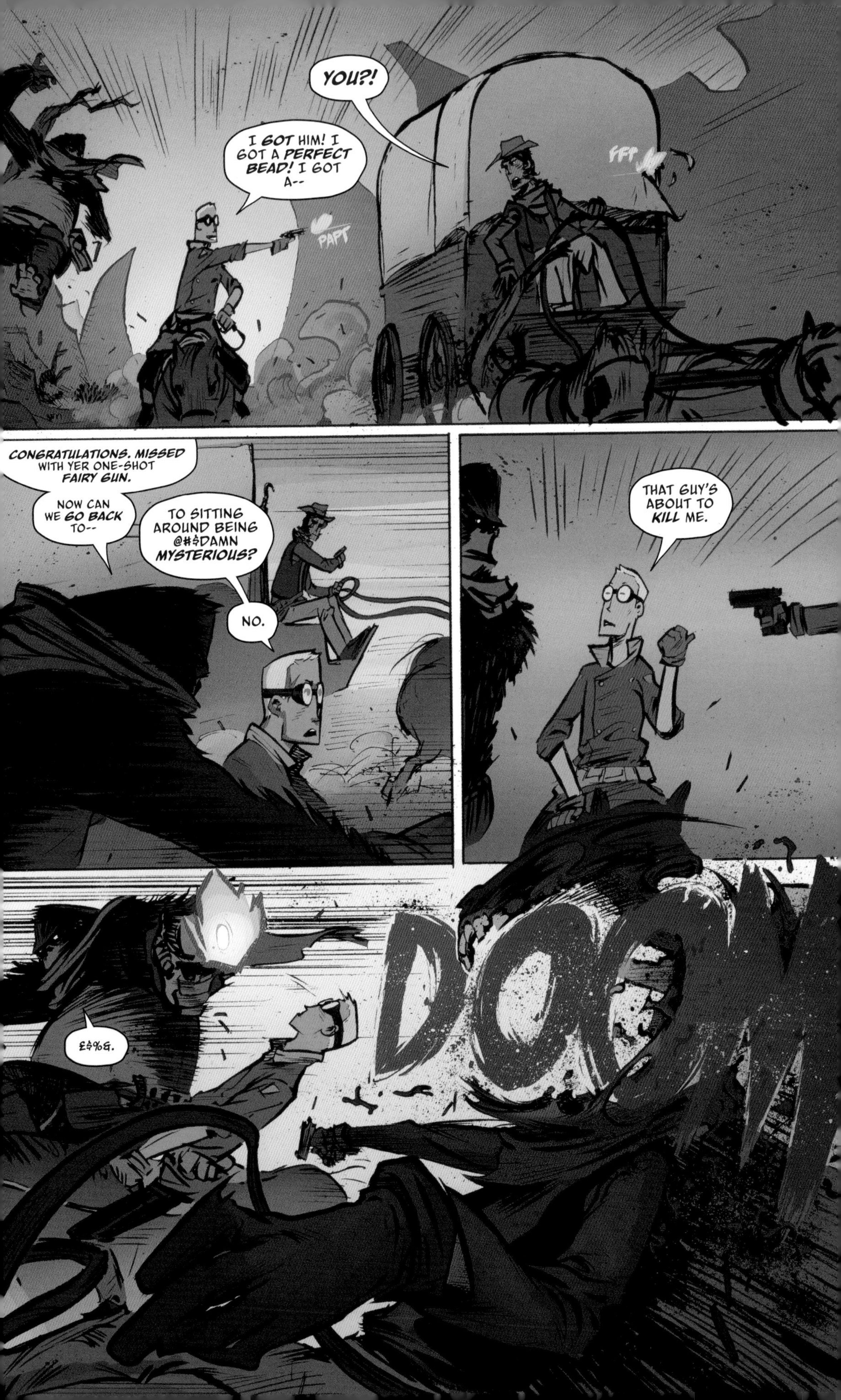

YOU?!
I GOT HIM! I GOT A PERFECT BEAD! I GOT A--
PAPT
CONGRATULATIONS. MISSED WITH YER ONE-SHOT FAIRY GUN.
NOW CAN WE GO BACK TO--
TO SITTING AROUND BEING @#$DAMN MYSTERIOUS?
NO.
THAT GUY'S ABOUT TO KILL ME.
£$%G.
DOOM

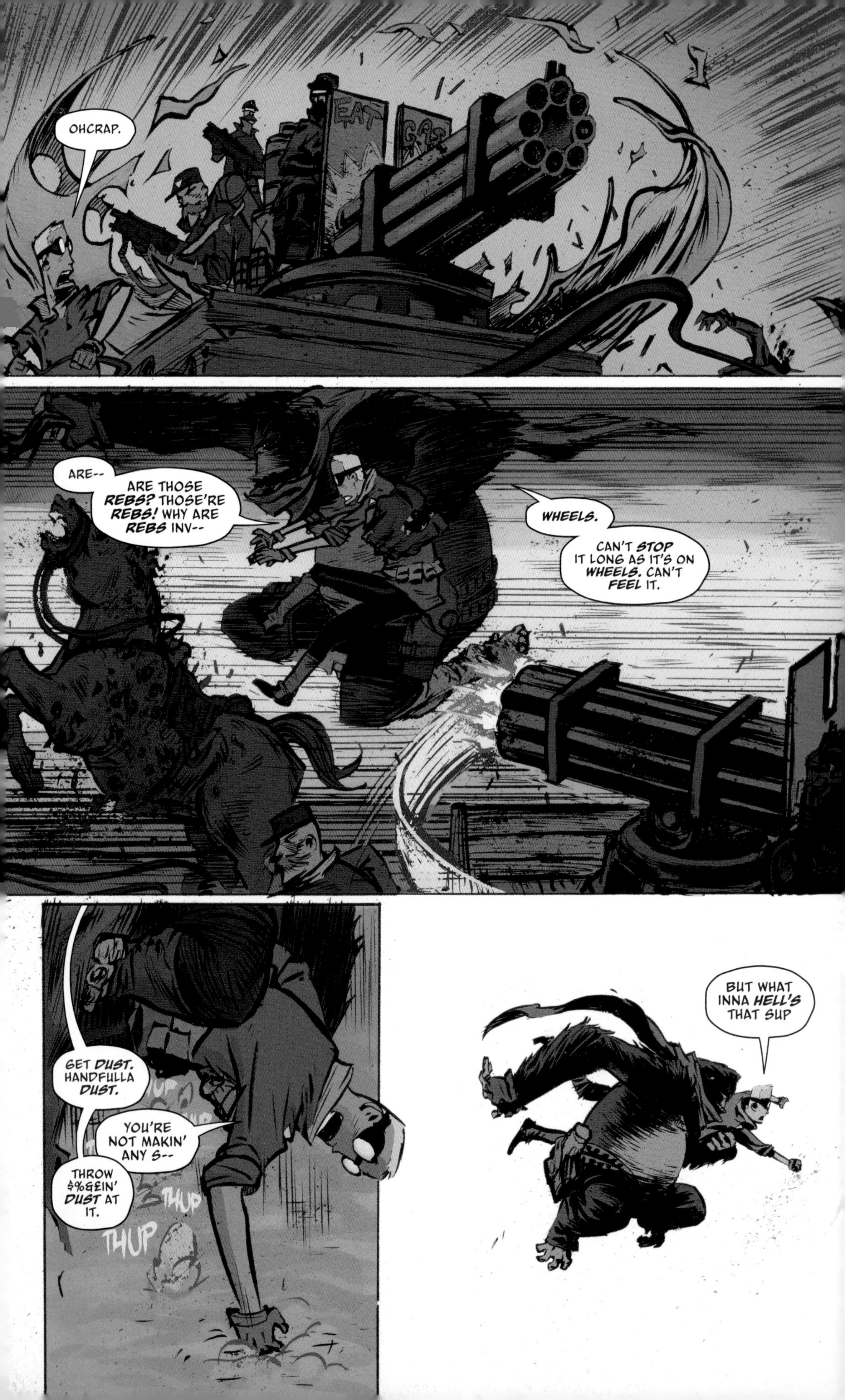
OHCRAP.
ARE--
ARE THOSE REBS? THOSE'RE REBS! WHY ARE REBS INV--
WHEELS.
CAN'T STOP IT LONG AS IT'S ON WHEELS. CAN'T FEEL IT.
GET DUST. HANDFULLA DUST.
YOU'RE NOT MAKIN' ANY S--
THROW $%&EIN' DUST AT IT.
THUP
THUP
THUP
THUP
BUT WHAT INNA HELL'S THAT SUP

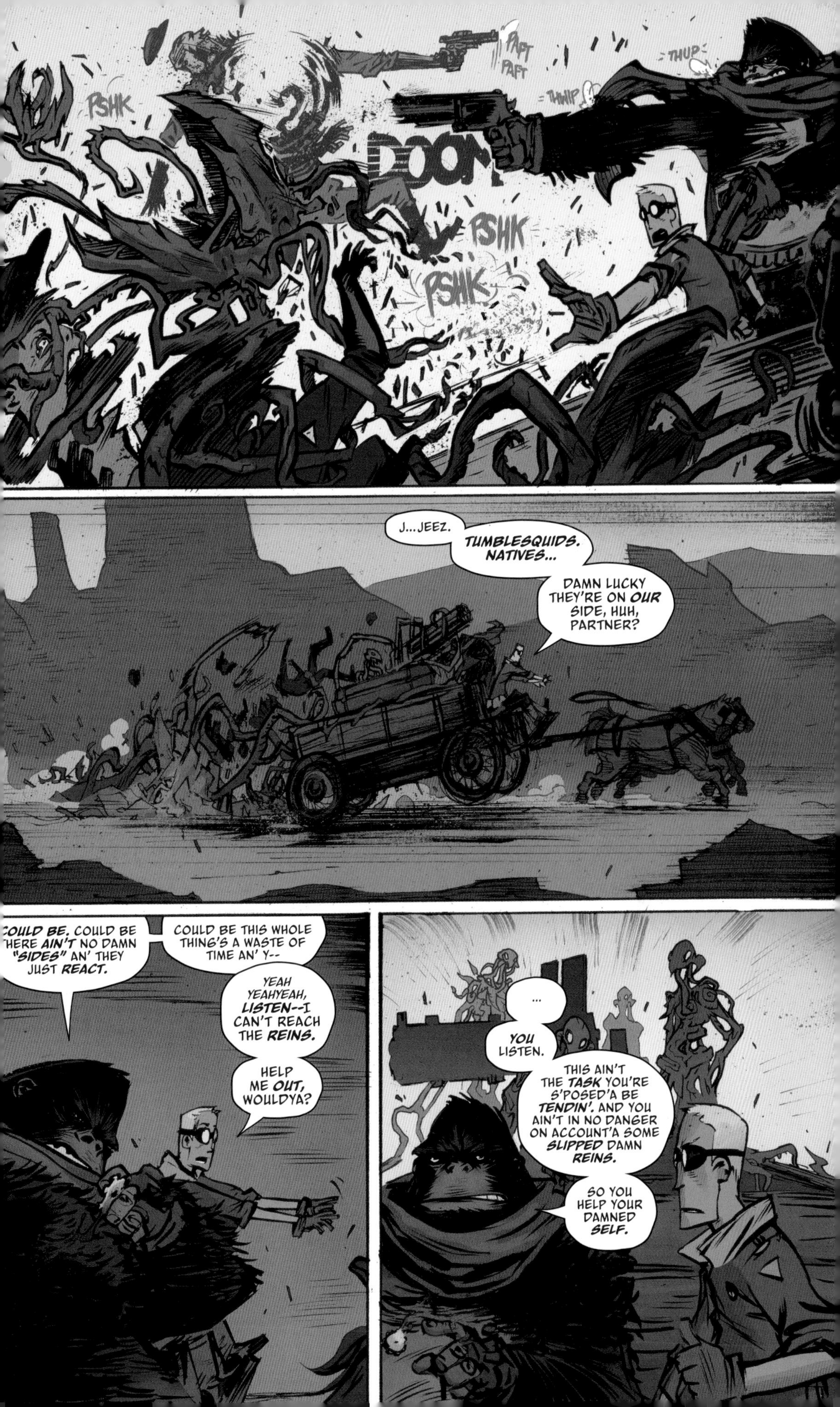
PAPT
PAPT
THUP
PSHK
THWIP
DOOM
PSHK
PSHK
J...JEEZ.
TUMBLESQUIDS. NATIVES...
DAMN LUCKY THEY'RE ON OUR SIDE, HUH, PARTNER?
COULD BE. COULD BE THERE AIN'T NO DAMN "SIDES" AN' THEY JUST REACT.
COULD BE THIS WHOLE THING'S A WASTE OF TIME AN' Y--
YEAH YEAHYEAH, LISTEN--I CAN'T REACH THE REINS.
HELP ME OUT, WOULDYA?
...
YOU LISTEN.
THIS AIN'T THE TASK YOU'RE S'POSED'A BE TENDIN'. AND YOU AIN'T IN NO DANGER ON ACCOUNT'A SOME SLIPPED DAMN REINS.
SO YOU HELP YOUR DAMNED SELF.

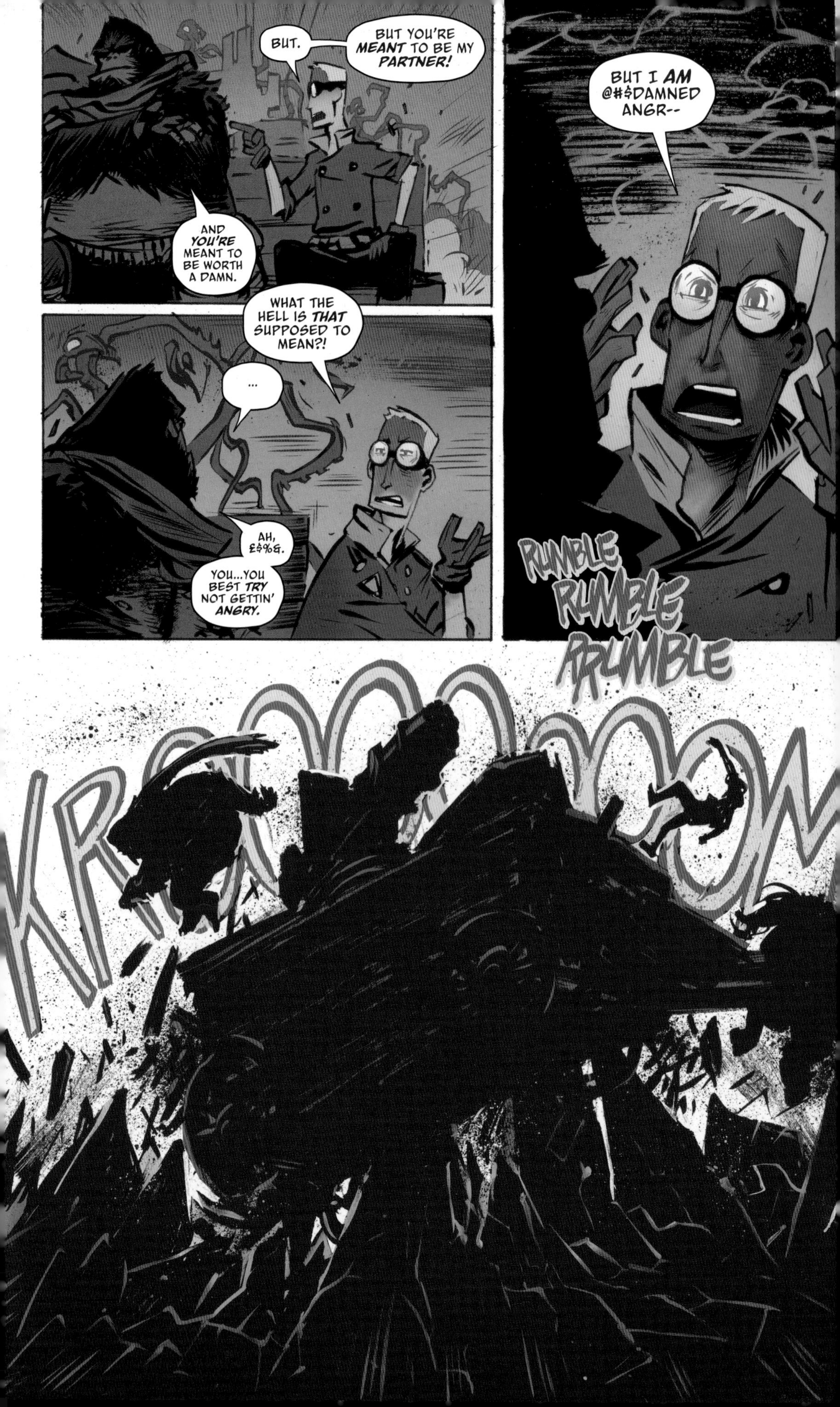

BUT.
BUT YOU'RE MEANT TO BE MY PARTNER!
AND YOU'RE MEANT TO BE WORTH A DAMN.
BUT I AM @#$DAMNED ANGR--
WHAT THE HELL IS THAT SUPPOSED TO MEAN?!
...
AH, £$%&.
YOU...YOU BEST TRY NOT GETTIN' ANGRY.
RUMBLE RUMBLE RUMBLE

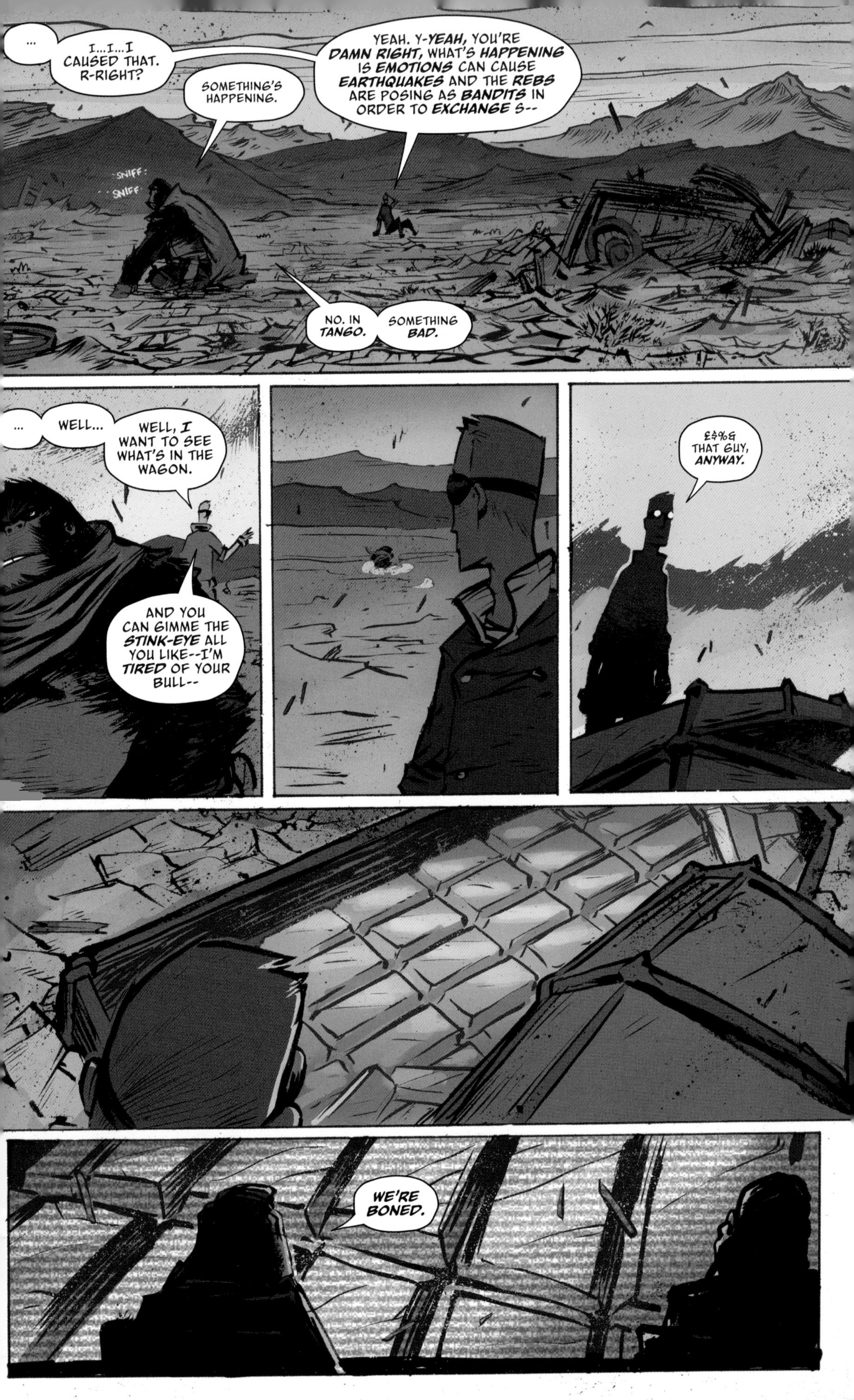
...
I...I...I CAUSED THAT. R-RIGHT?
SOMETHING'S HAPPENING.
YEAH. Y-YEAH, YOU'RE DAMN RIGHT, WHAT'S HAPPENING IS EMOTIONS CAN CAUSE EARTHQUAKES AND THE REBS ARE POSING AS BANDITS IN ORDER TO EXCHANGE S--
SNIFF
SNIFF
NO. IN TANGO.
SOMETHING BAD.
...
WELL...
WELL, I WANT TO SEE WHAT'S IN THE WAGON.
AND YOU CAN GIMME THE STINK-EYE ALL YOU LIKE--I'M TIRED OF YOUR BULL--
£$%& THAT GUY, ANYWAY.
WE'RE BONED.

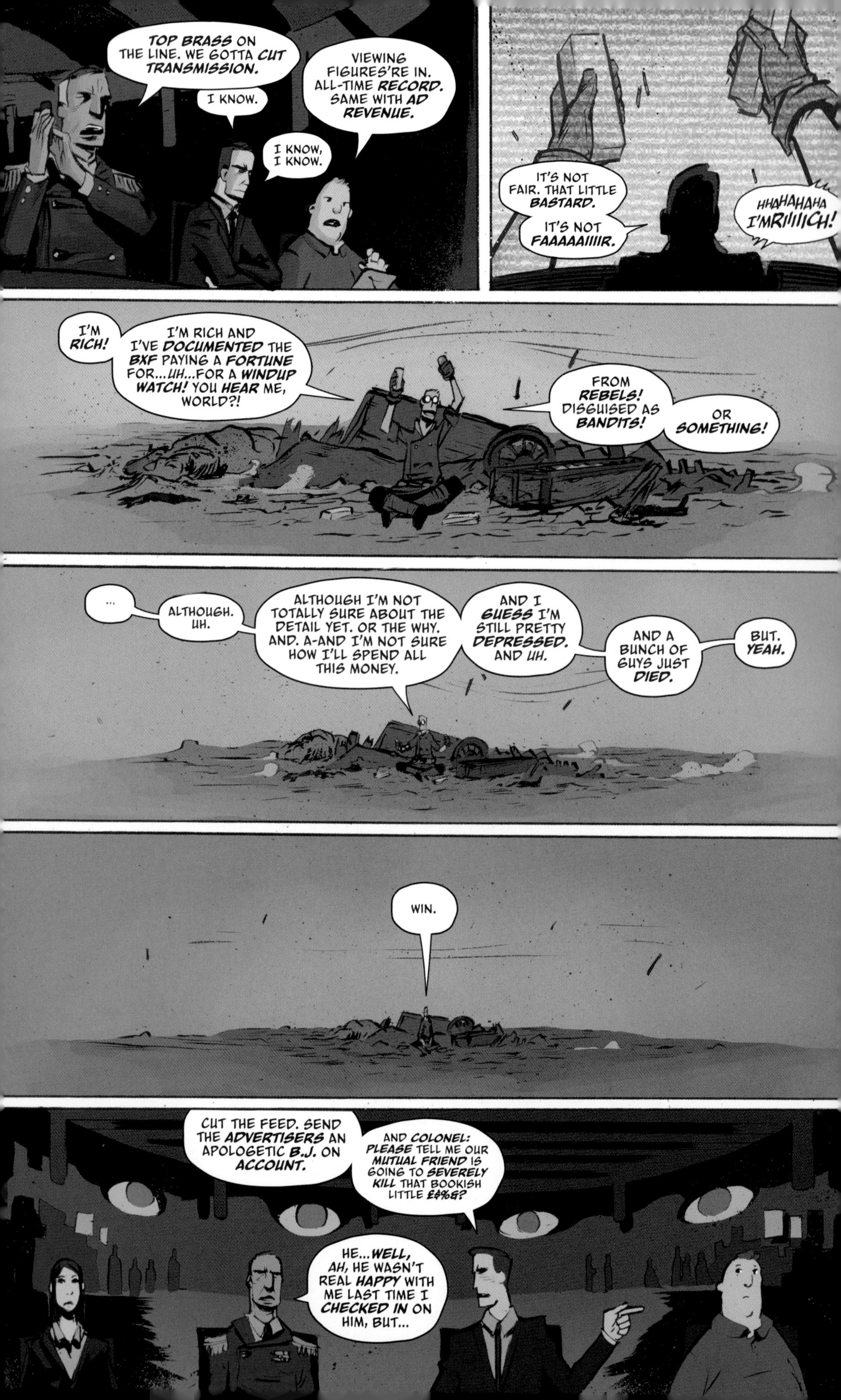
TOP BRASS ON THE LINE. WE GOTTA CUT TRANSMISSION.
I KNOW.
VIEWING FIGURES'RE IN. ALL-TIME RECORD. SAME WITH AD REVENUE.
I KNOW, I KNOW.
IT'S NOT FAIR. THAT LITTLE BASTARD.
IT'S NOT FAAAAAIIIIR.
HHAHAHAHA I'MRIIIIICH!
I'M RICH!
I'M RICH AND I'VE DOCUMENTED THE BXF PAYING A FORTUNE FOR...UH...FOR A WINDUP WATCH! YOU HEAR ME, WORLD?!
FROM REBELS! DISGUISED AS BANDITS!
OR SOMETHING!
...
ALTHOUGH. UH.
ALTHOUGH I'M NOT TOTALLY SURE ABOUT THE DETAIL YET. OR THE WHY. AND. A-AND I'M NOT SURE HOW I'LL SPEND ALL THIS MONEY.
AND I GUESS I'M STILL PRETTY DEPRESSED. AND UH.
AND A BUNCH OF GUYS JUST DIED.
BUT. YEAH.
WIN.
CUT THE FEED. SEND THE ADVERTISERS AN APOLOGETIC B.J. ON ACCOUNT.
AND COLONEL: PLEASE TELL ME OUR MUTUAL FRIEND IS GOING TO SEVERELY KILL THAT BOOKISH LITTLE £$%&?
HE...WELL, AH, HE WASN'T REAL HAPPY WITH ME LAST TIME I CHECKED IN ON HIM, BUT...

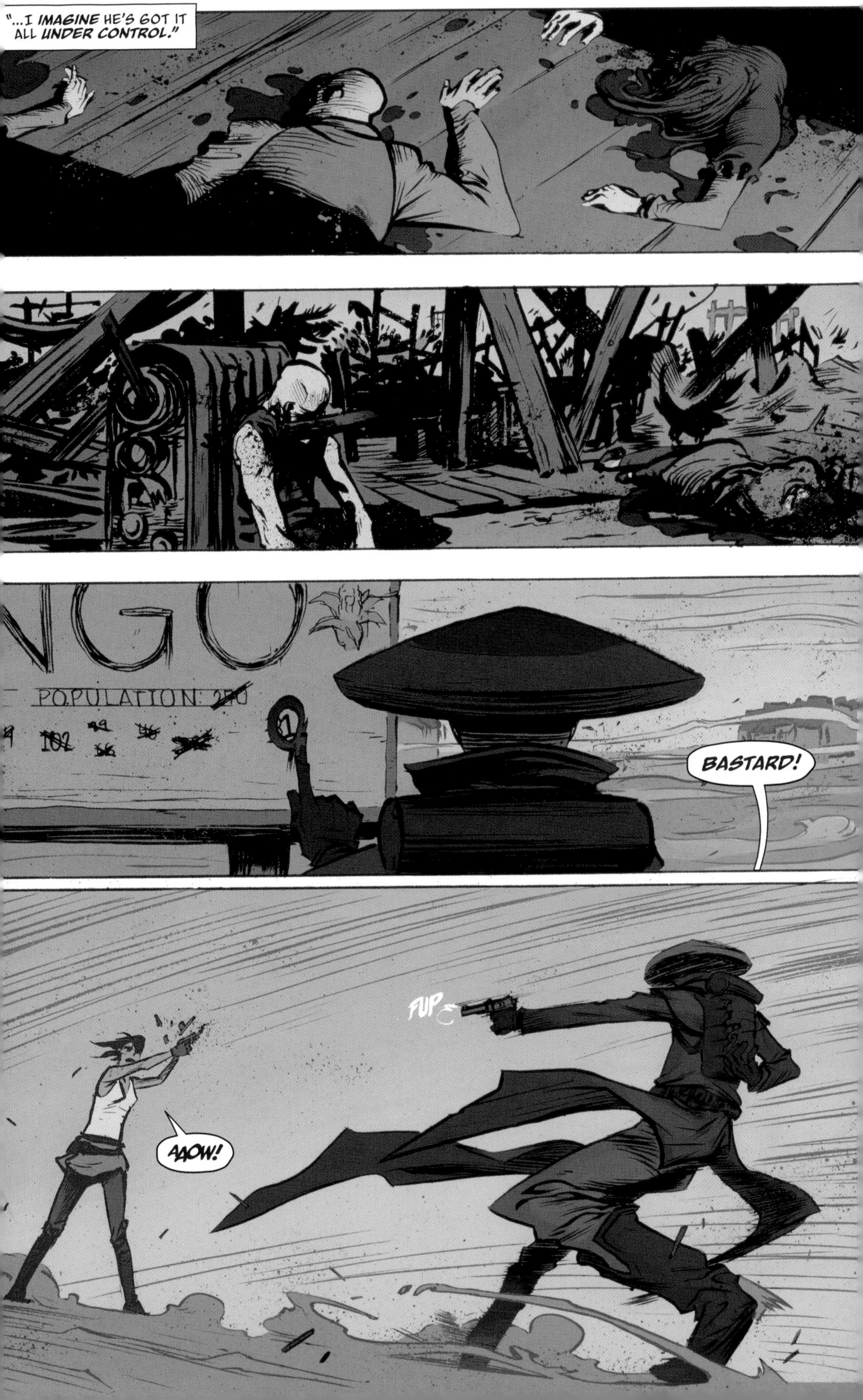
"...I IMAGINE HE'S GOT IT ALL UNDER CONTROL."
NGO
POPULATION:
BASTARD!
FUP
AAOW!

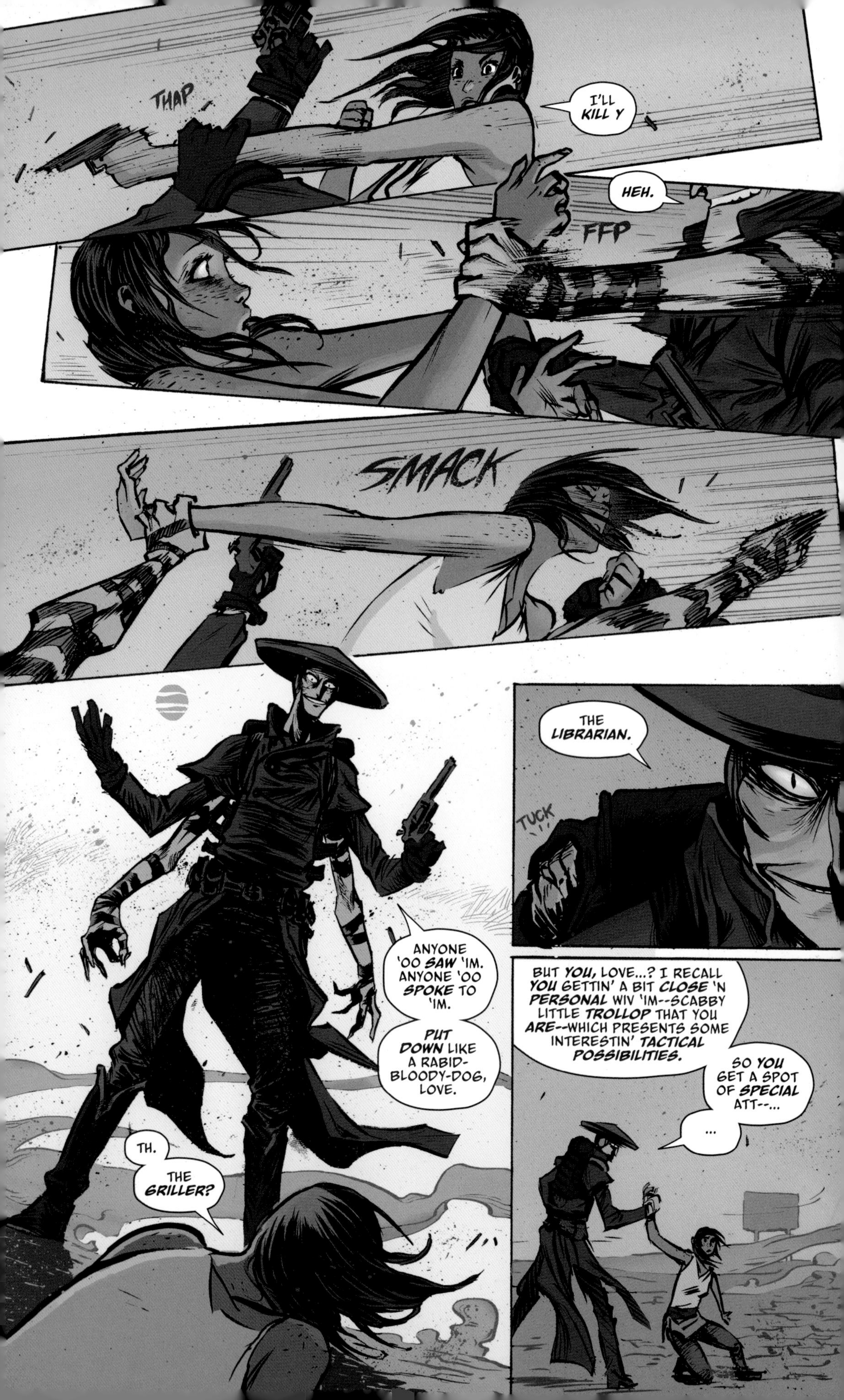
THAP
I'LL KILL Y
HEH.
FFP
SMACK
ANYONE 'OO SAW 'IM. ANYONE 'OO SPOKE TO 'IM.
PUT DOWN LIKE A RABID-BLOODY-DOG, LOVE.
TH.
THE GRILLER?
THE LIBRARIAN.
TUCK
BUT YOU, LOVE...? I RECALL YOU GETTIN' A BIT CLOSE 'N PERSONAL WIV 'IM--SCABBY LITTLE TROLLOP THAT YOU ARE--WHICH PRESENTS SOME INTERESTIN' TACTICAL POSSIBILITIES.
SO YOU GET A SPOT OF SPECIAL ATT--...
...

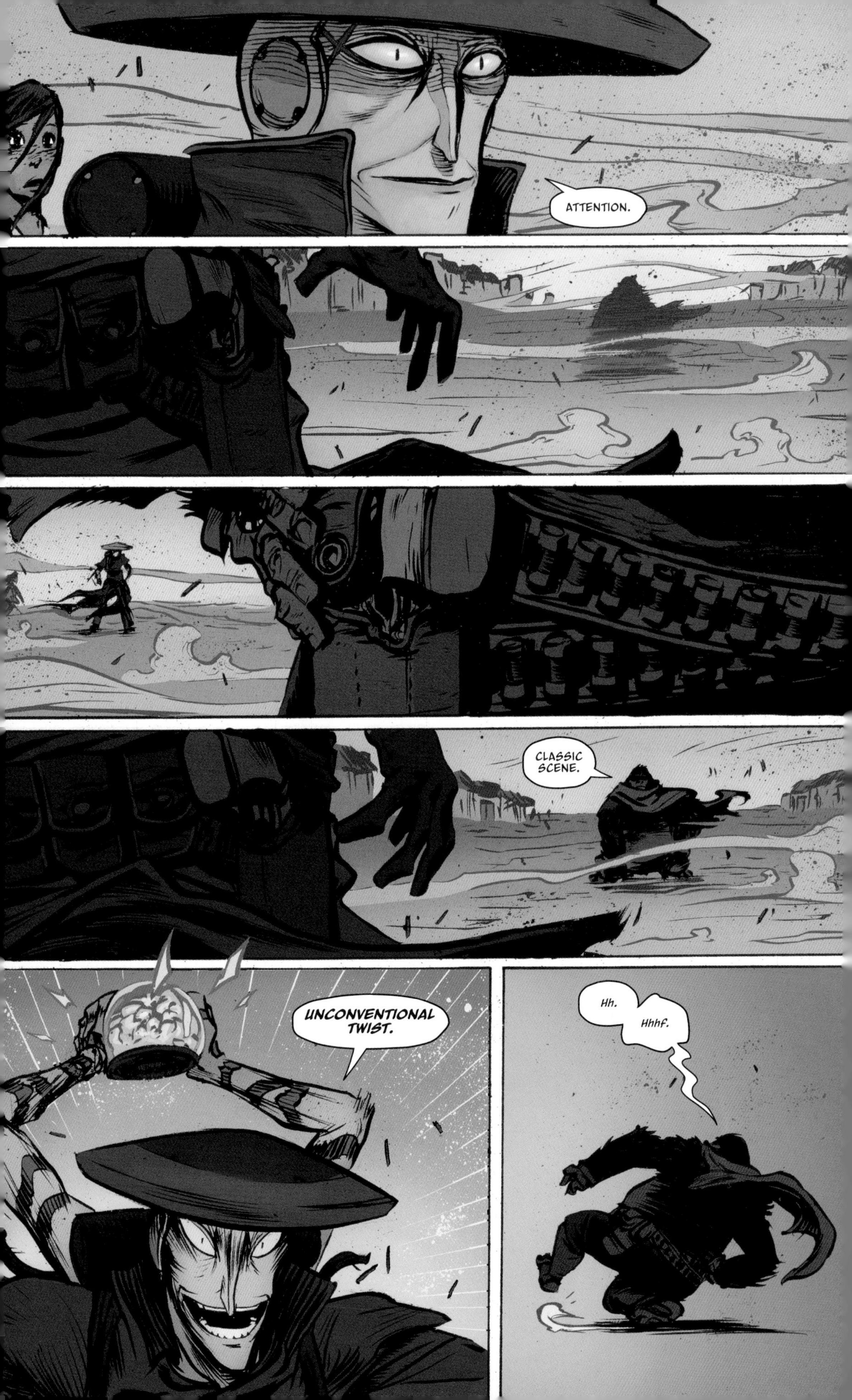
ATTENTION.
CLASSIC SCENE.
UNCONVENTIONAL TWIST.
Hh.
Hhhf.

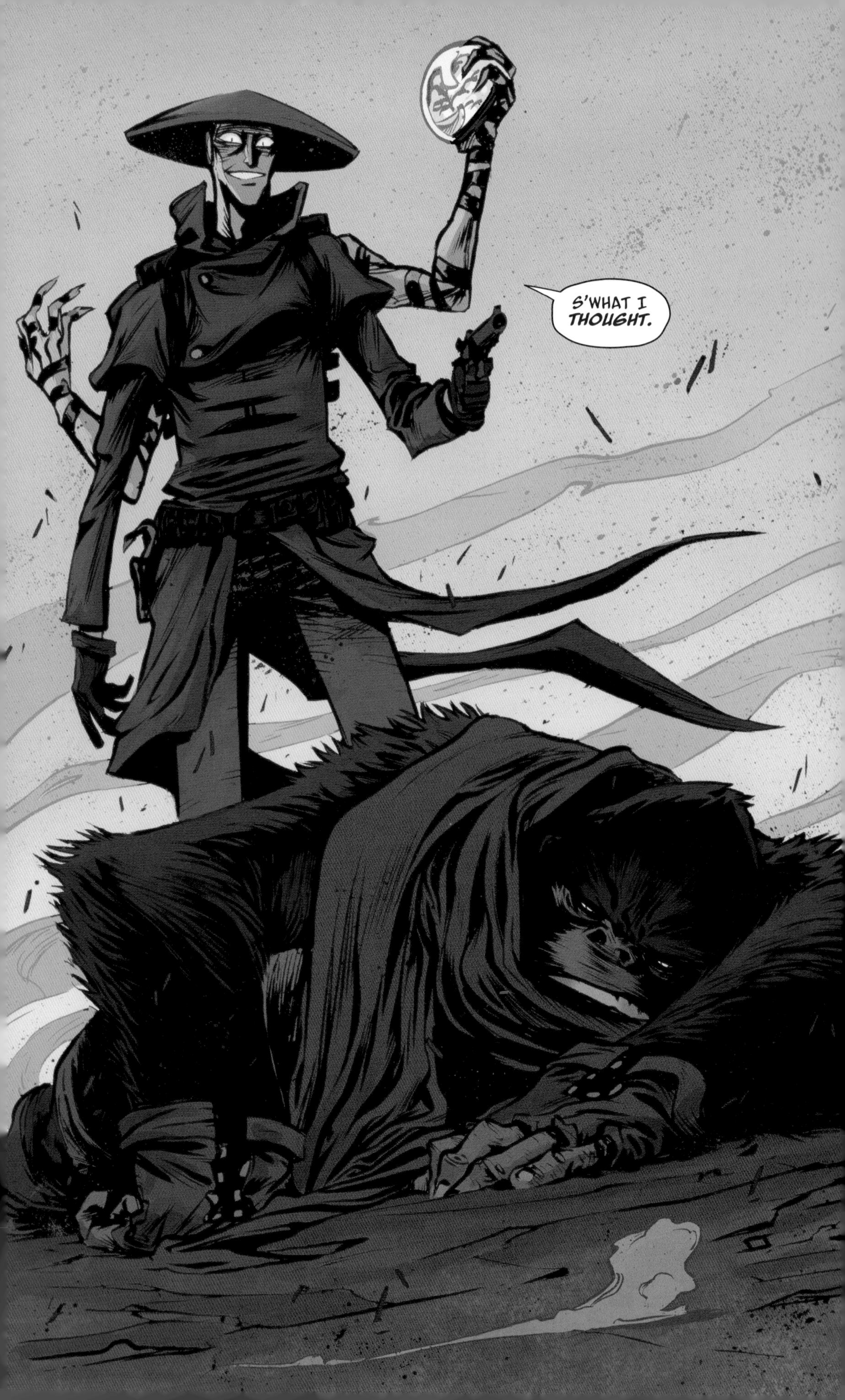
S'WHAT I THOUGHT.

CHAPTER FIVE

# SIX-GUN GORILLA

(Continued from page 8.)

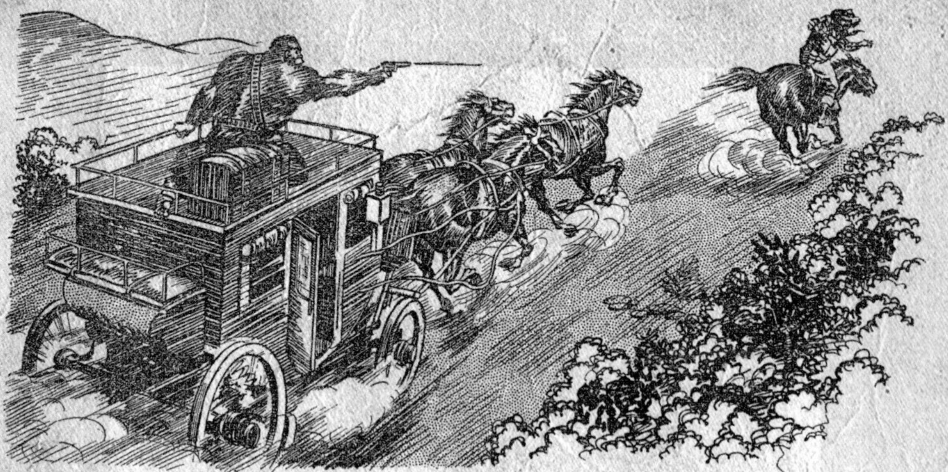



STAMPS.—300 different, including Airmail, beautiful uncommon sets, pictorials, Colonials. You'll be delighted. Price 6d. White, Stamps, Lye, Stourbridge.

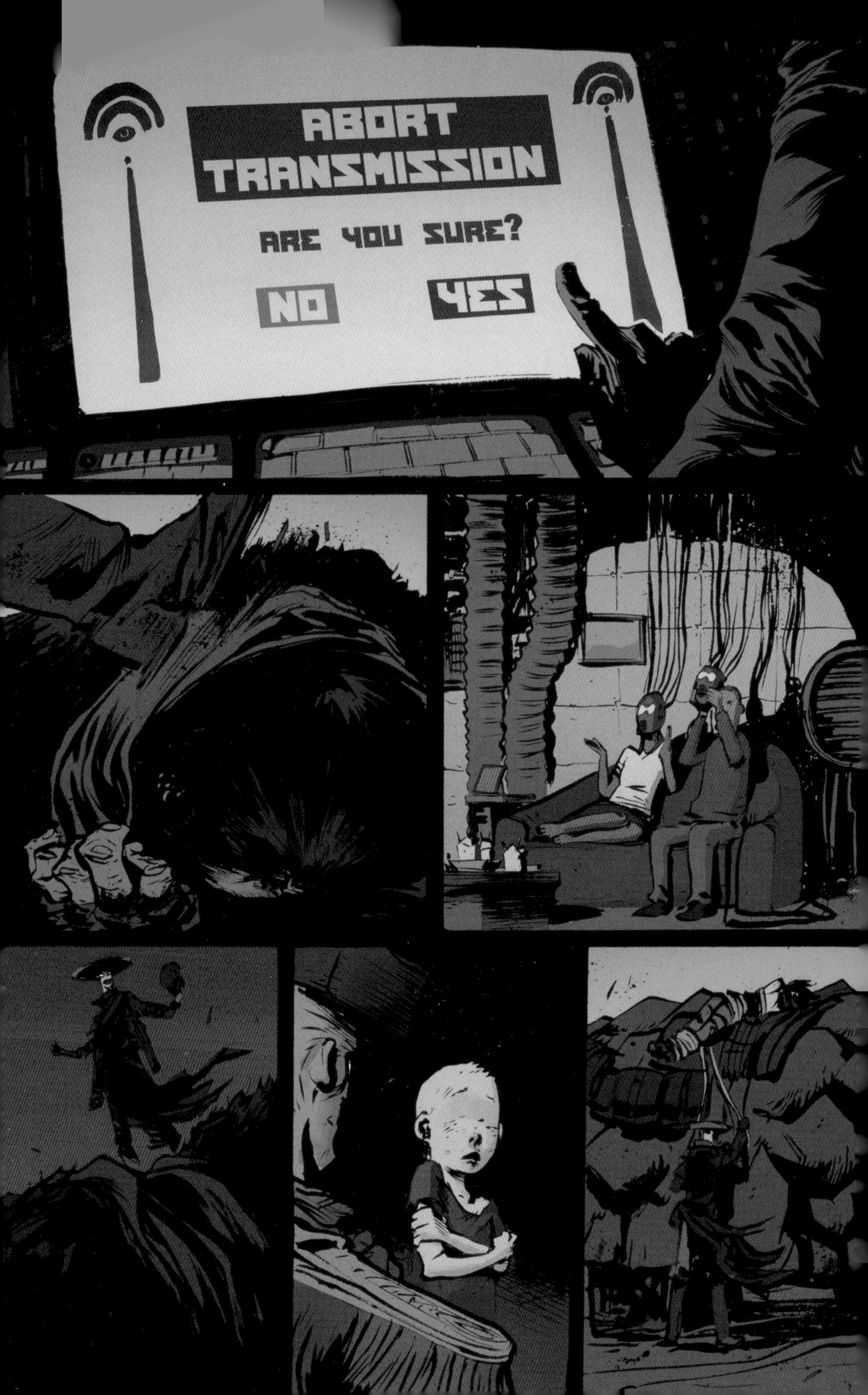
ABORT TRANSMISSION
ARE YOU SURE?
NO
YES

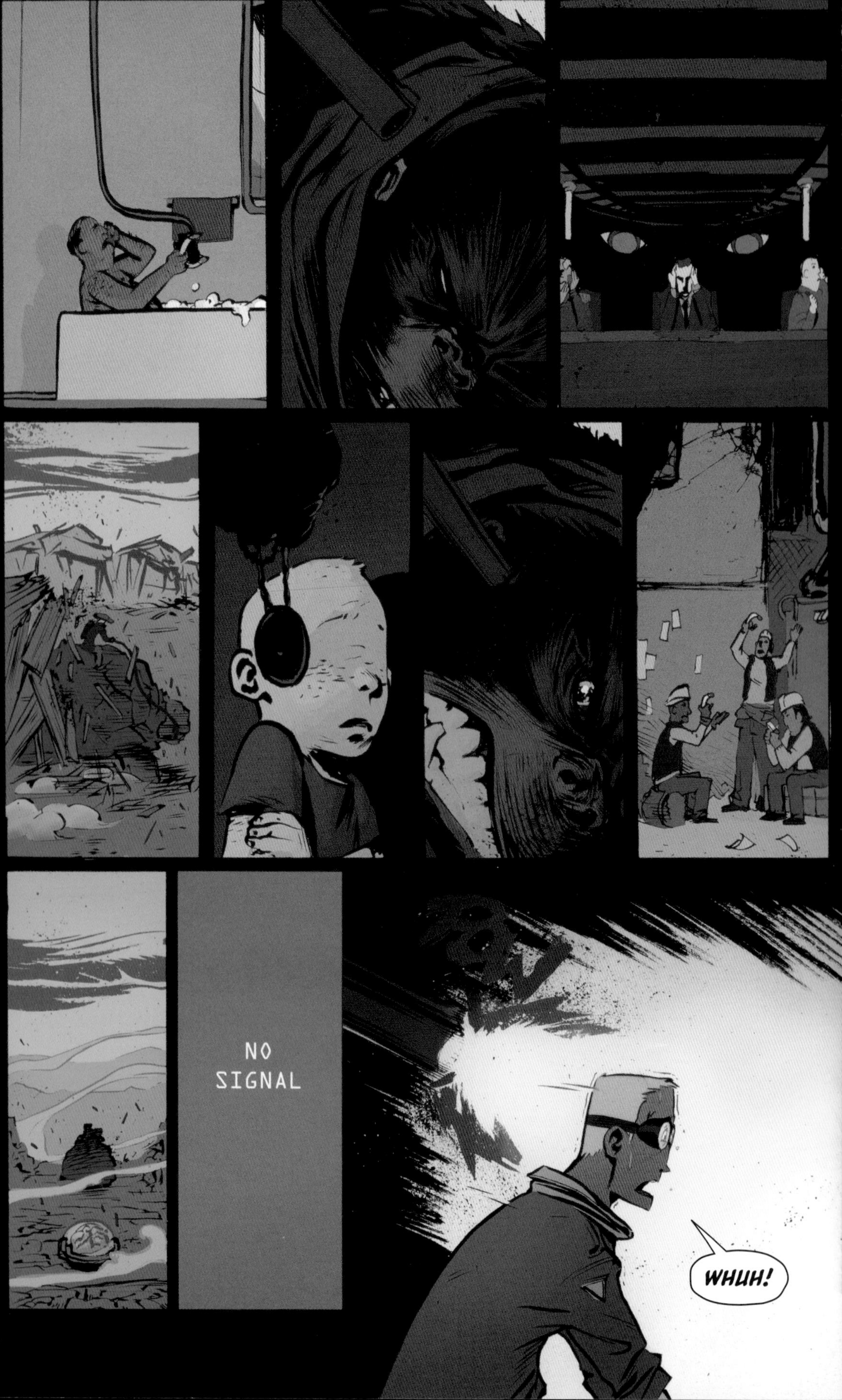
NO SIGNAL
WHUH!

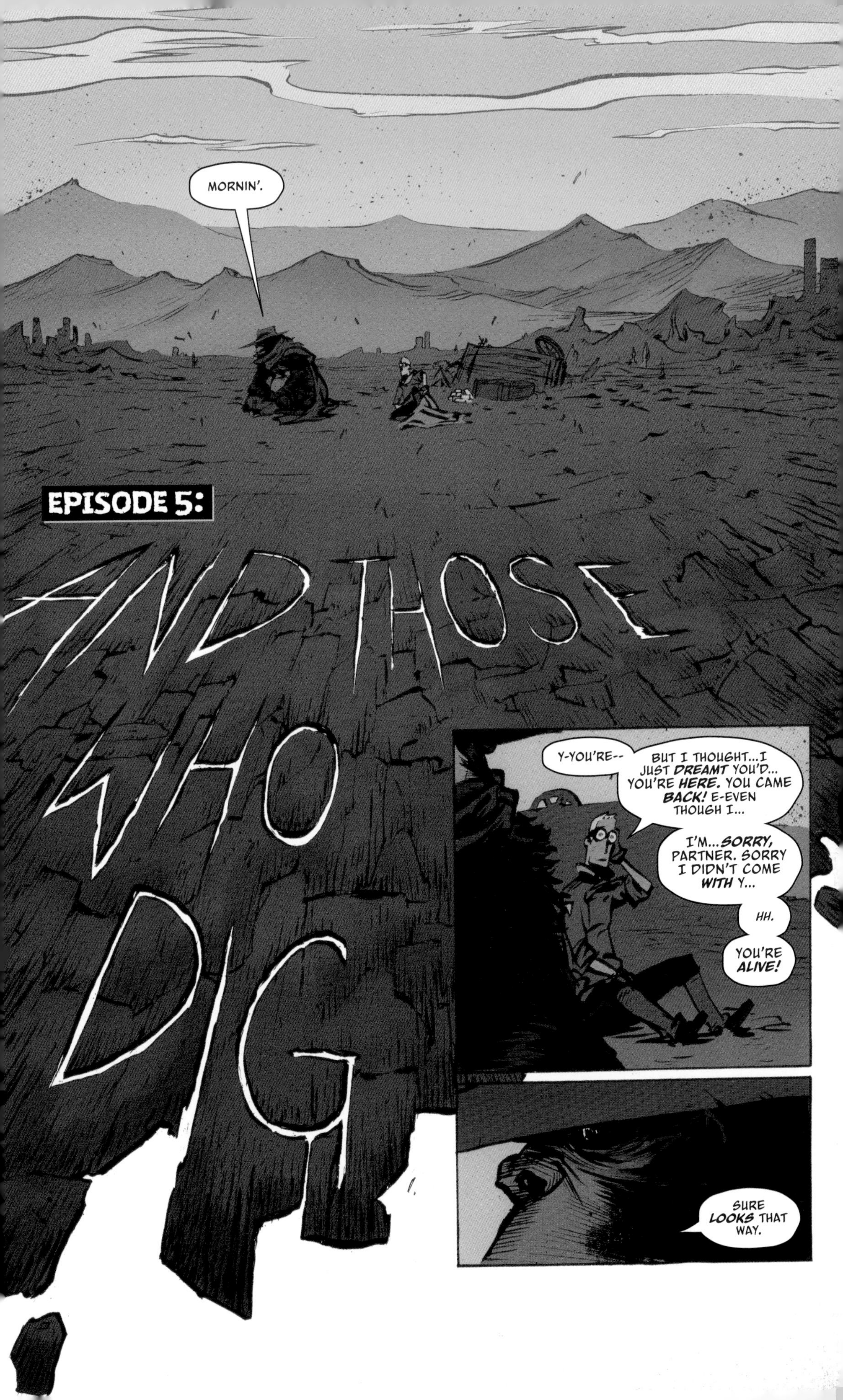
MORNIN'.
EPISODE 5:
AND THOSE WHO DIG
Y-YOU'RE--
BUT I THOUGHT...I JUST DREAMT YOU'D... YOU'RE HERE. YOU CAME BACK! E-EVEN THOUGH I...
I'M...SORRY, PARTNER. SORRY I DIDN'T COME WITH Y...
HH.
YOU'RE ALIVE!
SURE LOOKS THAT WAY.

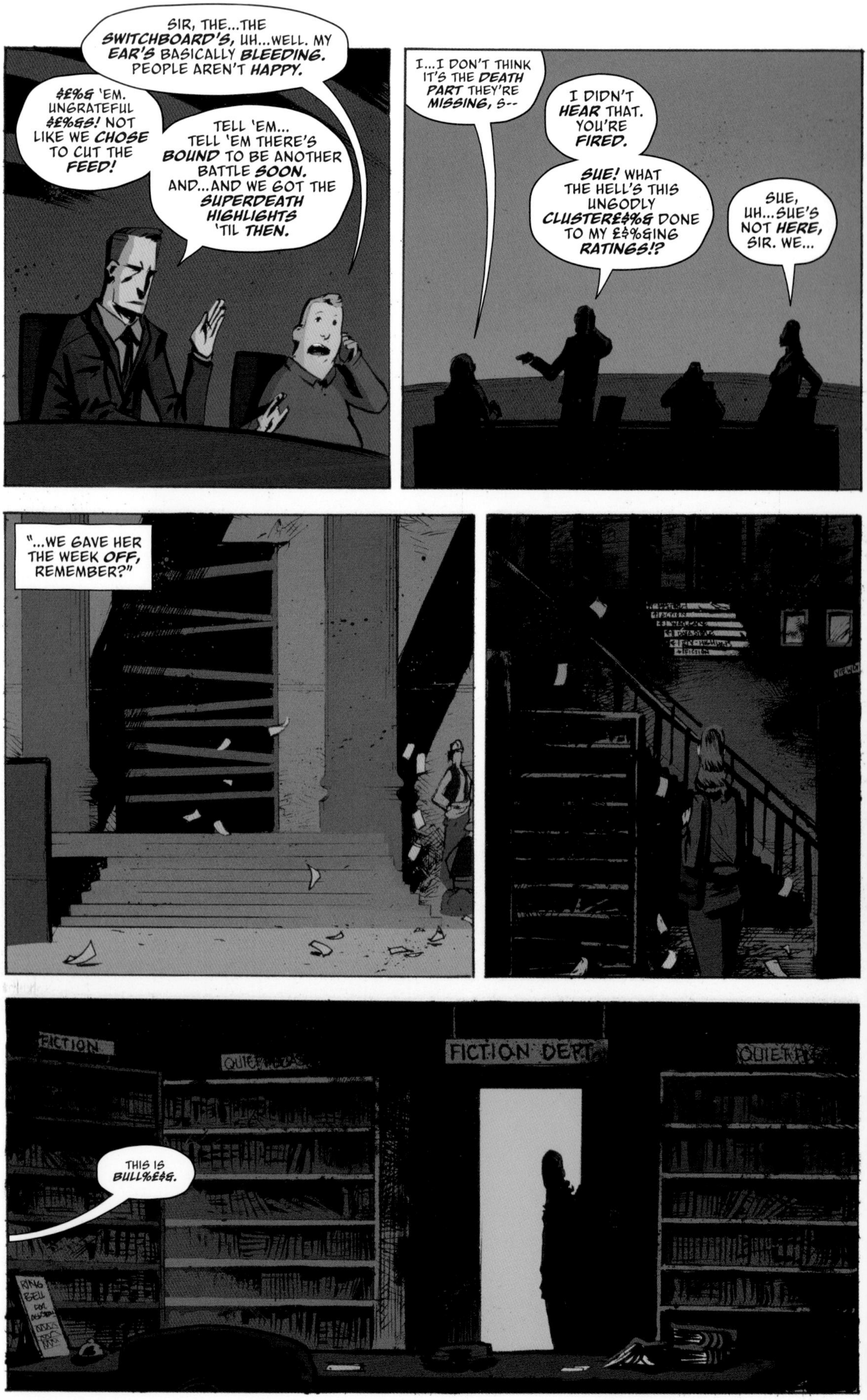
SIR, THE...THE SWITCHBOARD'S, UH...WELL. MY EAR'S BASICALLY BLEEDING. PEOPLE AREN'T HAPPY.
$£%& 'EM. UNGRATEFUL $£%&S! NOT LIKE WE CHOSE TO CUT THE FEED!
TELL 'EM... TELL 'EM THERE'S BOUND TO BE ANOTHER BATTLE SOON. AND...AND WE GOT THE SUPERDEATH HIGHLIGHTS 'TIL THEN.
I...I DON'T THINK IT'S THE DEATH PART THEY'RE MISSING, S--
I DIDN'T HEAR THAT. YOU'RE FIRED.
SUE! WHAT THE HELL'S THIS UNGODLY CLUSTER£$%& DONE TO MY £$%&ING RATINGS!?
SUE, UH...SUE'S NOT HERE, SIR. WE...
"...WE GAVE HER THE WEEK OFF, REMEMBER?"
FICTION
FICTION DEPT
THIS IS BULL%£$&.

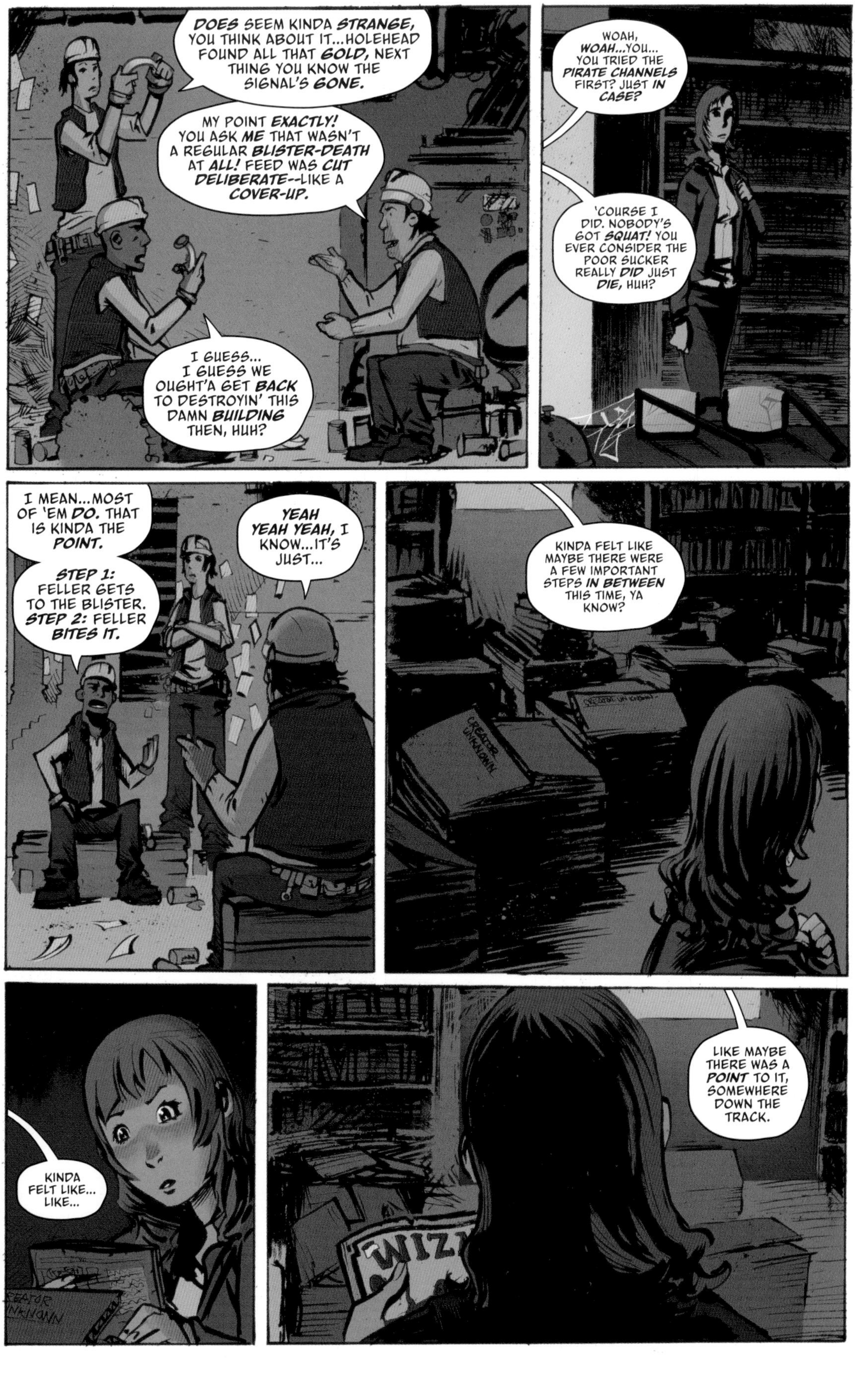
DOES SEEM KINDA STRANGE, YOU THINK ABOUT IT...HOLEHEAD FOUND ALL THAT GOLD, NEXT THING YOU KNOW THE SIGNAL'S GONE.
MY POINT EXACTLY! YOU ASK ME THAT WASN'T A REGULAR BLISTER-DEATH AT ALL! FEED WAS CUT DELIBERATE--LIKE A COVER-UP.
I GUESS... I GUESS WE OUGHT'A GET BACK TO DESTROYIN' THIS DAMN BUILDING THEN, HUH?
WOAH, WOAH...YOU... YOU TRIED THE PIRATE CHANNELS FIRST? JUST IN CASE?
'COURSE I DID. NOBODY'S GOT SQUAT! YOU EVER CONSIDER THE POOR SUCKER REALLY DID JUST DIE, HUH?
I MEAN...MOST OF 'EM DO. THAT IS KINDA THE POINT.
STEP 1: FELLER GETS TO THE BLISTER. STEP 2: FELLER BITES IT.
YEAH YEAH YEAH, I KNOW...IT'S JUST...
KINDA FELT LIKE MAYBE THERE WERE A FEW IMPORTANT STEPS IN BETWEEN THIS TIME, YA KNOW?
CREATOR UNKNOWN
KINDA FELT LIKE... LIKE...
LIKE MAYBE THERE WAS A POINT TO IT, SOMEWHERE DOWN THE TRACK.

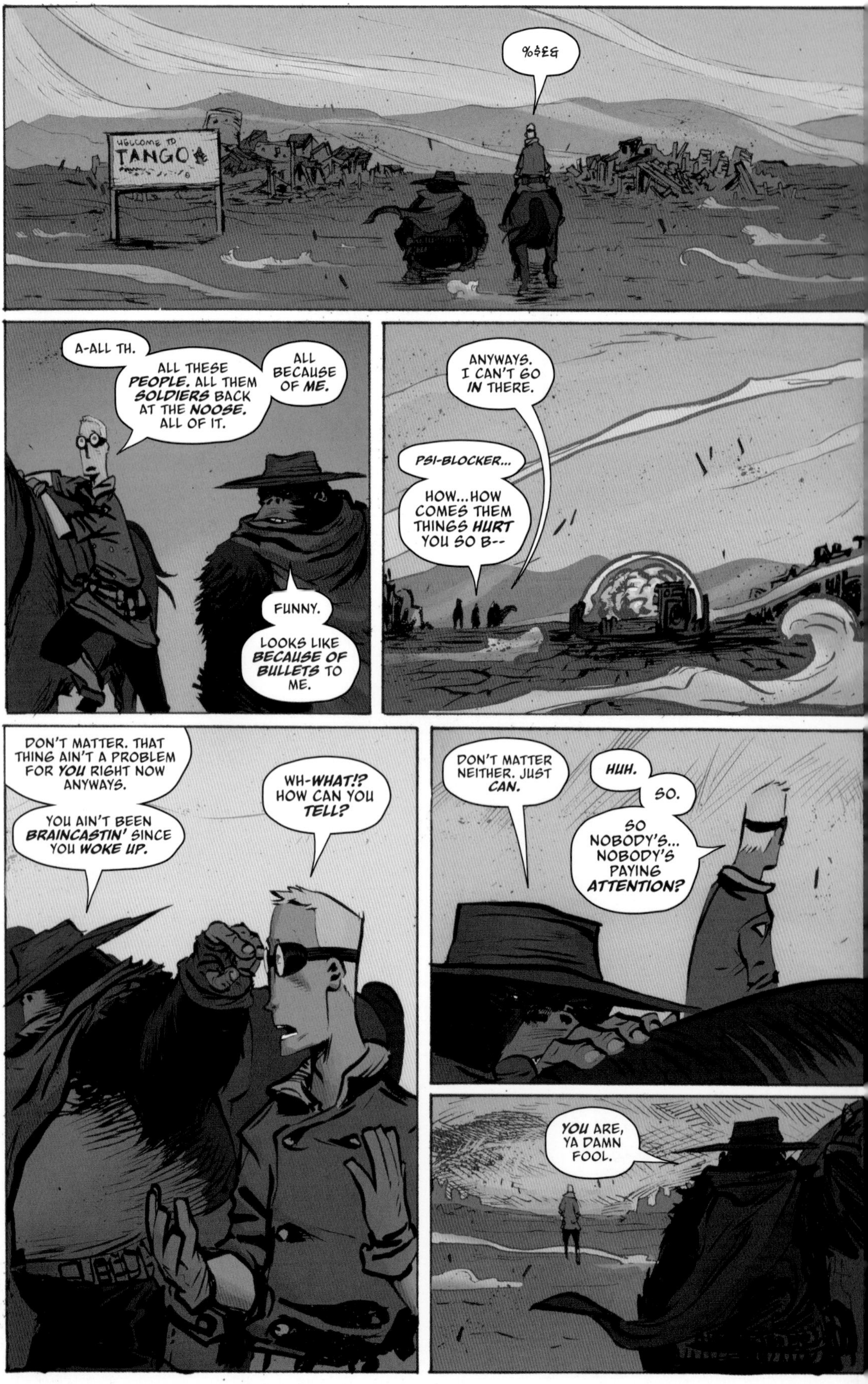
TANGO
%$£&
A-ALL TH.
ALL THESE PEOPLE. ALL THEM SOLDIERS BACK AT THE NOOSE. ALL OF IT.
ALL BECAUSE OF ME.
FUNNY.
LOOKS LIKE BECAUSE OF BULLETS TO ME.
ANYWAYS. I CAN'T GO IN THERE.
PSI-BLOCKER...
HOW...HOW COMES THEM THINGS HURT YOU SO B--
DON'T MATTER. THAT THING AIN'T A PROBLEM FOR YOU RIGHT NOW ANYWAYS.
YOU AIN'T BEEN BRAINCASTIN' SINCE YOU WOKE UP.
WH-WHAT!? HOW CAN YOU TELL?
DON'T MATTER NEITHER. JUST CAN.
HUH.
SO.
SO NOBODY'S... NOBODY'S PAYING ATTENTION?
YOU ARE, YA DAMN FOOL.

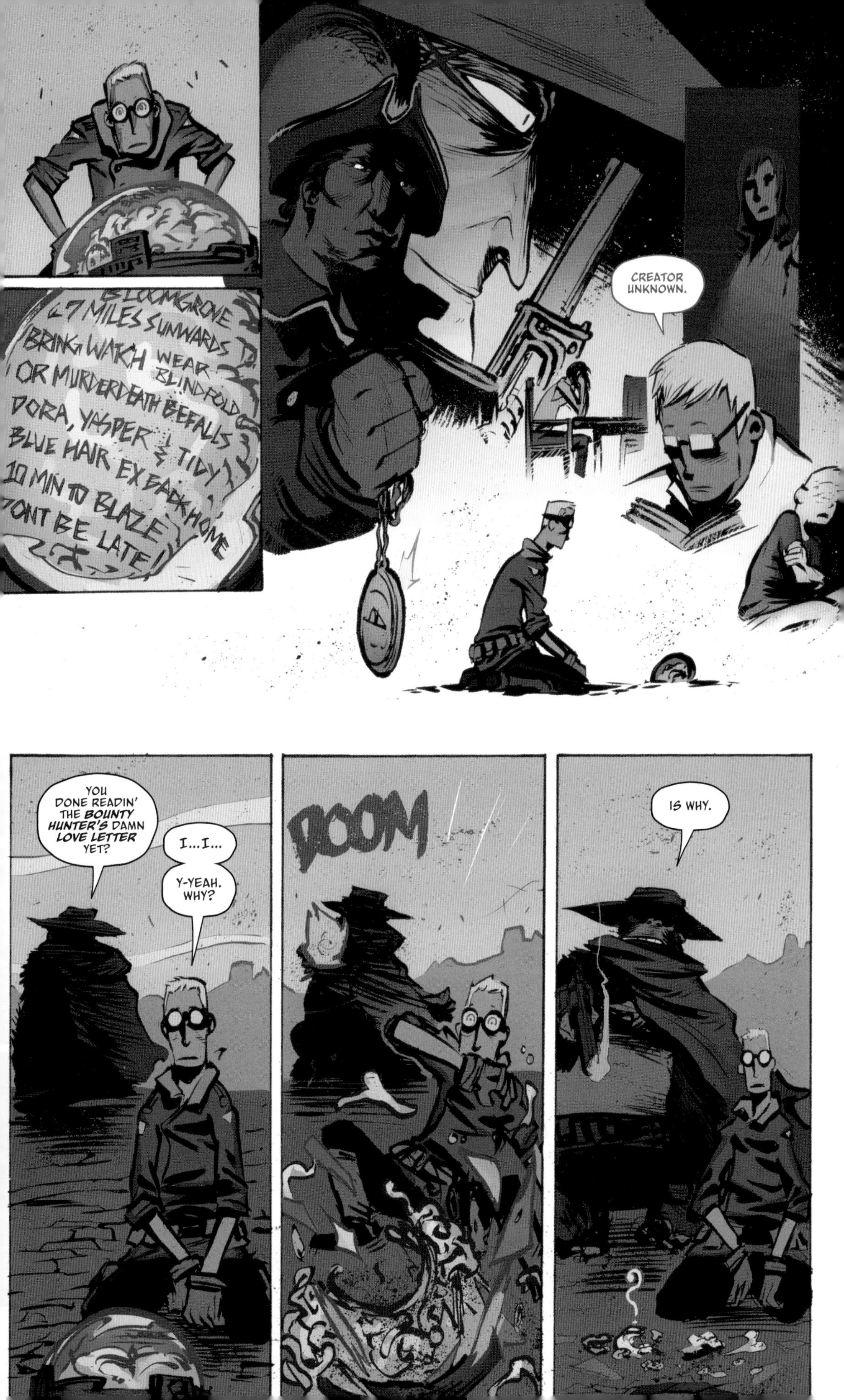
BLOOMGROVE
7 MILES SUNWARDS
BRING WATCH WEAR BLINDFOLD
OR MURDERDEATH BEFALLS
DORA, YASPER & TIDY
BLUE HAIR EX BACK HOME
10 MIN TO BLAZE
DONT BE LATE!
CREATOR UNKNOWN.
YOU DONE READIN' THE BOUNTY HUNTER'S DAMN LOVE LETTER YET?
I... I...
Y-YEAH. WHY?
DOOM
IS WHY.

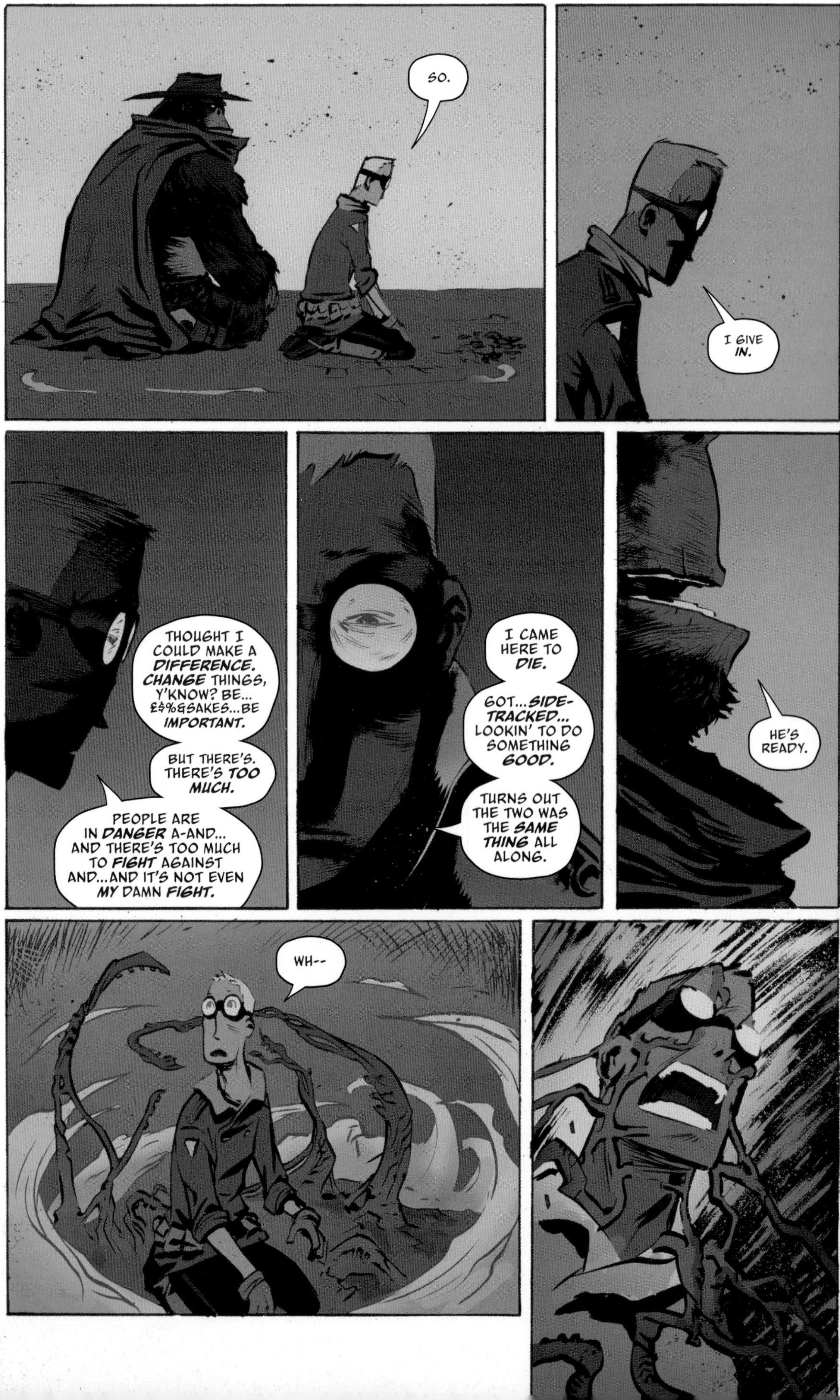
SO.
I GIVE IN.
THOUGHT I COULD MAKE A DIFFERENCE. CHANGE THINGS, Y'KNOW? BE... £$%&SAKES...BE IMPORTANT.
BUT THERE'S. THERE'S TOO MUCH.
PEOPLE ARE IN DANGER A-AND... AND THERE'S TOO MUCH TO FIGHT AGAINST AND...AND IT'S NOT EVEN MY DAMN FIGHT.
I CAME HERE TO DIE.
GOT...SIDE-TRACKED... LOOKIN' TO DO SOMETHING GOOD.
TURNS OUT THE TWO WAS THE SAME THING ALL ALONG.
HE'S READY.
WH--

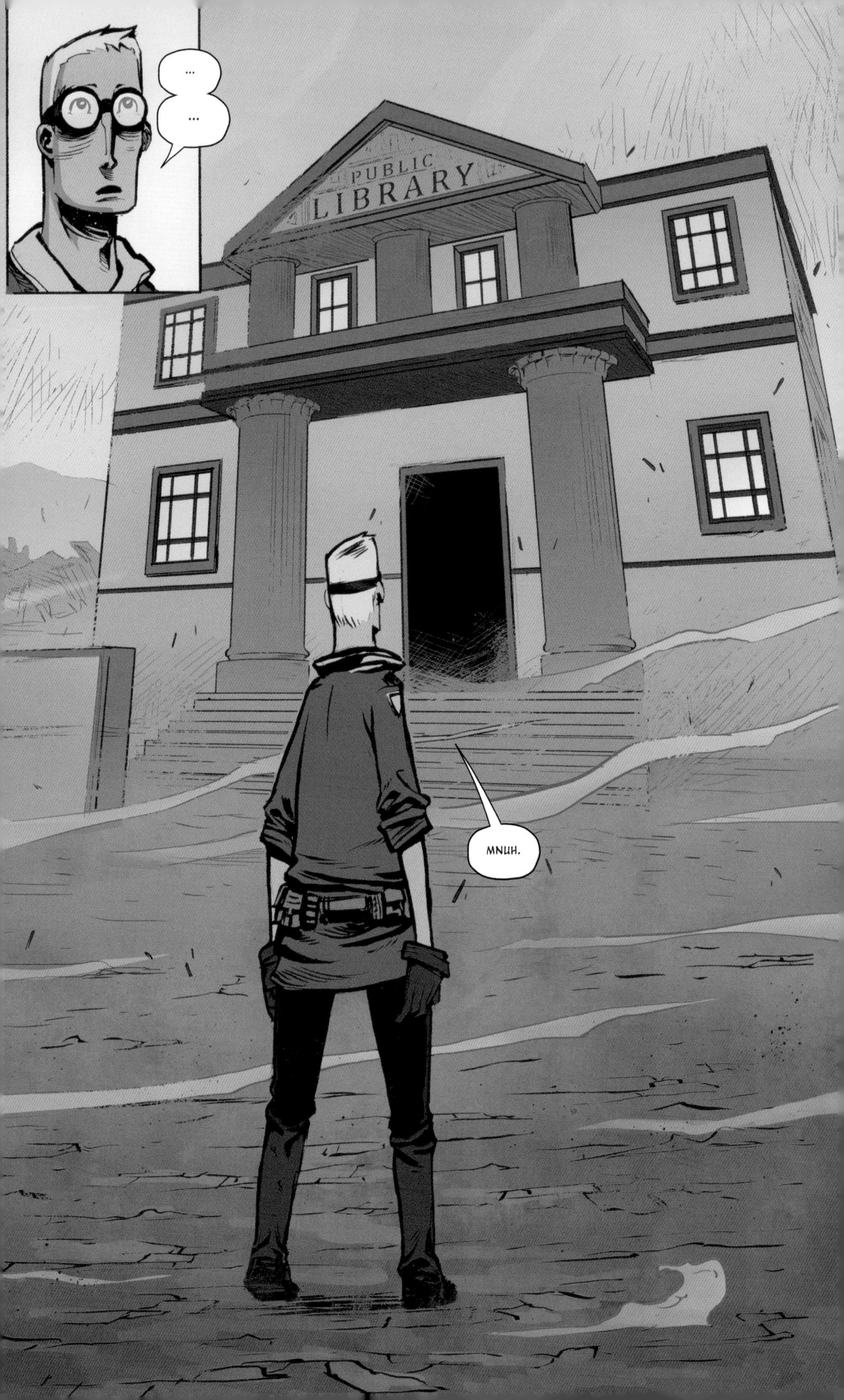
...
...
PUBLIC LIBRARY
MNUH.

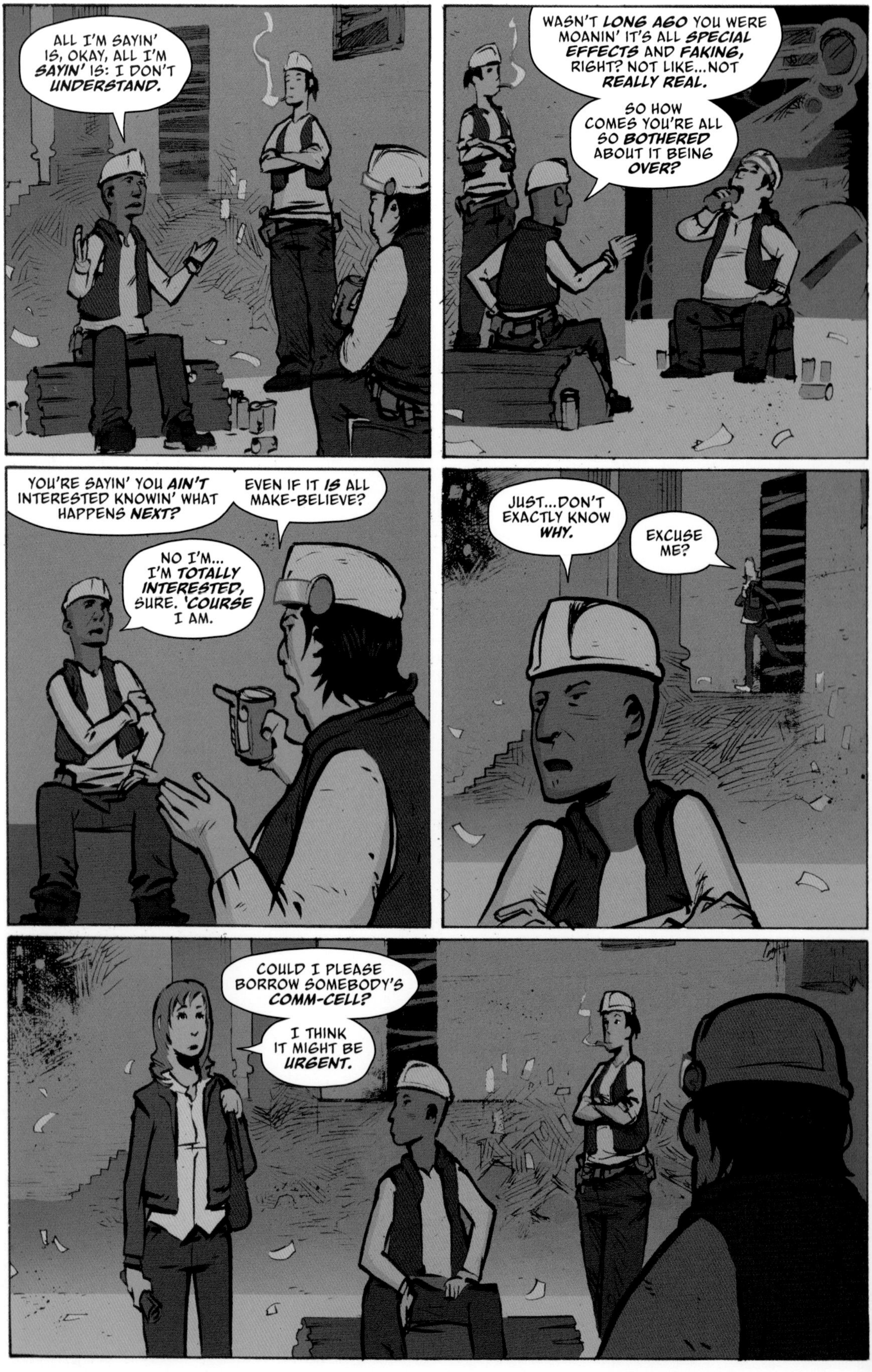
ALL I'M SAYIN' IS, OKAY, ALL I'M SAYIN' IS: I DON'T UNDERSTAND.
WASN'T LONG AGO YOU WERE MOANIN' IT'S ALL SPECIAL EFFECTS AND FAKING, RIGHT? NOT LIKE...NOT REALLY REAL.
SO HOW COMES YOU'RE ALL SO BOTHERED ABOUT IT BEING OVER?
YOU'RE SAYIN' YOU AIN'T INTERESTED KNOWIN' WHAT HAPPENS NEXT?
EVEN IF IT IS ALL MAKE-BELIEVE?
NO I'M... I'M TOTALLY INTERESTED, SURE. 'COURSE I AM.
JUST...DON'T EXACTLY KNOW WHY.
EXCUSE ME?
COULD I PLEASE BORROW SOMEBODY'S COMM-CELL?
I THINK IT MIGHT BE URGENT.

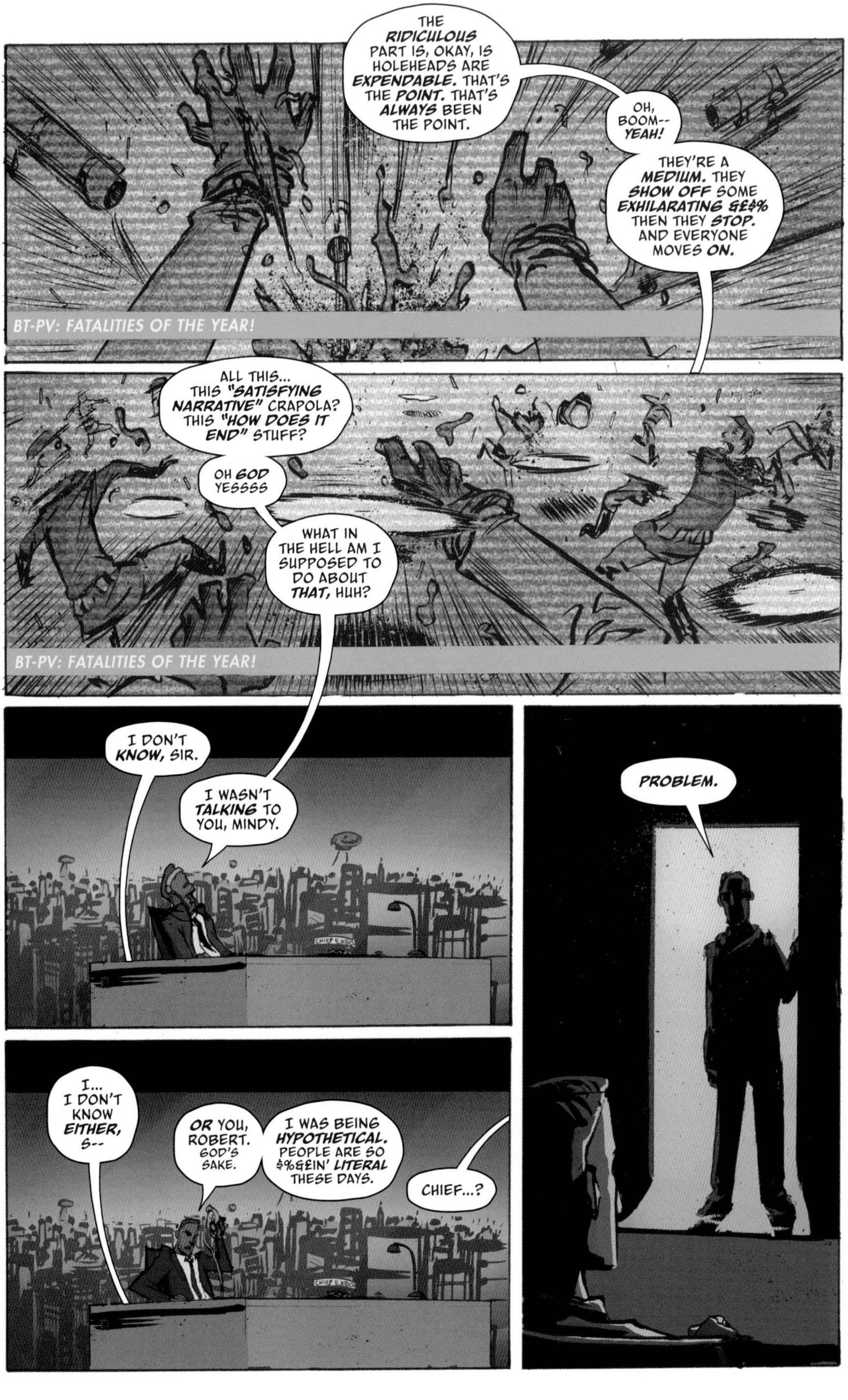
THE RIDICULOUS PART IS, OKAY, IS HOLEHEADS ARE EXPENDABLE. THAT'S THE POINT. THAT'S ALWAYS BEEN THE POINT.
OH, BOOM--YEAH!
THEY'RE A MEDIUM. THEY SHOW OFF SOME EXHILARATING &&$% THEN THEY STOP. AND EVERYONE MOVES ON.
BT-PV: FATALITIES OF THE YEAR!
ALL THIS... THIS "SATISFYING NARRATIVE" CRAPOLA? THIS "HOW DOES IT END" STUFF?
OH GOD YESSSS
WHAT IN THE HELL AM I SUPPOSED TO DO ABOUT THAT, HUH?
BT-PV: FATALITIES OF THE YEAR!
I DON'T KNOW, SIR.
I WASN'T TALKING TO YOU, MINDY.
I... I DON'T KNOW EITHER, S--
OR YOU, ROBERT. GOD'S SAKE.
I WAS BEING HYPOTHETICAL. PEOPLE ARE SO $%&EIN' LITERAL THESE DAYS.
CHIEF...?
PROBLEM.

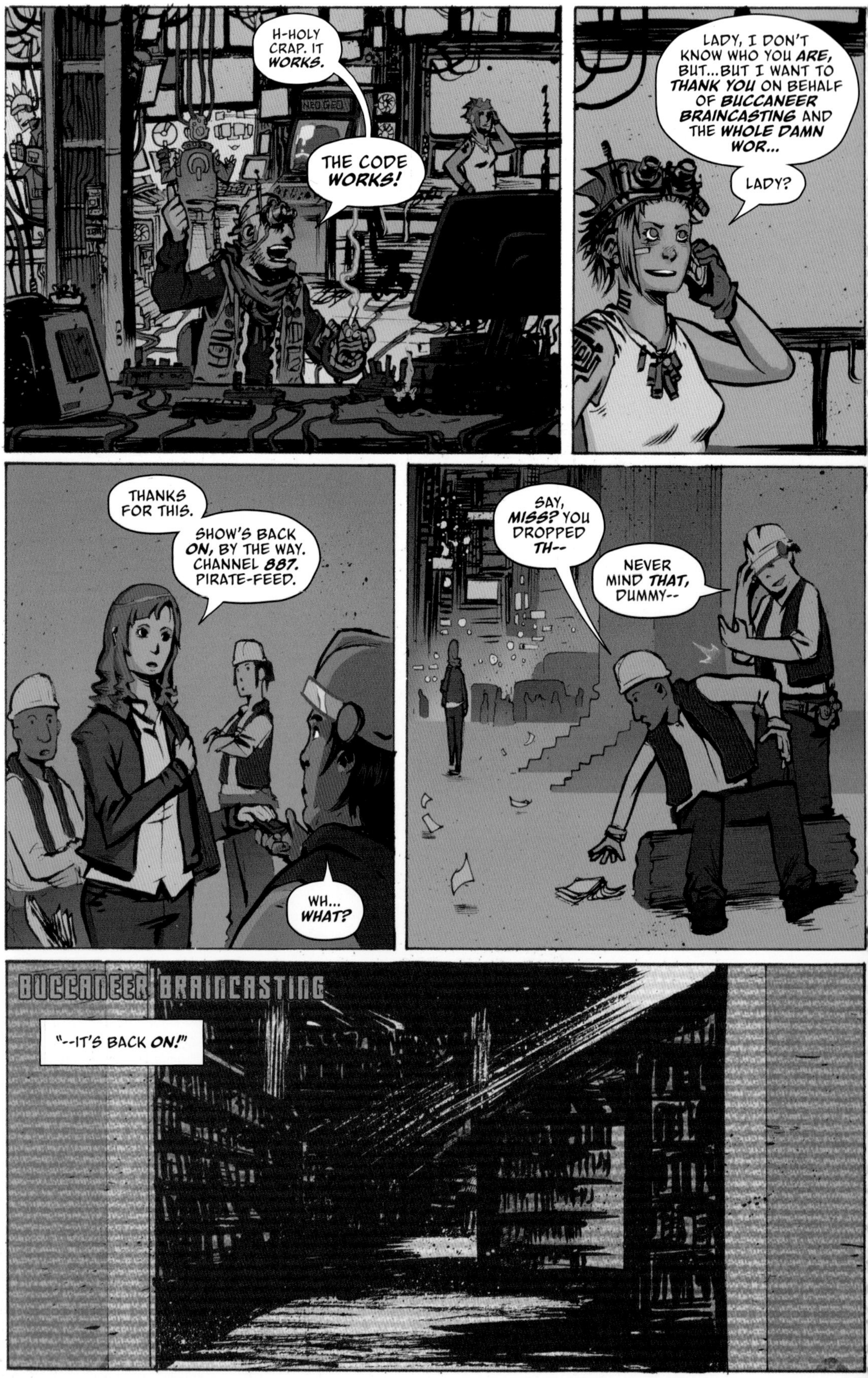

H-HOLY CRAP. IT WORKS.
THE CODE WORKS!
LADY, I DON'T KNOW WHO YOU ARE, BUT...BUT I WANT TO THANK YOU ON BEHALF OF BUCCANEER BRAINCASTING AND THE WHOLE DAMN WOR...
LADY?
THANKS FOR THIS.
SHOW'S BACK ON, BY THE WAY. CHANNEL 887. PIRATE-FEED.
WH... WHAT?
SAY, MISS? YOU DROPPED TH--
NEVER MIND THAT, DUMMY--
BUCCANEER BRAINCASTING
"--IT'S BACK ON!"

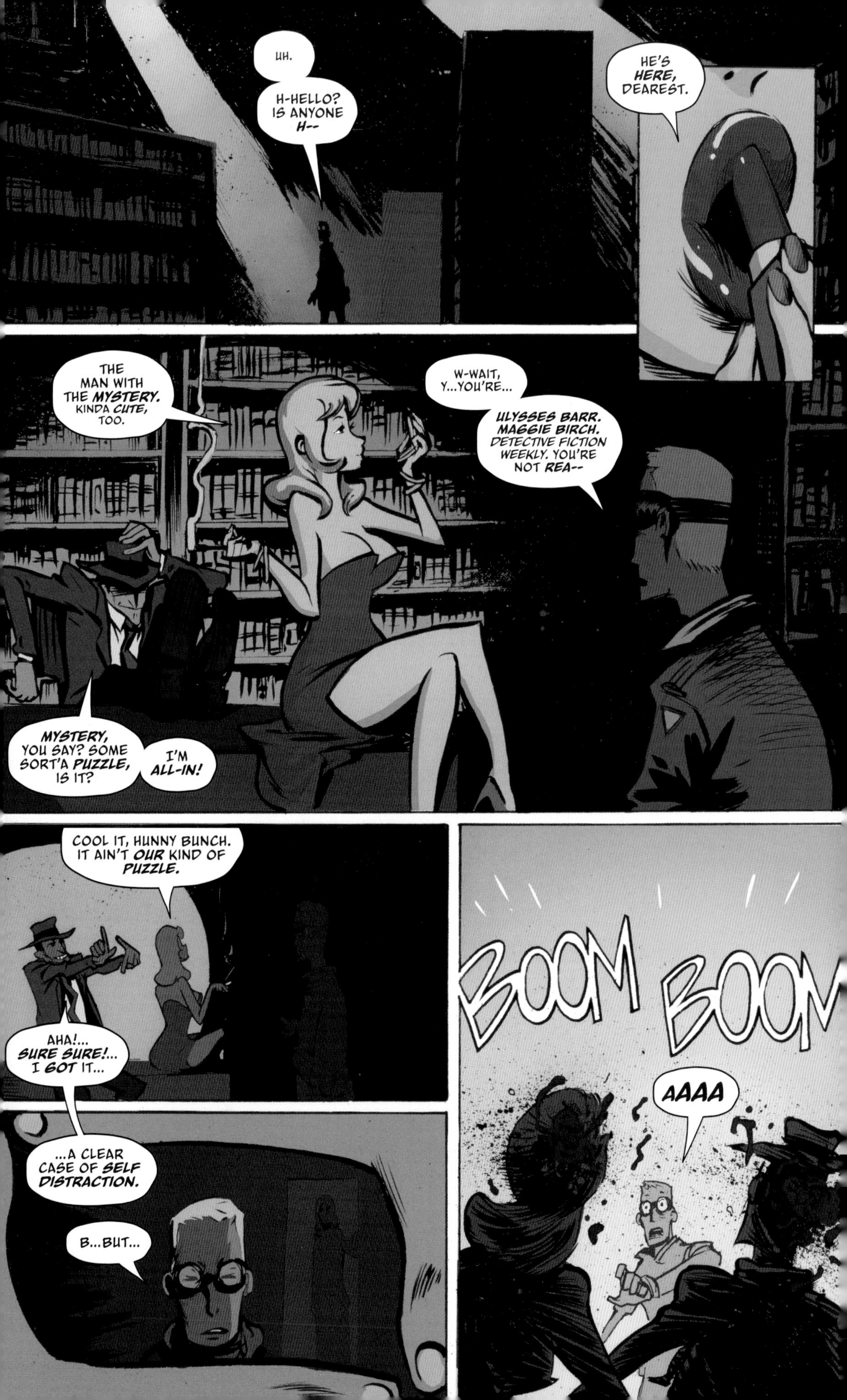
UH.
H-HELLO? IS ANYONE H--
HE'S HERE, DEAREST.
THE MAN WITH THE MYSTERY. KINDA CUTE, TOO.
W-WAIT, Y...YOU'RE...
ULYSSES BARR. MAGGIE BIRCH. DETECTIVE FICTION WEEKLY. YOU'RE NOT REA--
MYSTERY, YOU SAY? SOME SORT'A PUZZLE, IS IT?
I'M ALL-IN!
COOL IT, HUNNY BUNCH. IT AIN'T OUR KIND OF PUZZLE.
AHA!... SURE SURE!... I GOT IT...
...A CLEAR CASE OF SELF DISTRACTION.
B...BUT...
BOOM BOOM
AAAA

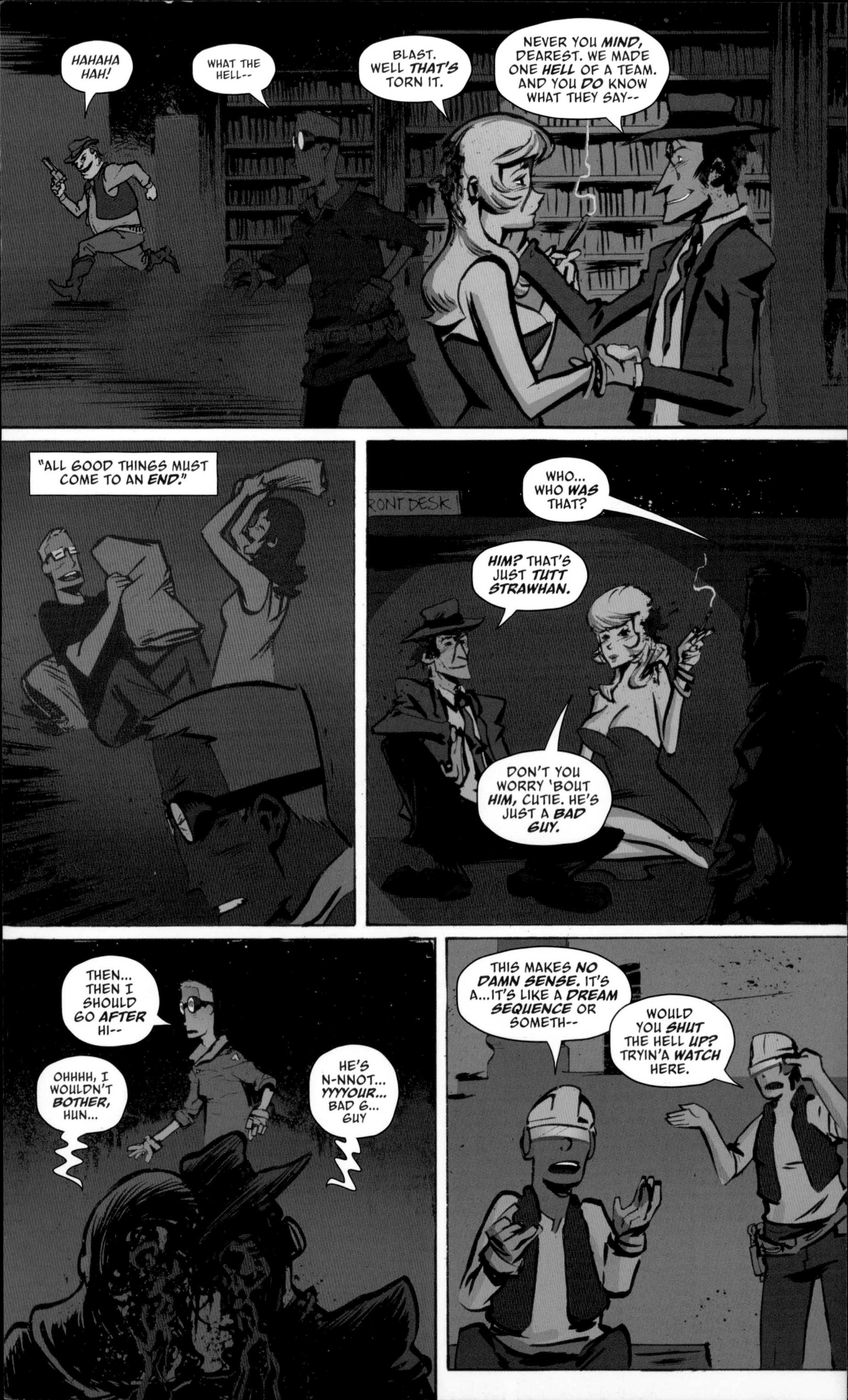
HAHAHA HAH!
WHAT THE HELL--
BLAST. WELL THAT'S TORN IT.
NEVER YOU MIND, DEAREST. WE MADE ONE HELL OF A TEAM. AND YOU DO KNOW WHAT THEY SAY--
"ALL GOOD THINGS MUST COME TO AN END."
RONT DESK
WHO... WHO WAS THAT?
HIM? THAT'S JUST TUTT STRAWHAN.
DON'T YOU WORRY 'BOUT HIM, CUTIE. HE'S JUST A BAD GUY.
THEN... THEN I SHOULD GO AFTER HI--
OHHHH, I WOULDN'T BOTHER, HUN...
HE'S N-NNOT... YYYYOUR... BAD G... GUY
THIS MAKES NO DAMN SENSE. IT'S A...IT'S LIKE A DREAM SEQUENCE OR SOMETH--
WOULD YOU SHUT THE HELL UP? TRYIN'A WATCH HERE.

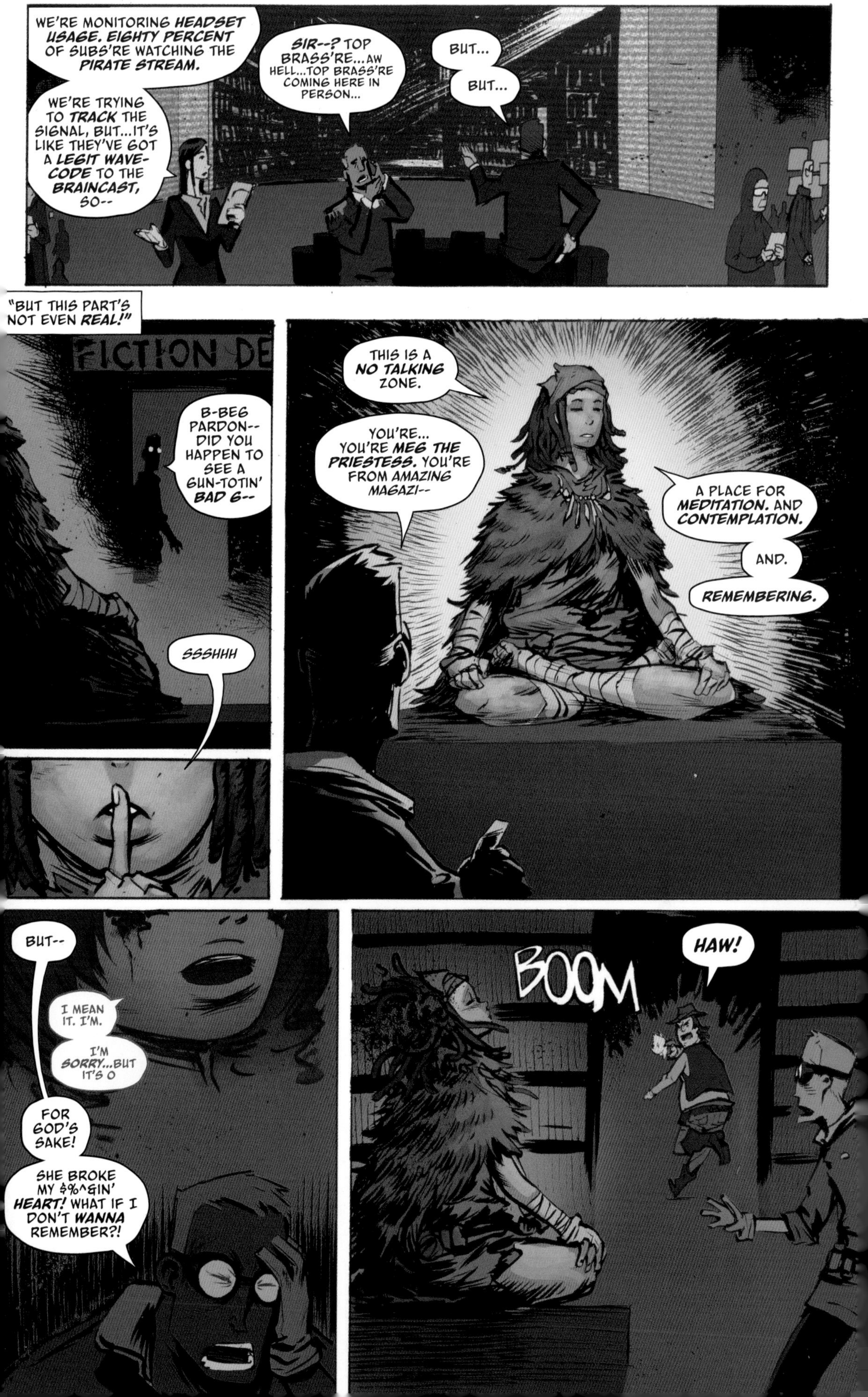
WE'RE MONITORING HEADSET USAGE. EIGHTY PERCENT OF SUBS'RE WATCHING THE PIRATE STREAM.
WE'RE TRYING TO TRACK THE SIGNAL, BUT...IT'S LIKE THEY'VE GOT A LEGIT WAVE-CODE TO THE BRAINCAST, SO--
SIR--? TOP BRASS'RE...AW HELL...TOP BRASS'RE COMING HERE IN PERSON...
BUT...
BUT...
"BUT THIS PART'S NOT EVEN REAL!"
FICTION DE
B-BEG PARDON--DID YOU HAPPEN TO SEE A GUN-TOTIN' BAD G--
SSSHHH
THIS IS A NO TALKING ZONE.
YOU'RE... YOU'RE MEG THE PRIESTESS. YOU'RE FROM AMAZING MAGAZI--
A PLACE FOR MEDITATION. AND CONTEMPLATION.
AND.
REMEMBERING.
BUT--
I MEAN IT. I'M.
I'M SORRY...BUT IT'S O
FOR GOD'S SAKE!
SHE BROKE MY $%^&IN' HEART! WHAT IF I DON'T WANNA REMEMBER?!
BOOM
HAW!

THEN ALL YOU'LL *HAVE* IS THE FACT IT *DIED.*

AND NOT THE FACT IT LIVED.

S... *STRAWHAN!*

KEEP IT *DAHN,* SQUIRE. CAN'T 'EAR THE BLUMMEN *MUSIC.*

WHOOPS! *SORRY!*

MARISE DUNCAN
CREATOR: DOROTHY CALTER

LANCELOT BIG
CREATOR: NELSON

BOOM BOOM

HAHA HA

BUT... BUT HE'S THE *BAD GUY!*

KSSH

VAL EMERY
GEORGE DILNOT

REALLY? *THAT* GHASTLY LITTLE OIK?

HE'S NOT *MY* BALLY BADDIE, BUSTER.

BOOM

*STRAWHAN!*

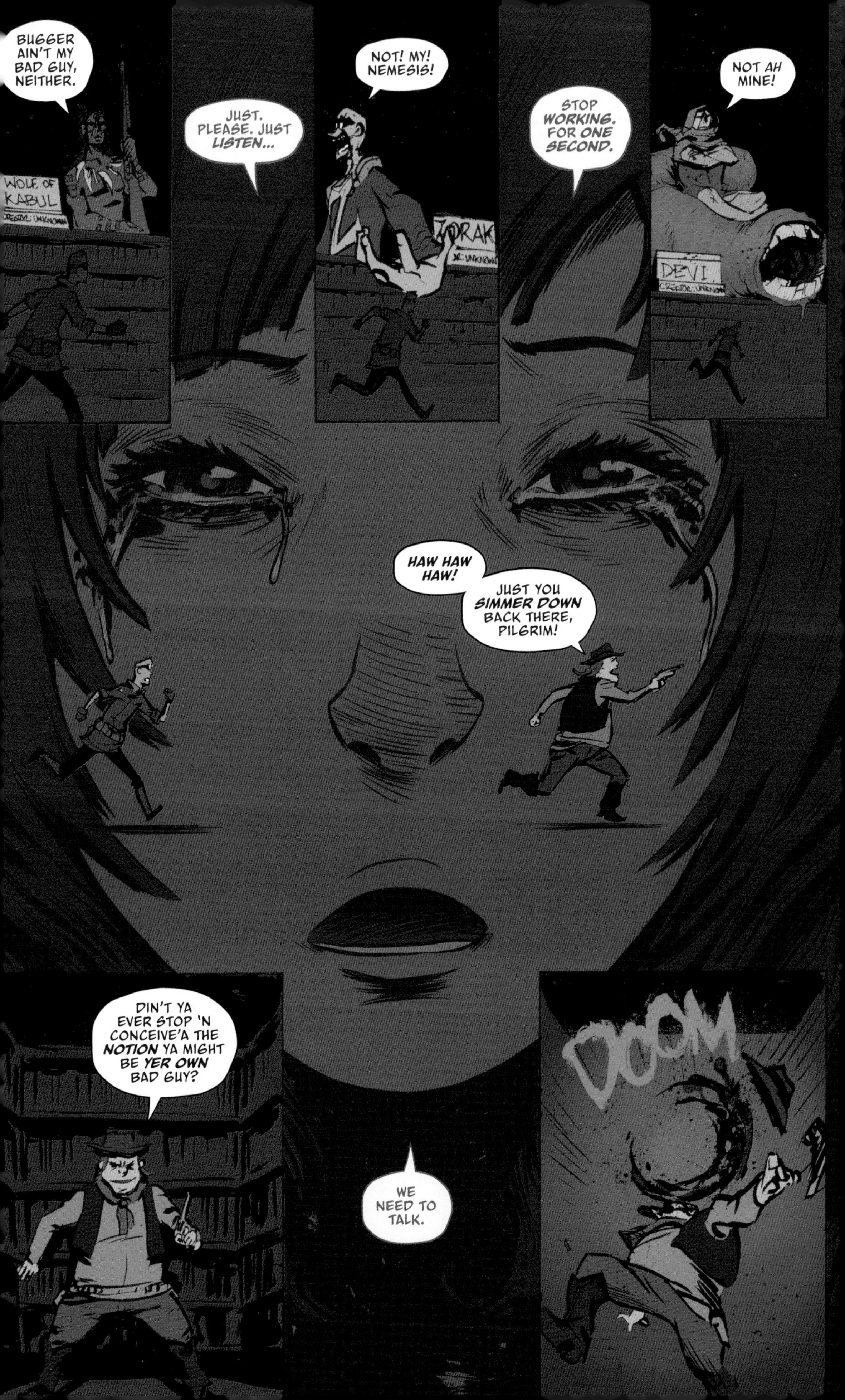
BUGGER AIN'T MY BAD GUY, NEITHER.
WOLF OF KABUL
CREATOR: UNKNOWN
JUST. PLEASE. JUST LISTEN...
NOT! MY! NEMESIS!
ZORAK
CR: UNKNOWN
STOP WORKING. FOR ONE SECOND.
NOT AH MINE!
DEVI.
CREATOR: UNKNOWN
HAW HAW HAW!
JUST YOU SIMMER DOWN BACK THERE, PILGRIM!
DIN'T YA EVER STOP 'N CONCEIVE'A THE NOTION YA MIGHT BE YER OWN BAD GUY?
WE NEED TO TALK.
DOOM

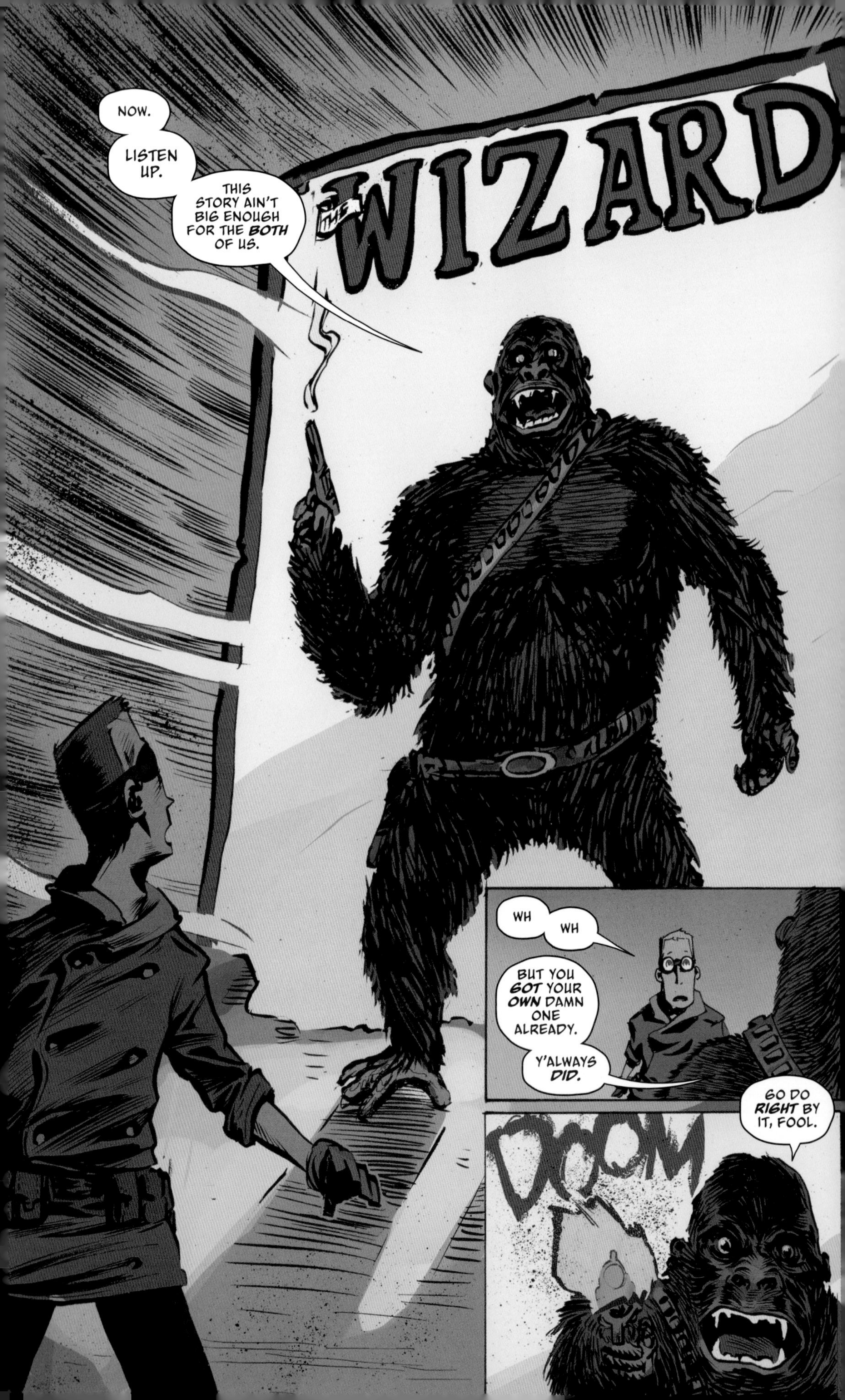

THE WIZARD
NOW.
LISTEN UP.
THIS STORY AIN'T BIG ENOUGH FOR THE BOTH OF US.
WH
WH
BUT YOU GOT YOUR OWN DAMN ONE ALREADY.
Y'ALWAYS DID.
GO DO RIGHT BY IT, FOOL.
DOOM

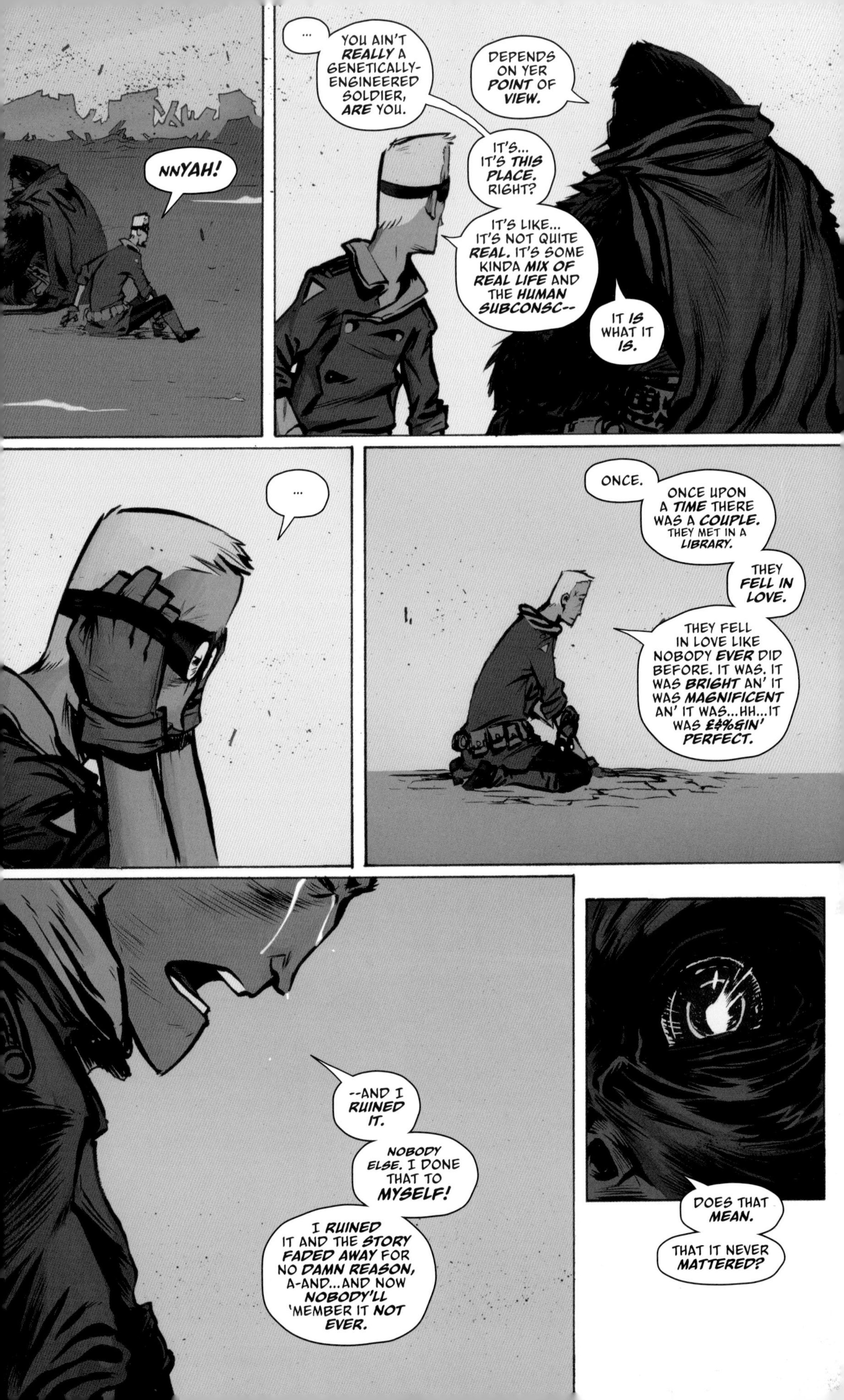
NNYAH!
...
YOU AIN'T REALLY A GENETICALLY-ENGINEERED SOLDIER, ARE YOU.
DEPENDS ON YER POINT OF VIEW.
IT'S... IT'S THIS PLACE. RIGHT?
IT'S LIKE... IT'S NOT QUITE REAL. IT'S SOME KINDA MIX OF REAL LIFE AND THE HUMAN SUBCONSC--
IT IS WHAT IT IS.
...
ONCE.
ONCE UPON A TIME THERE WAS A COUPLE. THEY MET IN A LIBRARY.
THEY FELL IN LOVE.
THEY FELL IN LOVE LIKE NOBODY EVER DID BEFORE. IT WAS. IT WAS BRIGHT AN' IT WAS MAGNIFICENT AN' IT WAS...HH...IT WAS £$%&IN' PERFECT.
--AND I RUINED IT.
NOBODY ELSE. I DONE THAT TO MYSELF!
I RUINED IT AND THE STORY FADED AWAY FOR NO DAMN REASON, A-AND...AND NOW NOBODY'LL 'MEMBER IT NOT EVER.
DOES THAT MEAN.
THAT IT NEVER MATTERED?

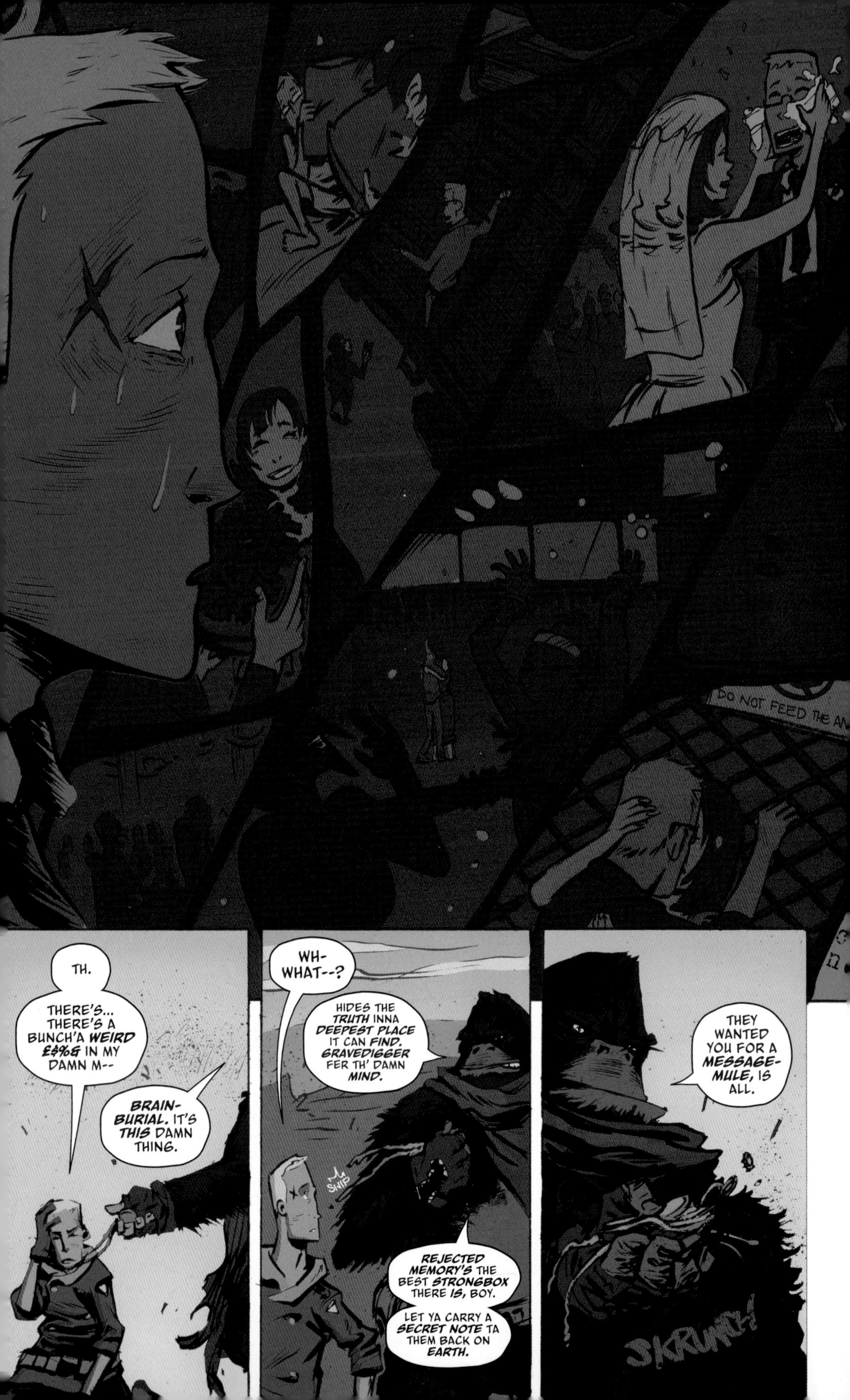
DO NOT FEED THE AN
TH.
THERE'S... THERE'S A BUNCH'A WEIRD £$%& IN MY DAMN M--
BRAIN-BURIAL. IT'S THIS DAMN THING.
WH-WHAT--?
HIDES THE TRUTH INNA DEEPEST PLACE IT CAN FIND. GRAVEDIGGER FER TH' DAMN MIND.
SNIP
REJECTED MEMORY'S THE BEST STRONGBOX THERE IS, BOY.
LET YA CARRY A SECRET NOTE TA THEM BACK ON EARTH.
THEY WANTED YOU FOR A MESSAGE-MULE, IS ALL.
SKRUNCH

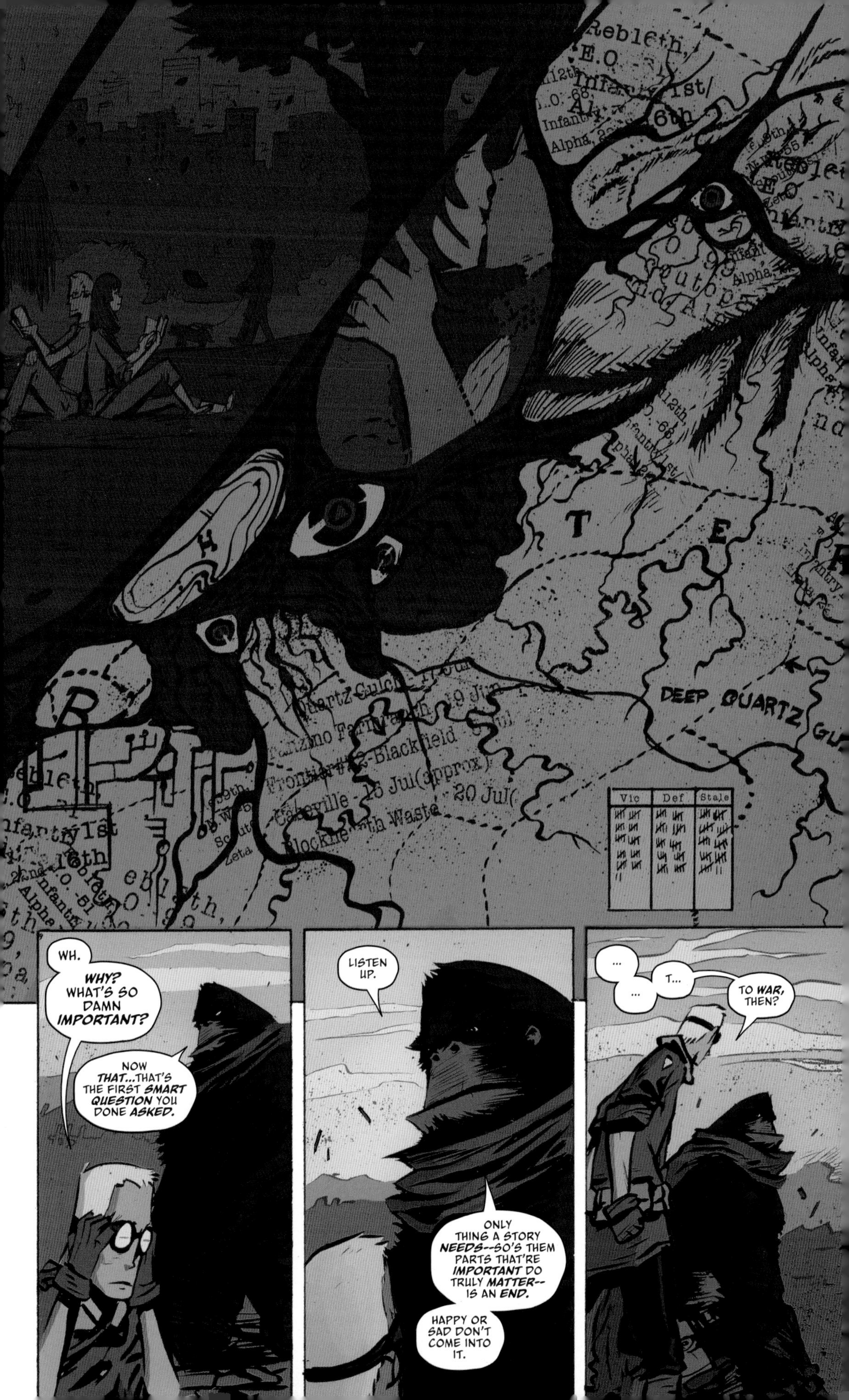
DEEP QUARTZ
Vic
Def
Stale
WH.
WHY? WHAT'S SO DAMN IMPORTANT?
NOW THAT...THAT'S THE FIRST SMART QUESTION YOU DONE ASKED.
LISTEN UP.
ONLY THING A STORY NEEDS--SO'S THEM PARTS THAT'RE IMPORTANT DO TRULY MATTER--IS AN END.
HAPPY OR SAD DON'T COME INTO IT.
...
...
T...
TO WAR, THEN?

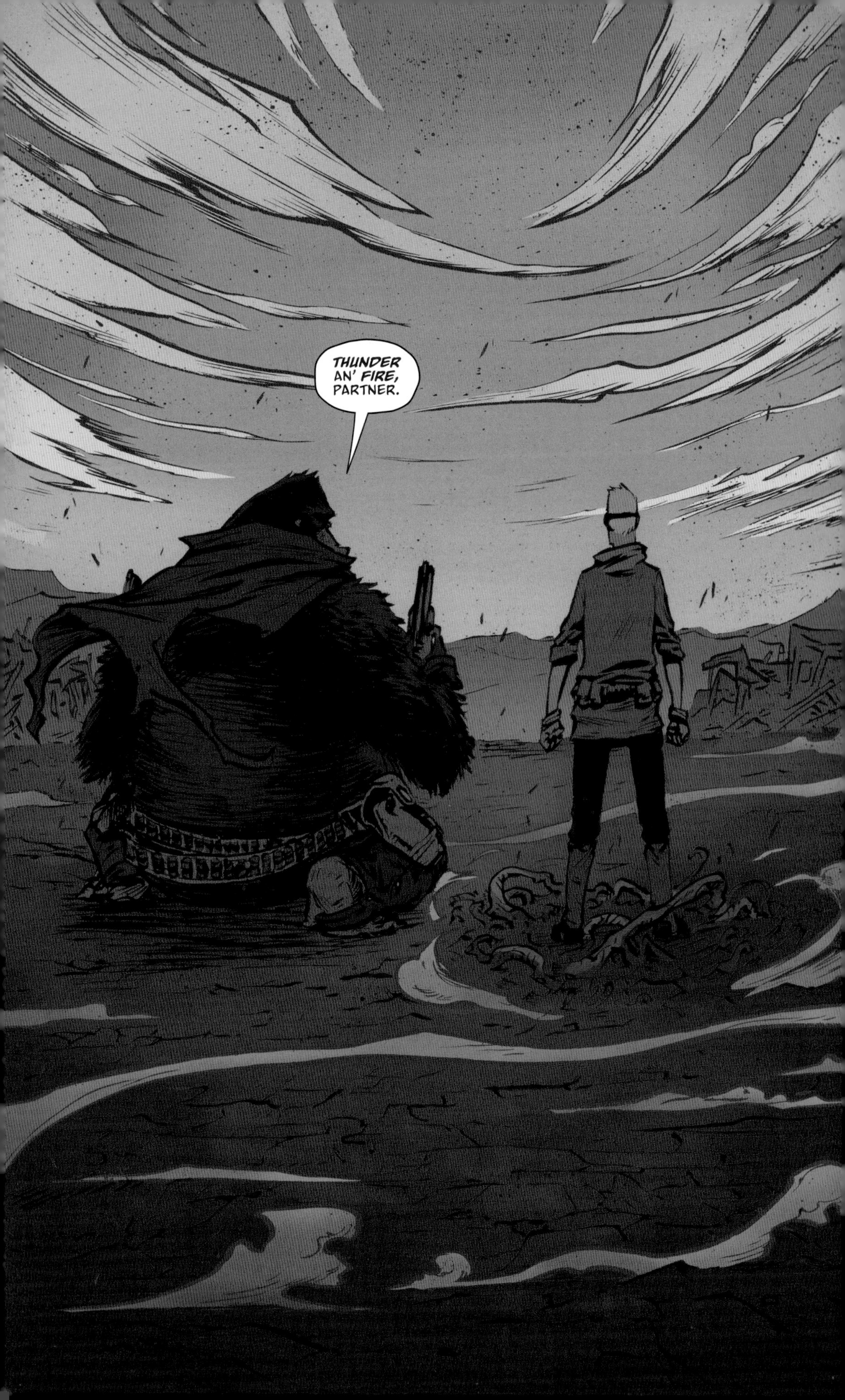
THUNDER AN' FIRE, PARTNER.

# CHAPTER SIX

# SIX-GUN GORILLA

(Continued from page 8.)

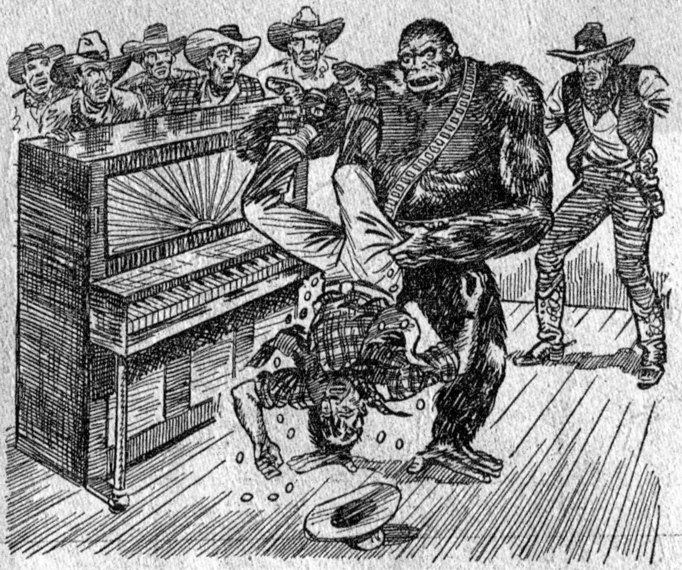



STAMPS.—300 different, including Airmail, beautiful uncommon sets, pictorials, Colonials. You'll be delighted. Price 6d. White, Stamps, Lye, Stourbridge.

ASTRID Packet Free.—Astrid (mourning) stamp, obsolete Morocco, Agencies (Windsor), fine set scarce Airmail, Belgium Tin Hat, Roumania (King Charles), 50 different, new large anniversary stamp. Remember we give 50% discount. Enclose 2d and request approvals. Robinson Bros. (D), Moreton, Wirral.

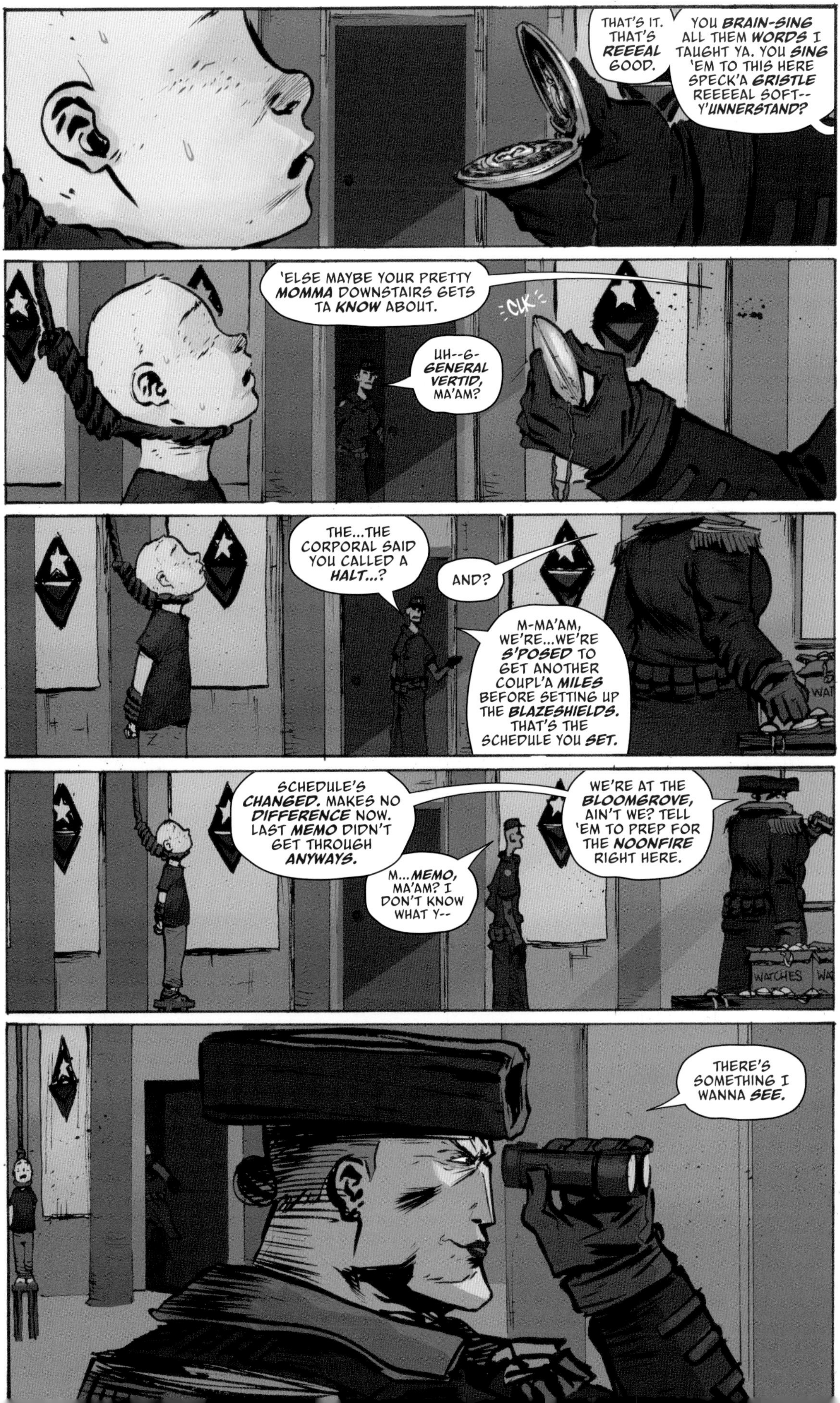
THAT'S IT. THAT'S REEEAL GOOD.
YOU BRAIN-SING ALL THEM WORDS I TAUGHT YA. YOU SING 'EM TO THIS HERE SPECK'A GRISTLE REEEEAL SOFT-- Y'UNNERSTAND?
'ELSE MAYBE YOUR PRETTY MOMMA DOWNSTAIRS GETS TA KNOW ABOUT.
CLK
UH--G-GENERAL VERTID, MA'AM?
THE...THE CORPORAL SAID YOU CALLED A HALT...?
AND?
M-MA'AM, WE'RE...WE'RE S'POSED TO GET ANOTHER COUPL'A MILES BEFORE SETTING UP THE BLAZESHIELDS. THAT'S THE SCHEDULE YOU SET.
SCHEDULE'S CHANGED. MAKES NO DIFFERENCE NOW. LAST MEMO DIDN'T GET THROUGH ANYWAYS.
M...MEMO, MA'AM? I DON'T KNOW WHAT Y--
WE'RE AT THE BLOOMGROVE, AIN'T WE? TELL 'EM TO PREP FOR THE NOONFIRE RIGHT HERE.
WATCHES
THERE'S SOMETHING I WANNA SEE.

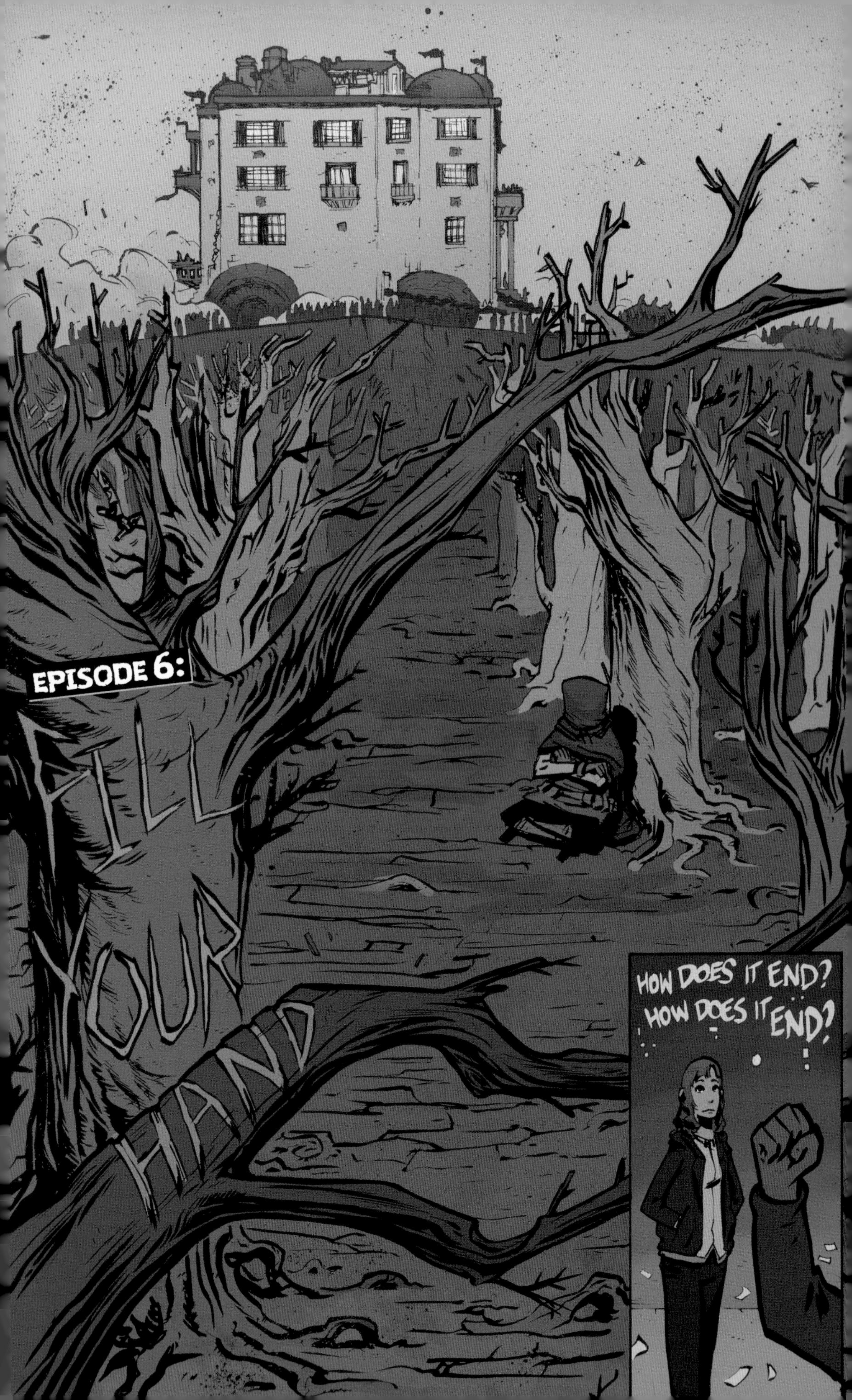
EPISODE 6:
FILL YOUR HAND
HOW DOES IT END?
HOW DOES IT END?

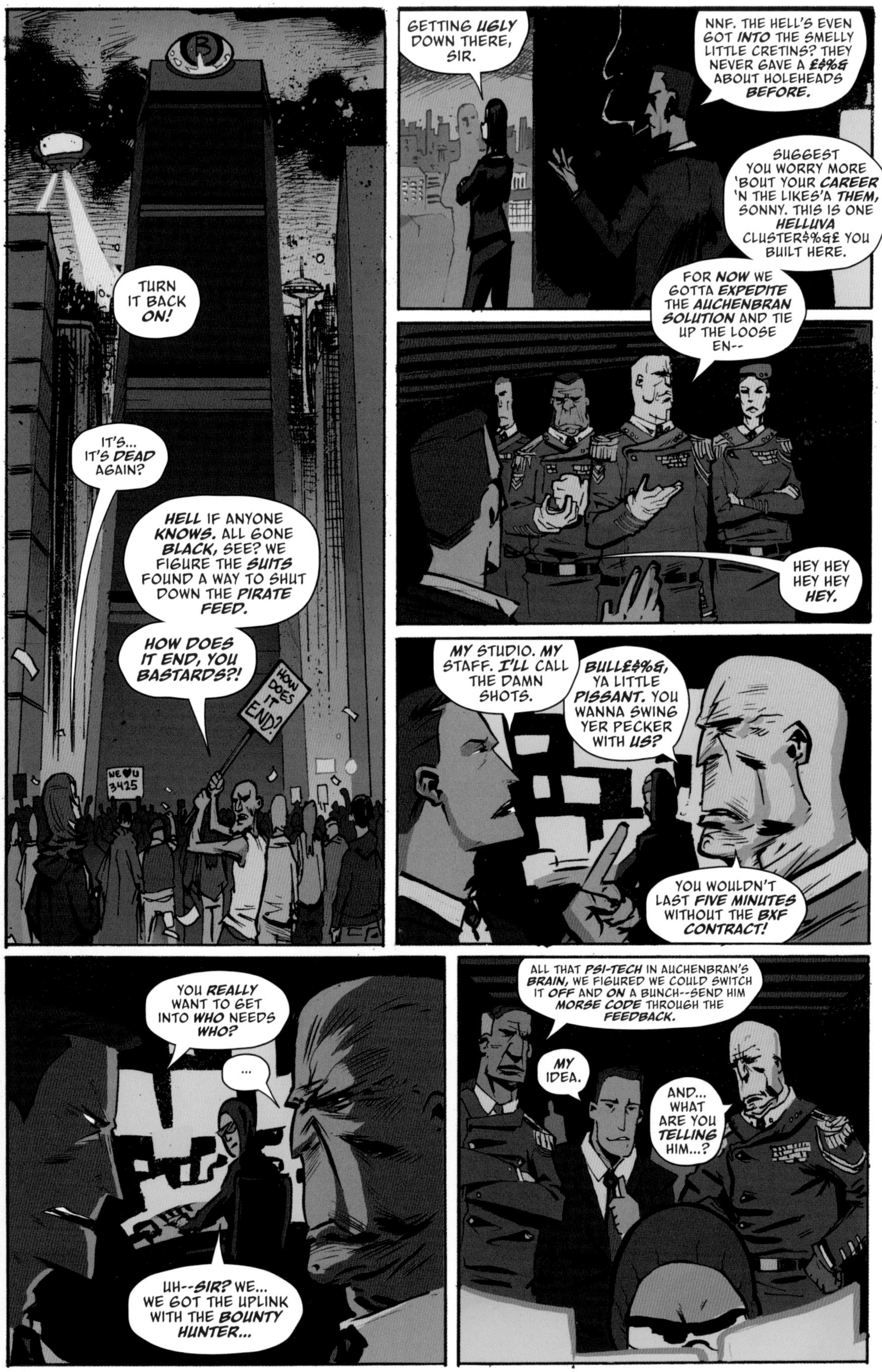
TURN IT BACK ON!
IT'S... IT'S DEAD AGAIN?
HELL IF ANYONE KNOWS. ALL GONE BLACK, SEE? WE FIGURE THE SUITS FOUND A WAY TO SHUT DOWN THE PIRATE FEED.
HOW DOES IT END, YOU BASTARDS?!
HOW DOES IT END?
WE ♥ U 3425
GETTING UGLY DOWN THERE, SIR.
NNF. THE HELL'S EVEN GOT INTO THE SMELLY LITTLE CRETINS? THEY NEVER GAVE A £$%G ABOUT HOLEHEADS BEFORE.
SUGGEST YOU WORRY MORE 'BOUT YOUR CAREER 'N THE LIKES'A THEM, SONNY. THIS IS ONE HELLUVA CLUSTER$%G£ YOU BUILT HERE.
FOR NOW WE GOTTA EXPEDITE THE AUCHENBRAN SOLUTION AND TIE UP THE LOOSE EN--
HEY HEY HEY HEY HEY.
MY STUDIO. MY STAFF. I'LL CALL THE DAMN SHOTS.
BULL£$%G, YA LITTLE PISSANT. YOU WANNA SWING YER PECKER WITH US?
YOU WOULDN'T LAST FIVE MINUTES WITHOUT THE BXF CONTRACT!
YOU REALLY WANT TO GET INTO WHO NEEDS WHO?
...
UH--SIR? WE... WE GOT THE UPLINK WITH THE BOUNTY HUNTER...
ALL THAT PSI-TECH IN AUCHENBRAN'S BRAIN, WE FIGURED WE COULD SWITCH IT OFF AND ON A BUNCH--SEND HIM MORSE CODE THROUGH THE FEEDBACK.
MY IDEA.
AND... WHAT ARE YOU TELLING HIM...?

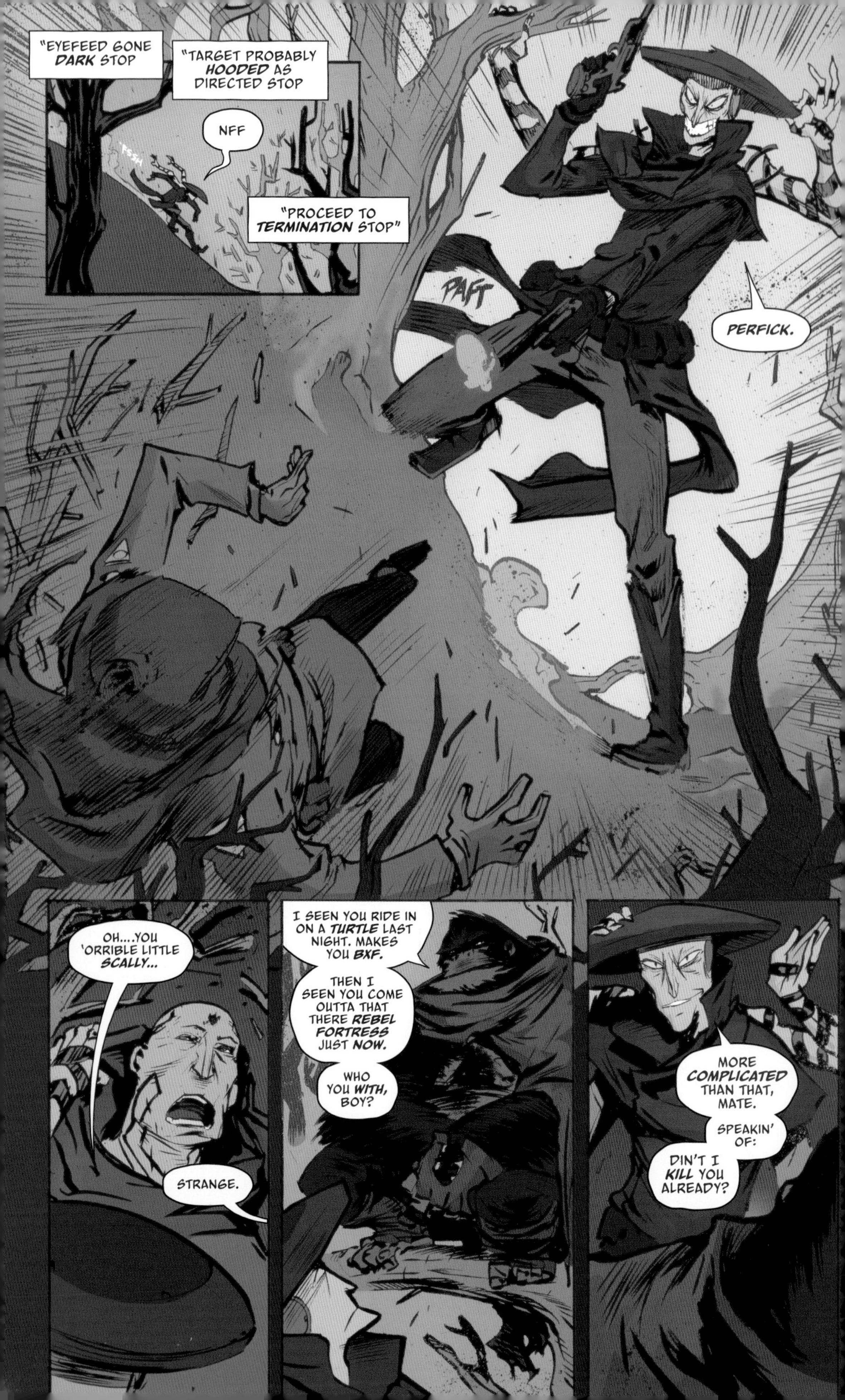

"EYEFEED GONE DARK STOP
"TARGET PROBABLY HOODED AS DIRECTED STOP
NFF
"PROCEED TO TERMINATION STOP"
PAFT
PERFICK.
OH....YOU 'ORRIBLE LITTLE SCALLY...
STRANGE.
I SEEN YOU RIDE IN ON A TURTLE LAST NIGHT. MAKES YOU BXF.
THEN I SEEN YOU COME OUTTA THAT THERE REBEL FORTRESS JUST NOW.
WHO YOU WITH, BOY?
MORE COMPLICATED THAN THAT, MATE.
SPEAKIN' OF:
DIN'T I KILL YOU ALREADY?

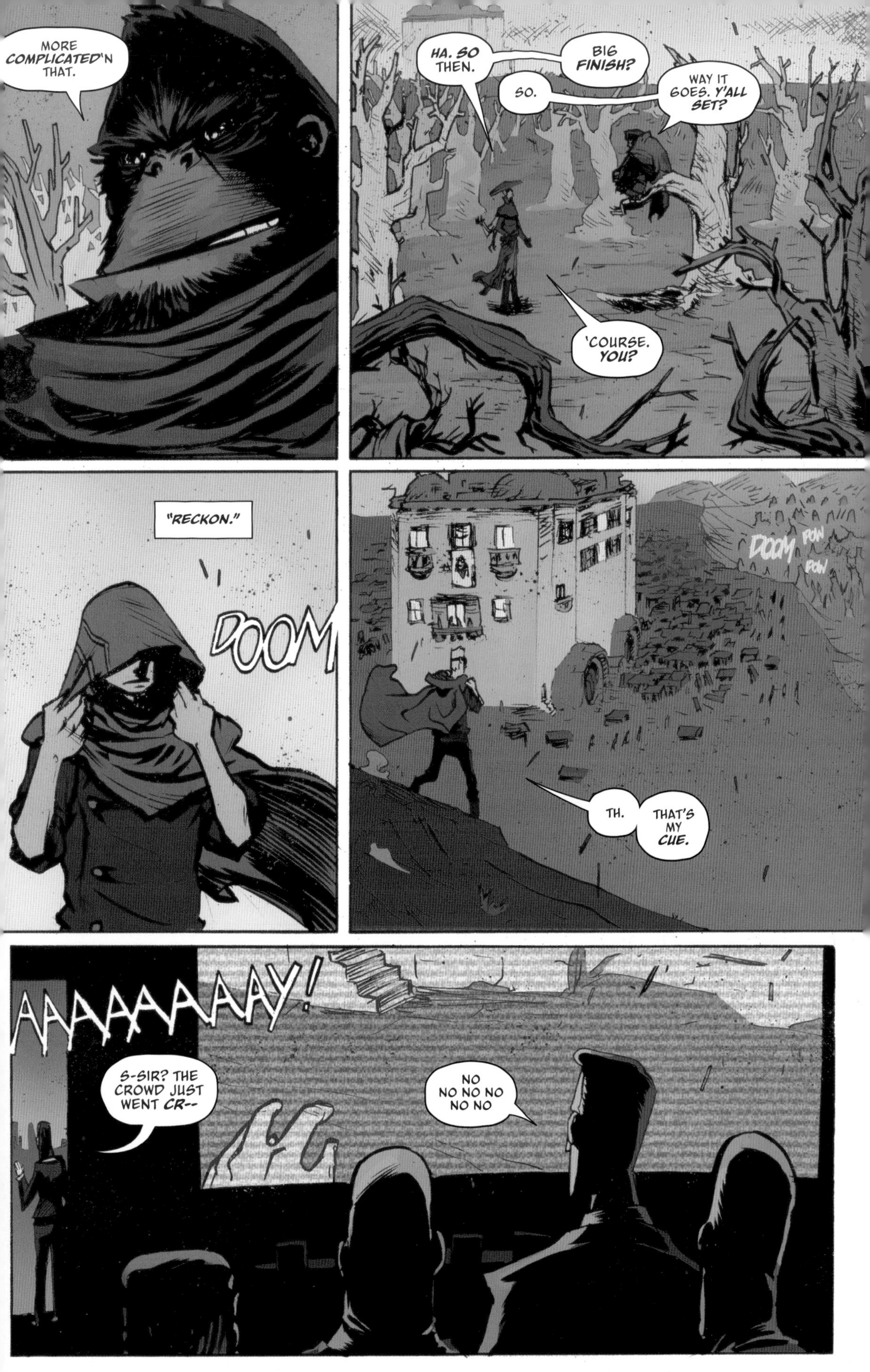
MORE COMPLICATED'N THAT.
HA. SO THEN.
BIG FINISH?
SO.
WAY IT GOES. Y'ALL SET?
'COURSE. YOU?
"RECKON."
DOOM
DOOM
POW
POW
TH.
THAT'S MY CUE.
AAAAAAAAY!
S-SIR? THE CROWD JUST WENT CR--
NO
NO NO NO
NO NO

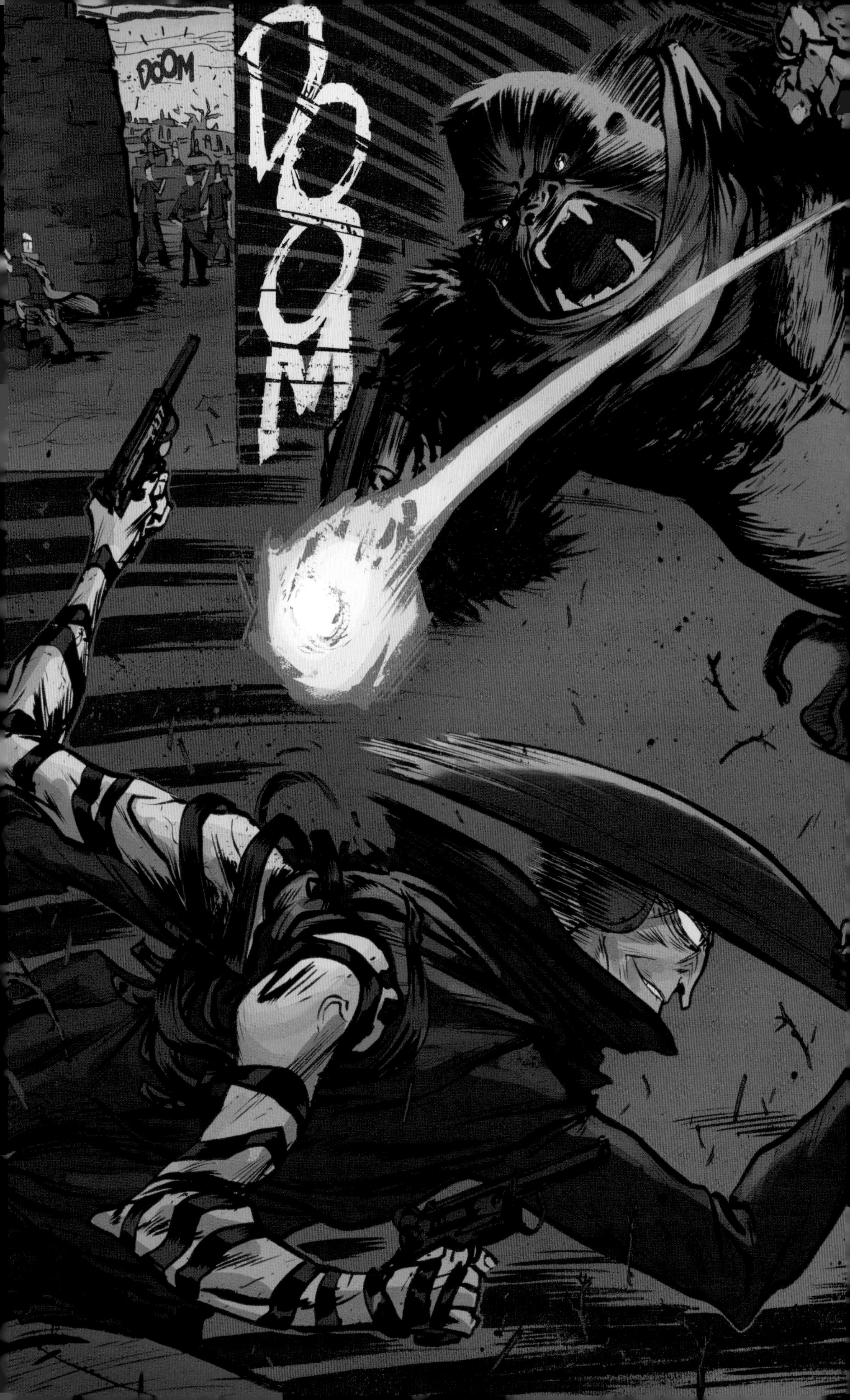
DOOM
DOOM

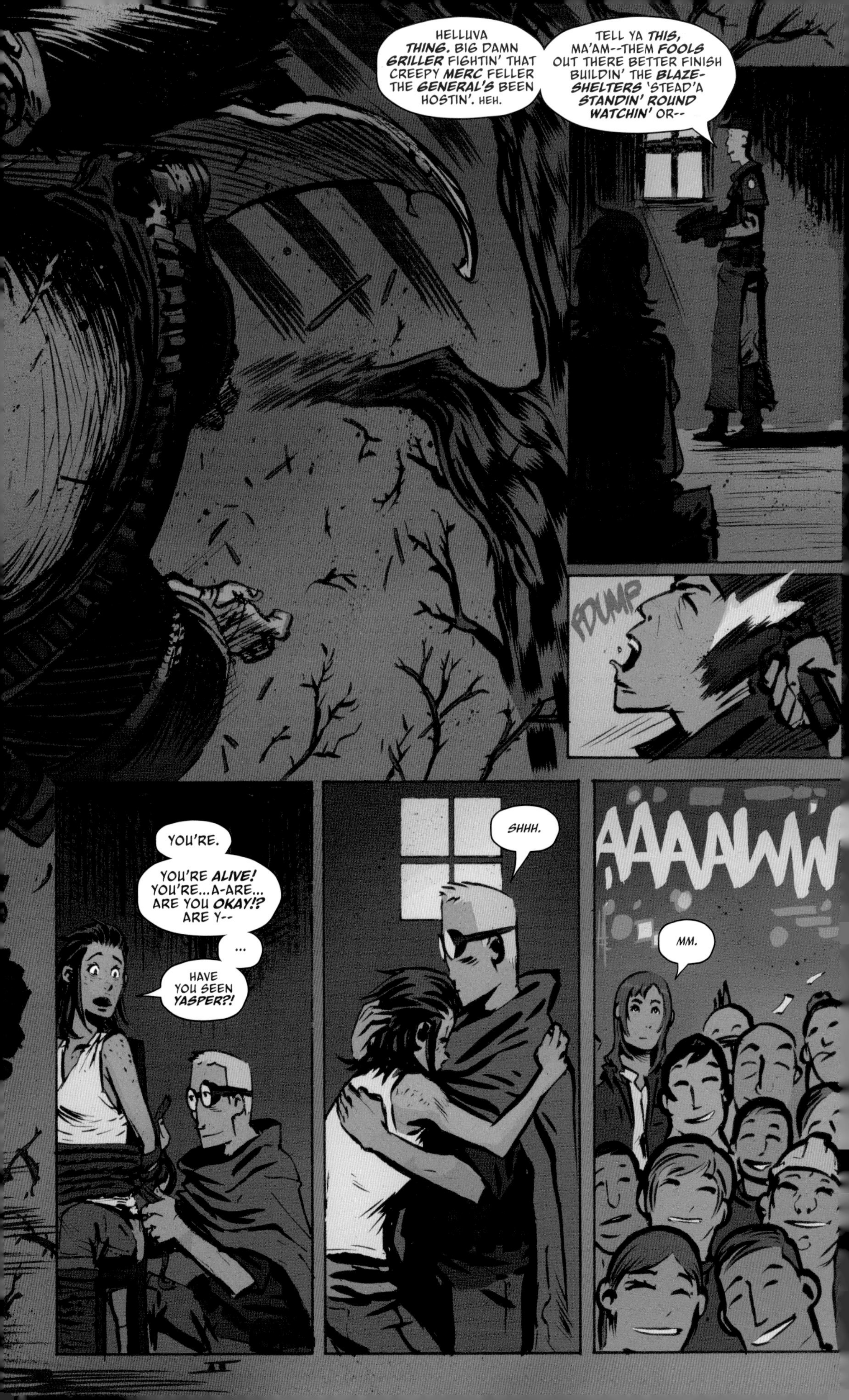
HELLUVA THING. BIG DAMN GRILLER FIGHTIN' THAT CREEPY MERC FELLER THE GENERAL'S BEEN HOSTIN'. HEH.
TELL YA THIS, MA'AM--THEM FOOLS OUT THERE BETTER FINISH BUILDIN' THE BLAZE-SHELTERS 'STEAD'A STANDIN' ROUND WATCHIN' OR--
FDUMP
YOU'RE.
YOU'RE ALIVE! YOU'RE...A-ARE... ARE YOU OKAY!? ARE Y--
...
HAVE YOU SEEN YASPER?!
SHHH.
AAAAWW
MM.

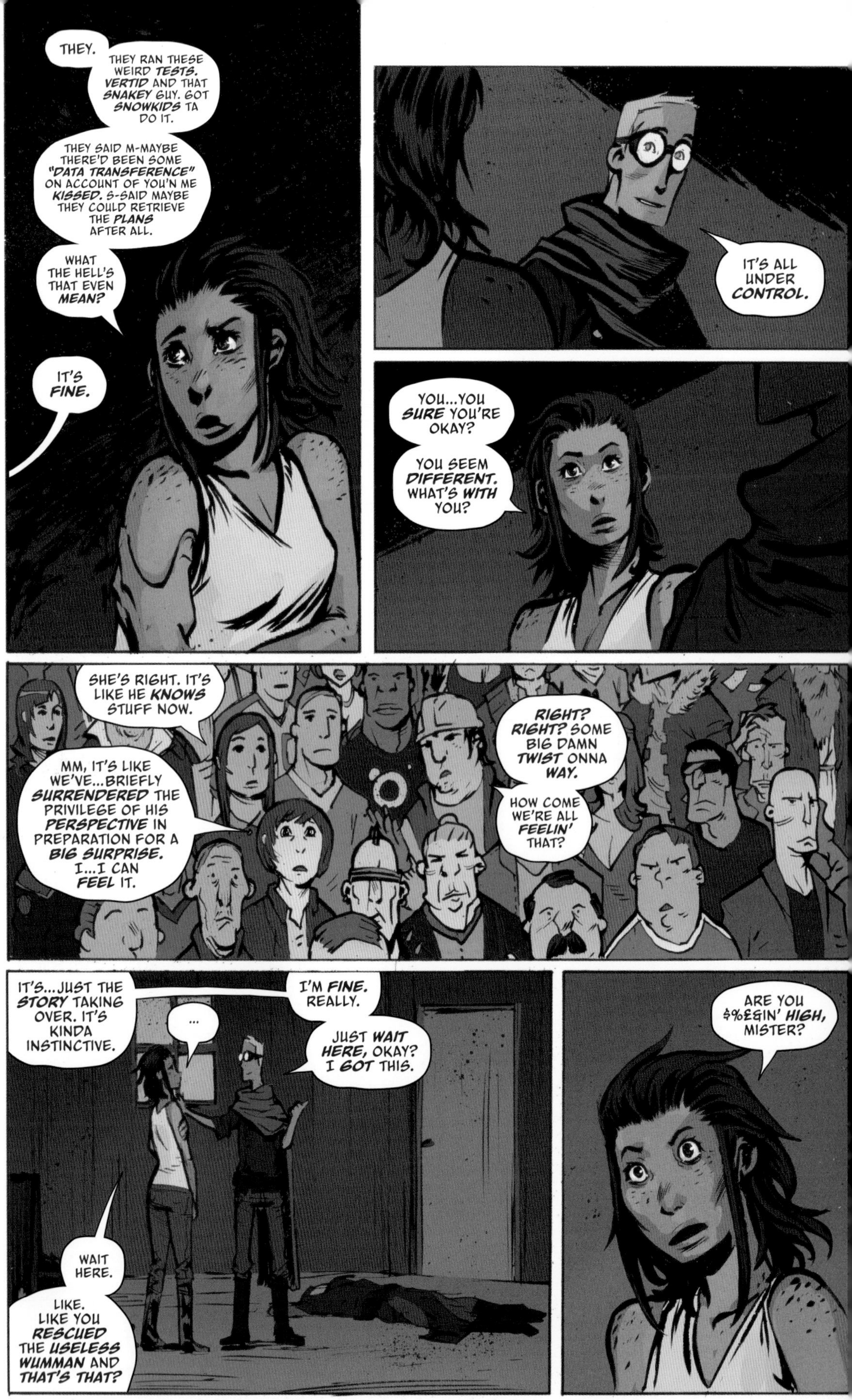
THEY.
THEY RAN THESE WEIRD TESTS. VERTID AND THAT SNAKEY GUY. GOT SNOWKIDS TA DO IT.
THEY SAID M-MAYBE THERE'D BEEN SOME "DATA TRANSFERENCE" ON ACCOUNT OF YOU'N ME KISSED. S-SAID MAYBE THEY COULD RETRIEVE THE PLANS AFTER ALL.
WHAT THE HELL'S THAT EVEN MEAN?
IT'S FINE.
IT'S ALL UNDER CONTROL.
YOU...YOU SURE YOU'RE OKAY?
YOU SEEM DIFFERENT. WHAT'S WITH YOU?
SHE'S RIGHT. IT'S LIKE HE KNOWS STUFF NOW.
MM, IT'S LIKE WE'VE...BRIEFLY SURRENDERED THE PRIVILEGE OF HIS PERSPECTIVE IN PREPARATION FOR A BIG SURPRISE. I...I CAN FEEL IT.
RIGHT? RIGHT? SOME BIG DAMN TWIST ONNA WAY.
HOW COME WE'RE ALL FEELIN' THAT?
IT'S...JUST THE STORY TAKING OVER. IT'S KINDA INSTINCTIVE.
...
I'M FINE. REALLY.
JUST WAIT HERE, OKAY? I GOT THIS.
WAIT HERE.
LIKE. LIKE YOU RESCUED THE USELESS WUMMAN AND THAT'S THAT?
ARE YOU $%£&IN' HIGH, MISTER?

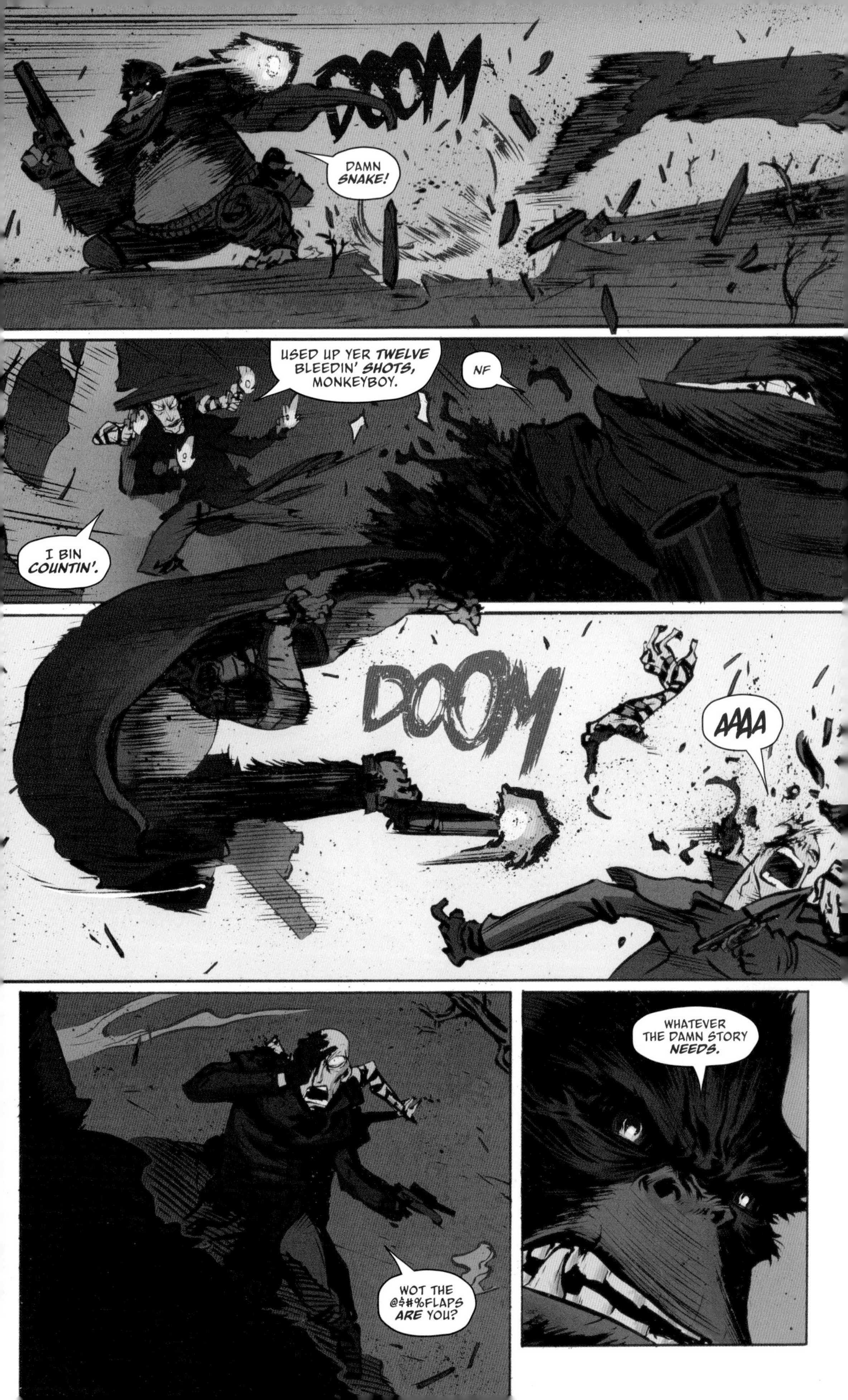
DOOM
DAMN SNAKE!
USED UP YER TWELVE BLEEDIN' SHOTS, MONKEYBOY.
NF
I BIN COUNTIN'.
DOOM
AAAA
WOT THE @$#%FLAPS ARE YOU?
WHATEVER THE DAMN STORY NEEDS.

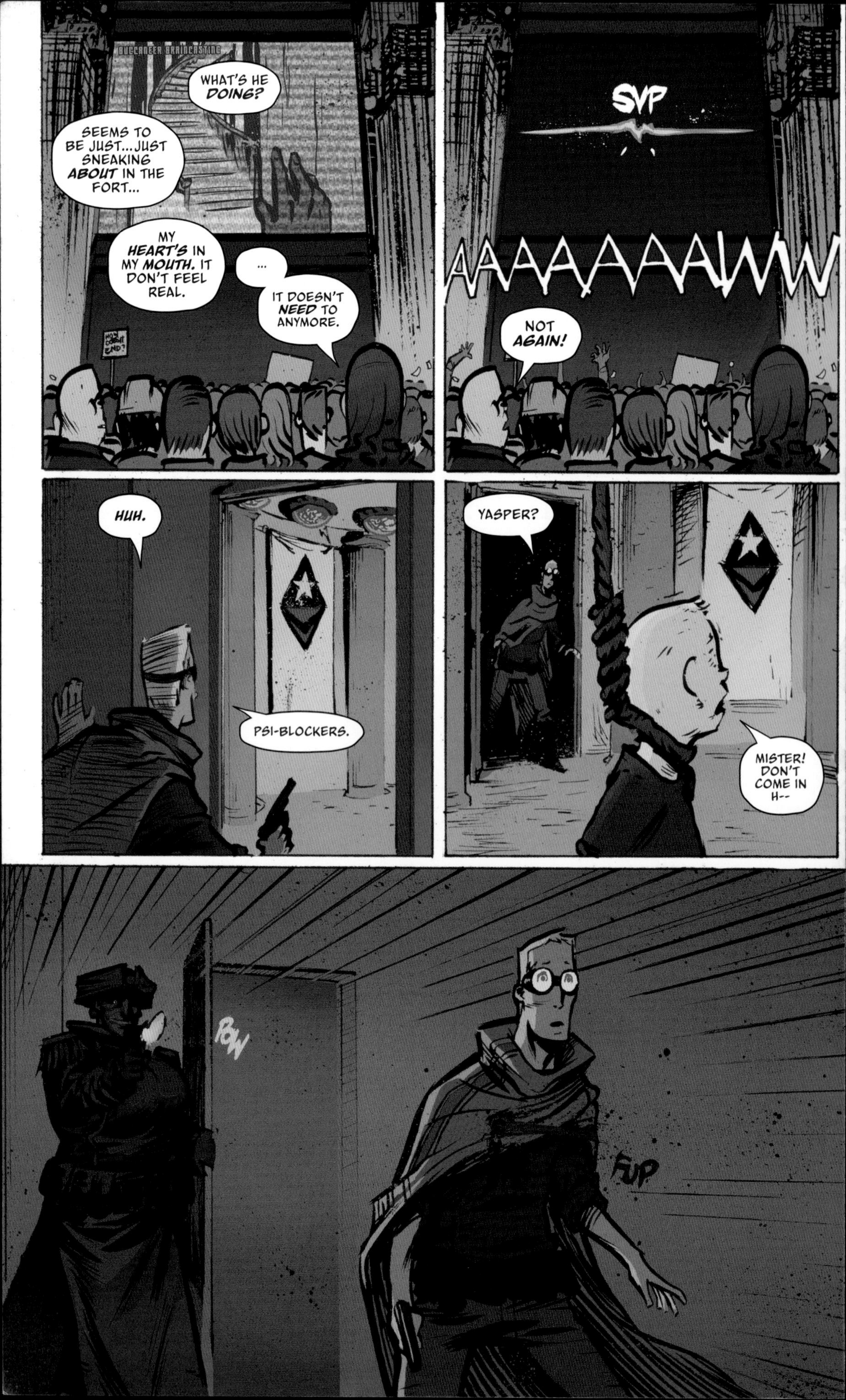
BUCCANEER BRAINCASTING
WHAT'S HE DOING?
SEEMS TO BE JUST...JUST SNEAKING ABOUT IN THE FORT...
MY HEART'S IN MY MOUTH. IT DON'T FEEL REAL.
...
IT DOESN'T NEED TO ANYMORE.
SVP
AAAAAAAWW
NOT AGAIN!
HUH.
PSI-BLOCKERS.
YASPER?
MISTER! DON'T COME IN H--
POW
FUP

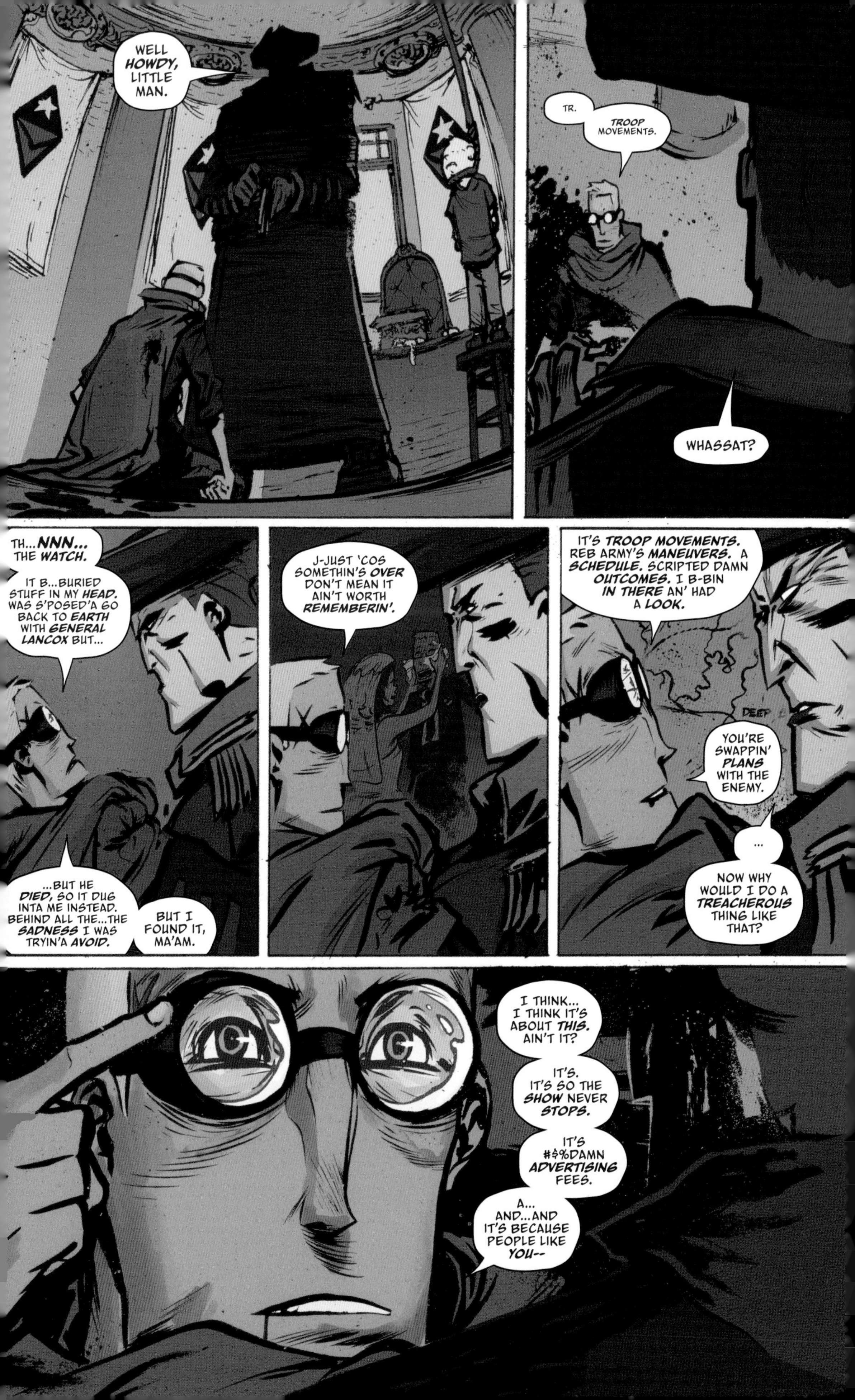
WELL HOWDY, LITTLE MAN.
TR.
TROOP MOVEMENTS.
WHASSAT?
TH...NNN... THE WATCH.
IT B...BURIED STUFF IN MY HEAD. WAS S'POSED'A GO BACK TO EARTH WITH GENERAL LANCOX BUT...
...BUT HE DIED, SO IT DUG INTA ME INSTEAD. BEHIND ALL THE...THE SADNESS I WAS TRYIN'A AVOID.
BUT I FOUND IT, MA'AM.
J-JUST 'COS SOMETHIN'S OVER DON'T MEAN IT AIN'T WORTH REMEMBERIN'.
IT'S TROOP MOVEMENTS. REB ARMY'S MANEUVERS. A SCHEDULE. SCRIPTED DAMN OUTCOMES. I B-BIN IN THERE AN' HAD A LOOK.
DEEP
YOU'RE SWAPPIN' PLANS WITH THE ENEMY.
...
NOW WHY WOULD I DO A TREACHEROUS THING LIKE THAT?
I THINK... I THINK IT'S ABOUT THIS. AIN'T IT?
IT'S. IT'S SO THE SHOW NEVER STOPS.
IT'S #$%DAMN ADVERTISING FEES.
A... AND...AND IT'S BECAUSE PEOPLE LIKE YOU--

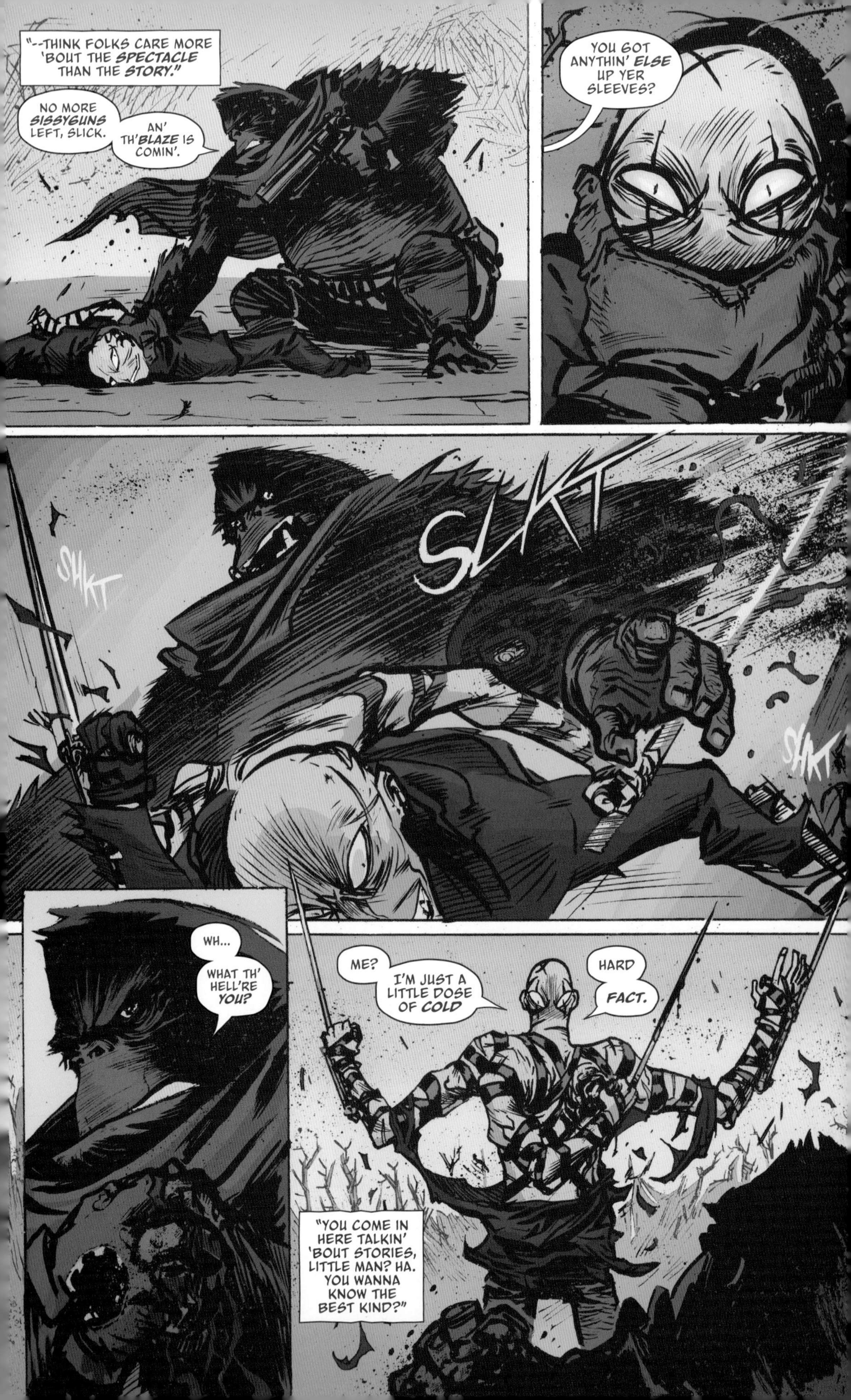
"--THINK FOLKS CARE MORE 'BOUT THE SPECTACLE THAN THE STORY."
NO MORE SISSYGUNS LEFT, SLICK.
AN' TH'BLAZE IS COMIN'.
YOU GOT ANYTHIN' ELSE UP YER SLEEVES?
SHKT
SLKT
SHKT
WH...
WHAT TH' HELL'RE YOU?
ME?
I'M JUST A LITTLE DOSE OF COLD
HARD FACT.
"YOU COME IN HERE TALKIN' 'BOUT STORIES, LITTLE MAN? HA. YOU WANNA KNOW THE BEST KIND?"

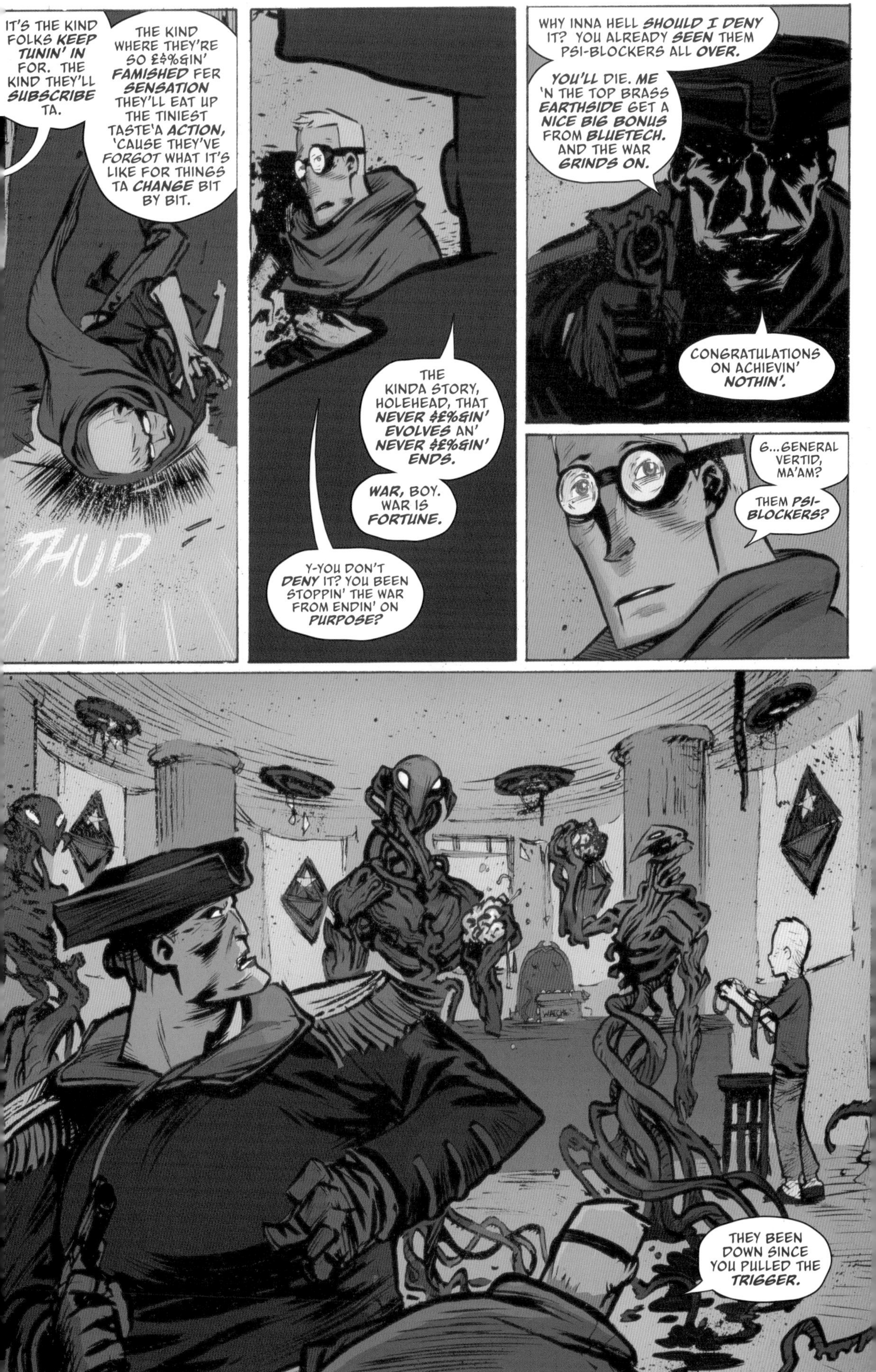
IT'S THE KIND FOLKS KEEP TUNIN' IN FOR. THE KIND THEY'LL SUBSCRIBE TA.
THE KIND WHERE THEY'RE SO £$%&GIN' FAMISHED FER SENSATION THEY'LL EAT UP THE TINIEST TASTE'A ACTION, 'CAUSE THEY'VE FORGOT WHAT IT'S LIKE FOR THINGS TA CHANGE BIT BY BIT.
THUD
THE KINDA STORY, HOLEHEAD, THAT NEVER $£%&GIN' EVOLVES AN' NEVER $£%&GIN' ENDS.
WAR, BOY. WAR IS FORTUNE.
Y-YOU DON'T DENY IT? YOU BEEN STOPPIN' THE WAR FROM ENDIN' ON PURPOSE?
WHY INNA HELL SHOULD I DENY IT? YOU ALREADY SEEN THEM PSI-BLOCKERS ALL OVER.
YOU'LL DIE. ME 'N THE TOP BRASS EARTHSIDE GET A NICE BIG BONUS FROM BLUETECH. AND THE WAR GRINDS ON.
CONGRATULATIONS ON ACHIEVIN' NOTHIN'.
G...GENERAL VERTID, MA'AM?
THEM PSI-BLOCKERS?
THEY BEEN DOWN SINCE YOU PULLED THE TRIGGER.

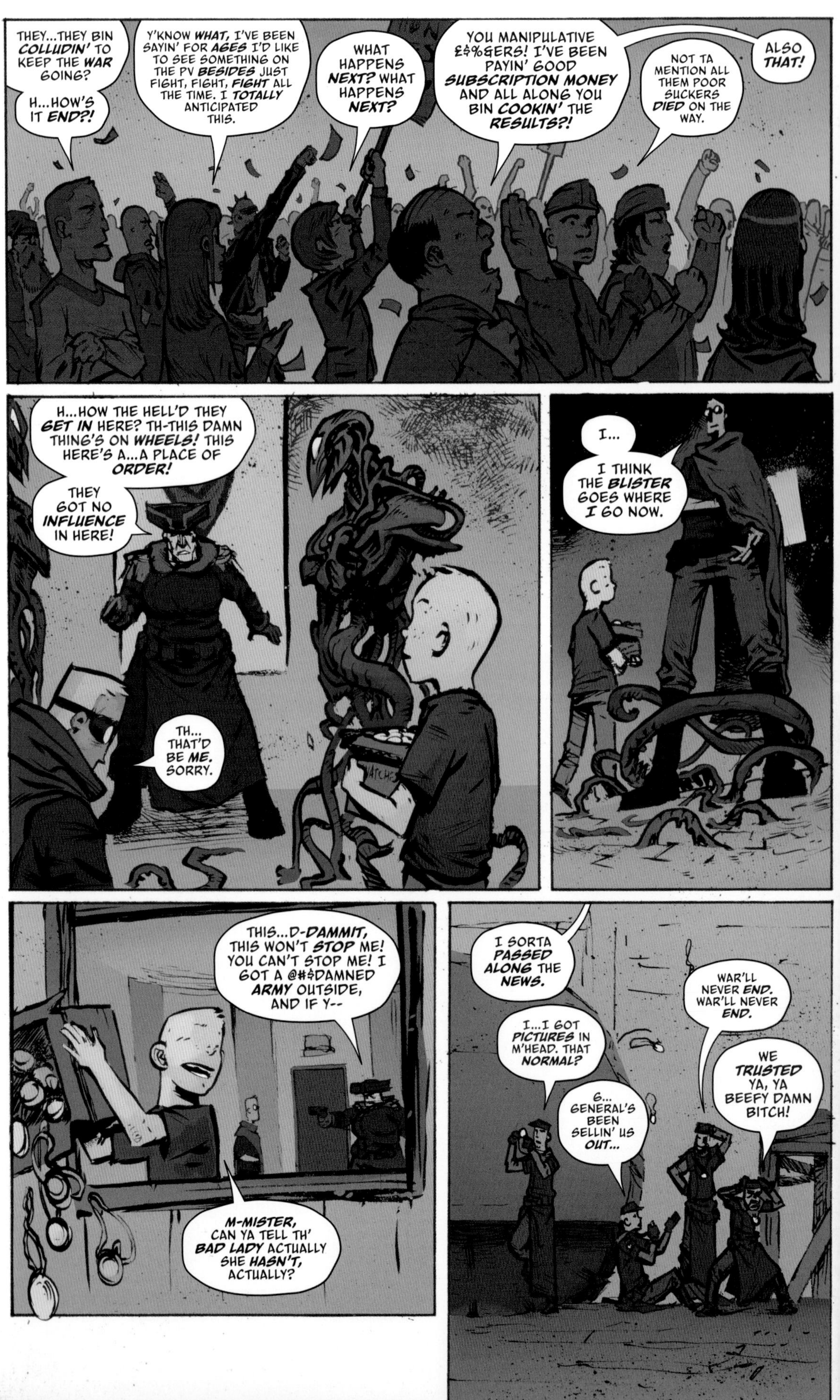
THEY...THEY BIN COLLUDIN' TO KEEP THE WAR GOING?
H...HOW'S IT END?!
Y'KNOW WHAT, I'VE BEEN SAYIN' FOR AGES I'D LIKE TO SEE SOMETHING ON THE PV BESIDES JUST FIGHT, FIGHT, FIGHT ALL THE TIME. I TOTALLY ANTICIPATED THIS.
WHAT HAPPENS NEXT? WHAT HAPPENS NEXT?
YOU MANIPULATIVE £$%&ERS! I'VE BEEN PAYIN' GOOD SUBSCRIPTION MONEY AND ALL ALONG YOU BIN COOKIN' THE RESULTS?!
ALSO THAT!
NOT TA MENTION ALL THEM POOR SUCKERS DIED ON THE WAY.
H...HOW THE HELL'D THEY GET IN HERE? TH-THIS DAMN THING'S ON WHEELS! THIS HERE'S A...A PLACE OF ORDER!
THEY GOT NO INFLUENCE IN HERE!
TH... THAT'D BE ME. SORRY.
I...
I THINK THE BLISTER GOES WHERE I GO NOW.
THIS...D-DAMMIT, THIS WON'T STOP ME! YOU CAN'T STOP ME! I GOT A @#$DAMNED ARMY OUTSIDE, AND IF Y--
M-MISTER, CAN YA TELL TH' BAD LADY ACTUALLY SHE HASN'T, ACTUALLY?
I SORTA PASSED ALONG THE NEWS.
I...I GOT PICTURES IN M'HEAD. THAT NORMAL?
G... GENERAL'S BEEN SELLIN' US OUT...
WAR'LL NEVER END. WAR'LL NEVER END.
WE TRUSTED YA, YA BEEFY DAMN BITCH!

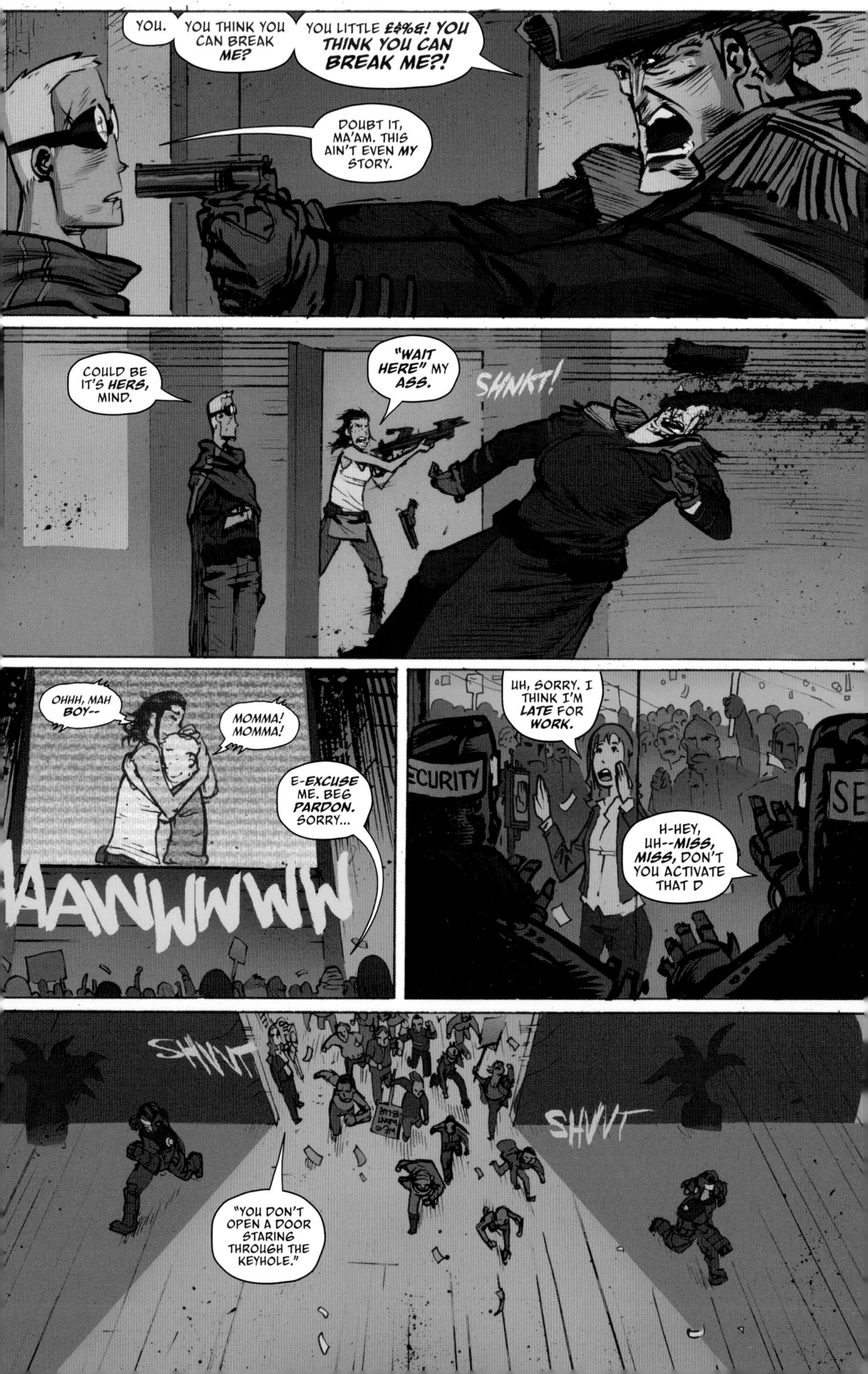
YOU.
YOU THINK YOU CAN BREAK ME?
YOU LITTLE £$%&! YOU THINK YOU CAN BREAK ME?!
DOUBT IT, MA'AM. THIS AIN'T EVEN MY STORY.
COULD BE IT'S HERS, MIND.
"WAIT HERE" MY ASS.
SHNKT!
OHHH, MAH BOY--
MOMMA! MOMMA!
AAWWWWW
E-EXCUSE ME. BEG PARDON. SORRY...
UH, SORRY. I THINK I'M LATE FOR WORK.
SECURITY
H-HEY, UH--MISS, MISS, DON'T YOU ACTIVATE THAT D
SHVVT
SHVVT
"YOU DON'T OPEN A DOOR STARING THROUGH THE KEYHOLE."

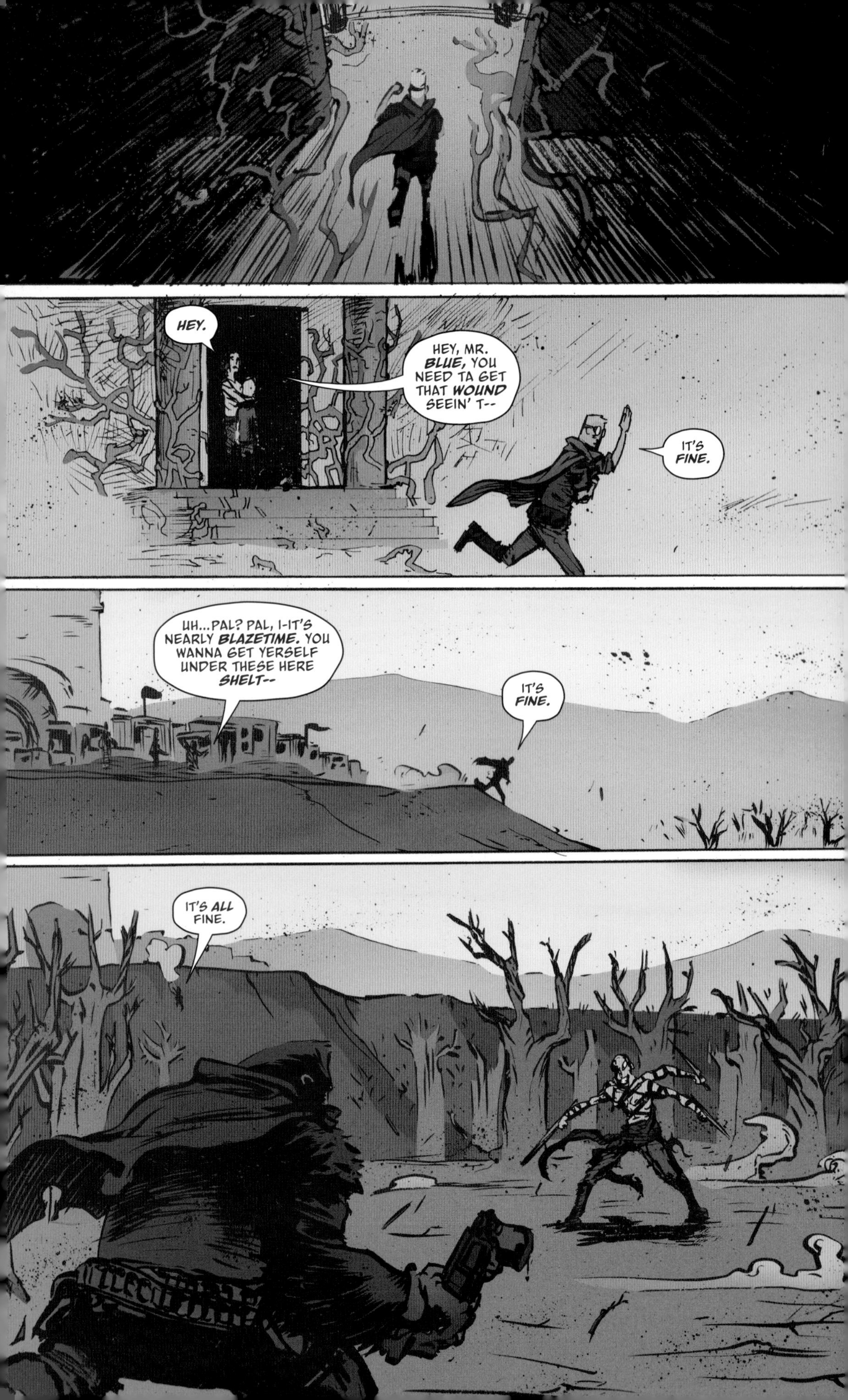
HEY.
HEY, MR. BLUE, YOU NEED TA GET THAT WOUND SEEIN' T--
IT'S FINE.
UH...PAL? PAL, I-IT'S NEARLY BLAZETIME. YOU WANNA GET YERSELF UNDER THESE HERE SHELT--
IT'S FINE.
IT'S ALL FINE.

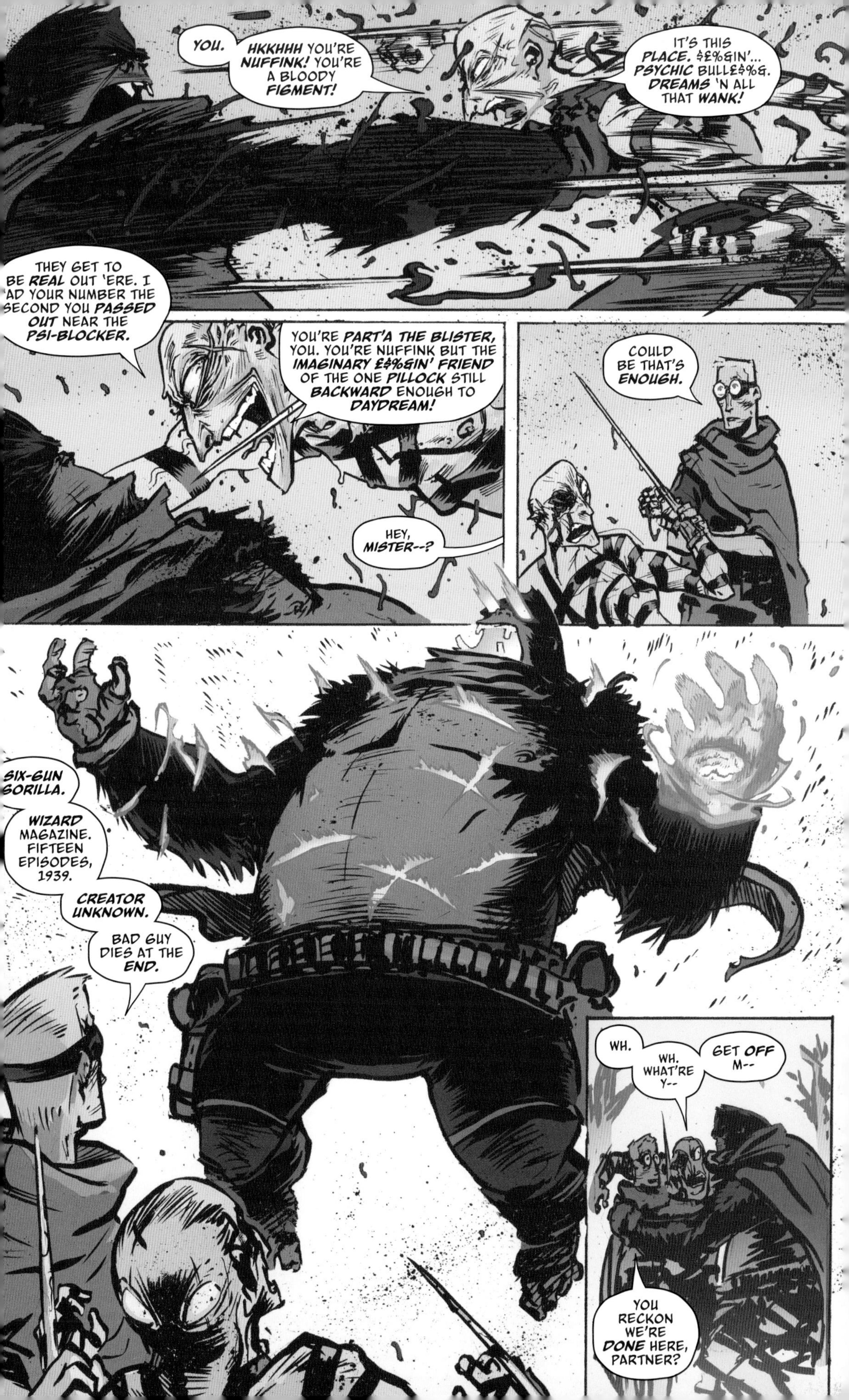
YOU.
HKKHHH YOU'RE NUFFINK! YOU'RE A BLOODY FIGMENT!
IT'S THIS PLACE. $£%&IN'... PSYCHIC BULL£$%&. DREAMS 'N ALL THAT WANK!
THEY GET TO BE REAL OUT 'ERE. I 'AD YOUR NUMBER THE SECOND YOU PASSED OUT NEAR THE PSI-BLOCKER.
YOU'RE PART'A THE BLISTER, YOU. YOU'RE NUFFINK BUT THE IMAGINARY £$%&IN' FRIEND OF THE ONE PILLOCK STILL BACKWARD ENOUGH TO DAYDREAM!
HEY, MISTER--?
COULD BE THAT'S ENOUGH.
SIX-GUN GORILLA.
WIZARD MAGAZINE. FIFTEEN EPISODES, 1939.
CREATOR UNKNOWN.
BAD GUY DIES AT THE END.
WH.
WH. WHAT'RE Y--
GET OFF M--
YOU RECKON WE'RE DONE HERE, PARTNER?

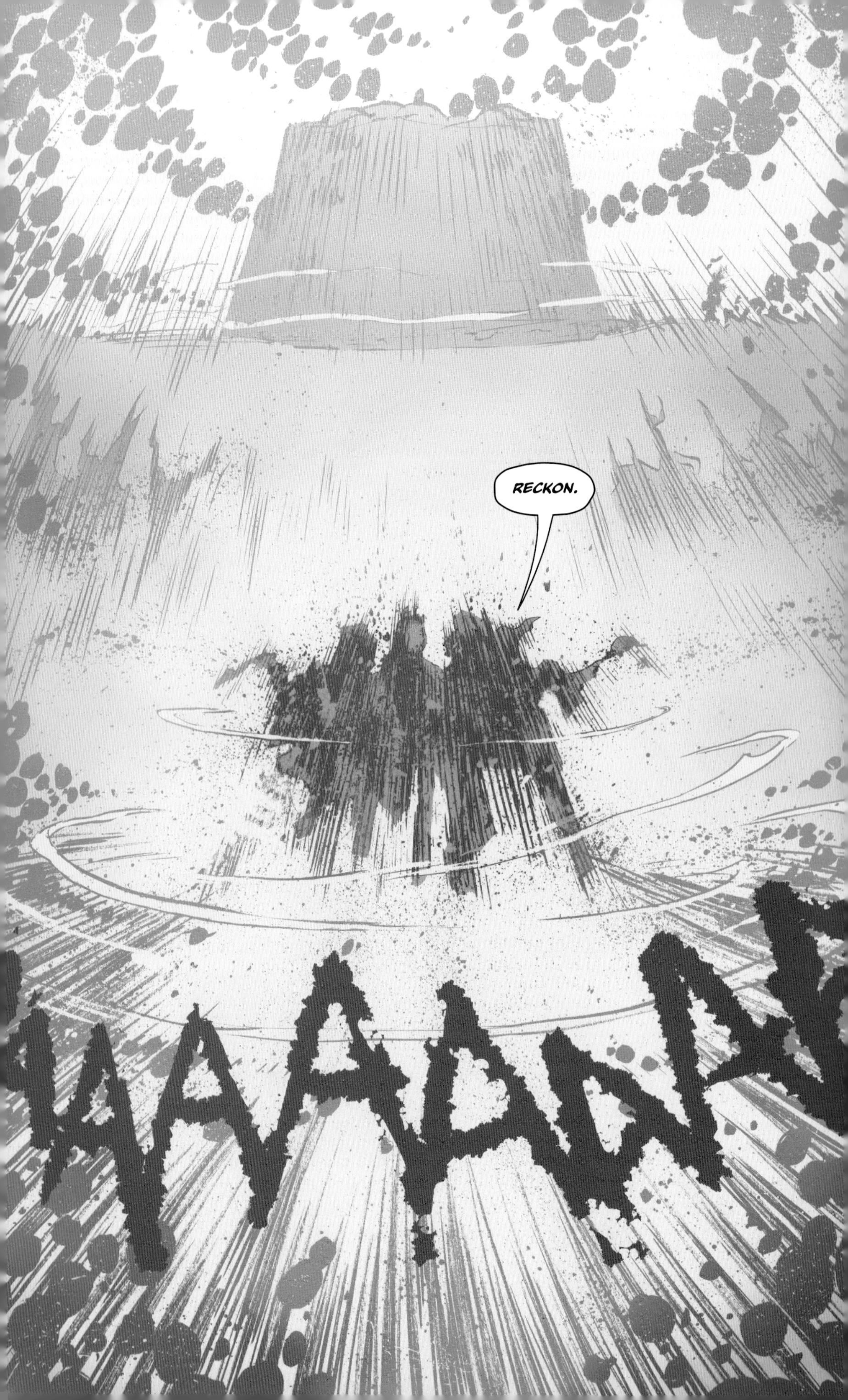
RECKON.

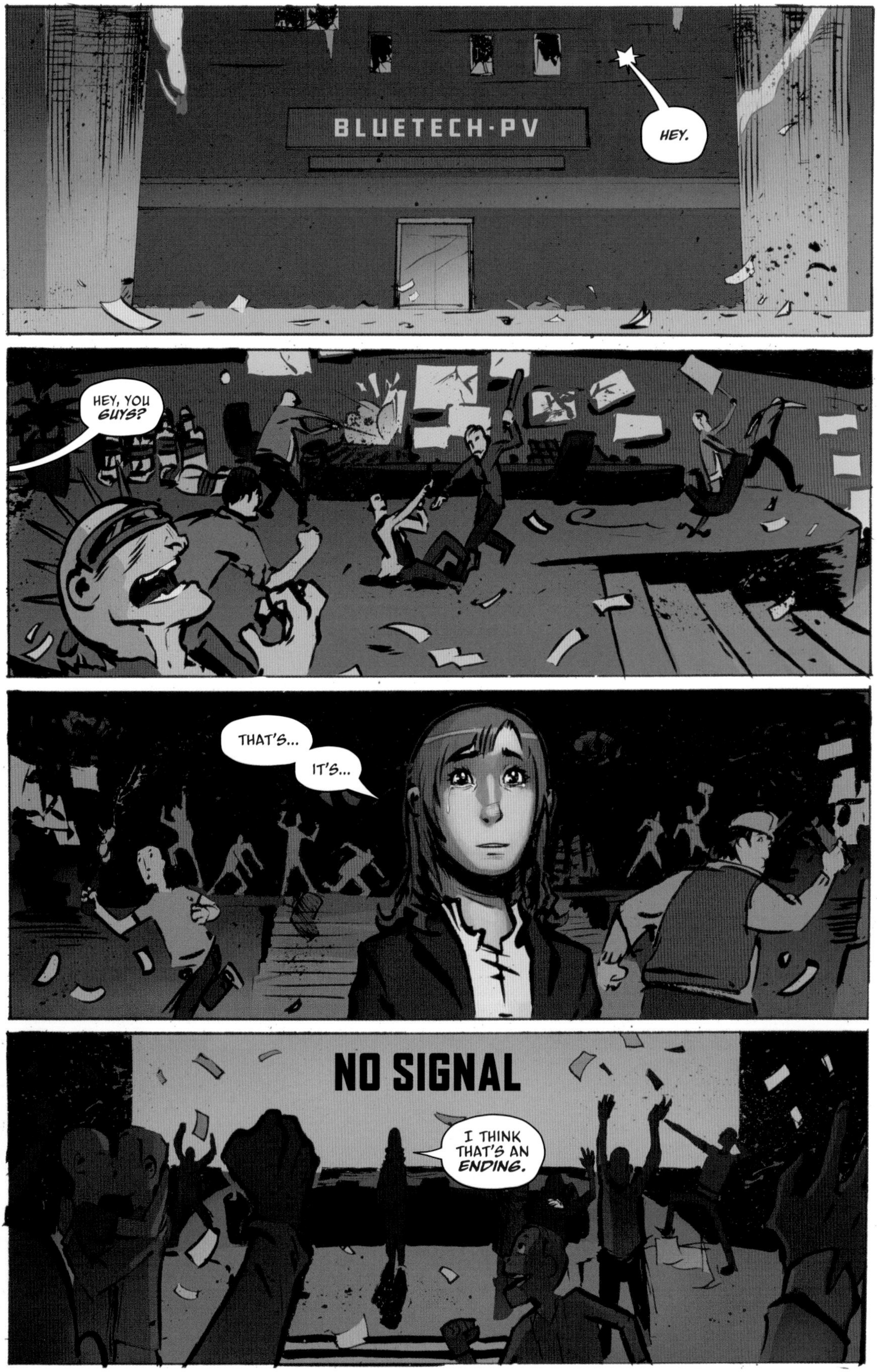
BLUETECH·PV
HEY.
HEY, YOU GUYS?
THAT'S...
IT'S...
NO SIGNAL
I THINK THAT'S AN ENDING.

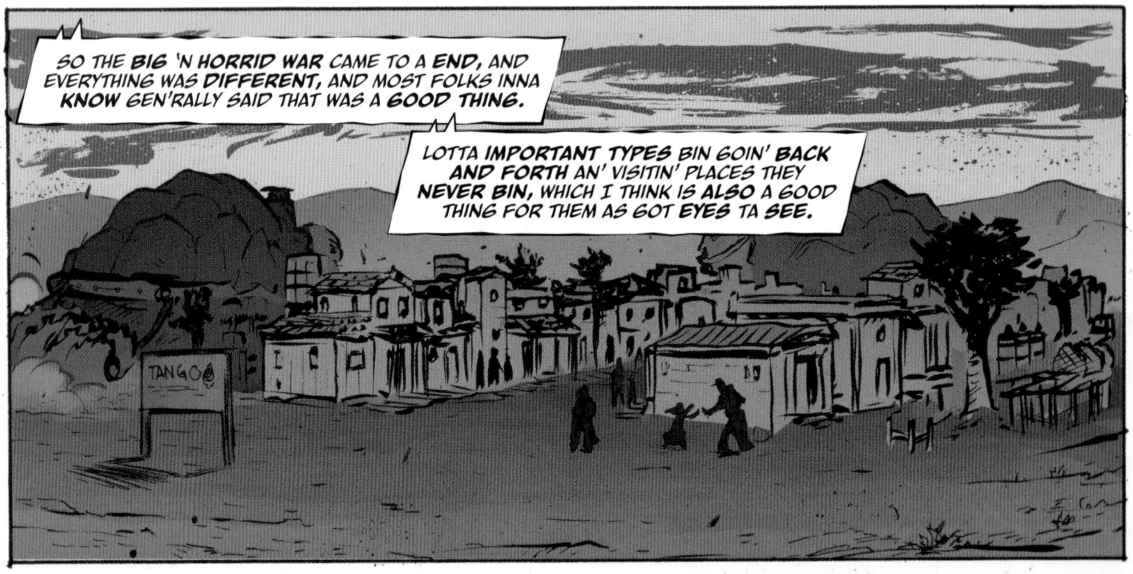
SO THE BIG 'N HORRID WAR CAME TO A END, AND EVERYTHING WAS DIFFERENT, AND MOST FOLKS INNA KNOW GEN'RALLY SAID THAT WAS A GOOD THING.
LOTTA IMPORTANT TYPES BIN GOIN' BACK AND FORTH AN' VISITIN' PLACES THEY NEVER BIN, WHICH I THINK IS ALSO A GOOD THING FOR THEM AS GOT EYES TA SEE.
TANGO

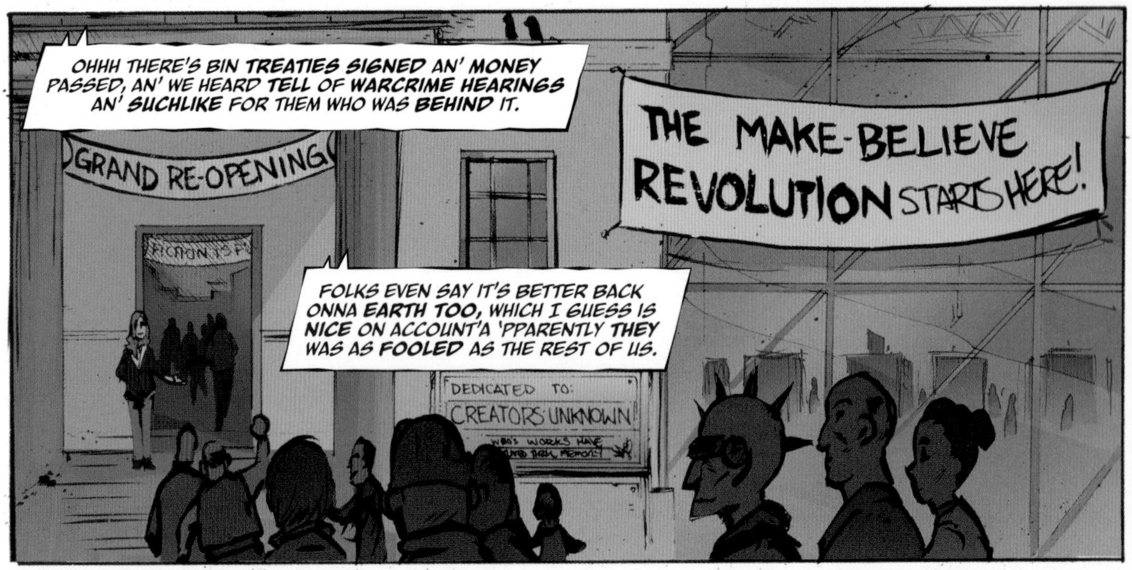
OHHH THERE'S BIN TREATIES SIGNED AN' MONEY PASSED, AN' WE HEARD TELL OF WARCRIME HEARINGS AN' SUCHLIKE FOR THEM WHO WAS BEHIND IT.
THE MAKE-BELIEVE REVOLUTION STARTS HERE!
GRAND RE-OPENING
FOLKS EVEN SAY IT'S BETTER BACK ONNA EARTH TOO, WHICH I GUESS IS NICE ON ACCOUNT'A 'PPARENTLY THEY WAS AS FOOLED AS THE REST OF US.
DEDICATED TO:
CREATORS UNKNOWN

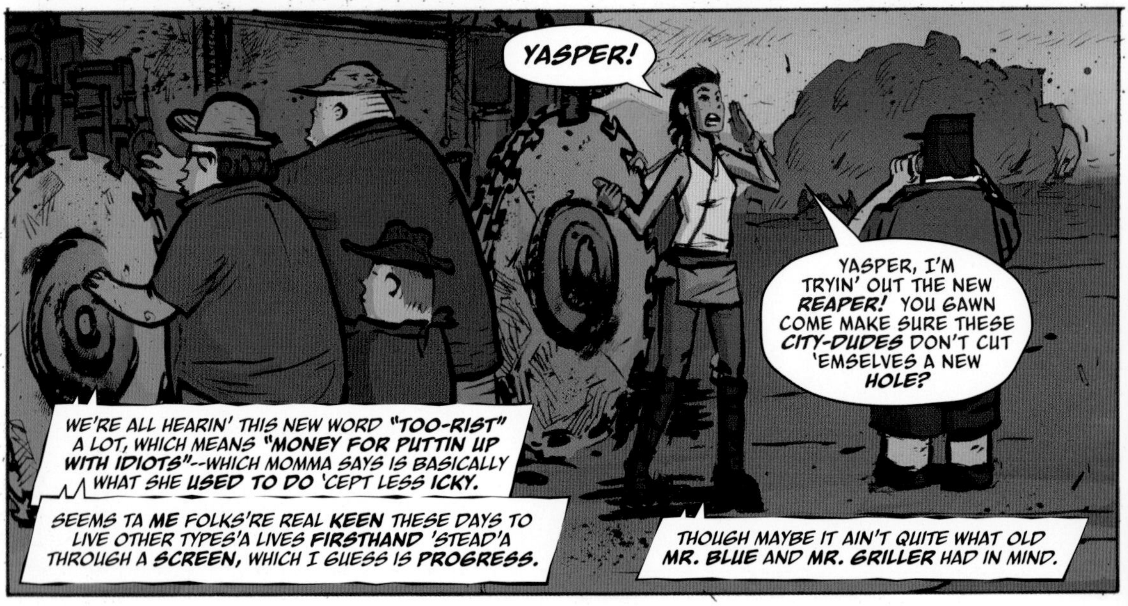
YASPER!
YASPER, I'M TRYIN' OUT THE NEW REAPER! YOU GAWN COME MAKE SURE THESE CITY-DUDES DON'T CUT 'EMSELVES A NEW HOLE?
WE'RE ALL HEARIN' THIS NEW WORD "TOO-RIST" A LOT, WHICH MEANS "MONEY FOR PUTTIN UP WITH IDIOTS"--WHICH MOMMA SAYS IS BASICALLY WHAT SHE USED TO DO 'CEPT LESS ICKY.
SEEMS TA ME FOLKS'RE REAL KEEN THESE DAYS TO LIVE OTHER TYPES'A LIVES FIRSTHAND 'STEAD'A THROUGH A SCREEN, WHICH I GUESS IS PROGRESS.
THOUGH MAYBE IT AIN'T QUITE WHAT OLD MR. BLUE AND MR. GRILLER HAD IN MIND.

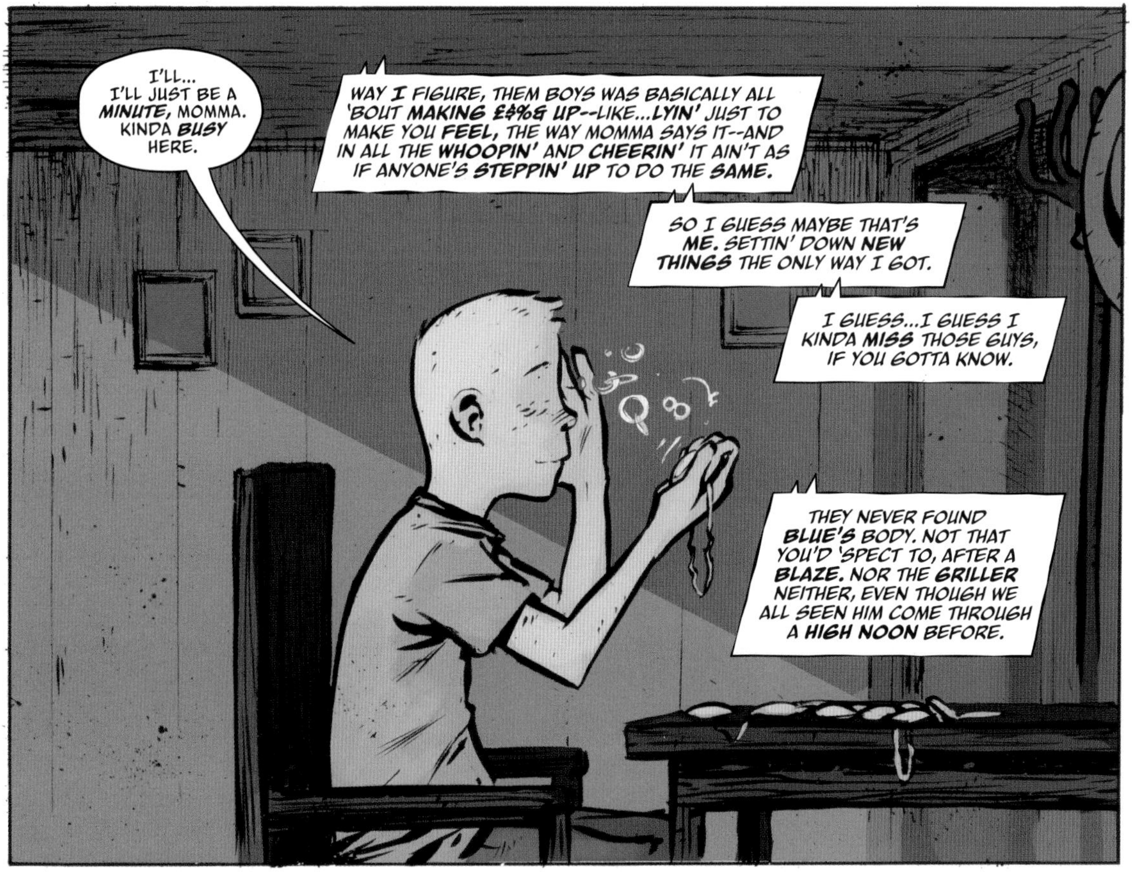

I'LL... I'LL JUST BE A MINUTE, MOMMA. KINDA BUSY HERE.
WAY I FIGURE, THEM BOYS WAS BASICALLY ALL 'BOUT MAKING £$%& UP--LIKE...LYIN' JUST TO MAKE YOU FEEL, THE WAY MOMMA SAYS IT--AND IN ALL THE WHOOPIN' AND CHEERIN' IT AIN'T AS IF ANYONE'S STEPPIN' UP TO DO THE SAME.
SO I GUESS MAYBE THAT'S ME. SETTIN' DOWN NEW THINGS THE ONLY WAY I GOT.
I GUESS...I GUESS I KINDA MISS THOSE GUYS, IF YOU GOTTA KNOW.
THEY NEVER FOUND BLUE'S BODY. NOT THAT YOU'D 'SPECT TO, AFTER A BLAZE. NOR THE GRILLER NEITHER, EVEN THOUGH WE ALL SEEN HIM COME THROUGH A HIGH NOON BEFORE.


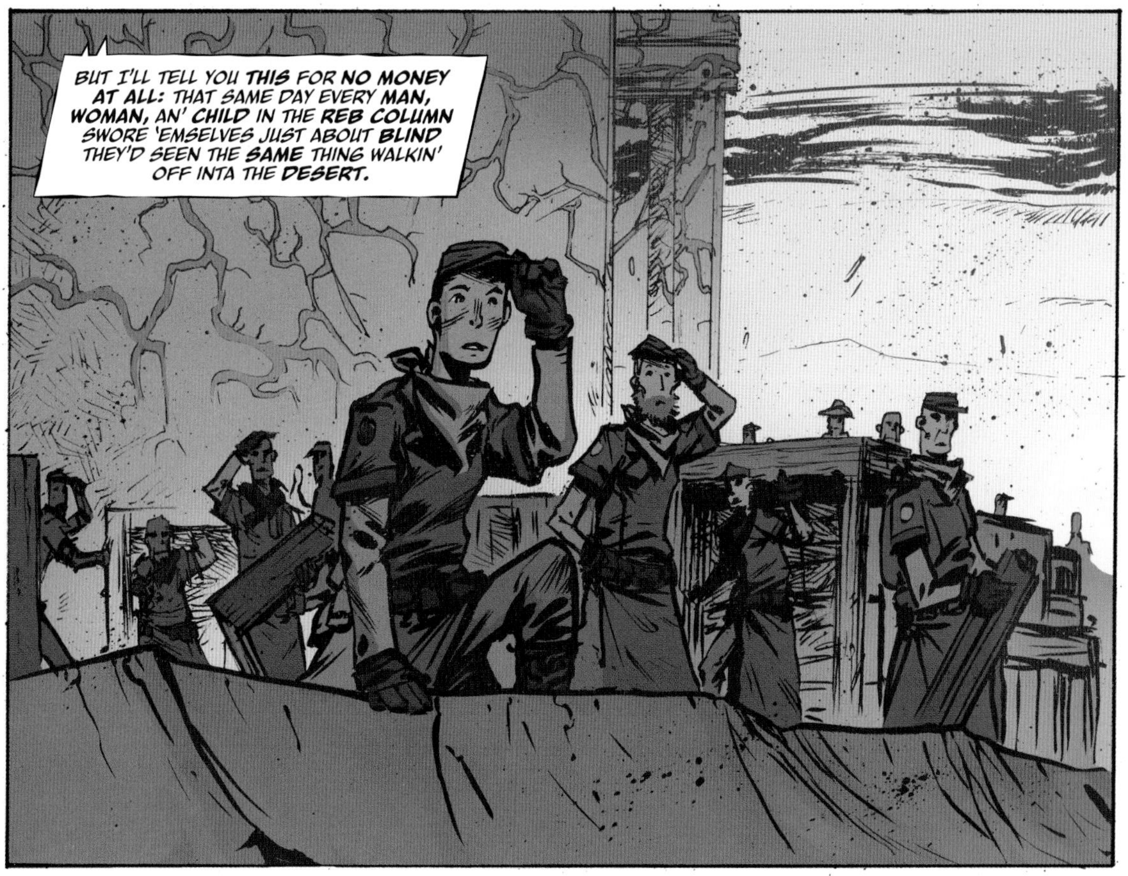

BUT I'LL TELL YOU THIS FOR NO MONEY AT ALL: THAT SAME DAY EVERY MAN, WOMAN, AN' CHILD IN THE REB COLUMN SWORE 'EMSELVES JUST ABOUT BLIND THEY'D SEEN THE SAME THING WALKIN' OFF INTA THE DESERT.

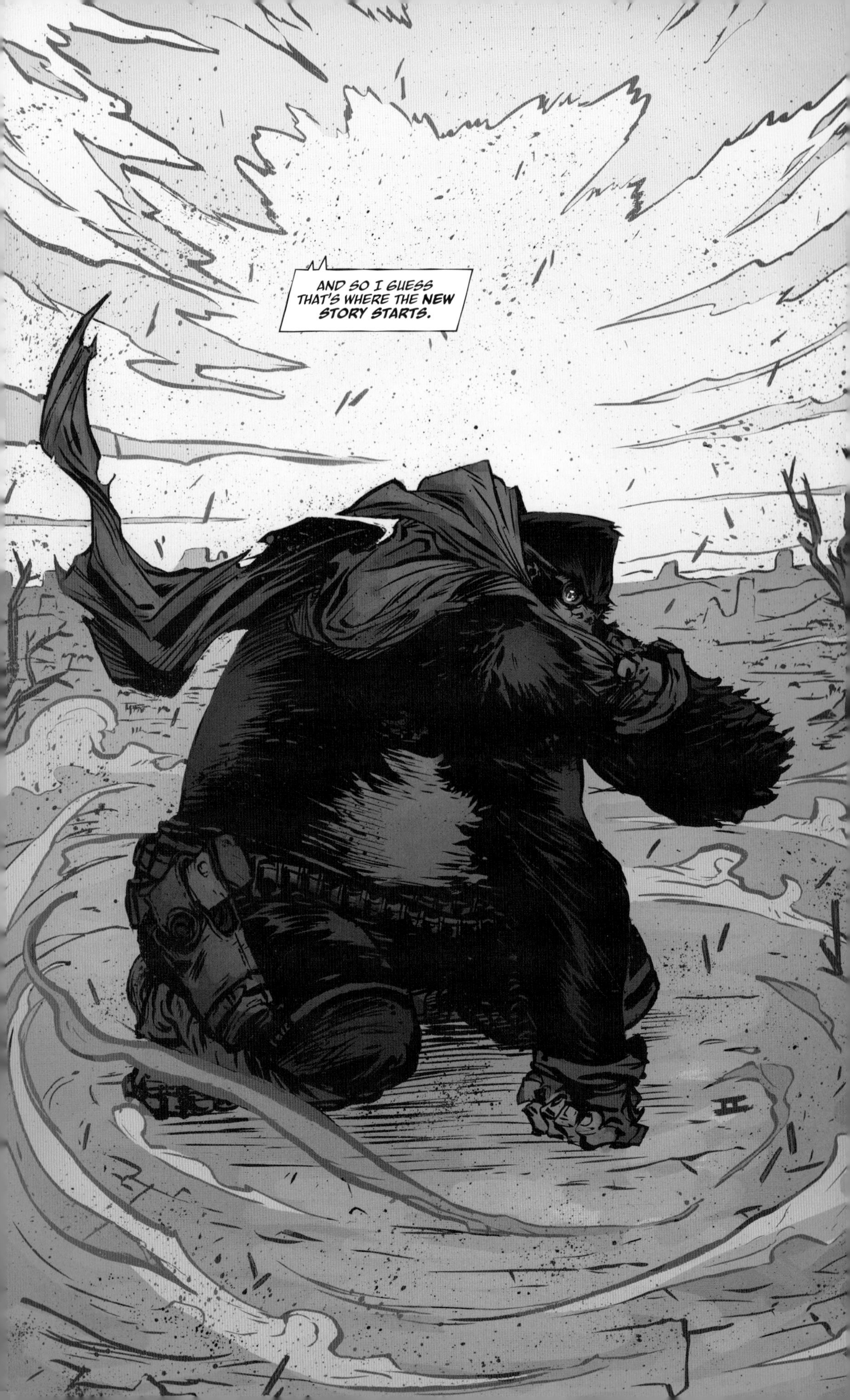
AND SO I GUESS THAT'S WHERE THE NEW STORY STARTS.

# COVER GALLERY

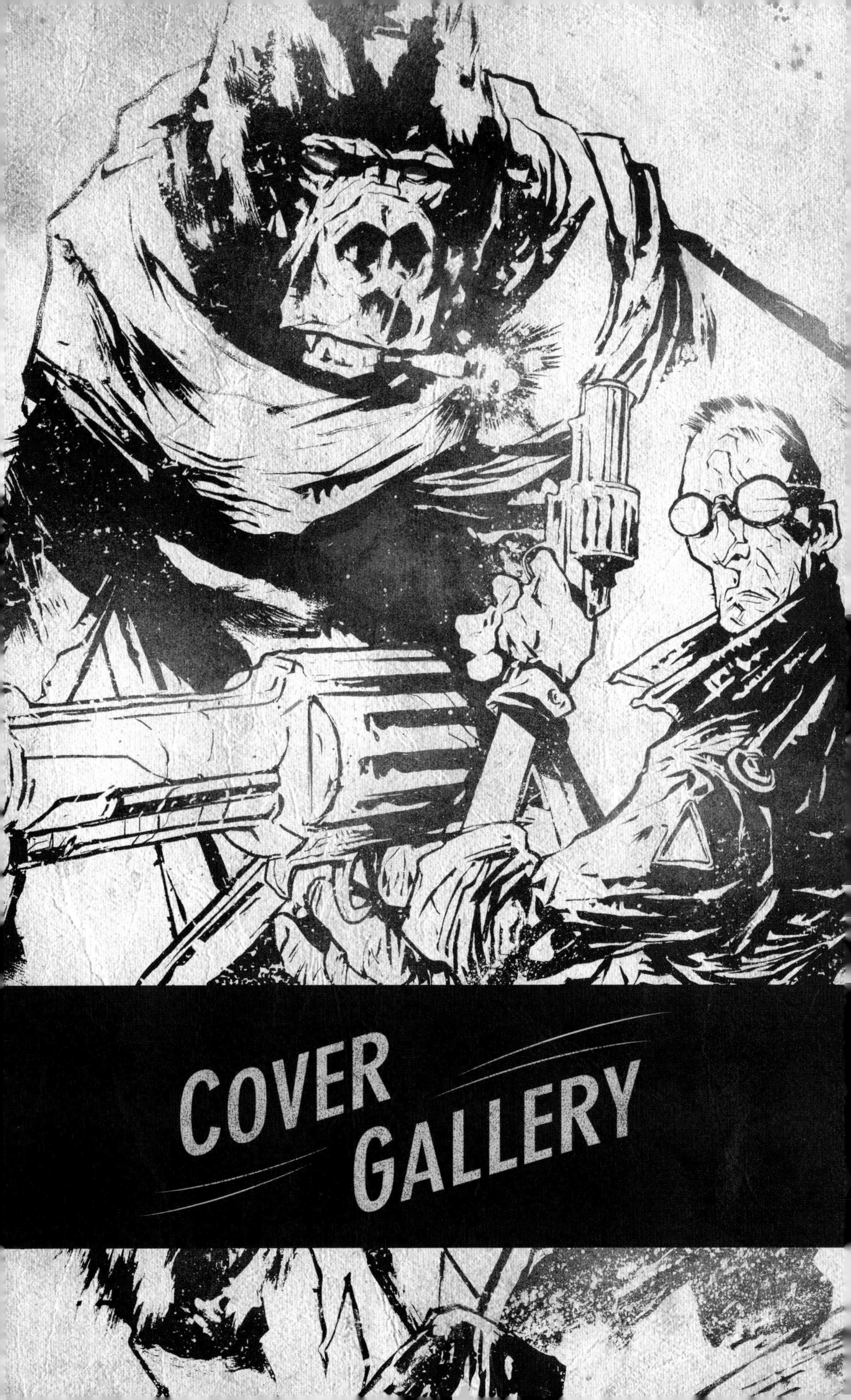

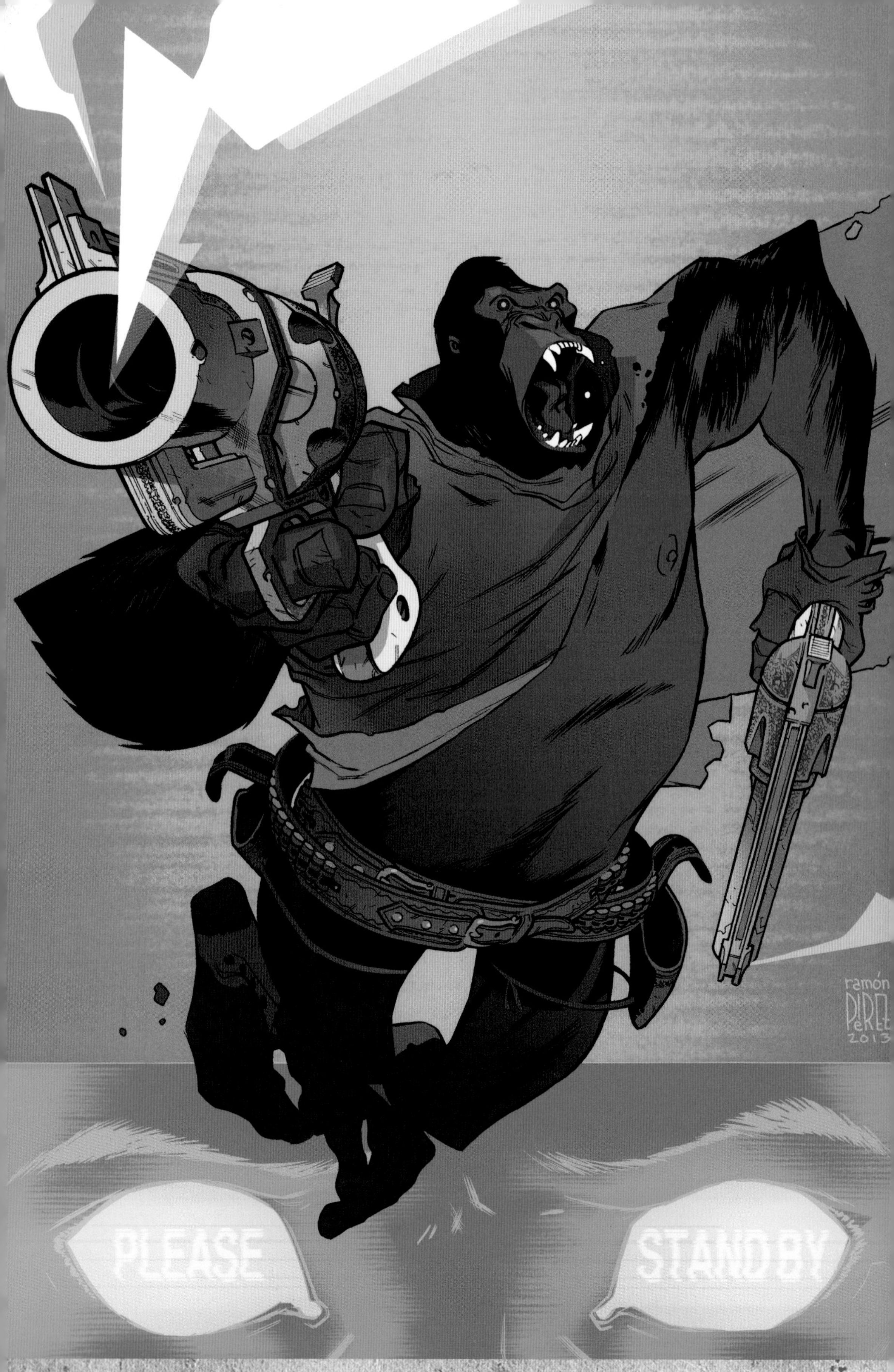
ramón PéREz 2013
PLEASE
STAND BY

ISSUE ONE COVER BY
**RAMÓN PÉREZ**

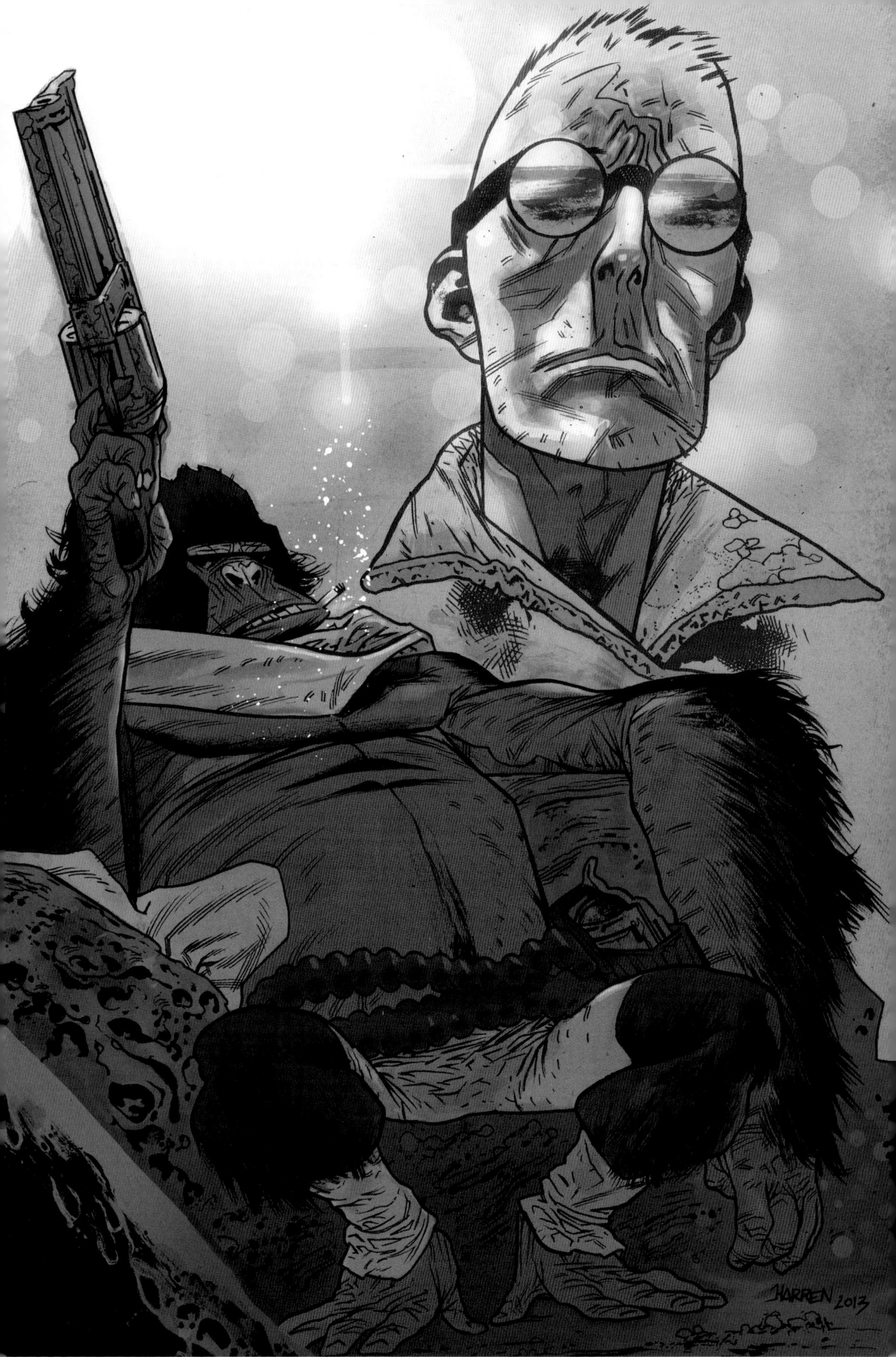
HARREN 2013

ISSUE ONE COVER BY
**JAMES HARREN** WITH **RICO RENZI**

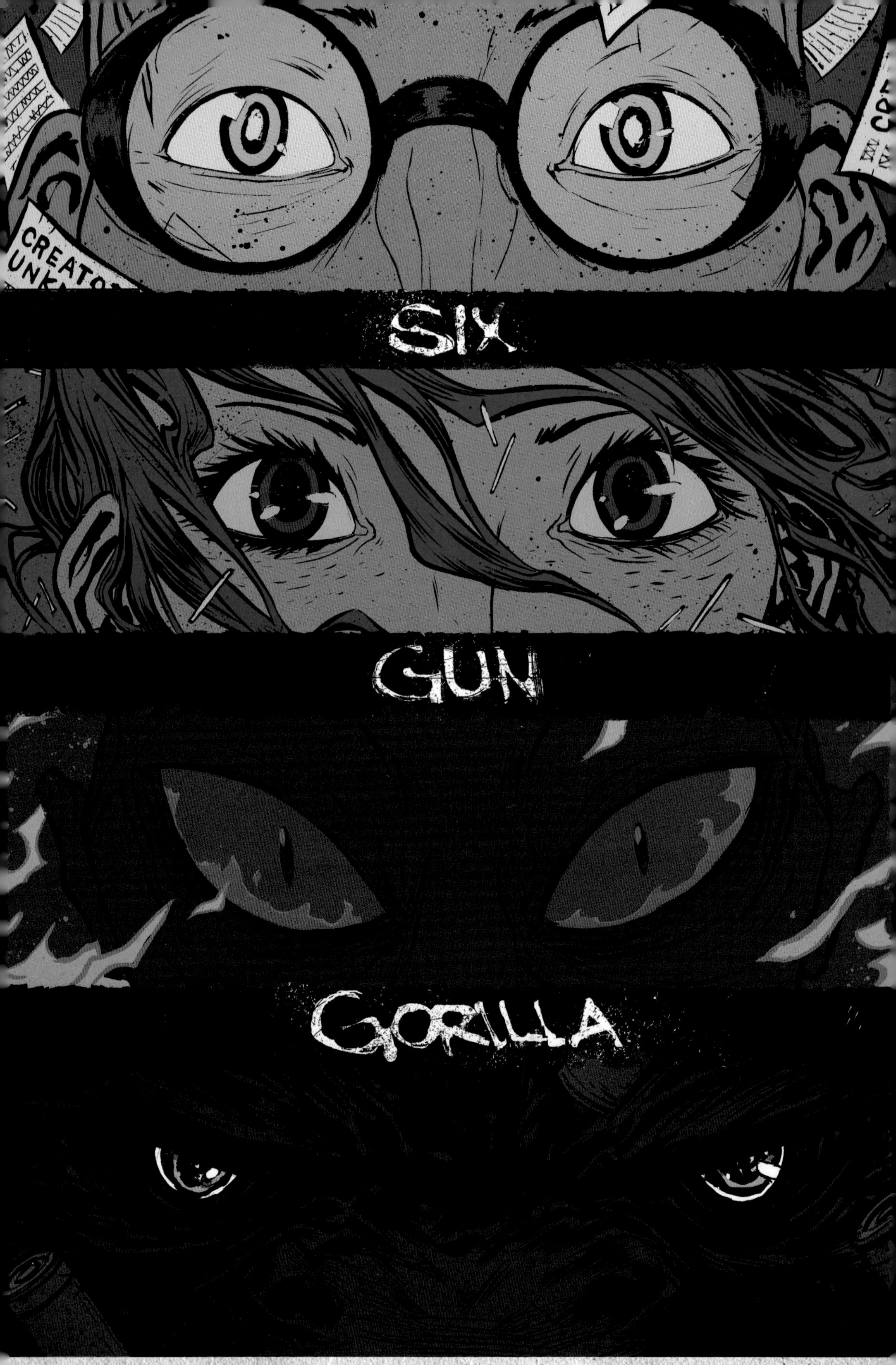
SIX
GUN
GORILLA

ISSUE ONE SDCC EXCLUSIVE COVER BY
**JEFF STOKELY** WITH **RICO RENZI**

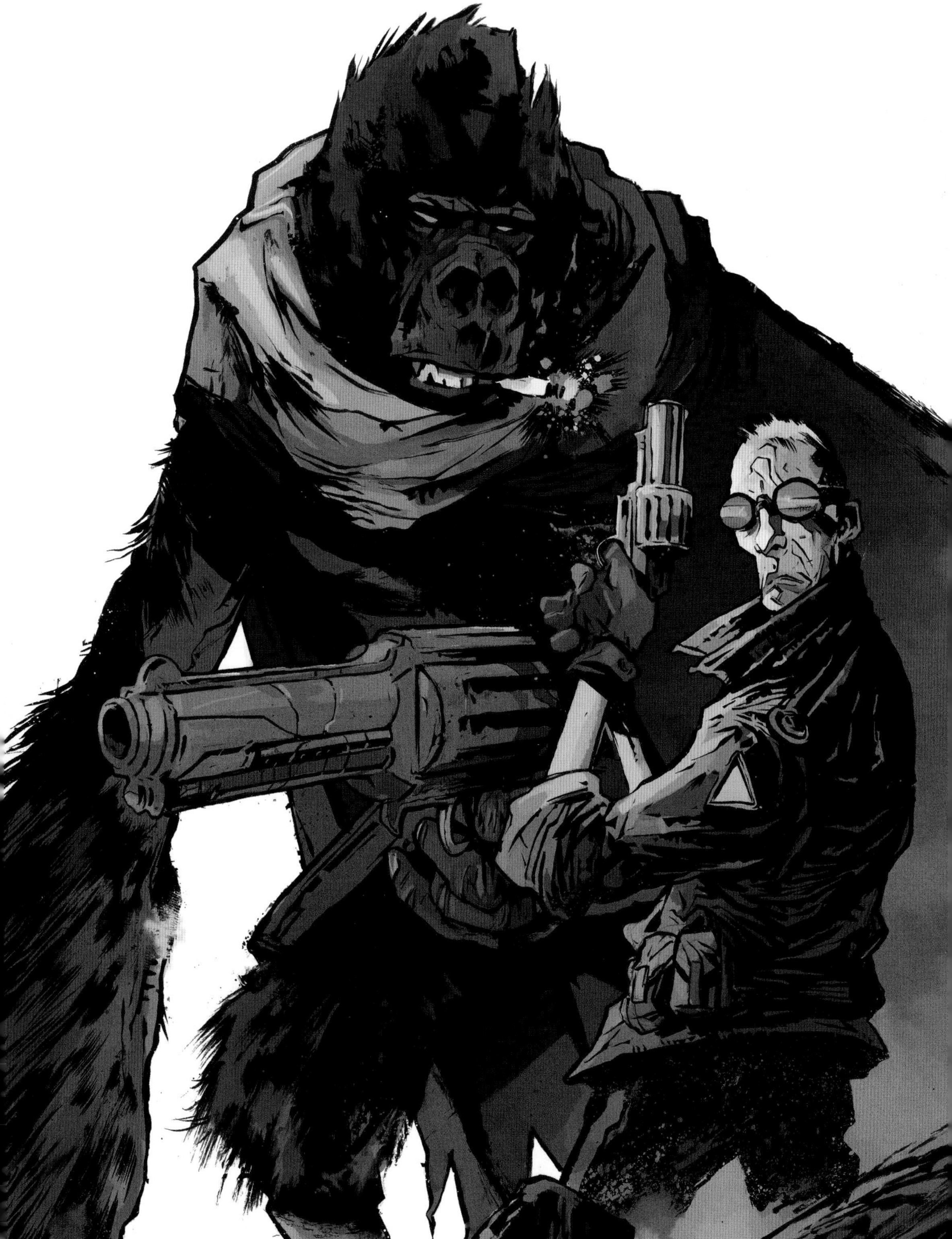

ISSUE ONE 2ND PRINT COVER BY
**JOE QUERIO**

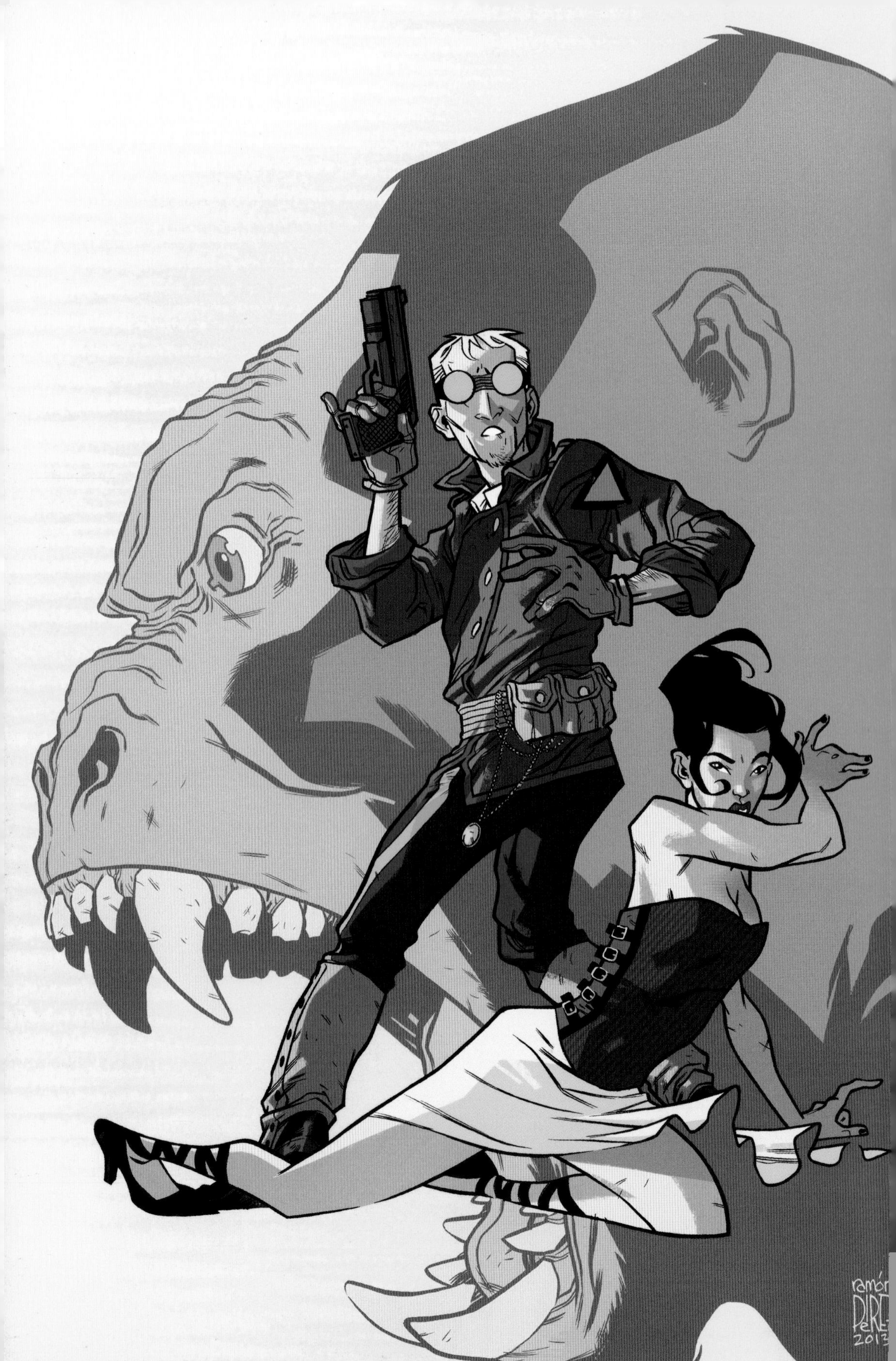

ISSUE TWO COVER BY
**RAMÓN PÉREZ**

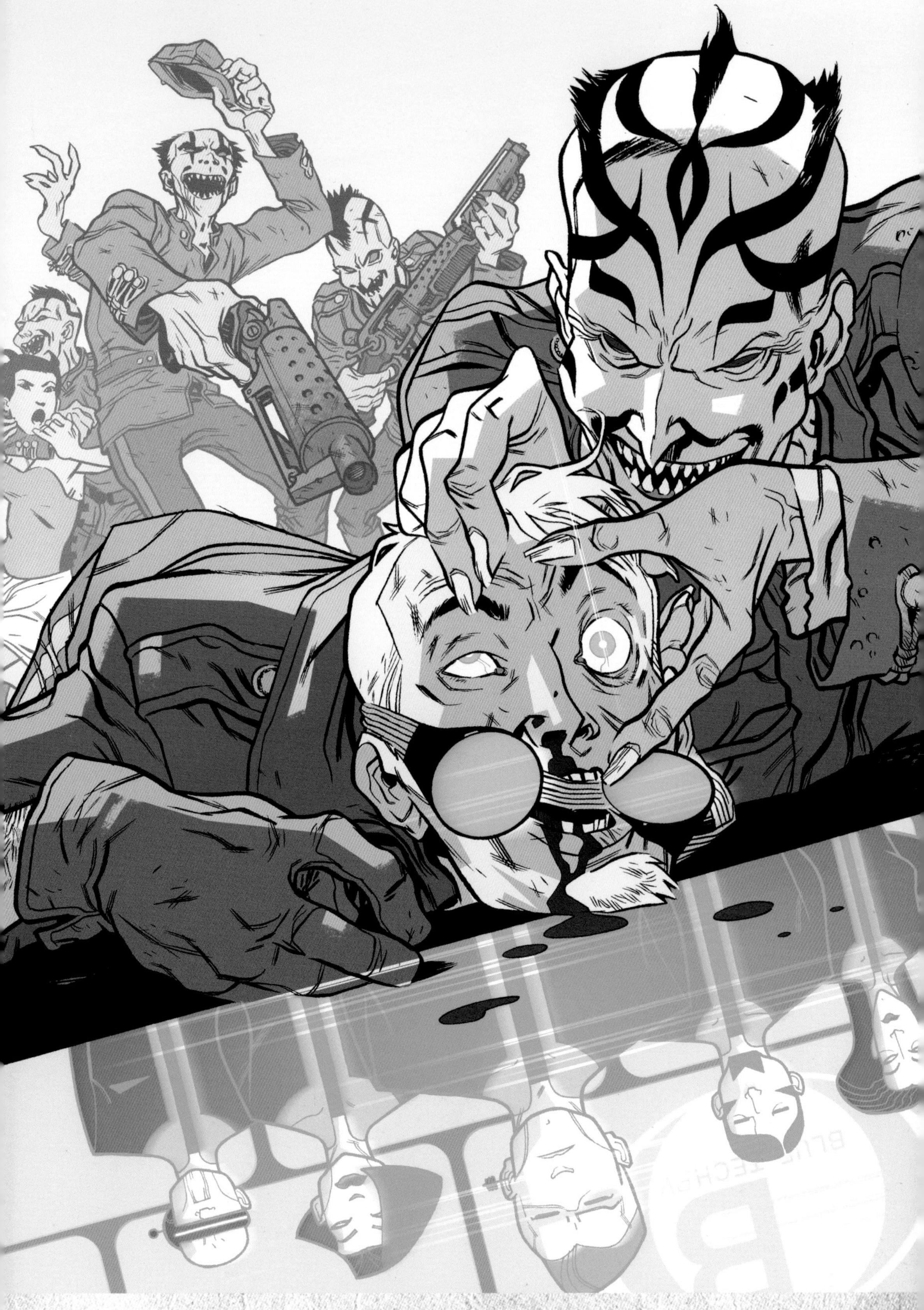

ISSUE THREE COVER BY
**RAMÓN PÉREZ**

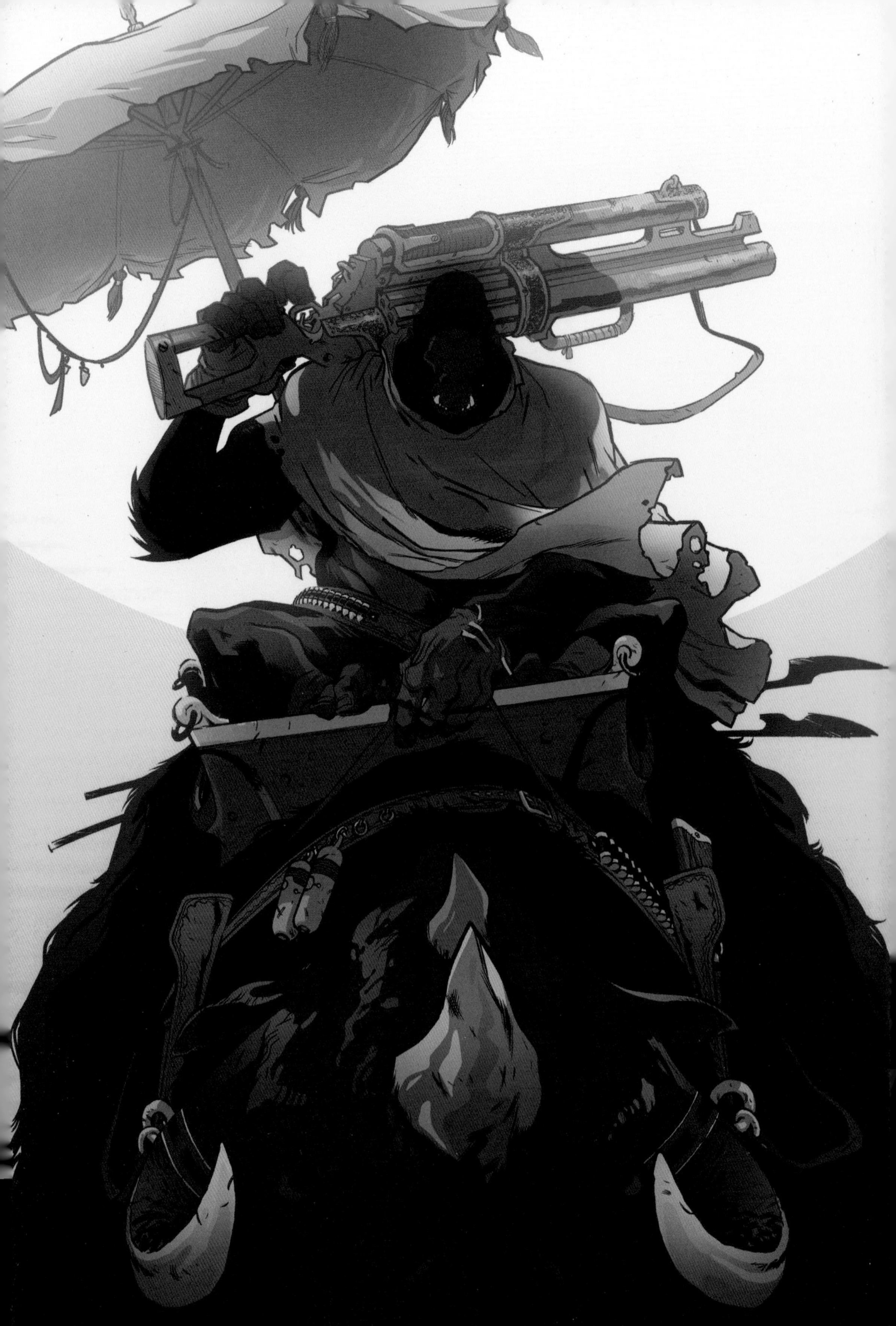

ISSUE FOUR COVER BY
**RAMÓN PÉREZ**

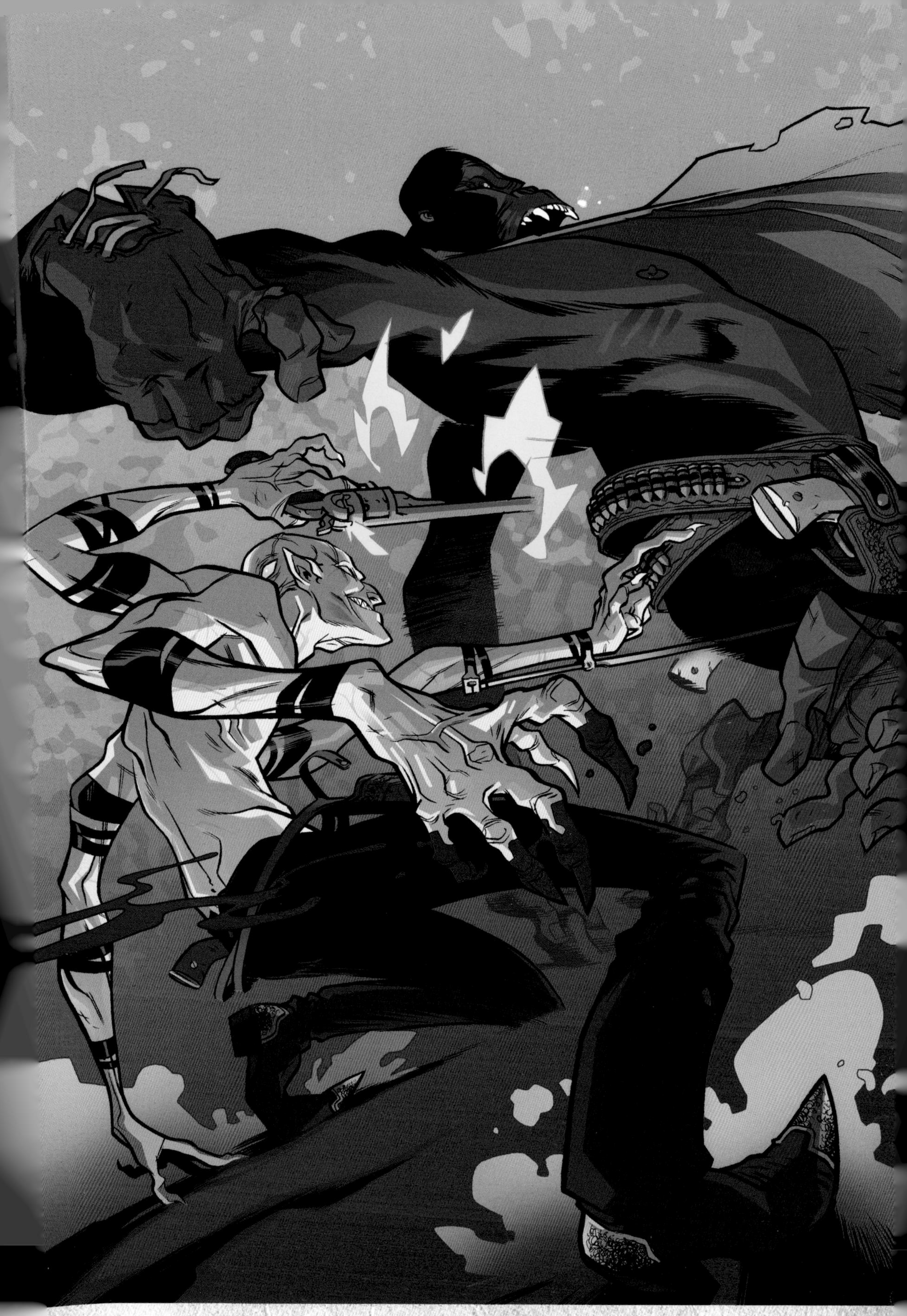

ISSUE FIVE COVER BY
**RAMÓN PÉREZ**

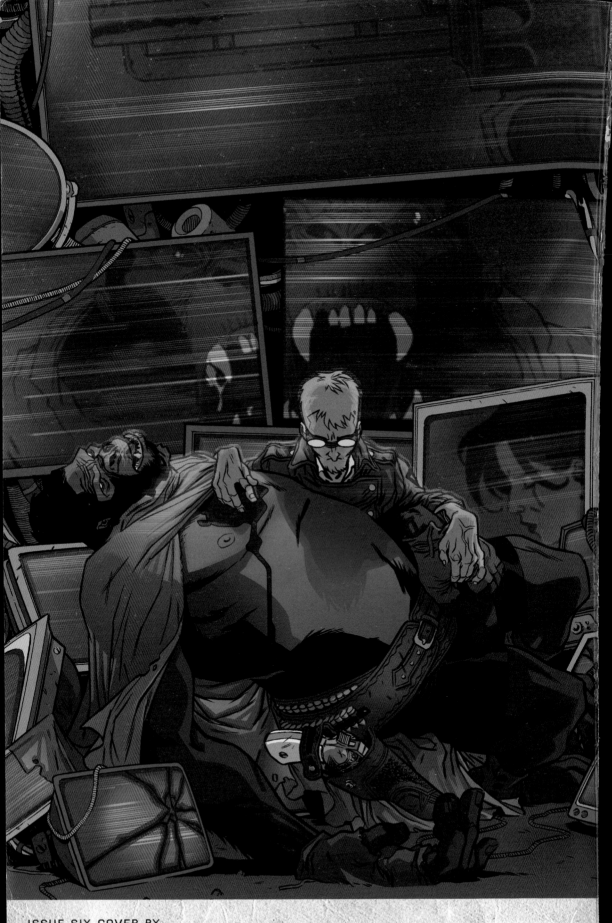

ISSUE SIX COVER BY
**RAMÓN PÉREZ**